GETTING STARTED

Welcome

Congratulations, you have just gained access to the highest quality practice Associate Certification Exam. These practice tests will prepare you thorough to pass first time with confidence.

There are 6 practice exams with 65 questions each and each set of practice exams includes questions from the five domains of the latest DVA-C01 exam. All 390 practice questions were designed to reflect the difficulty of the real AWS exam. With these Practice Tests, you'll know when you are ready to pass your AWS Developer Associate exam first time! We recommend re-taking these practice tests until you consistently score 80% or higher - that's when you're ready to sit the exam and achieve a great score!

If you want easy to pass questions, then these Practice Tests are <u>not</u> for you! Our students love these high-quality practice tests because they match the level of difficulty and exam pattern of the actual certification exam and help them understand the AWS concepts. Students who have recently passed the AWS exam confirm that these AWS practice questions are the most similar to the real AWS exam.

I hope you get great value from this resource and feel confident that you'll ace your AWS Certified Developer Associate exam through diligent study of these questions.

Wishing you all the best with your AWS Certification exam.

Neal Davis

AWS Solution Architect & Founder of Digital Cloud Training

How to best use this resource

We have organized the practice questions into 6 sets and each set is repeated once <u>without</u> answers and explanations and once <u>with</u> answers and explanations. This allows you to choose from two methods of preparation.

1. Exam simulation

To simulate the exam experience, use the "PRACTICE QUESTIONS ONLY" sets. Grab a pen and paper to record your answers for all 65 questions. After completing each set, check your answers using the "PRACTICE QUESTIONS, ANSWERS & EXPLANATIONS" section.

To calculate your total score, sum up the number of correct answers and multiply them by 1.54 (weighting out of 100%) to get your percentage score out of 100%. For example, if you got 50 questions right, the calculation would be 50 x 1.54 = 77%. The pass mark of the official AWS exam is 72%.

2. Training mode

To use the practice questions as a learning tool, use the "PRACTICE QUESTIONS, ANSWERS & EXPLANATIONS" sets to view the answers and read the in-depth explanations as you move through the questions.

Key Training Advice

AIM FOR A MINIMUM SCORE OF 80%: Although the actual AWS exam has a pass mark of 72%, we recommend that you repeatedly retake our AWS practice exams until you consistently score 80% or higher. We encourage you to put in the work and study the explanations in detail! Once you achieve the recommended score in the practice tests - you are ready to sit the exam and achieve a great score!

CONFORM WITH EXAM BLUEPRINT: Using our AWS Certified Developer practice exams helps you gain experience with the test question format and how the questions in the real AWS exam are structured. With our practice tests, you will be adequately prepared for the real AWS exam.

DEEPEN YOUR KNOWLEDGE: Please note that though we match the AWS exam pattern, our AWS practice exams are NOT brain dumps. Please don't expect to pass the real AWS certification exam by simply memorizing answers. Instead, we encourage you to use our AWS Developer Associate practice tests to deepen your knowledge. This is your best chance to successfully pass your exam no matter what questions you are presented with in your real exam.

Your Pathway to Success

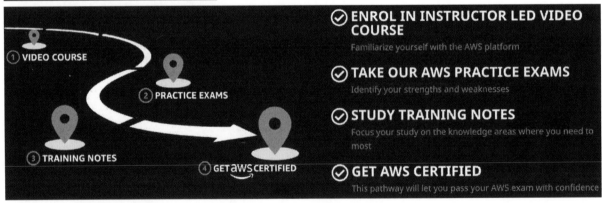

Instructor-led Video Course

If you're new to AWS, we'd suggest first enrolling in the online instructor-led AWS Certified Developer Associate Video Course from Digital Cloud Training to familiarize yourself with the AWS platform before assessing your exam readiness with these practice exams.

Training Notes

Use the <u>Training Notes</u> for the AWS Certified Developer Associate from Digital Cloud to get a more detailed understanding of the AWS services and focus your study on the knowledge areas where you need to most. Deep dive into the DVA-C01 exam objectives with 340 pages of detailed facts, tables and diagrams to shortcut your time to success.

Limited Time Bonus Offer

As a special bonus, we are now offering **FREE Access to the Exam Simulator** on the Digital Cloud Training website. The exam simulator randomly selects 65 questions from our pool of 390 questions - mimicking the real AWS exam environment. The practice exam has the same format, style, time limit, and passing score as the real AWS exam. Navigate to the BONUS OFFER section at end of this book for instructions on how to claim your bonus.

Download your FREE PDF version of this book

Based on the feedback we've received from our Amazon clients, we understand that studying complex diagrams in black and white or accessing reference links from a kindle may NOT offer the best learning experience.

That's why we've decided to provide you with a PDF of this book at no additional charge. This extended version includes additional diagrams, images and reference links that will enable you to access additional information. To access your free PDF version, simply navigate to the Conclusion of this book for download instructions.

Contact, Feedback & Sharing

We want you to get great value from these training resources. If for any reason you are not 100% satisfied, please contact us at feedback@digitalcloud.training. We promise to address all questions and concerns, typically within 24hrs. We really want you to have a 5-star learning experience!

The AWS platform is evolving quickly, and the exam tracks these changes with a typical lag of around 6 months. We are therefore reliant on student feedback to keep track of what is appearing in the exam. If there are any topics in your exam that weren't covered in our training resources, please provide us with feedback using this form https://digitalcloud.training/student-feedback/. We appreciate any feedback that will help us further improve our AWS training resources.

If you enjoy reading reviews, please consider paying it forward. Reviews really matter - they guide students and help us continuously improve our courses. We celebrate every honest review and truly appreciate it. We'd be thrilled if you could leave a rating at amazon.com/ryp or your local amazon store (e.g. amazon.co.uk/ryp).

Our private Facebook group is a great place to ask questions and share knowledge and exam tips with the AWS community. Join the AWS Certification QA group on Facebook and share your exam feedback with the AWS community: https://www.facebook.com/groups/awscertificationqa

To join the discussion about all things related to Amazon Web Services on Slack, visit: https://digitalcloud.training/contact/ for instructions.

TABLE OF CONTENTS

SET 1: PRACTICE QUESTIONS ONLY

For training purposes, go directly to Set 1: Practice Questions, Answers & Explanations

1. Question

A developer is planning to use a Lambda function to process incoming requests from an Application Load Balancer (ALB). How can this be achieved?

1: Create a target group and register the Lambda function using the AWS CLI

2: Create an Auto Scaling Group (ASG) and register the Lambda function in the launch configuration

3: Setup an API in front of the ALB using API Gateway and use an integration request to map the request to the Lambda function

4: Configure an event-source mapping between the ALB and the Lambda function

2. Question

A developer is troubleshooting problems with a Lambda function that is invoked by Amazon SNS and repeatedly fails. How can the developer save discarded events for further processing?

1: Enable CloudWatch Logs for the Lambda function

2: Configure a Dead Letter Queue (DLQ)

3: Enable Lambda streams

4: Enable SNS notifications for failed events

3. Question

A company will be uploading several terabytes of data to Amazon S3. What is the SIMPLEST solution to ensure that the data is encrypted before it is sent to S3 and whilst in transit?

1: Use client-side encryption with a KMS managed CMK and SSL

2: Use server-side encryption with client provided keys

3: Use client-side encryption and a hardware VPN to a VPC and an S3 endpoint

4: Use server-side encryption with S3 managed keys and SSL

4. Question

An EC2 instance is allowed to access several buckets in an AWS account. The IAM policy attached to the EC2 instance profile's IAM role was replaced a few hours ago and restricts access to a single S3 bucket. However, the instance is still able to access all buckets. What is the MOST likely explanation for this? (Select TWO)

1: There is another policy attached to the IAM role that allows access

2: The evaluation logic checked the IAM user identity-based policy and found an allow

3: A resource-based policy attached to the S3 bucket is allowing access

4: IAM is eventually consistent, the changes may not have synchronized yet

5: It is not possible to restrict access to multiple buckets from a single policy

5. Question

A company is setting up a Lambda function that will process events from a DynamoDB stream. The Lambda function has been created and a stream has been enabled. What else needs to be done for this solution to work?

1: An alarm should be created in CloudWatch that sends a notification to Lambda when a new entry is added to the DynamoDB stream

2: An event-source mapping must be created on the DynamoDB side to associate the DynamoDB stream with the Lambda function

3: An event-source mapping must be created on the Lambda side to associate the DynamoDB stream with the Lambda function

4: Update the CloudFormation template to map the DynamoDB stream to the Lambda function

6. Question

A developer is preparing to deploy a Docker container to Amazon ECS using CodeDeploy. The developer has defined the deployment actions in a JSON file. What should the developer name the file?

1: buildspec.yml

3: appspec.yaml

3: cron.yml

4: appspec.yml

7. Question

A decoupled application is using an Amazon SQS queue. The processing layer that is retrieving messages from the queue is not able to keep up with the number of messages being placed in the queue. What is the FIRST step the developer should take to increase the number of messages the application receives?

1: Use the API to update the WaitTimeSeconds parameter to a value other than 0

2: Add additional Amazon SQS queues and have the application poll those queues

3: Use the ReceiveMessage API to retrieve up to 10 messages at a time

4: Configure the queue to use short polling

8. Question

An application uses AWS Lambda which makes remote to several downstream services. A developer wishes to add data to custom subsegments in AWS X-Ray that can be used with filter expressions. Which type of data should be used?

1: Metadata

2: Annotations

3: Trace ID

4: Daemon

9. Question

An application component writes thousands of item-level changes to a DynamoDB table per day. The developer requires that a record is maintained of the items before they were modified. What MUST the developer do to retain this information? (Select TWO)

1: Create a CloudWatch alarm that sends a notification when an item is modified

2: Enable DynamoDB Streams for the table

3: Set the StreamViewType to OLD_IMAGE

4: Set the StreamViewType to NEW_AND_OLD_IMAGES

5: Use an AWS Lambda function to extract the item records from the notification and write to an S3 bucket

10. Question

An X-Ray daemon is being used on an Amazon ECS cluster to assist with debugging stability issues. A developer requires more detailed timing information and data related to downstream calls to AWS services.

What should the developer use to obtain this extra detail?

1: Subsegments

2: Annotations

3: Metadata

4: Filter expressions

11. Question

A developer has deployed an application on an Amazon EC2 instance in a private subnet within a VPC. The subnet does not have Internet connectivity. The developer would like to write application logs to an Amazon S3 bucket. What MUST be configured to enable connectivity?

1: An IAM role must be added to the instance that has permissions to write to the S3 bucket

2: A bucket policy needs to be added specifying the principles that are allowed to write data to the bucket

3: A VPN should be established to enable private connectivity to S3

4: A VPC endpoint should be provisioned for S3

12. Question

A Developer wants to encrypt new objects that are being uploaded to an Amazon S3 bucket by an application. There must be an audit trail of who has used the key during this process. There should be no change to the performance of the application. Which type of encryption meets these requirements?

1: Server-side encryption using S3-managed keys

2: Server-side encryption with AWS KMS-managed keys

3: Client-side encryption with a client-side symmetric master key

4: Client-side encryption with AWS KMS-managed keys

13. Question

A serverless application uses an Amazon API Gateway and AWS Lambda. The application processes data submitted in a form by users of the application and certain data must be stored and available to subsequent function calls. What is the BEST solution for storing this data?

1: Store the data in an Amazon Kinesis Data Stream

2: Store the data in the /tmp directory

3: Store the data in an Amazon DynamoDB table

4: Store the data in an Amazon SQS queue

14. Question

A Development team need to push an update to an application that is running on AWS Elastic Beanstalk. The business SLA states that the application must maintain full performance capabilities during updates whilst minimizing cost. Which Elastic Beanstalk deployment policy should the development team select?

1: Immutable

2: Rolling

3: All at once

4: Rolling with additional batch

15. Question

An organization developed an application that uses a set of APIs that are being served through Amazon API Gateway. The API calls must be authenticated based on OpenID identity providers such as Amazon, Google, or Facebook. The APIs should allow access based on a custom authorization model. Which is the simplest and MOST secure design to use to build an authentication and authorization model for the APIs?

1: Use Amazon ElastiCache to store user credentials and pass them to the APIs for authentication and authorization

2: Use Amazon DynamoDB to store user credentials and have the application retrieve temporary credentials from AWS STS. Make API calls by passing user credentials to the APIs for authentication and authorization

3: Use Amazon Cognito user pools and a custom authorizer to authenticate and authorize users based on JSON Web Tokens

4: Build an OpenID token broker with Amazon and Facebook. Users will authenticate with these identify providers and pass the JSON Web Token to the API to authenticate each API call

16. Question

An AWS Lambda function has been packaged for deployment to multiple environments including development, test, and production. The Lambda function uses an Amazon RDS MySQL database for storing data. Each environment has a different RDS MySQL database. How can a Developer configure the Lambda function package to ensure the correct database connection string is used for each environment?

1: Use a separate function for development and production

2: Include the resources in the function code

3: Use environment variables for the database connection strings

4: Use layers for storing the database connection strings

17. Question

An application is being deployed on an Amazon EC2 instance running Linux. The EC2 instance will need to manage other AWS services. How can the EC2 instance be configured to make API calls to AWS service securely?

1: Run the "aws configure" AWS CLI command and specify the access key ID and secret access key

2: Create an AWS IAM Role, attach a policy with the necessary privileges and attach the role to the instance's instance profile

3: Store a users' console login credentials in the application code so the application can call AWS STS and gain temporary security credentials

4: Store the access key ID and secret access key as encrypted AWS Lambda environment variables and invoke Lambda for each API call

18. Question

A Developer is building an application that will store data relating to financial transactions in multiple DynamoDB tables. The Developer needs to ensure the transactions provide atomicity, isolation, and durability (ACID) and that changes are committed following an all-or nothing paradigm. What write API should be used for the DynamoDB table?

1: Standard

2: Strongly consistent

3: Transactional

4: Eventually consistent

19. Question

A Developer will be launching several Docker containers on a new Amazon ECS cluster using the EC2 Launch Type. The containers will all run a web service on port 80. What is the EASIEST way the Developer can configure the task definition to ensure the web services run correctly and there are no port conflicts on the host instances?

1: Specify port 80 for the container port and a unique port number for the host port

2: Specify a unique port number for the container port and port 80 for the host port

3: Specify port 80 for the container port and port 0 for the host port

4: Leave both the container port and host port configuration blank

20. Question

A Developer is designing a fault-tolerant application that will use Amazon EC2 instances and an Elastic Load Balancer. The Developer needs to ensure that if an EC2 instance fails session data is not lost. How can this be achieved?

1: Enable Sticky Sessions on the Elastic Load Balancer

2: Use an EC2 Auto Scaling group to automatically launch new instances

3: Use Amazon DynamoDB to perform scalable session handling

4: Use Amazon SQS to save session data

21. Question

A CloudFormation stack needs to be deployed in several regions and requires a different Amazon Machine Image (AMI) in each region. Which AWS CloudFormation template key can be used to specify the correct AMI for each region?

1: Outputs

2: Parameters

3: Resources

4: Mappings

22. Question

A company has an application that logs all information to Amazon S3. Whenever there is a new log file, an AWS Lambda function is invoked to process the log files. The code works, gathering all of the necessary information. However, when checking the Lambda function logs, duplicate entries with the same request ID are found. What is the BEST explanation for the duplicate entries?

1: The S3 bucket name was specified incorrectly

2: The Lambda function failed, and the Lambda service retried the invocation with a delay

3: There was an S3 outage, which caused duplicate entries of the same log file

4: The application stopped intermittently and then resumed

23. Question

An AWS Lambda function authenticates to an external web site using a regularly rotated user name and password. The credentials need to be stored securely and must not be stored in the function code.

What combination of AWS services can be used to achieve this requirement? (Select TWO)

1: AWS Certificate Manager (ACM)

2: AWS Systems Manager Parameter Store

3: AWS Key Management Store (KMS)

4: AWS Artifact

5: Amazon GuardDuty

24. Question

A Development team would use a GitHub repository and would like to migrate their application code to AWS CodeCommit. What needs to be created before they can migrate a cloned repository to CodeCommit over HTTPS?

1: A GitHub secure authentication token

2: A public and private SSH key file

3: A set of Git credentials generated with IAM

4: An Amazon EC2 IAM role with CodeCommit permissions

25. Question

A company has a large Amazon DynamoDB table which they scan periodically so they can analyze several attributes. The scans are consuming a lot of provisioned throughput. What technique can a Developer use to minimize the impact of the scan on the table's provisioned throughput?

1: Set a smaller page size for the scan

2: Use parallel scans

3: Define a range key on the table

4: Prewarm the table by updating all items

26. Question

A Developer is deploying an application in a microservices architecture on Amazon ECS. The Developer needs to choose the best task placement strategy to MINIMIZE the number of instances that are used. Which task placement strategy should be used?

1: spread

2: random

3: binpack

4: weighted

27. Question

A company has created a set of APIs using Amazon API Gateway and exposed them to partner companies. The APIs have caching enabled for all stages. The partners require a method of invalidating the cache that they can build into their applications. What can the partners use to invalidate the API cache?

1: They can pass the HTTP header Cache-Control: max-age=0

2: They can use the query string parameter INVALIDATE_CACHE

3: They must wait for the TTL to expire

4: They can invoke an AWS API endpoint which invalidates the cache

28. Question

A Developer is deploying an AWS Lambda update using AWS CodeDeploy. In the appspec.yml file, which of the following is a valid structure for the order of hooks that should be specified?

1: BeforeInstall > AfterInstall > AfterAllowTestTraffic > BeforeAllowTraffic > AfterAllowTraffic

2: BeforeInstall > AfterInstall > ApplicationStart > ValidateService

3: BeforeAllowTraffic > AfterAllowTraffic

4: BeforeBlockTraffic > AfterBlockTraffic > BeforeAllowTraffic > AfterAllowTraffic

29. Question

A Developer needs to scan a full DynamoDB 50GB table within non-peak hours. About half of the strongly consistent RCUs are typically used during non-peak hours and the scan duration must be minimized. How can the Developer optimize the scan execution time without impacting production workloads?

1: Use sequential scans

2: Use parallel scans while limiting the rate

3: Increase the RCUs during the scan operation

4: Change to eventually consistent RCUs during the scan operation

30. Question

A Development team is involved with migrating an on-premises MySQL database to Amazon RDS. The database usage is very read-heavy. The Development team wants re-factor the application code to achieve optimum read performance for queries. How can this objective be met?

1: Add database retries to the code and vertically scale the Amazon RDS database

2: Use Amazon RDS with a multi-AZ deployment

3: Add a connection string to use an Amazon RDS read replica for read queries

4: Add a connection string to use a read replica on an Amazon EC2 instance

31. Question

To reduce the cost of API actions performed on an Amazon SQS queue, a Developer has decided to implement long polling. Which of the following modifications should the Developer make to the API actions?

1: Set the ReceiveMessage API with a WaitTimeSeconds of 20

2: Set the SetQueueAttributes API with a DelaySeconds of 20

3: Set the ReceiveMessage API with a VisibilityTimeout of 30

4: Set the SetQueueAttributes with a MessageRetentionPeriod of 60

32. Question

A company is deploying an Amazon Kinesis Data Streams application that will collect streaming data from a gaming application. Consumers will run on Amazon EC2 instances. In this architecture, what can be deployed on consumers to act as an intermediary between the record processing logic and Kinesis Data Streams and instantiate a record processor for each shard?

1: Amazon Kinesis API

2: AWS CLI

3: Amazon Kinesis CLI

4: Amazon Kinesis Client Library (KCL)

33. Question

A serverless application uses an AWS Lambda function to process Amazon S3 events. The Lambda function executes 20 times per second and takes 20 seconds to complete each execution. How many concurrent executions will the Lambda function require?

1: 5

2: 400

3: 40

4: 20

34. Question

A Developer needs to be notified by email when a new object is uploaded to a specific Amazon S3 bucket. What is the EASIEST way for the Developer to enable these notifications?

1: Add an event to the S3 bucket for PUT and POST events and use an Amazon SNS Topic

2: Add an event to the S3 bucket for PUT and POST events and use an Amazon SQS queue

3: Add an event to the S3 bucket for PUT and POST events and use an AWS Lambda function

4: Add an event to the S3 bucket for all object create events and use AWS Step Functions

35. Question

A Developer is setting up a code update to Amazon ECS using AWS CodeDeploy. The Developer needs to complete the code update quickly. Which of the following deployment types should the Developer use?

1: In-place

2: Canary

3: Blue/green

4: Linear

36. Question

Change management procedures at an organization require that a log is kept recording activity within AWS accounts. The activity that must be recorded includes API activity related to creating, modifying or deleting AWS resources. Which AWS service should be used to record this information?

1: Amazon CloudWatch

2: Amazon CloudTrail

3: AWS X-Ray

4: AWS OpsWorks

37. Question

A company is deploying an on-premise application server that will connect to several AWS services. What is the BEST way to provide the application server with permissions to authenticate to AWS services?

1: Create an IAM role with the necessary permissions and assign it to the application server

2: Create an IAM user and generate access keys. Create a credentials file on the application server

3: Create an IAM group with the necessary permissions and add the on-premise application server to the group

4: Create an IAM user and generate a key pair. Use the key pair in API calls to AWS services

38. Question

A Developer is creating an application that will run on Amazon EC2 instances. The application will process encrypted files. The files must be decrypted prior to processing. Which of the following steps should be taken to securely decrypt the data? (Select TWO)

1: Pass the encrypted data key to the Decrypt operation

2: Use the encrypted data key to decrypt the data and then remove the encrypted data key from memory as soon as possible

3: Use the plaintext data key to decrypt the data and then remove the plaintext data key from memory as soon as possible

4: Use the plaintext data key to decrypt the data and then remove the encrypted data key from memory as soon as possible

5: Pass the plaintext data key to the Decrypt operation

39. Question

A Developer needs to launch a serverless static website. The Developer needs to get the website up and running quickly and easily. What should the Developer do?

1: Configure an Amazon S3 bucket as a static website

2: Configure an Amazon EC2 instance with Apache

3: Create an AWS Lambda function with an API Gateway front-end

4: Share an Amazon EFS volume as a static website

40. Question

A Developer requires a multi-threaded in-memory cache to place in front of an Amazon RDS database. Which caching solution should the Developer choose?

1: Amazon DynamoDB DAX

2: Amazon ElastiCache Redis

3: Amazon ElastiCache Memcached

4: Amazon RedShift

41. Question

A Developer needs to write a small amount of temporary log files from an application running on an Amazon EC2 instance. The log files will be automatically deleted every 24 hours. What is the SIMPLEST solution for storing this data that will not require additional code?

1: Write the log files to an attached Amazon EBS volume

2: Write the log files to an Amazon EFS volume

3: Write the log files to an Amazon DynamoDB database

4: Write the log files to an Amazon S3 bucket

42. Question

A Developer has recently created an application that uses an AWS Lambda function, an Amazon DynamoDB table, and also sends notifications using Amazon SNS. The application is not working as expected and the Developer needs to analyze what is happening across all components of the application. What is the BEST way to analyze the issue?

1: Enable X-Ray tracing for the Lambda function

2: Create an Amazon CloudWatch Events rule

3: Assess the application with Amazon Inspector

4: Monitor the application with AWS Trusted Advisor

43. Question

A company needs to store sensitive documents on Amazon S3. The documents should be encrypted in transit using SSL/TLS and then be encrypted for storage at the destination. The company do not want to manage any of the encryption infrastructure or customer master keys and require the most cost-effective solution. What is the MOST suitable option to encrypt the data?

1: Server-Side Encryption with Amazon S3-Managed Keys (SSE-S3)

2: Server-Side Encryption with Customer Master Keys (CMKs) Stored in AWS Key Management Service (SSE-KMS) using customer managed CMKs

3: Server-Side Encryption with Customer-Provided Keys (SSE-C)

4: Client-side encryption with Amazon S3 managed keys

44. Question

A Developer is building a three-tier web application that must be able to handle a minimum of 10,000 requests per minute. The requirements state that the web tier should be completely stateless while the application maintains session state data for users. How can the session state data be maintained externally, whilst keeping latency at the LOWEST possible value?

1: Create an Amazon RedShift instance, then implement session handling at the application level to leverage a database inside the RedShift database instance for session data storage

2: Implement a shared Amazon EFS file system solution across the underlying Amazon EC2 instances, then implement session handling at the application level to leverage the EFS file system for session data storage

3: Create an Amazon ElastiCache Redis cluster, then implement session handling at the application level to leverage the cluster for session data storage

4: Create an Amazon DynamoDB table, then implement session handling at the application level to leverage the table for session data storage

45. Question

A Developer is writing an imaging microservice on AWS Lambda. The service is dependent on several libraries that are not available in the Lambda runtime environment. Which strategy should the Developer follow to create the Lambda deployment package?

1: Create a ZIP file with the source code and all dependent libraries

2: Create a ZIP file with the source code and a script that installs the dependent libraries at runtime

3: Create a ZIP file with the source code and an appspec.yml file. Add the libraries to the appspec.yml file and upload to Amazon S3. Deploy using CloudFormation

4: Create a ZIP file with the source code and a buildspec.yml file that installs the dependent libraries on AWS Lambda

46. Question

An e-commerce web application that shares session state on-premises is being migrated to AWS. The application must be fault tolerant, natively highly scalable, and any service interruption should not affect the user experience. What is the best option to store the session state?

1: Store the session state in Amazon ElastiCache

2: Store the session state in Amazon CloudFront

3: Store the session state in Amazon S3

4: Enable session stickiness using elastic load balancers

47. Question

A Developer is writing a serverless application that will process data uploaded to a file share. The Developer has created an AWS Lambda function and requires the function to be invoked every 15 minutes to process the data. What is an automated and serverless way to trigger the function?

1: Deploy an Amazon EC2 instance based on Linux, and edit it's /etc/crontab file by adding a command to periodically invoke the Lambda function

2: Configure an environment variable named PERIOD for the Lambda function. Set the value at 600

3: Create an Amazon CloudWatch Events rule that triggers on a regular schedule to invoke the Lambda function

4: Create an Amazon SNS topic that has a subscription to the Lambda function with a 600-second timer

48. Question

A Developer attempted to run an AWS CodeBuild project, and received an error. The error stated that the length of all environment variables exceeds the limit for the combined maximum of characters. What is the recommended solution?

1: Add the export LC_ALL="en_US.utf8" command to the pre_build section to ensure POSIX localization

2: Use Amazon Cognito to store key-value pairs for large numbers of environment variables

3: Update the settings for the build project to use an Amazon S3 bucket for large numbers of environment variables

4: Use AWS Systems Manager Parameter Store to store large numbers of environment variables

49. Question

A Development team wants to run their container workloads on Amazon ECS. Each application container needs to share data with another container to collect logs and metrics. What should the Development team do to meet these requirements?

1: Create two pod specifications. Make one to include the application container and the other to include the other container. Link the two pods together

2: Create two task definitions. Make one to include the application container and the other to include the other container. Mount a shared volume between the two tasks

3: Create one task definition. Specify both containers in the definition. Mount a shared volume between those two containers

4: Create a single pod specification. Include both containers in the specification. Mount a persistent volume to both containers

50. Question

An application deployed on AWS Elastic Beanstalk experienced increased error rates during deployments of new application versions, resulting in service degradation for users. The Development team believes that this is because of the reduction in capacity during the deployment steps. The team would like to change the deployment policy configuration of the environment to an option that maintains full capacity during deployment while using the existing instances. Which deployment policy will meet these requirements while using the existing instances?

1: All at once

2: Rolling

3: Rolling with additional batch

4: Immutable

51. Question

A company has implemented AWS CodePipeline to automate its release pipelines. The Development team is writing an AWS Lambda function that will send notifications for state changes of each of the actions in the stages. Which steps must be taken to associate the Lambda function with the event source?

1: Create a trigger that invokes the Lambda function from the Lambda console by selecting CodePipeline as the event source

2: Create an event trigger and specify the Lambda function from the CodePipeline console

3: Create an Amazon CloudWatch alarm that monitors status changes in CodePipeline and triggers the Lambda function

4: Create an Amazon CloudWatch Events rule that uses CodePipeline as an event source

52. Question

A Developer has made an update to an application. The application serves users around the world and uses Amazon CloudFront for caching content closer to users. It has been reported that after deploying the application updates, users are not able to see the latest changes. How can the Developer resolve this issue?

1: Remove the origin from the CloudFront configuration and add it again

2: Disable forwarding of query strings and request headers from the CloudFront distribution configuration

3: Invalidate all the application objects from the edge caches

4: Disable the CloudFront distribution and enable it again to update all the edge locations

53. Question

A company has three different environments: Development, QA, and Production. The company wants to deploy its code first in the Development environment, then QA, and then Production. Which AWS service can be used to meet this requirement?

1: Use AWS CodeCommit to create multiple repositories to deploy the application

2: Use AWS CodeBuild to create, configure, and deploy multiple build application projects

3: Use AWS Data Pipeline to create multiple data pipeline provisions to deploy the application

4: Use AWS CodeDeploy to create multiple deployment groups

54. Question

A Developer has been tasked by a client to create an application. The client has provided the following requirements for the application:

- **Performance efficiency of seconds with up to a minute of latency**
- **Data storage requirements will be up to thousands of terabytes**
- **Per-message sizes may vary between 100 KB and 100 MB**
- **Data can be stored as key/value stores supporting eventual consistency**

What is the MOST cost-effective AWS service to meet these requirements?

1: Amazon DynamoDB

3: Amazon S3

3: Amazon RDS (with a MySQL engine)

4: Amazon ElastiCache

55. Question

An application on-premises uses Linux servers and a relational database using PostgreSQL. The company will be migrating the application to AWS and require a managed service that will take care of capacity provisioning, load balancing, and auto-scaling. Which combination of services should the Developer use? (Select TWO)

1: AWS Elastic Beanstalk

2: Amazon EC2 with Auto Scaling

3: Amazon EC2 with PostgreSQL

4: Amazon RDS with PostrgreSQL

5: AWS Lambda with CloudWatch Events

56. Question

A company runs many microservices applications that use Docker containers. The company are planning to migrate the containers to Amazon ECS. The workloads are highly variable and therefore the company prefers to be charged per running task. Which solution is the BEST fit for the company's requirements?

1: Amazon ECS with the EC2 launch type

2: Amazon ECS with the Fargate launch type

3: An Amazon ECS Service with Auto Scaling

4: An Amazon ECS Cluster with Auto Scaling

57. Question

A team of Developers require read-only access to an Amazon DynamoDB table. The Developers have been added to a group. What should an administrator do to provide the team with access whilst following the principal of least privilege?

1: Assign the AmazonDynamoDBReadOnlyAccess AWS managed policy to the group

2: Create a customer managed policy with read only access to DynamoDB and specify the ARN of the table for the "Resource" element. Attach the policy to the group

3: Assign the AWSLambdaDynamoDBExecutionRole AWS managed policy to the group

4: Create a customer managed policy with read/write access to DynamoDB for all resources. Attach the policy to the group

58. Question

A Developer is reviewing the permissions attached to an AWS Lambda function's execution role. What are the minimum permissions required for Lambda to create an Amazon CloudWatch Logs group and stream and write logs into the stream?

1: "logs:CreateLogGroup", "logs:CreateLogStream", "logs:PutLogEvents"

2: "logs:CreateLogGroup", "logs:CreateLogStream", "logs:PutDestination"

3: "logs:CreateExportTask", "logs:CreateLogStream", "logs:PutLogEvents"

4: "logs:GetLogEvents", "logs:GetLogRecord", "logs:PutLogEvents"

59. Question

An application needs to generate SMS text messages and emails for a large number of subscribers. Which AWS service can be used to send these messages to customers?

1: Amazon SES

2: Amazon SQS

3: Amazon SWF

4: Amazon SNS

60. Question

A website is deployed in several AWS regions. A Developer needs to direct global users to the website that provides the best performance. How can the Developer achieve this?

1: Create Alias records in AWS Route 53 and direct the traffic to an Elastic Load Balancer

2: Create A records in AWS Route 53 and use a weighted routing policy

3: Create A records in AWS Route 53 and use a latency-based routing policy

4: Create CNAME records in AWS Route 53 and direct traffic to Amazon CloudFront

61. Question

An IAM user is unable to assume an IAM role. The policy statement includes the "Effect": "Allow" and "Resource": "arn:aws:iam::*5123399432*:role/*MyCARole*" elements. Which other element MUST be included to allow the role to be assumed?

1: "Action": "ec2:AssumeRole

2: "Action": "sts:AssumeRole"

3: "Action": "sts:GetSessionToken"

4: "Action": "sts:GetAccessKeyInfo"

62. Question

An existing IAM user needs access to AWS resources in another account from an insecure environment for a short-term need (around 15 minutes). What would be the MOST secure method to provide the required access?

1: Use the AssumeRoleWithWebIdentity API operation to assume a role in the other account that has the required permissions

2: Use the AssumeRole API operation to assume a role in the other account that has the required permissions

3: Use the GetFederationToken API operation to return a set of temporary security credentials

4: Use the GetSessionToken API operation to return a set of temporary security credentials and specify 900 seconds in the DurationSeconds parameter

63. Question

A Developer has created a task definition that includes the following JSON code:

```
"placementStrategy": [
  {
    "field": "attribute:ecs.availability-zone",
    "type": "spread"
  },
  {
    "field": "instanceId",
    "type": "spread"
  }
]
```

What is the effect of this task placement strategy?

1: It distributes tasks evenly across Availability Zones and then distributes tasks evenly across the instances within each Availability Zone

2: It distributes tasks evenly across Availability Zones and then bin packs tasks based on memory within each Availability Zone

3: It distributes tasks evenly across Availability Zones and then distributes tasks evenly across distinct instances within each Availability Zone

4: It distributes tasks evenly across Availability Zones and then distributes tasks randomly across instances within each Availability Zone

64. Question

What is the most suitable storage solution for files up to 1 GB in size that must be stored for long periods of time that are accessed directly by applications with varying frequency?

1: Amazon S3 Glacier

2: Amazon DynamoDB

3: Amazon S3 Standard

4: Amazon RDS

65. Question

Users of an application using Amazon API Gateway, AWS Lambda and Amazon DynamoDB have reported errors when using the application. Which metrics should a Developer monitor in Amazon CloudWatch to determine the number of client-side and server-side errors?

1: 4XXError and 5XXError

2: CacheHitCount and CacheMissCount

3: IntegrationLatency and Latency

4: Errors

SET 1: PRACTICE QUESTIONS, ANSWERS & EXPLANATIONS

1. Question

A developer is planning to use a Lambda function to process incoming requests from an Application Load Balancer (ALB). How can this be achieved?

1: Create a target group and register the Lambda function using the AWS CLI

2: Create an Auto Scaling Group (ASG) and register the Lambda function in the launch configuration

3: Setup an API in front of the ALB using API Gateway and use an integration request to map the request to the Lambda function

4: Configure an event-source mapping between the ALB and the Lambda function

Answer: 1

Explanation:

You can register your Lambda functions as targets and configure a listener rule to forward requests to the target group for your Lambda function. When the load balancer forwards the request to a target group with a Lambda function as a target, it invokes your Lambda function and passes the content of the request to the Lambda function, in JSON format.

You need to create a target group, which is used in request routing, and register a Lambda function to the target group. If the request content matches a listener rule with an action to forward it to this target group, the load balancer invokes the registered Lambda function.

CORRECT: "Create a target group and register the Lambda function using the AWS CLI" is the correct answer.

INCORRECT: "Create an Auto Scaling Group (ASG) and register the Lambda function in the launch configuration" is incorrect as launch configurations and ASGs are used for launching Amazon EC2 instances, you cannot use an ASG with a Lambda function.

INCORRECT: "Setup an API in front of the ALB using API Gateway and use an integration request to map the request to the Lambda function" is incorrect as it is not a common design pattern to map an API Gateway API to a Lambda function when using an ALB. Though technically possible, typically you would choose to put API Gateway or an ALB in front of your application, not both.

INCORRECT: "Configure an event-source mapping between the ALB and the Lambda function" is incorrect as you cannot configure an event-source mapping between and ALB and a Lambda function.

2. Question

A developer is troubleshooting problems with a Lambda function that is invoked by Amazon SNS and repeatedly fails. How can the developer save discarded events for further processing?

1: Enable CloudWatch Logs for the Lambda function

2: Configure a Dead Letter Queue (DLQ)

3: Enable Lambda streams

4: Enable SNS notifications for failed events

Answer: 2

Explanation:

You can configure a dead letter queue (DLQ) on AWS Lambda to give you more control over message handling for all asynchronous invocations, including those delivered via AWS events (S3, SNS, IoT, etc.).

A dead-letter queue saves discarded events for further processing. A dead-letter queue acts the same as an on-failure destination in that it is used when an event fails all processing attempts or expires without being processed.

However, a dead-letter queue is part of a function's version-specific configuration, so it is locked in when you publish a version. On-failure destinations also support additional targets and include details about the function's response in the invocation record.

You can setup a DLQ by configuring the 'DeadLetterConfig' property when creating or updating your Lambda function. You can provide an SQS queue or an SNS topic as the 'TargetArn' for your DLQ, and AWS Lambda will write the event object invoking the Lambda function to this endpoint after the standard retry policy (2 additional retries on failure) is exhausted.

CORRECT: "Configure a Dead Letter Queue (DLQ)" is the correct answer.

INCORRECT: "Enable CloudWatch Logs for the Lambda function" is incorrect as CloudWatch logs will record metrics about the function but will not record records of the discarded events.

INCORRECT: "Enable Lambda streams" is incorrect as this is not something that exists (*DynamoDB* streams does exist).

INCORRECT: "Enable SNS notifications for failed events" is incorrect. Sending notifications from SNS will not include the data required for troubleshooting. A DLQ is the correct solution.

3. Question

A company will be uploading several terabytes of data to Amazon S3. What is the SIMPLEST solution to ensure that the data is encrypted before it is sent to S3 and whilst in transit?

1: Use client-side encryption with a KMS managed CMK and SSL

2: Use server-side encryption with client provided keys

3: Use client-side encryption and a hardware VPN to a VPC and an S3 endpoint

4: Use server-side encryption with S3 managed keys and SSL

Answer: 1

Explanation:

Client-side encryption is the act of encrypting data before sending it to Amazon S3. You have the following options:

- Use a customer master key (CMK) stored in AWS Key Management Service (AWS KMS).
- Use a master key you store within your application.

Additionally, using HTTPS/SSL to encrypt the data as it is transmitted over the Internet adds an additional layer of protection.

CORRECT: "Use client-side encryption with a KMS managed CMK and SSL" is the correct answer.

INCORRECT: "Use server-side encryption with client provided keys" is incorrect as this will encrypt the data as it is written to the S3 bucket. The questions states that you need to encrypt date *before* it is sent to S3.

INCORRECT: "Use client-side encryption and a hardware VPN to a VPC and an S3 endpoint" is incorrect. You can configure a hardware VPN to a VPC and configure an S3 endpoint to access S3 privately (rather than across the Internet). However, this is certainly not the simplest solution. Encrypting the data using client-side encryption and then using HTTPS/SSL to transmit the data is operationally easier to configure and manage and provides ample security.

INCORRECT: "Use server-side encryption with S3 managed keys and SSL" is incorrect as this does not encrypt the data before it is sent to S3 which is a requirement.

4. Question

An EC2 instance is allowed to access several buckets in an AWS account. The IAM policy attached to the EC2 instance profile's IAM role was replaced a few hours ago and restricts access to a single S3 bucket. However, the instance is still able to access all buckets. What is the MOST likely explanation for this? (Select TWO)

1: There is another policy attached to the IAM role that allows access

2: The evaluation logic checked the IAM user identity-based policy and found an allow

3: A resource-based policy attached to the S3 bucket is allowing access

4: IAM is eventually consistent, the changes may not have synchronized yet

5: It is not possible to restrict access to multiple buckets from a single policy

Answer: 1,3

Explanation:

Assume that a principal sends a request to AWS to access a resource in the same account as the principal's entity. The AWS enforcement code decides whether the request should be allowed or denied. AWS gathers all of the policies that apply to the request context. The following is a high-level summary of the AWS evaluation logic on those policies within a single account.

- By default, all requests are implicitly denied.
- An explicit allow in an identity-based or resource-based policy overrides this default.
- If a permissions boundary, Organizations SCP, or session policy is present, it might override the allow with an implicit deny.
- An explicit deny in any policy overrides any allows.

In this case the most likely explanation is that either another policy attached to the role has an allow rule allowing access to the buckets, or the bucket has a resource-based policy attached to it that is allowing access to the buckets.

CORRECT: "There is another policy attached to the IAM role that allows access" is a correct answer.

CORRECT: "A resource-based policy attached to the S3 bucket is allowing access" is also a correct answer.

INCORRECT: "The evaluation logic checked the IAM user identity-based policy and found an allow" is incorrect as the EC2 instance is using a role, not a user account.

INCORRECT: "IAM is eventually consistent, the changes may not have synchronized yet" is incorrect. Yes, IAM is eventually consistent however the question states that the changes were made a few hours ago which is ample time for IAM to synchronize.

INCORRECT: "It is not possible to restrict access to multiple buckets from a single policy" is incorrect. This is not true; you can certainly do this using multiple resources in the policy.

5. Question

A company is setting up a Lambda function that will process events from a DynamoDB stream. The Lambda function has been created and a stream has been enabled. What else needs to be done for this solution to work?

1: An alarm should be created in CloudWatch that sends a notification to Lambda when a new entry is added to the DynamoDB stream

2: An event-source mapping must be created on the DynamoDB side to associate the DynamoDB stream with the Lambda function

3: An event-source mapping must be created on the Lambda side to associate the DynamoDB stream with the Lambda function

4: Update the CloudFormation template to map the DynamoDB stream to the Lambda function

Answer: 3

Explanation:

An event source mapping is an AWS Lambda resource that reads from an event source and invokes a Lambda function. You can use event source mappings to process items from a stream or queue in services that don't invoke Lambda functions directly. Lambda provides event source mappings for the following services.

Services That Lambda Reads Events From

- Amazon Kinesis

- Amazon DynamoDB
- Amazon Simple Queue Service

An event source mapping uses permissions in the function's execution role to read and manage items in the event source. Permissions, event structure, settings, and polling behavior vary by event source.

The configuration of the event source mapping for stream-based services (DynamoDB, Kinesis), and Amazon SQS, is made on the Lambda side.

Note: for other services, such as Amazon S3 and SNS, the function is invoked asynchronously and the configuration is made on the source (S3/SNS) rather than Lambda.

CORRECT: "An event-source mapping must be created on the Lambda side to associate the DynamoDB stream with the Lambda function" is the correct answer.

INCORRECT: "An alarm should be created in CloudWatch that sends a notification to Lambda when a new entry is added to the DynamoDB stream" is incorrect as you should use an event-source mapping between Lambda and DynamoDB instead.

INCORRECT: "An event-source mapping must be created on the DynamoDB side to associate the DynamoDB stream with the Lambda function" is incorrect because for stream-based services that don't invoke Lambda functions directly, the configuration should be made on the Lambda side.

INCORRECT: "Update the CloudFormation template to map the DynamoDB stream to the Lambda function" is incorrect as CloudFormation may not even be used in this scenario (it wasn't mentioned) and wouldn't continuously send events from DynamoDB streams to Lambda either.

6. Question

A developer is preparing to deploy a Docker container to Amazon ECS using CodeDeploy. The developer has defined the deployment actions in a JSON file. What should the developer name the file?

1: buildspec.yml

3: appspec.yaml

3: cron.yml

4: appspec.yml

Answer: 2

Explanation:

The application specification file (AppSpec file) is a YAML-formatted or JSON-formatted file used by CodeDeploy to manage a deployment. The AppSpec file defines the deployment actions you want AWS CodeDeploy to execute.

The name of the AppSpec file for an EC2/On-Premises deployment must be appspec.yml. The name of the AppSpec file for an Amazon ECS or AWS Lambda deployment must be appspec.yaml.

Therefore, as this is an ECS deployment the file name must be appspec.yaml.

CORRECT: "appspec.yaml" is the correct answer.

INCORRECT: "buildspec.yml" is incorrect as this is the file name you should use for the file that defines the build instructions for AWS CodeBuild.

INCORRECT: "cron.yml" is incorrect. This is a file you can use with Elastic Beanstalk if you want to deploy a worker application that processes periodic background tasks.

INCORRECT: "appspec.yml" is incorrect as the file extension for ECS or Lambda deployments should be ".yaml", not ".yml".

7. Question

A decoupled application is using an Amazon SQS queue. The processing layer that is retrieving messages from the queue is not able to keep up with the number of messages being placed in the queue. What is the FIRST step the developer should take to increase the number of messages the application receives?

1: Use the API to update the WaitTimeSeconds parameter to a value other than 0

2: Add additional Amazon SQS queues and have the application poll those queues

3: Use the ReceiveMessage API to retrieve up to 10 messages at a time

4: Configure the queue to use short polling

Answer: 3

Explanation:

The ReceiveMessage API call retrieves one or more messages (up to 10), from the specified queue. This should be the first step to resolve the issue. With more messages received with each call the application should be able to process messages faster.

If the application still fails to keep up with the messages, and speed is important (remember this is one of the reasons for using an SQS queue, to shield your processing layer for the front-end), then additional queues can be added to scale horizontally.

CORRECT: "Use the ReceiveMessage API to retrieve up to 10 messages at a time" is the correct answer.

INCORRECT: "Use the API to update the WaitTimeSeconds parameter to a value other than 0" is incorrect as this is used to configure long polling.

INCORRECT: "Add additional Amazon SQS queues and have the application poll those queues" is incorrect as this may not be the first step. It would be simpler to update the application code to pull more messages at a time before adding queues.

INCORRECT: "Configure the queue to use short polling" is incorrect as this will not help the application to receive more messages.

8. Question

An application uses AWS Lambda which makes remote to several downstream services. A developer wishes to add data to custom subsegments in AWS X-Ray that can be used with filter expressions. Which type of data should be used?

1: Metadata

2: Annotations

3: Trace ID

4: Daemon

Answer: 2

Explanation:

AWS X-Ray helps developers analyze and debug production, distributed applications, such as those built using a microservices architecture. With X-Ray, you can understand how your application and its underlying services are performing to identify and troubleshoot the root cause of performance issues and errors. X-Ray provides an end-to-end view of requests as they travel through your application and shows a map of your application's underlying components.

You can record additional information about requests, the environment, or your application with annotations and metadata. You can add annotations and metadata to the segments that the X-Ray SDK creates, or to custom subsegments that you create.

Annotations are key-value pairs with string, number, or Boolean values. Annotations are indexed for use with filter expressions. Use annotations to record data that you want to use to group traces in the console, or when calling the GetTraceSummaries API.

CORRECT: "Annotations" is the correct answer.

INCORRECT: "Metadata" is incorrect. Metadata are key-value pairs that can have values of any type, including objects and lists, but are not indexed for use with filter expressions. Use metadata to record additional data that you want stored in the trace but don't need to use with search.

INCORRECT: "Trace ID" is incorrect. An X-Ray trace ID is used to group a set of data points in AWS X-Ray.

INCORRECT: "Daemon" is incorrect as this is a software application that listens for traffic on UDP port 2000, gathers raw segment data, and relays it to the AWS X-Ray API.

9. Question

An application component writes thousands of item-level changes to a DynamoDB table per day. The developer requires that a record is maintained of the items before they were modified. What MUST the developer do to retain this information? (Select TWO)

1: Create a CloudWatch alarm that sends a notification when an item is modified

2: Enable DynamoDB Streams for the table

3: Set the StreamViewType to OLD_IMAGE

4: Set the StreamViewType to NEW_AND_OLD_IMAGES

5: Use an AWS Lambda function to extract the item records from the notification and write to an S3 bucket

Answer: 2,3

Explanation:

DynamoDB Streams captures a time-ordered sequence of item-level modifications in any DynamoDB table and stores this information in a log for up to 24 hours. Applications can access this log and view the data items as they appeared before and after they were modified, in near-real time.

You can also use the CreateTable or UpdateTable API operations to enable or modify a stream. The StreamSpecification parameter determines how the stream is configured:

StreamEnabled — Specifies whether a stream is enabled (true) or disabled (false) for the table.

StreamViewType — Specifies the information that will be written to the stream whenever data in the table is modified:

- KEYS_ONLY — Only the key attributes of the modified item.
- NEW_IMAGE — The entire item, as it appears after it was modified.
- OLD_IMAGE — The entire item, as it appeared before it was modified.
- NEW_AND_OLD_IMAGES — Both the new and the old images of the item.

In this scenario, we only need to keep a copy of the items before they were modified. Therefore, the solution is to enable DynamoDB streams and set the StreamViewType to OLD_IMAGES.

CORRECT: "Enable DynamoDB Streams for the table" is the correct answer.

CORRECT: "Set the StreamViewType to OLD_IMAGE" is the correct answer.

INCORRECT: "Create a CloudWatch alarm that sends a notification when an item is modified" is incorrect as DynamoDB streams is the best way to capture a time-ordered sequence of item-level modifications in a DynamoDB table.

INCORRECT: "Set the StreamViewType to NEW_AND_OLD_IMAGES" is incorrect as we only need to keep a record of the items before they were modified. This setting would place a record in the stream that includes the item before and after modification.

INCORRECT: "Use an AWS Lambda function to extract the item records from the notification and write to an S3 bucket" is incorrect. There is no requirement to write the updates to S3 and if you did want to do this with Lambda you would need to extract the information from the stream, not a notification.

10. Question

An X-Ray daemon is being used on an Amazon ECS cluster to assist with debugging stability issues. A developer requires more detailed timing information and data related to downstream calls to AWS services. What should the developer use to obtain this extra detail?

1: Subsegments

2: Annotations

3: Metadata

4: Filter expressions

Answer: 1

Explanation:

A segment can break down the data about the work done into subsegments. Subsegments provide more granular timing information and details about downstream calls that your application made to fulfill the original request.

A subsegment can contain additional details about a call to an AWS service, an external HTTP API, or an SQL database. You can even define arbitrary subsegments to instrument specific functions or lines of code in your application.

CORRECT: "Subsegments" is the correct answer.

INCORRECT: "Annotations" is incorrect. Annotations are simple key-value pairs that are indexed for use with filter expressions. Use annotations to record data that you want to use to group traces in the console, or when calling the the GetTraceSummaries API.

INCORRECT: "Metadata" is incorrect. Metadata are key-value pairs with values of any type, including objects and lists, but that are not indexed. Use metadata to record data you want to store in the trace but don't need to use for searching traces.

INCORRECT: "Filter expressions" is incorrect. You can use filter expressions to find traces related to specific paths or users.

11. Question

A developer has deployed an application on an Amazon EC2 instance in a private subnet within a VPC. The subnet does not have Internet connectivity. The developer would like to write application logs to an Amazon S3 bucket. What MUST be configured to enable connectivity?

1: An IAM role must be added to the instance that has permissions to write to the S3 bucket

2: A bucket policy needs to be added specifying the principles that are allowed to write data to the bucket

3: A VPN should be established to enable private connectivity to S3

4: A VPC endpoint should be provisioned for S3

Answer: 4

Explanation:

Please note that the question specifically asks how to enable connectivity so this is not about permissions. When using a private subnet with no Internet connectivity there are only two options available for connecting to Amazon S3 (which remember, is a service with a public endpoint, it's not in your VPC).

The first option is to enable Internet connectivity through either a NAT Gateway or a NAT Instance. However, there is no answer offering either of these as a solution. The other option is to enable a VPC endpoint for S3.

The specific type of VPC endpoint to S3 is a Gateway Endpoint. EC2 instances running in private subnets of a VPC can use the endpoint to enable controlled access to S3 buckets, objects, and API functions that are in the same region as the VPC. You can then use an S3 bucket policy to indicate which VPCs and which VPC Endpoints have access to your S3 buckets.

In the following diagram, instances in subnet 2 can access Amazon S3 through the gateway endpoint.

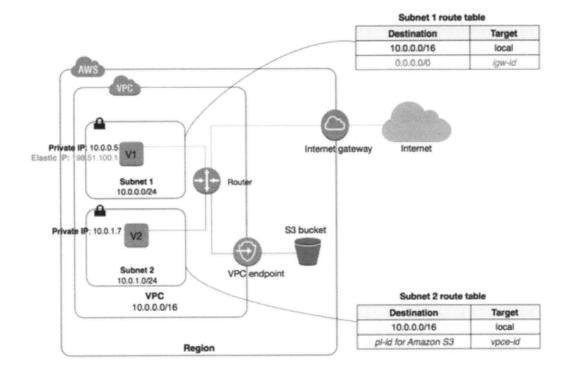

Subnet 1 route table	
Destination	Target
10.0.0.0/16	local
0.0.0.0/0	igw-id

Subnet 2 route table	
Destination	Target
10.0.0.0/16	local
pl-id for Amazon S3	vpce-id

Therefore, the only answer that presents a solution to this challenge is to provision an VPC endpoint for S3.

CORRECT: "A VPC endpoint should be provisioned for S3" is the correct answer.

INCORRECT: "An IAM role must be added to the instance that has permissions to write to the S3 bucket" is incorrect. You do need to do this, but the question is asking about connectivity, not permissions.

INCORRECT: "A bucket policy needs to be added specifying the principles that are allowed to write data to the bucket" is incorrect. You may choose to use a bucket policy to enable permissions but the question is asking about connectivity, not permissions.

INCORRECT: "A VPN should be established to enable private connectivity to S3" is incorrect. You can create a VPN to establish an encrypted tunnel into a VPC from a location outside of AWS. However, you cannot create a VPN connection from a subnet within a VPC to Amazon S3.

12. Question

A Developer wants to encrypt new objects that are being uploaded to an Amazon S3 bucket by an application. There must be an audit trail of who has used the key during this process. There should be no change to the performance of the application. Which type of encryption meets these requirements?

1: Server-side encryption using S3-managed keys

2: Server-side encryption with AWS KMS-managed keys

3: Client-side encryption with a client-side symmetric master key

4: Client-side encryption with AWS KMS-managed keys

Answer: 2

Explanation:

Server-Side Encryption with Customer Master Keys (CMKs) Stored in AWS Key Management Service (SSE-KMS) is similar to SSE-S3, but with some additional benefits and charges for using this service. There are separate permissions for the use of a CMK that provides added protection against unauthorized access of your objects in Amazon S3. SSE-KMS also provides you with an audit trail that shows when your CMK was used and by whom.

Therefore, the key to answering this question correctly is understanding that you do not get an audit trail of key usage when using S3-managed keys. You can still track API usage if you're using S3-managed keys, but not key usage. For this solution we need to use server-side encryption and AWS KMS-managed keys.

CORRECT: "Server-side encryption with AWS KMS-managed keys" is the correct answer.

INCORRECT: "Server-side encryption using S3-managed keys" is incorrect as S3-managed keys will not provide an audit trail of key usage as described above.

INCORRECT: "Client-side encryption with a client-side symmetric master key" is incorrect as server-side encryption should be used with a KMS-managed key so we get the audit trail of key usage.

INCORRECT: "Client-side encryption with AWS KMS-managed keys" is incorrect as the encryption should take place server-side so we do not impose any additional processing on the application that may affect performance.

13. Question

A serverless application uses an Amazon API Gateway and AWS Lambda. The application processes data submitted in a form by users of the application and certain data must be stored and available to subsequent function calls. What is the BEST solution for storing this data?

1: Store the data in an Amazon Kinesis Data Stream

2: Store the data in the /tmp directory

3: Store the data in an Amazon DynamoDB table

4: Store the data in an Amazon SQS queue

Answer: 3

Explanation:

AWS Lambda is a stateless compute service and so you cannot store session data in AWS Lambda itself. You can store a limited amount of information (up to 512 MB) in the /tmp directory. This information is preserved if the function is reused (i.e. the execution context is reused). However, it is not guaranteed that the execution context will be reused so the data could be destroyed.

The /tmp should only be used for data that can be regenerated or for operations that require a local filesystem, but not as a permanent storage solution. It is ideal for setting up database connections that will be needed across invocations of the function as the connection is made once and preserved across invocations.

Amazon DynamoDB is a good solution for this scenario as it is a low-latency NoSQL database that is often used for storing session state data. Amazon S3 would also be a good fit for this scenario but is not offered as an option.

With both Amazon DynamoDB and Amazon S3 you can store data long-term and it is available for multiple invocations of your function as well as being available from multiple invocations simultaneously.

CORRECT: "Store the data in an Amazon DynamoDB table" is the correct answer.

INCORRECT: "Store the data in an Amazon Kinesis Data Stream" is incorrect as this service is used for streaming data. It is not used for session-store use cases.

INCORRECT: "Store the data in the /tmp directory" is incorrect as any data stored in the /tmp may not be available for subsequent calls to your function. The /tmp directory content remains when the execution context is frozen, providing transient cache that can be used for multiple invocations. However, it is not guaranteed that the execution context will be reused so the data could be lost.

INCORRECT: "Store the data in an Amazon SQS queue" is incorrect as a message queue is not used for long-term storage of data.

14. Question

A Development team need to push an update to an application that is running on AWS Elastic Beanstalk. The business SLA states that the application must maintain full performance capabilities during updates whilst minimizing cost. Which Elastic Beanstalk deployment policy should the development team select?

1: Immutable

2: Rolling

3: All at once

4: Rolling with additional batch

Answer: 4

Explanation:

AWS Elastic Beanstalk provides several options for how deployments are processed, including deployment policies (**All at once**, **Rolling**, **Rolling with additional batch**, and **Immutable**) and options that let you configure batch size and health check behavior during deployments.

For this scenario we need to ensure we do not reduce the capacity of the application but we also need to minimize cost.

The **Rolling with additional batch** deployment policy does require extra cost but the extra cost is the size of a batch of instances, therefore you can reduce cost by reducing the batch size. The **Immutable** deployment policy requires a total deployment of new instances – i.e. if you have 4 instances this will double to 8 instances.

Therefore, the best deployment policy to use for this scenario is the **Rolling with additional batch**.

CORRECT: "Rolling with additional batch" is the correct answer.

INCORRECT: "Immutable" is incorrect as this would require a higher cost as you need a total deployment of new instances.

INCORRECT: "Rolling" is incorrect as this will result in a reduction in capacity which will affect performance.

INCORRECT: "All at once" is incorrect as this results in a total reduction in capacity, i.e. your entire application is taken down at once while the application update is installed.

15. Question

An organization developed an application that uses a set of APIs that are being served through Amazon API Gateway. The API calls must be authenticated based on OpenID identity providers such as Amazon, Google, or Facebook. The APIs should allow access based on a custom authorization model. Which is the simplest and MOST secure design to use to build an authentication and authorization model for the APIs?

1: Use Amazon ElastiCache to store user credentials and pass them to the APIs for authentication and authorization

2: Use Amazon DynamoDB to store user credentials and have the application retrieve temporary credentials from AWS STS. Make API calls by passing user credentials to the APIs for authentication and authorization

3: Use Amazon Cognito user pools and a custom authorizer to authenticate and authorize users based on JSON Web Tokens

4: Build an OpenID token broker with Amazon and Facebook. Users will authenticate with these identify providers and pass the JSON Web Token to the API to authenticate each API call

Answer: 3

Explanation:

With Amazon Cognito User Pools your app users can sign in either directly through a user pool or federate through a third-party identity provider (IdP). The user pool manages the overhead of handling the tokens that are returned from social sign-in through Facebook, Google, Amazon, and Apple, and from OpenID Connect (OIDC) and SAML IdPs.

After successful authentication, Amazon Cognito returns user pool tokens to your app. You can use the tokens to grant your users access to your own server-side resources, or to the Amazon API Gateway. Or, you can exchange them for AWS credentials to access other AWS services.

The ID token is a JSON Web Token (JWT) that contains claims about the identity of the authenticated user such as name, email, and phone_number. You can use this identity information inside your application. The ID token can also be used to authenticate users against your resource servers or server applications.

CORRECT: "Use Amazon Cognito user pools and a custom authorizer to authenticate and authorize users based on JSON Web Tokens" is the correct answer.

INCORRECT: "Use Amazon ElastiCache to store user credentials and pass them to the APIs for authentication and authorization" is incorrect. This option does not provide a solution for authenticating based on Open ID providers and is not secure as there is no mechanism mentioned for ensuring the secrecy of the credentials.

INCORRECT: "Use Amazon DynamoDB to store user credentials and have the application retrieve temporary credentials from AWS STS. Make API calls by passing user credentials to the APIs for authentication and authorization" is incorrect. This option also does not solve the requirement of integrating with Open ID providers and also suffers from the same security concerns as the option above.

INCORRECT: "Build an OpenID token broker with Amazon and Facebook. Users will authenticate with these identify providers and pass the JSON Web Token to the API to authenticate each API call" is incorrect. This may be a workable and secure solution however it is definitely not the simplest as it would require significant custom development.

16. Question

An AWS Lambda function has been packaged for deployment to multiple environments including development, test, and production. The Lambda function uses an Amazon RDS MySQL database for storing data. Each environment has a different RDS MySQL database. How can a Developer configure the Lambda function package to ensure the correct database connection string is used for each environment?

1: Use a separate function for development and production

2: Include the resources in the function code

3: Use environment variables for the database connection strings

4: Use layers for storing the database connection strings

Answer: 3

Explanation:

You can use environment variables to store secrets securely and adjust your function's behavior without updating code. An environment variable is a pair of strings that are stored in a function's version-specific configuration.

Use environment variables to pass environment-specific settings to your code. For example, you can have two functions with the same code but different configuration. One function connects to a test database, and the other connects to a production database.

In this situation, you use environment variables to tell the function the hostname and other connection details for the database. You might also set an environment variable to configure your test environment to use more verbose logging or more detailed tracing.

You set environment variables on the unpublished version of your function by specifying a key and value. When you publish a version, the environment variables are locked for that version along with other version-specific configuration.

It is possible to create separate versions of a function with different environment variables referencing the relevant database connection strings. Aliases can then be used to differentiate the environments and be used for connecting to the functions.

Therefore, using environment variables is the best way to ensure the environment-specific database connection strings are available in a single deployment package.

CORRECT: "Use environment variables for the database connection strings" is the correct answer.

INCORRECT: "Use a separate function for development and production" is incorrect as there's a single deployment package that must contain the connection strings for multiple environments. Therefore, using environment variables is necessary.

INCORRECT: "Include the resources in the function code" is incorrect. It would not be secure to include the database connection strings in the function code. With environment variables the password string can be encrypted using KMS which is much more secure.

INCORRECT: "Use layers for storing the database connection strings" is incorrect. Layers are used for adding external libraries to your functions.

<u>**17. Question**</u>

An application is being deployed on an Amazon EC2 instance running Linux. The EC2 instance will need to manage other AWS services. How can the EC2 instance be configured to make API calls to AWS service securely?

1: Run the "aws configure" AWS CLI command and specify the access key ID and secret access key

2: Create an AWS IAM Role, attach a policy with the necessary privileges and attach the role to the instance's instance profile

3: Store a users' console login credentials in the application code so the application can call AWS STS and gain temporary security credentials

4: Store the access key ID and secret access key as encrypted AWS Lambda environment variables and invoke Lambda for each API call

Answer: 2

Explanation:

Applications must sign their API requests with AWS credentials. Therefore, if you are an application developer, you need a strategy for managing credentials for your applications that run on EC2 instances. For example, you can securely distribute your AWS credentials to the instances, enabling the applications on those instances to use your credentials to sign requests, while protecting your credentials from other users.

However, it's challenging to securely distribute credentials to each instance, especially those that AWS creates on your behalf, such as Spot Instances or instances in Auto Scaling groups. You must also be able to update the credentials on each instance when you rotate your AWS credentials.

IAM roles are designed so that your applications can securely make API requests from your instances, without requiring you to manage the security credentials that the applications use.

Instead of creating and distributing your AWS credentials, you can delegate permission to make API requests using IAM roles as follows:

- Create an IAM role.
- Define which accounts or AWS services can assume the role.
- Define which API actions and resources the application can use after assuming the role.
- Specify the role when you launch your instance or attach the role to an existing instance.
- Have the application retrieve a set of temporary credentials and use them.

For example, you can use IAM roles to grant permissions to applications running on your instances that need to use a bucket in Amazon S3. You can specify permissions for IAM roles by creating a policy in JSON format. These are similar to the policies that you create for IAM users. If you change a role, the change is propagated to all instances.

Therefore, the best solution is to create an AWS IAM Role with the necessary privileges (through an IAM policy) and attach the role to the instance's instance profile.

CORRECT: "Create an AWS IAM Role, attach a policy with the necessary privileges and attach the role to the instance's instance profile" is the correct answer.

INCORRECT: "Run the "aws configure" AWS CLI command and specify the access key ID and secret access key" is incorrect as this in insecure as the access key ID and secret access key are stored in plaintext on the instance's local disk.

INCORRECT: "Store a users' console login credentials in the application code so the application can call AWS STS and gain temporary security credentials" is incorrect. This is a nonsense solution that would not work for multiple reasons. Firstly, the user console login credentials and not used for API access; secondly the STS service will not accept user login credentials and return temporary access credentials.

INCORRECT: "Store the access key ID and secret access key as encrypted AWS Lambda environment variables and invoke Lambda for each API call" is incorrect. You can encrypt Lambda variables with KMS keys; however, this is not an ideal solution as you will still need to decrypt the keys through the Lambda code and then pass them to the EC2 instance. There could be security risks in this process. This is generally a poor use case for Lambda and IAM Roles are a far superior way of providing the necessary access.

18. Question

A Developer is building an application that will store data relating to financial transactions in multiple DynamoDB tables. The Developer needs to ensure the transactions provide atomicity, isolation, and durability (ACID) and that changes are committed following an all-or nothing paradigm. What write API should be used for the DynamoDB table?

1: Standard

2: Strongly consistent

3: Transactional

4: Eventually consistent

Answer: 3

Explanation:

Amazon DynamoDB transactions simplify the developer experience of making coordinated, all-or-nothing changes to multiple items both within and across tables. Transactions provide atomicity, consistency, isolation, and durability (ACID) in DynamoDB, helping you to maintain data correctness in your applications.

You can use the DynamoDB transactional read and write APIs to manage complex business workflows that require adding, updating, or deleting multiple items as a single, all-or-nothing operation. For example, a video game developer can ensure that players' profiles are updated correctly when they exchange items in a game or make in-game purchases.

With the transaction write API, you can group multiple Put, Update, Delete, and ConditionCheck actions. You can then submit the actions as a single TransactWriteItems operation that either succeeds or fails as a unit. The same is true for multiple Get actions, which you can group and submit as a single TransactGetItems operation.

There is no additional cost to enable transactions for your DynamoDB tables. You pay only for the reads or writes that are part of your transaction. DynamoDB performs two underlying reads or writes of every item in the transaction: one to prepare the transaction and one to commit the transaction. These two underlying read/write operations are visible in your Amazon CloudWatch metrics.

CORRECT: "Transactional" is the correct answer.

INCORRECT: "Standard" is incorrect as this will not provide the ACID / all-or nothing transactional writes that are required for this solution.

INCORRECT: "Strongly consistent" is incorrect as this applies to reads only, not writes.

INCORRECT: "Eventually consistent" is incorrect as this applies to reads only, not writes.

19. Question

A Developer will be launching several Docker containers on a new Amazon ECS cluster using the EC2 Launch Type. The containers will all run a web service on port 80. What is the EASIEST way the Developer can configure the task definition to ensure the web services run correctly and there are no port conflicts on the host instances?

1: Specify port 80 for the container port and a unique port number for the host port

2: Specify a unique port number for the container port and port 80 for the host port

3: Specify port 80 for the container port and port 0 for the host port

4: Leave both the container port and host port configuration blank

Answer: 3

Explanation:

Port mappings allow containers to access ports on the host container instance to send or receive traffic. Port mappings are specified as part of the container definition. The container port is the port number on the container that is bound to the user-specified or automatically assigned host port. The host port is the port number on the container instance to reserve for your container.

As we cannot have multiple services bound to the same host port, we need to ensure that each container port mapping uses a different host port. The easiest way to do this is to set the host port number to 0 and ECS will automatically assign an available port. We also need to assign port 80 to the container port so that the web service is able to run.

CORRECT: "Specify port 80 for the container port and port 0 for the host port" is the correct answer.

INCORRECT: "Specify port 80 for the container port and a unique port number for the host port" is incorrect as this is more difficult to manage as you have to manually assign the port number.

INCORRECT: "Specify a unique port number for the container port and port 80 for the host port" is incorrect as the web service on the container needs to run on pot 80 and you can only bind one container to port 80 on the host so this would not allow more than one container to work.

INCORRECT: "Leave both the container port and host port configuration blank" is incorrect as this would mean that ECS would dynamically assign both the container and host port. As the web service must run on port 80 this would not work correctly.

20. Question

A Developer is designing a fault-tolerant application that will use Amazon EC2 instances and an Elastic Load Balancer. The Developer needs to ensure that if an EC2 instance fails session data is not lost. How can this be achieved?

1: Enable Sticky Sessions on the Elastic Load Balancer

2: Use an EC2 Auto Scaling group to automatically launch new instances

3: Use Amazon DynamoDB to perform scalable session handling

4: Use Amazon SQS to save session data

Answer: 3

Explanation:

For this scenario the key requirement is to ensure the data is not lost. Therefore, the data must be stored in a durable data store outside of the EC2 instances. Amazon DynamoDB is a suitable solution for storing session data. DynamoDB has a session handling capability for multiple languages as in the below example for PHP:

"The **DynamoDB Session Handler** is a custom session handler for PHP that allows developers to use Amazon DynamoDB as a session store. Using DynamoDB for session storage alleviates issues that occur with session handling in a distributed web application by moving sessions off of the local file system and into a shared location. DynamoDB is fast, scalable, easy to setup, and handles replication of your data automatically."

Therefore, the best answer is to use DynamoDB to store the session data.

CORRECT: "Use Amazon DynamoDB to perform scalable session handling" is the correct answer.

INCORRECT: "Enable Sticky Sessions on the Elastic Load Balancer" is incorrect. Sticky sessions attempts to direct a user that has reconnected to the application to the same EC2 instance that they connected to previously. However, this does not ensure that the session data is going to be available.

INCORRECT: "Use an EC2 Auto Scaling group to automatically launch new instances" is incorrect as this does not provide a solution for storing the session data.

INCORRECT: "Use Amazon SQS to save session data" is incorrect as Amazon SQS is not suitable for storing session data.

21. Question

A CloudFormation stack needs to be deployed in several regions and requires a different Amazon Machine Image (AMI) in each region. Which AWS CloudFormation template key can be used to specify the correct AMI for each region?

1: Outputs

2: Parameters

3: Resources

4: Mappings

Answer: 4

Explanation:

The optional Mappings section matches a key to a corresponding set of named values. For example, if you want to set values based on a region, you can create a mapping that uses the region name as a key and contains the values you want to specify for each specific region. You use the Fn::FindInMap intrinsic function to retrieve values in a map.

The following example shows a Mappings section with a map RegionMap, which contains five keys that map to name-value pairs containing single string values. The keys are region names. Each name-value pair is the AMI ID for the HVM64 AMI in the region represented by the key.

CORRECT: "Mappings" is the correct answer.

INCORRECT: "Outputs" is incorrect. The optional Outputs section declares output values that you can import into other stacks (to create cross-stack references), return in response (to describe stack calls), or view on the AWS CloudFormation console.

INCORRECT: "Parameters" is incorrect. Parameters enable you to input custom values to your template each time you create or update a stack.

INCORRECT: "Resources" is incorrect. The required Resources section declares the AWS resources that you want to include in the stack, such as an Amazon EC2 instance or an Amazon S3 bucket.

22. Question

A company has an application that logs all information to Amazon S3. Whenever there is a new log file, an AWS Lambda function is invoked to process the log files. The code works, gathering all of the necessary information. However, when checking the Lambda function logs, duplicate entries with the same request ID are found. What is the BEST explanation for the duplicate entries?

1: The S3 bucket name was specified incorrectly

2: The Lambda function failed, and the Lambda service retried the invocation with a delay

3: There was an S3 outage, which caused duplicate entries of the same log file

4: The application stopped intermittently and then resumed

Answer: 2

Explanation:

From the AWS documentation:

"When an error occurs, your function may be invoked multiple times. Retry behavior varies by error type, client, event source, and invocation type. For example, if you invoke a function asynchronously and it returns an error, Lambda executes the function up to two more times. For more information, see Retry Behavior.

For asynchronous invocation, Lambda adds events to a queue before sending them to your function. If your function does not have enough capacity to keep up with the queue, events may be lost. Occasionally, your function may receive the same event multiple times, even if no error occurs. To retain events that were not processed, configure your function with a dead-letter queue."

Therefore, the most likely explanation is that the function failed, and Lambda retried the invocation.

CORRECT: "The Lambda function failed, and the Lambda service retried the invocation with a delay" is the correct answer.

INCORRECT: "The S3 bucket name was specified incorrectly" is incorrect. If this was the case all attempts would fail but this is not the case.

INCORRECT: "There was an S3 outage, which caused duplicate entries of the same log file" is incorrect. There cannot be duplicate log files in Amazon S3 as every object must be unique within a bucket. Therefore, if the same log file was uploaded twice it would just overwrite the previous version of the file. Also, if a separate request was made to Lambda it would have a different request ID.

INCORRECT: "The application stopped intermittently and then resumed" is incorrect. The issue is duplicate entries of the same request ID.

23. Question

An AWS Lambda function authenticates to an external web site using a regularly rotated user name and password. The credentials need to be stored securely and must not be stored in the function code. What combination of AWS services can be used to achieve this requirement? (Select TWO)

1: AWS Certificate Manager (ACM)

2: AWS Systems Manager Parameter Store

3: AWS Key Management Store (KMS)

4: AWS Artifact

5: Amazon GuardDuty

Answer: 2,3

Explanation:

With AWS Systems Manager Parameter Store, you can create secure string parameters, which are parameters that have a plaintext parameter name and an encrypted parameter value. Parameter Store uses AWS KMS to encrypt and decrypt the parameter values of secure string parameters.

With Parameter Store you can create, store, and manage data as parameters with values. You can create a parameter in Parameter Store and use it in multiple applications and services subject to policies and permissions that you design. When you need to change a parameter value, you change one instance, rather than managing error-prone changes to numerous sources. Parameter Store supports a hierarchical structure for parameter names, so you can qualify a parameter for specific uses.

To manage sensitive data, you can create secure string parameters. Parameter Store uses AWS KMS customer master keys (CMKs) to encrypt the parameter values of secure string parameters when you create or change them. It also uses CMKs to decrypt the parameter values when you access them. You can use the AWS managed CMK that Parameter Store creates for your account or specify your own customer managed CMK.

Therefore, you can use a combination of AWS Systems Manager Parameter Store and AWS Key Management Store to store the credentials securely. These keys can be then be referenced in the Lambda function code or through environment variables.

NOTE: Systems Manager Parameter Store does not natively perform rotation of credentials so this must be done in the application. AWS Secrets Manager does perform credential rotation however it is not an answer option for this question.

CORRECT: "AWS Systems Manager Parameter Store" is a correct answer.

CORRECT: "AWS Key Management Store (KMS)" is also a correct answer.

INCORRECT: "AWS Certificate Manager (ACM)" is incorrect as this service is used to issue SSL/TLS certificates not encryption keys.

INCORRECT: "AWS Artifact" is incorrect as this is a service to view compliance information about the AWS platform

INCORRECT: "Amazon GuardDuty" is incorrect. Amazon GuardDuty is a threat detection service that continuously monitors for malicious activity and unauthorized behavior to protect your AWS accounts and workloads.

24. Question

A Development team would use a GitHub repository and would like to migrate their application code to AWS CodeCommit. What needs to be created before they can migrate a cloned repository to CodeCommit over HTTPS?

1: A GitHub secure authentication token

2: A public and private SSH key file

3: A set of Git credentials generated with IAM

4: An Amazon EC2 IAM role with CodeCommit permissions

Answer: 3

Explanation:

AWS CodeCommit is a managed version control service that hosts private Git repositories in the AWS cloud. To use CodeCommit, you configure your Git client to communicate with CodeCommit repositories. As part of this configuration, you provide IAM credentials that CodeCommit can use to authenticate you. IAM supports CodeCommit with three types of credentials:

- Git credentials, an IAM -generated user name and password pair you can use to communicate with CodeCommit repositories over HTTPS.

- SSH keys, a locally generated public-private key pair that you can associate with your IAM user to communicate with CodeCommit repositories over SSH.

- AWS access keys, which you can use with the credential helper included with the AWS CLI to communicate with CodeCommit repositories over HTTPS.

In this scenario the Development team need to connect to CodeCommit using HTTPS so they need either AWS access keys to use the AWS CLI or Git credentials generated by IAM. Access keys are not offered as an answer choice so the best answer is that they need to create a set of Git credentials generated with IAM

CORRECT: "A set of Git credentials generated with IAM" is the correct answer.

INCORRECT: "A GitHub secure authentication token" is incorrect as they need to authenticate to AWS CodeCommit, not GitHub (they have already accessed and cloned the repository).

INCORRECT: "A public and private SSH key file" is incorrect as these are used to communicate with CodeCommit repositories using SSH, not HTTPS.

INCORRECT: "An Amazon EC2 IAM role with CodeCommit permissions" is incorrect as you need the Git credentials generated through IAM to connect to CodeCommit.

25. Question

A company has a large Amazon DynamoDB table which they scan periodically so they can analyze several attributes. The scans are consuming a lot of provisioned throughput. What technique can a Developer use to minimize the impact of the scan on the table's provisioned throughput?

1: Set a smaller page size for the scan

2: Use parallel scans

3: Define a range key on the table

4: Prewarm the table by updating all items

Answer: 1

Explanation:

In general, Scan operations are less efficient than other operations in DynamoDB. A Scan operation always scans the entire table or secondary index. It then filters out values to provide the result you want, essentially adding the extra step of removing data from the result set.

If possible, you should avoid using a Scan operation on a large table or index with a filter that removes many results. Also, as a table or index grows, the Scan operation slows. The Scan operation examines every item for the requested values and can use up the provisioned throughput for a large table or index in a single operation.

Instead of using a large Scan operation, you can use the following techniques to minimize the impact of a scan on a table's provisioned throughput.

- **Reduce page size**

Because a Scan operation reads an entire page (by default, 1 MB), you can reduce the impact of the scan operation by setting a smaller page size. The Scan operation provides a *Limit* parameter that you can use to set the page size for your request. Each Query or Scan request that has a smaller page size uses fewer read operations and creates a "pause" between each request.

- **Isolate scan operations**

DynamoDB is designed for easy scalability. As a result, an application can create tables for distinct purposes, possibly even duplicating content across several tables. You want to perform scans on a table that is not taking "mission-critical" traffic. Some applications handle this load by rotating traffic hourly between two tables—one for critical traffic, and one for bookkeeping. Other applications can do this by performing every write on two tables: a "mission-critical" table, and a "shadow" table.

Therefore, the best option to reduce the impact of the scan on the table's provisioned throughput is to set a smaller page size for the scan.

CORRECT: "Set a smaller page size for the scan" is the correct answer.

INCORRECT: "Use parallel scans" is incorrect as this will return results faster but place more burden on the table's provisioned throughput.

INCORRECT: "Define a range key on the table" is incorrect. A range key is a composite key that includes the hash key and another attribute. This is of limited use in this scenario as the table is being scanned to analyze multiple attributes.

INCORRECT: "Prewarm the table by updating all items" is incorrect as updating all items would incur significant costs in terms of provisioned throughput and would not be advantageous.

26. Question

A Developer is deploying an application in a microservices architecture on Amazon ECS. The Developer needs to choose the best task placement strategy to MINIMIZE the number of instances that are used. Which task placement strategy should be used?

1: spread

2: random

3: binpack

4: weighted

Answer: 3

Explanation:

A *task placement strategy* is an algorithm for selecting instances for task placement or tasks for termination. Task placement strategies can be specified when either running a task or creating a new service.

Amazon ECS supports the following task placement strategies:

binpack - Place tasks based on the least available amount of CPU or memory. This minimizes the number of instances in use.

random - Place tasks randomly.

spread - Place tasks evenly based on the specified value. Accepted values are instanceId (or host, which has the same effect), or any platform or custom attribute that is applied to a container instance, such as attribute:ecs.availability-zone. Service tasks are spread based on the tasks from that service. Standalone tasks are spread based on the tasks from the same task group.

The **binpack** task placement strategy is the most suitable for this scenario as it minimizes the number of instances used which is a requirement for this solution.

CORRECT: "binpack" is the correct answer.

INCORRECT: "random" is incorrect as this would assign tasks randomly to EC2 instances which would not result in minimizing the number of instances used.

INCORRECT: "spread" is incorrect as this would spread the tasks based on a specified value. This is not used for minimizing the number of instances used.

INCORRECT: "weighted" is incorrect as this is not an ECS task placement strategy. Weighted is associated with Amazon Route 53 routing policies.

27. Question

A company has created a set of APIs using Amazon API Gateway and exposed them to partner companies. The APIs have caching enabled for all stages. The partners require a method of invalidating the cache that they can build into their applications. What can the partners use to invalidate the API cache?

1: They can pass the HTTP header Cache-Control: max-age=0

2: They can use the query string parameter INVALIDATE_CACHE

3: They must wait for the TTL to expire

4: They can invoke an AWS API endpoint which invalidates the cache

Answer: 1

Explanation:

You can enable API caching in Amazon API Gateway to cache your endpoint's responses. With caching, you can reduce the number of calls made to your endpoint and also improve the latency of requests to your API.

When you enable caching for a stage, API Gateway caches responses from your endpoint for a specified time-to-live (TTL) period, in seconds. API Gateway then responds to the request by looking up the endpoint response from the cache instead of making a request to your endpoint. The default TTL value for API caching is 300 seconds. The maximum TTL value is 3600 seconds. TTL=0 means caching is disabled.

A client of your API can invalidate an existing cache entry and reload it from the integration endpoint for individual requests. The client must send a request that contains the Cache-Control: max-age=0 header.

The client receives the response directly from the integration endpoint instead of the cache, provided that the client is authorized to do so. This replaces the existing cache entry with the new response, which is fetched from the integration endpoint.

To grant permission for a client, attach a policy of the following format to an IAM execution role for the user.

```
{
  "Version": "2012-10-17",
  "Statement": [
    {
      "Effect": "Allow",
      "Action": [
        "execute-api:InvalidateCache"
      ],
      "Resource": [
        "arn:aws:execute-api:region:account-id:api-id/stage-name/GET/resource-path-specifier"
      ]
    }
  ]
}
```

This policy allows the API Gateway execution service to invalidate the cache for requests on the specified resource (or resources).

Therefore, as described above the solution is to get the partners to pass the HTTP header Cache-Control: max-age=0.

CORRECT: "They can pass the HTTP header Cache-Control: max-age=0" is the correct answer.

INCORRECT: "They can use the query string parameter INVALIDATE_CACHE" is incorrect. This is not a valid method of invalidating the cache with API Gateway.

INCORRECT: "They must wait for the TTL to expire" is incorrect as this is not true, you do not need to wait as you can pass the HTTP header Cache-Control: max-age=0 whenever you need to in order to invalidate the cache.

INCORRECT: "They can invoke an AWS API endpoint which invalidates the cache" is incorrect. This is not a valid method of invalidating the cache with API Gateway.

28. Question

A Developer is deploying an AWS Lambda update using AWS CodeDeploy. In the appspec.yml file, which of the following is a valid structure for the order of hooks that should be specified?

1: BeforeInstall > AfterInstall > AfterAllowTestTraffic > BeforeAllowTraffic > AfterAllowTraffic

2: BeforeInstall > AfterInstall > ApplicationStart > ValidateService

3: BeforeAllowTraffic > AfterAllowTraffic

4: BeforeBlockTraffic > AfterBlockTraffic > BeforeAllowTraffic > AfterAllowTraffic

Answer: 3

Explanation:

The content in the 'hooks' section of the AppSpec file varies, depending on the compute platform for your deployment. The 'hooks' section for an EC2/On-Premises deployment contains mappings that link deployment lifecycle event hooks to one or more scripts.

The 'hooks' section for a Lambda or an Amazon ECS deployment specifies Lambda validation functions to run during a deployment lifecycle event. If an event hook is not present, no operation is executed for that event. This section is required only if you are running scripts or Lambda validation functions as part of the deployment.

CORRECT: "BeforeAllowTraffic > AfterAllowTraffic" is the correct answer.

INCORRECT: "BeforeInstall > AfterInstall > ApplicationStart > ValidateService" is incorrect as this would be valid for Amazon EC2.

INCORRECT: "BeforeInstall > AfterInstall > AfterAllowTestTraffic > BeforeAllowTraffic > AfterAllowTraffic" is incorrect as this would be valid for Amazon ECS.

INCORRECT: "BeforeBlockTraffic > AfterBlockTraffic > BeforeAllowTraffic > AfterAllowTraffic" is incorrect as this is a partial listing of hooks for Amazon EC2 but is incomplete.

29. Question

A Developer needs to scan a full DynamoDB 50GB table within non-peak hours. About half of the strongly consistent RCUs are typically used during non-peak hours and the scan duration must be minimized. How can the Developer optimize the scan execution time without impacting production workloads?

1: Use sequential scans

2: Use parallel scans while limiting the rate

3: Increase the RCUs during the scan operation

4: Change to eventually consistent RCUs during the scan operation

Answer: 2

Explanation:

Performing a scan on a table consumes a lot of RCUs. A Scan operation always scans the entire table or secondary index. It then filters out values to provide the result you want, essentially adding the extra step of removing data from the result set. To reduce the amount of RCUs used by the scan so it doesn't affect production workloads whilst minimizing the execution time, there are a couple of recommendations the Developer can follow.

Firstly, the *Limit* parameter can be used to reduce the page size. The Scan operation provides a *Limit* parameter that you can use to set the page size for your request. Each Query or Scan request that has a smaller page size uses fewer read operations and creates a "pause" between each request.

Secondly, the Developer can configure parallel scans. With parallel scans the Developer can maximize usage of the available throughput and have the scans distributed across the table's partitions.

A parallel scan can be the right choice if the following conditions are met:

- The table size is 20 GB or larger.
- The table's provisioned read throughput is not being fully used.
- Sequential Scan operations are too slow.

Therefore, to optimize the scan operation the Developer should use parallel scans while limiting the rate as this will ensure that the scan operation does not affect the performance of production workloads and still have it complete in the minimum time.

CORRECT: "Use parallel scans while limiting the rate" is the correct answer.

INCORRECT: "Use sequential scans" is incorrect as this is slower than parallel scans and the Developer needs to minimize scan execution time.

INCORRECT: "Increase the RCUs during the scan operation" is incorrect as the table is only using half of the RCUs during non-peak hours so there are RCUs available. You could increase RCUs and perform the scan faster, but this would be more expensive. The better solution is to use parallel scans with the limit parameter.

INCORRECT: "Change to eventually consistent RCUs during the scan operation" is incorrect as this does not provide a solution for preventing impact to the production workloads. The limit parameter should be used to ensure the tables RCUs are not fully used.

30. Question

A Development team is involved with migrating an on-premises MySQL database to Amazon RDS. The database usage is very read-heavy. The Development team wants re-factor the application code to achieve optimum read performance for queries. How can this objective be met?

1: Add database retries to the code and vertically scale the Amazon RDS database

2: Use Amazon RDS with a multi-AZ deployment

3: Add a connection string to use an Amazon RDS read replica for read queries

Answer: 3

Explanation:

Amazon RDS uses the MariaDB, MySQL, Oracle, and PostgreSQL DB engines' built-in replication functionality to create a special type of DB instance called a Read Replica from a source DB instance. Updates made to the source DB instance are asynchronously copied to the Read Replica.

You can reduce the load on your source DB instance by routing read queries from your applications to the Read Replica. Using Read Replicas, you can elastically scale out beyond the capacity constraints of a single DB instance for read-heavy database workloads.

A primary Amazon RDS database server allows reads and writes while a Read Replica can be used for running read-only workloads such as BI/reporting. This reduces the load on the primary database.

It is necessary to add logic to your code to direct read traffic to the Read Replica and write traffic to the primary database. Therefore, in this scenario the Development team will need to "Add a connection string to use an Amazon RDS read replica for read queries".

CORRECT: "Add a connection string to use an Amazon RDS read replica for read queries" is the correct answer.

INCORRECT: "Add database retries to the code and vertically scale the Amazon RDS database" is incorrect as this is not a good way to scale reads as you will likely hit a ceiling at some point in terms of cost or instance type. Scaling reads can be better implemented with horizontal scaling using a Read Replica.

INCORRECT: "Use Amazon RDS with a multi-AZ deployment" is incorrect as this creates a standby copy of the database in another AZ that can be failed over to in a failure scenario. This is used for DR not (at least not primarily) used for scaling performance. It is possible for certain RDS engines to use a multi-AZ standby as a read replica however the requirements in this solution do not warrant this configuration.

INCORRECT: "Add a connection string to use a read replica on an Amazon EC2 instance" is incorrect as Read Replicas are something you create on Amazon RDS, not on an EC2 instance.

31. Question

To reduce the cost of API actions performed on an Amazon SQS queue, a Developer has decided to implement long polling. Which of the following modifications should the Developer make to the API actions?

1: Set the ReceiveMessage API with a WaitTimeSeconds of 20

2: Set the SetQueueAttributes API with a DelaySeconds of 20

3: Set the ReceiveMessage API with a VisibilityTimeout of 30

4: Set the SetQueueAttributes with a MessageRetentionPeriod of 60

Answer: 1

Explanation:

The process of consuming messages from a queue depends on whether you use short or long polling. By default, Amazon SQS uses *short polling*, querying only a subset of its servers (based on a weighted random distribution) to determine whether any messages are available for a response. You can use *long polling* to reduce your costs while allowing your consumers to receive messages as soon as they arrive in the queue.

When you consume messages from a queue using short polling, Amazon SQS samples a subset of its servers (based on a weighted random distribution) and returns messages from only those servers. Thus, a particular ReceiveMessage request might not return all of your messages. However, if you have fewer than 1,000 messages in your queue, a subsequent request will return your messages. If you keep consuming from your queues, Amazon SQS samples all of its servers, and you receive all of your messages.

When the wait time for the ReceiveMessage API action is greater than 0, *long polling* is in effect. The maximum long polling wait time is 20 seconds. Long polling helps reduce the cost of using Amazon SQS by eliminating the number of empty responses (when there are no messages available for a ReceiveMessage request) and false empty responses (when messages are available but aren't included in a response).

Long polling occurs when the WaitTimeSeconds parameter of a ReceiveMessage request is set to a value greater than 0 in one of two ways:

- The ReceiveMessage call sets WaitTimeSeconds to a value greater than 0.
- The ReceiveMessage call doesn't set WaitTimeSeconds, but the queue attribute ReceiveMessageWaitTimeSeconds is set to a value greater than 0.

Therefore, the Developer should set the ReceiveMessage API with a WaitTimeSeconds of 20.

CORRECT: "Set the ReceiveMessage API with a WaitTimeSeconds of 20" is the correct answer.

INCORRECT: "Set the SetQueueAttributes API with a DelaySeconds of 20" is incorrect as this would be used to configure a delay queue where the delivery of messages in the queue is delayed.

INCORRECT: "Set the ReceiveMessage API with a VisibilityTimeout of 30" is incorrect as this would configure the visibility timeout which is the length of time a message that has been received is invisible.

INCORRECT: "Set the SetQueueAttributes with a MessageRetentionPeriod of 60" is incorrect as this would configure how long messages are retained in the queue.

32. Question

A company is deploying an Amazon Kinesis Data Streams application that will collect streaming data from a gaming application. Consumers will run on Amazon EC2 instances. In this architecture, what can be deployed on consumers to act as an intermediary between the record processing logic and Kinesis Data Streams and instantiate a record processor for each shard?

1: Amazon Kinesis API

2: AWS CLI

3: Amazon Kinesis CLI

4: Amazon Kinesis Client Library (KCL)

Answer: 4

Explanation:

The Kinesis Client Library (KCL) helps you consume and process data from a Kinesis data stream. This type of application is also referred to as a *consumer*. The KCL takes care of many of the complex tasks associated with distributed computing, such as load balancing across multiple instances, responding to instance failures, checkpointing processed records, and reacting to resharding. The KCL enables you to focus on writing record-processing logic.

The KCL is different from the Kinesis Data Streams API that is available in the AWS SDKs. The Kinesis Data Streams API helps you manage many aspects of Kinesis Data Streams (including creating streams, resharding, and putting and getting records). The KCL provides a layer of abstraction specifically for processing data in a consumer role.

Therefore, the correct answer is to use the Kinesis Client Library.

CORRECT: "Amazon Kinesis Client Library (KCL)" is the correct answer.

INCORRECT: "Amazon Kinesis API" is incorrect. You can work with Kinesis Data Streams directly from your consumers using the API but this is does not deploy an intermediary component as required.

INCORRECT: "AWS CLI" is incorrect. The AWS CLI can be used to work directly with the Kinesis API but this does not deploy an intermediary component as required.

INCORRECT: "Amazon Kinesis CLI" is incorrect as this does not exist. The AWS CLI has commands for working with Kinesis.

33. Question

A serverless application uses an AWS Lambda function to process Amazon S3 events. The Lambda function executes 20 times per second and takes 20 seconds to complete each execution. How many concurrent executions will the Lambda function require?

1: 5

2: 400

3: 40

4: 20

Answer: 2

Explanation:

Concurrency is the number of requests that your function is serving at any given time. When your function is invoked, Lambda allocates an instance of it to process the event. When the function code finishes running, it can handle another request. If the function is invoked again while a request is still being processed, another instance is allocated, which increases the function's concurrency.

To calculate the concurrency requirements for the Lambda function simply multiply the number of executions per second (20) by the time it takes to complete the execution (20).

Therefore, for this scenario the calculation is 20 x 20 = 400.

CORRECT: "400" is the correct answer.

INCORRECT: "5" is incorrect. Please use the formula above to calculate concurrency requirements.

INCORRECT: "40" is incorrect. Please use the formula above to calculate concurrency requirements.

INCORRECT: "20" is incorrect. Please use the formula above to calculate concurrency requirements.

34. Question

A Developer needs to be notified by email when a new object is uploaded to a specific Amazon S3 bucket. What is the EASIEST way for the Developer to enable these notifications?

1: Add an event to the S3 bucket for PUT and POST events and use an Amazon SNS Topic

2: Add an event to the S3 bucket for PUT and POST events and use an Amazon SQS queue

3: Add an event to the S3 bucket for PUT and POST events and use an AWS Lambda function

4: Add an event to the S3 bucket for all object create events and use AWS Step Functions

Answer: 1

Explanation:

The Amazon S3 notification feature enables you to receive notifications when certain events happen in your bucket. To enable notifications, you must first add a notification configuration that identifies the events you want Amazon S3 to publish and the destinations where you want Amazon S3 to send the notifications. You store this configuration in the *notification* subresource that is associated with a bucket.

Amazon Simple Notification Service (SNS) is a service that allows you to send notifications from the cloud in a publisher / subscriber model. It supports multiple transport protocols including email.

The easiest option presented is therefore to add an event to the S3 bucket for PUT and POST events and use an Amazon SNS Topic.

CORRECT: "Add an event to the S3 bucket for PUT and POST events and use an Amazon SNS Topic" is the correct answer.

INCORRECT: "Add an event to the S3 bucket for PUT and POST events and use an Amazon SQS queue" is incorrect as SQS is a message queue and is not suitable for when you want to trigger an email notification.

INCORRECT: "Add an event to the S3 bucket for PUT and POST events and use an AWS Lambda function" is incorrect as this would also not be the best service for triggering an email notification.

INCORRECT: "Add an event to the S3 bucket for all object create events and use AWS Step Functions" is incorrect as this service is involved with the coordination of serverless workflows, it is not used for triggering email notifications.

35. Question

A Developer is setting up a code update to Amazon ECS using AWS CodeDeploy. The Developer needs to complete the code update quickly. Which of the following deployment types should the Developer use?

1: In-place

2: Canary

3: Blue/green

4: Linear

Answer: 3

Explanation:

CodeDeploy provides two deployment type options – in-place and blue/green. Note that AWS Lambda and Amazon ECS deployments cannot use an in-place deployment type.

The Blue/green deployment type on an Amazon ECS compute platform works like this:

- Traffic is shifted from the task set with the original version of an application in an Amazon ECS service to a replacement task set in the same service.
- You can set the traffic shifting to linear or canary through the deployment configuration.
- The protocol and port of a specified load balancer listener is used to reroute production traffic.
- During a deployment, a test listener can be used to serve traffic to the replacement task set while validation tests are run.

CORRECT: "Blue/green" is the correct answer.

INCORRECT: "Canary" is incorrect as this is a traffic shifting option, not a deployment type. Traffic is shifted in two increments.

INCORRECT: "Linear" is incorrect as this is a traffic shifting option, not a deployment type. Traffic is shifted in two increments.

INCORRECT: "In-place" is incorrect as AWS Lambda and Amazon ECS deployments cannot use an in-place deployment type.

36. Question

Change management procedures at an organization require that a log is kept recording activity within AWS accounts. The activity that must be recorded includes API activity related to creating, modifying or deleting AWS resources. Which AWS service should be used to record this information?

1: Amazon CloudWatch

2: Amazon CloudTrail

3: AWS X-Ray

4: AWS OpsWorks

Answer: 2

Explanation:

AWS CloudTrail is a service that enables governance, compliance, operational auditing, and risk auditing of your AWS account. With CloudTrail, you can log, continuously monitor, and retain account activity related to actions across your AWS infrastructure. CloudTrail provides event history of your AWS account activity, including actions taken through the AWS Management Console, AWS SDKs, command line tools, and other AWS services.

This event history simplifies security analysis, resource change tracking, and troubleshooting. In addition, you can use CloudTrail to detect unusual activity in your AWS accounts. These capabilities help simplify operational analysis and troubleshooting.

Therefore, Amazon CloudTrail is the most suitable service for the requirements in this scenario.

CORRECT: "Amazon CloudTrail" is the correct answer.

INCORRECT: "Amazon CloudWatch" is incorrect as this service is used for performance monitoring, not recording API actions.

INCORRECT: "AWS X-Ray" is incorrect as this is used for tracing application activity for performance and operational statistics.

INCORRECT: "AWS OpsWorks" is incorrect as this is a configuration management service that helps you build and operate highly dynamic applications and propagate changes instantly.

37. Question

A company is deploying an on-premise application server that will connect to several AWS services. What is the BEST way to provide the application server with permissions to authenticate to AWS services?

1: Create an IAM role with the necessary permissions and assign it to the application server

2: Create an IAM user and generate access keys. Create a credentials file on the application server

3: Create an IAM group with the necessary permissions and add the on-premise application server to the group

4: Create an IAM user and generate a key pair. Use the key pair in API calls to AWS services

Answer: 2

Explanation:

Access keys are long-term credentials for an IAM user or the AWS account root user. You can use access keys to sign programmatic requests to the AWS CLI or AWS API (directly or using the AWS SDK).

Access keys are stored in one of the locations on a client that needs to make authenticated API calls to AWS services:

- Linux: ~/.aws/credentials
- Windows: %UserProfile%\.aws\credentials

In this scenario the application server is running on-premises. Therefore, you cannot assign an IAM role (which would be the preferable solution for Amazon EC2 instances). In this case it is therefore better to use access keys.

CORRECT: "Create an IAM user and generate access keys. Create a credentials file on the application server" is the correct answer.

INCORRECT: "Create an IAM role with the necessary permissions and assign it to the application server" is incorrect. This is an on-premises server so it is not possible to use an IAM role. If it was an EC2 instance, this would be the preferred (best practice) option.

INCORRECT: "Create an IAM group with the necessary permissions and add the on-premise application server to the group" is incorrect. You cannot add a server to an IAM group. You put IAM users into groups and assign permissions to them using a policy.

INCORRECT: "Create an IAM user and generate a key pair. Use the key pair in API calls to AWS services" is incorrect as key pairs are used for SSH access to Amazon EC2 instances. You cannot use them in API calls to AWS services.

38. Question

A Developer is creating an application that will run on Amazon EC2 instances. The application will process encrypted files. The files must be decrypted prior to processing. Which of the following steps should be taken to securely decrypt the data? (Select TWO)

1: Pass the encrypted data key to the Decrypt operation

2: Use the encrypted data key to decrypt the data and then remove the encrypted data key from memory as soon as possible

3: Use the plaintext data key to decrypt the data and then remove the plaintext data key from memory as soon as possible

4: Use the plaintext data key to decrypt the data and then remove the encrypted data key from memory as soon as possible

5: Pass the plaintext data key to the Decrypt operation

Answer: 1,3

Explanation:

When you encrypt your data, your data is protected, but you have to protect your encryption key. One strategy is to encrypt it. *Envelope encryption* is the practice of encrypting plaintext data with a data key, and then encrypting the data key under another key.

You can even encrypt the data encryption key under another encryption key and encrypt that encryption key under another encryption key. But, eventually, one key must remain in plaintext so you can decrypt the keys and your data. This top-level plaintext key encryption key is known as the *master key*.

To decrypt your data, pass the encrypted data key to the Decrypt operation. AWS KMS uses your CMK to decrypt the data key and then it returns the plaintext data key. Use the plaintext data key to decrypt your data and then remove the plaintext data key from memory as soon as possible.

CORRECT: "Pass the encrypted data key to the Decrypt operation" is a correct answer.

CORRECT: "Use the plaintext data key to decrypt the data and then remove the plaintext data key from memory as soon as possible" is also a correct answer.

INCORRECT: "Use the encrypted data key to decrypt the data and then remove the encrypted data key from memory as soon as possible" is incorrect as you can only decrypt data with an unencrypted data key.

INCORRECT: "Use the plaintext data key to decrypt the data and then remove the encrypted data key from memory as soon as possible" is incorrect as it's the plaintext data key that must be removed from memory as it's a security concern.

INCORRECT: "Pass the plaintext data key to the Decrypt operation" is incorrect as the encrypted data key should be passed to the Decrypt operation.

39. Question

A Developer needs to launch a serverless static website. The Developer needs to get the website up and running quickly and easily. What should the Developer do?

1: Configure an Amazon S3 bucket as a static website

2: Configure an Amazon EC2 instance with Apache

3: Create an AWS Lambda function with an API Gateway front-end

4: Share an Amazon EFS volume as a static website

Answer: 1

Explanation:

You can use Amazon S3 to host a static website. On a *static* website, individual webpages include static content. They might also contain client-side scripts.

To host a static website on Amazon S3, you configure an Amazon S3 bucket for website hosting and then upload your website content to the bucket. When you configure a bucket as a static website, you enable static website hosting, set permissions, and add an index document. Depending on your website requirements, you can also configure other options, including redirects, web traffic logging, and custom error documents.

CORRECT: "Configure an Amazon S3 bucket as a static website" is the correct answer.

INCORRECT: "Configure an Amazon EC2 instance with Apache" is incorrect as this is not a serverless solution.

INCORRECT: "Create an AWS Lambda function with an API Gateway front-end" is incorrect as this is not the easiest way to create a static website. Using Amazon S3 would be easier.

INCORRECT: "Share an Amazon EFS volume as a static website" is incorrect as you cannot share an Amazon EFS volume as a static website.

40. Question

A Developer requires a multi-threaded in-memory cache to place in front of an Amazon RDS database. Which caching solution should the Developer choose?

1: Amazon DynamoDB DAX

2: Amazon ElastiCache Redis

3: Amazon ElastiCache Memcached

4: Amazon RedShift

Answer: 3

Explanation:

Amazon ElastiCache is a fully managed implementation of two popular in-memory data stores – Redis and Memcached. The in-memory caching provided by ElastiCache can be used to significantly improve latency and throughput for many read-heavy application workloads or compute-intensive workloads.

There are two types of engine you can choose from: Memcached, Redis:

MEMCACHED

- Simplest model and can run large nodes.

- Can be scaled in and out and cache objects such as DBs.

- Widely adopted memory object caching system.

- Multi-threaded.

REDIS

- Open-source in-memory key-value store.

- Supports more complex data structures: sorted sets and lists.

- Supports master / slave replication and multi-AZ for cross-AZ redundancy.

- Support automatic failover and backup/restore.

As the Developer requires a multi-threaded cache, the best choice is Memcached.

CORRECT: "Amazon ElastiCache Memcached" is the correct answer.

INCORRECT: "Amazon ElastiCache Redis" is incorrect as Redis it not multi-threaded.

INCORRECT: "Amazon DynamoDB DAX" is incorrect as this is more suitable for use with an Amazon DynamoDB table.

INCORRECT: "Amazon RedShift" is incorrect as this is not an in-memory caching engine, it is a data warehouse.

41. Question

A Developer needs to write a small amount of temporary log files from an application running on an Amazon EC2 instance. The log files will be automatically deleted every 24 hours. What is the SIMPLEST solution for storing this data that will not require additional code?

1: Write the log files to an attached Amazon EBS volume

2: Write the log files to an Amazon EFS volume

3: Write the log files to an Amazon DynamoDB database

4: Write the log files to an Amazon S3 bucket

Answer: 1

Explanation:

Amazon Elastic Block Store (Amazon EBS) provides block level storage volumes for use with EC2 instances. EBS volumes behave like raw, unformatted block devices.

You can mount these volumes as devices on your instances. You can mount multiple volumes on the same instance, and you can mount a volume to multiple instances at a time.

You can create a file system on top of these volumes or use them in any way you would use a block device (like a hard drive). You can dynamically change the configuration of a volume attached to an instance.

The simplest solution for this scenario is to choose a local Elastic Block Store (EBS) volume to write the log files to. This requires no additional coding.

CORRECT: "Write the log files to an attached Amazon EBS volume" is the correct answer.

INCORRECT: "Write the log files to an Amazon EFS volume" is incorrect as this is not the simplest solution and is better suited to use cases where you need to share the data with other instances.

INCORRECT: "Write the log files to an Amazon DynamoDB database" is incorrect as this is not the simplest solution as it would require additional code in the application compared to just writing the data to a local volume.

INCORRECT: "Write the log files to an Amazon S3 bucket" is incorrect as this is not the simplest solution as it would require additional code in the application compared to just writing the data to a local volume.

42. Question

A Developer has recently created an application that uses an AWS Lambda function, an Amazon DynamoDB table, and also sends notifications using Amazon SNS. The application is not working as expected and the Developer needs to analyze what is happening across all components of the application. What is the BEST way to analyze the issue?

1: Enable X-Ray tracing for the Lambda function

2: Create an Amazon CloudWatch Events rule

3: Assess the application with Amazon Inspector

4: Monitor the application with AWS Trusted Advisor

Answer: 1

Explanation:

AWS X-Ray makes it easy for developers to analyze the behavior of their production, distributed applications with end-to-end tracing capabilities. You can use X-Ray to identify performance bottlenecks, edge case errors, and other hard to detect issues.

AWS X-Ray provides an end-to-end, cross-service view of requests made to your application. It gives you an application-centric view of requests flowing through your application by aggregating the data gathered from individual services in your application into a single unit called a trace. You can use this trace to follow the path of an individual request as it passes through each service or tier in your application so that you can pinpoint where issues are occurring.

AWS X-Ray will assist the developer with visually analyzing the end-to-end view of connectivity between the application components and how they are performing using a Service Map. X-Ray also provides aggregated data about the application.

CORRECT: "Enable X-Ray tracing for the Lambda function" is the correct answer.

INCORRECT: "Create an Amazon CloudWatch Events rule" is incorrect as this feature of CloudWatch is used to trigger actions based on changes in the state of AWS services.

INCORRECT: "Assess the application with Amazon Inspector" is incorrect. Amazon Inspector is an automated security assessment service that helps improve the security and compliance of applications deployed on AWS.

INCORRECT: "Monitor the application with AWS Trusted Advisor" is incorrect. **AWS Trusted Advisor** is an online tool that provides you real time guidance to help you provision your resources following AWS best practices.

43. Question

A company needs to store sensitive documents on Amazon S3. The documents should be encrypted in transit using SSL/TLS and then be encrypted for storage at the destination. The company do not want to manage any of the encryption infrastructure or customer master keys and require the most cost-effective solution. What is the MOST suitable option to encrypt the data?

1: Server-Side Encryption with Amazon S3-Managed Keys (SSE-S3)

2: Server-Side Encryption with Customer Master Keys (CMKs) Stored in AWS Key Management Service (SSE-KMS) using customer managed CMKs

3: Server-Side Encryption with Customer-Provided Keys (SSE-C)

4: Client-side encryption with Amazon S3 managed keys

Answer: 1

Explanation:

Server-side encryption is the encryption of data at its destination by the application or service that receives it. Amazon S3 encrypts your data at the object level as it writes it to disks in its data centers and decrypts it for you when you access it. As long as you authenticate your request and you have access permissions, there is no difference in the way you access encrypted or unencrypted objects.

There are three options for server-side encryption:

- **Server-Side Encryption with Amazon S3-Managed Keys (SSE-S3)** – the data is encrypted by Amazon S3 using keys that are managed through S3

- **Server-Side Encryption with Customer Master Keys (CMKs) Stored in AWS Key Management Service (SSE-KMS)** – this options uses CMKs managed in AWS KMS. There are additional benefits such as auditing and permissions associated with the CMKs but also additional charges

- **Server-Side Encryption with Customer-Provided Keys (SSE-C)** – you manage the encryption keys and Amazon S3 manages the encryption, as it writes to disks, and decryption, when you access your objects.

The most suitable option for the requirements in this scenario is to use Server-Side Encryption with Amazon S3-Managed Keys (SSE-S3) as the company do not want to manage CMKs and require a simple solution.

CORRECT: "Server-Side Encryption with Amazon S3-Managed Keys (SSE-S3)" is the correct answer.

INCORRECT: "Server-Side Encryption with Customer Master Keys (CMKs) Stored in AWS Key Management Service (SSE-KMS) using customer managed CMKs" is incorrect as the company do not want to manage CMKs and they need the most cost-effective option and this does add additional costs.

INCORRECT: "Server-Side Encryption with Customer-Provided Keys (SSE-C)" is incorrect as with this option the customer must manage the keys or use keys managed in AWS KMS (which adds cost and complexity).

INCORRECT: "Client-side encryption with Amazon S3 managed keys" is incorrect as you cannot use Amazon S3 managed keys for client-side encryption and the encryption does not need to take place client-side for this solution.

44. Question

A Developer is building a three-tier web application that must be able to handle a minimum of 10,000 requests per minute. The requirements state that the web tier should be completely stateless while the application maintains session state data for users. How can the session state data be maintained externally, whilst keeping latency at the LOWEST possible value?

1: Create an Amazon RedShift instance, then implement session handling at the application level to leverage a database inside the RedShift database instance for session data storage

2: Implement a shared Amazon EFS file system solution across the underlying Amazon EC2 instances, then implement session handling at the application level to leverage the EFS file system for session data storage

3: Create an Amazon ElastiCache Redis cluster, then implement session handling at the application level to leverage the cluster for session data storage

4: Create an Amazon DynamoDB table, then implement session handling at the application level to leverage the table for session data storage

Answer: 3

Explanation:

It is common to use key/value stores for storing session state data. The two options presented in the answers are Amazon DynamoDB and Amazon ElastiCache Redis. Of these two, ElastiCache will provide the lowest latency as it is an in-memory database.

Therefore, the best answer is to create an Amazon ElastiCache Redis cluster, then implement session handling at the application level to leverage the cluster for session data storage.

CORRECT: "Create an Amazon ElastiCache Redis cluster, then implement session handling at the application level to leverage the cluster for session data storage" is the correct answer.

INCORRECT: "Create an Amazon DynamoDB table, then implement session handling at the application level to leverage the table for session data storage" is incorrect as though this is a good solution for storing session state data, the latency will not be as low as with ElastiCache.

INCORRECT: "Create an Amazon RedShift instance, then implement session handling at the application level to leverage a database inside the RedShift database instance for session data storage" is incorrect. RedShift is a data warehouse that is used for OLAP use cases, not for storing session state data.

INCORRECT: "Implement a shared Amazon EFS file system solution across the underlying Amazon EC2 instances, then implement session handling at the application level to leverage the EFS file system for session data storage" is incorrect. For session state data a key/value store such as DynamoDB or ElastiCache will provide better performance.

45. Question

A Developer is writing an imaging microservice on AWS Lambda. The service is dependent on several libraries that are not available in the Lambda runtime environment. Which strategy should the Developer follow to create the Lambda deployment package?

1: Create a ZIP file with the source code and all dependent libraries

2: Create a ZIP file with the source code and a script that installs the dependent libraries at runtime

3: Create a ZIP file with the source code and an appspec.yml file. Add the libraries to the appspec.yml file and upload to Amazon S3. Deploy using CloudFormation

4: Create a ZIP file with the source code and a buildspec.yml file that installs the dependent libraries on AWS Lambda

Answer: 1

Explanation:

A deployment package is a ZIP archive that contains your function code and dependencies. You need to create a deployment package if you use the Lambda API to manage functions, or if you need to include libraries and dependencies other than the AWS SDK.

You can upload the package directly to Lambda, or you can use an Amazon S3 bucket, and then upload it to Lambda. If the deployment package is larger than 50 MB, you must use Amazon S3.

CORRECT: "Create a ZIP file with the source code and all dependent libraries" is the correct answer.

INCORRECT: "Create a ZIP file with the source code and a script that installs the dependent libraries at runtime" is incorrect as the Developer should not run a script at runtime as this will cause latency. Instead, the Developer should include the dependent libraries in the ZIP package.

INCORRECT: "Create a ZIP file with the source code and an appspec.yml file. Add the libraries to the appspec.yml file and upload to Amazon S3. Deploy using CloudFormation" is incorrect. The appspec.yml file is used with CodeDeploy, you cannot add libraries into it, and it is not deployed using CloudFormation.

INCORRECT: "Create a ZIP file with the source code and a buildspec.yml file that installs the dependent libraries on AWS Lambda" is incorrect as the buildspec.yml file is used with CodeBuild for compiling source code and running tests. It cannot be used to install dependent libraries within Lambda.

46. Question

An e-commerce web application that shares session state on-premises is being migrated to AWS. The application must be fault tolerant, natively highly scalable, and any service interruption should not affect the user experience. What is the best option to store the session state?

1: Store the session state in Amazon ElastiCache

2: Store the session state in Amazon CloudFront

3: Store the session state in Amazon S3

4: Enable session stickiness using elastic load balancers

Answer: 1

Explanation:

There are various ways to manage user sessions including storing those sessions locally to the node responding to the HTTP request or designating a layer in your architecture which can store those sessions in a scalable and robust manner. Common approaches used include utilizing Sticky sessions or using a Distributed Cache for your session management.

In this scenario, a distributed cache is suitable for storing session state data. ElastiCache can perform this role and with the Redis engine replication is also supported. Therefore, the solution is fault-tolerant and natively highly scalable.

CORRECT: "Store the session state in Amazon ElastiCache" is the correct answer.

INCORRECT: "Store the session state in Amazon CloudFront" is incorrect as CloudFront is not suitable for storing session state data, it is used for caching content for better global performance.

INCORRECT: "Store the session state in Amazon S3" is incorrect as though you can store session data in Amazon S3 and replicate the data to another bucket, this would result in a service interruption if the S3 bucket was not accessible.

INCORRECT: "Enable session stickiness using elastic load balancers" is incorrect as this feature directs sessions from a specific client to a specific EC2 instances. Therefore, if the instance fails the user must be redirected to another EC2 instance and the session state data would be lost.

47. Question

A Developer is writing a serverless application that will process data uploaded to a file share. The Developer has created an AWS Lambda function and requires the function to be invoked every 15 minutes to process the data. What is an automated and serverless way to trigger the function?

1: Deploy an Amazon EC2 instance based on Linux, and edit it's /etc/crontab file by adding a command to periodically invoke the Lambda function

2: Configure an environment variable named PERIOD for the Lambda function. Set the value at 600

3: Create an Amazon CloudWatch Events rule that triggers on a regular schedule to invoke the Lambda function

4: Create an Amazon SNS topic that has a subscription to the Lambda function with a 600-second timer

Answer: 3

Explanation:

Amazon CloudWatch Events help you to respond to state changes in your AWS resources. When your resources change state, they automatically send events into an event stream. You can create rules that match selected events in the stream and route them to your AWS Lambda function to take action.

You can create a Lambda function and direct AWS Lambda to execute it on a regular schedule. You can specify a fixed rate (for example, execute a Lambda function every hour or 15 minutes), or you can specify a Cron expression.

Therefore, the Developer should create an Amazon CloudWatch Events rule that triggers on a regular schedule to invoke the Lambda function. This is a serverless and automated solution.

CORRECT: "Create an Amazon CloudWatch Events rule that triggers on a regular schedule to invoke the Lambda function" is the correct answer.

INCORRECT: "Deploy an Amazon EC2 instance based on Linux, and edit it's /etc/crontab file by adding a command to periodically invoke the Lambda function" is incorrect as EC2 is not a serverless solution.

INCORRECT: "Configure an environment variable named PERIOD for the Lambda function. Set the value at 600" is incorrect as you cannot cause a Lambda function to execute based on a value in an environment variable.

INCORRECT: "Create an Amazon SNS topic that has a subscription to the Lambda function with a 600-second timer" is incorrect as SNS does not run on a timer, CloudWatch Events should be used instead.

48. Question

A Developer attempted to run an AWS CodeBuild project, and received an error. The error stated that the length of all environment variables exceeds the limit for the combined maximum of characters. What is the recommended solution?

1: Add the export LC_ALL="en_US.utf8" command to the pre_build section to ensure POSIX localization

2: Use Amazon Cognito to store key-value pairs for large numbers of environment variables

3: Update the settings for the build project to use an Amazon S3 bucket for large numbers of environment variables

4: Use AWS Systems Manager Parameter Store to store large numbers of environment variables

Answer: 4

Explanation:

In this case the build is using environment variables that are too large for AWS CodeBuild. CodeBuild can raise errors when the length of all environment variables (all names and values added together) reach a combined maximum of around 5,500 characters.

The recommended solution is to use Amazon EC2 Systems Manager Parameter Store to store large environment variables and then retrieve them from your buildspec file. Amazon EC2 Systems Manager Parameter Store can store an individual environment variable (name and value added together) that is a combined 4,096 characters or less.

CORRECT: "Use AWS Systems Manager Parameter Store to store large numbers of environment variables" is the correct answer.

INCORRECT: "Add the export LC_ALL="en_US.utf8" command to the pre_build section to ensure POSIX localization" is incorrect as this is used to set the locale and will not affect the limits that have been reached.

INCORRECT: "Use Amazon Cognito to store key-value pairs for large numbers of environment variables" is incorrect as Cognito is used for authentication and authorization and is not suitable for this purpose.

INCORRECT: "Update the settings for the build project to use an Amazon S3 bucket for large numbers of environment variables" is incorrect as Systems Manager Parameter Store is designed for this purpose and is a better fit.

49. Question

A Development team wants to run their container workloads on Amazon ECS. Each application container needs to share data with another container to collect logs and metrics. What should the Development team do to meet these requirements?

1: Create two pod specifications. Make one to include the application container and the other to include the other container. Link the two pods together

2: Create two task definitions. Make one to include the application container and the other to include the other container. Mount a shared volume between the two tasks

3: Create one task definition. Specify both containers in the definition. Mount a shared volume between those two containers

4: Create a single pod specification. Include both containers in the specification. Mount a persistent volume to both containers

Answer: 3

Explanation:

Amazon ECS tasks support Docker volumes. To use data volumes, you must specify the volume and mount point configurations in your task definition. Docker volumes are supported for the EC2 launch type only.

To configure a Docker volume, in the task definition volumes section, define a data volume with name and DockerVolumeConfiguration values. In the containerDefinitions section, define multiple containers with mountPoints values that reference the name of the defined volume and the containerPath value to mount the volume at on the container.

The containers should both be specified in the same task definition. Therefore, the Development team should create one task definition, specify both containers in the definition and then mount a shared volume between those two containers

CORRECT: "Create one task definition. Specify both containers in the definition. Mount a shared volume between those two containers" is the correct answer.

INCORRECT: "Create two pod specifications. Make one to include the application container and the other to include the other container. Link the two pods together" is incorrect as pods are a concept associated with the Elastic Kubernetes Service (EKS).

INCORRECT: "Create two task definitions. Make one to include the application container and the other to include the other container. Mount a shared volume between the two tasks" is incorrect as a single task definition should be created with both containers.

INCORRECT: "Create a single pod specification. Include both containers in the specification. Mount a persistent volume to both containers" is incorrect as pods are a concept associated with the Elastic Kubernetes Service (EKS).

50. Question

An application deployed on AWS Elastic Beanstalk experienced increased error rates during deployments of new application versions, resulting in service degradation for users. The Development team believes that this is because of the reduction in capacity during the deployment steps. The team would like to change the deployment policy configuration of the environment to an option that maintains full capacity during deployment while using the existing instances. Which deployment policy will meet these requirements while using the existing instances?

1: All at once

2: Rolling

3: Rolling with additional batch

4: Immutable

Answer: 3

Explanation:

AWS Elastic Beanstalk provides several options for how deployments are processed, including deployment policies and options that let you configure batch size and health check behavior during deployments.

All at once:

- Deploys the new version to all instances simultaneously.

Rolling:

- Update a few instances at a time (bucket), and then move onto the next bucket once the first bucket is healthy (downtime for 1 bucket at a time).

Rolling with additional batch:

- Like Rolling but launches new instances in a batch ensuring that there is full availability.

Immutable:

- Launches new instances in a new ASG and deploys the version update to these instances before swapping traffic to these instances once healthy.
- Zero downtime.

Blue / Green deployment:

- Zero downtime and release facility.
- Create a new "stage" environment and deploy updates there.

The rolling with additional batch launches a new batch to ensure capacity is not reduced and then updates the existing instances. Therefore, this is the best option to use for these requirements.

CORRECT: "Rolling with additional batch" is the correct answer.

INCORRECT: "Rolling" is incorrect as this will only use the existing instances without introducing an extra batch and therefore this will reduce the capacity of the application while the updates are taking place.

INCORRECT: "All at once" is incorrect as this will run the updates on all instances at the same time causing a total outage.

INCORRECT: "Immutable" is incorrect as this installs the updates on new instances, not existing instances.

51. Question

A company has implemented AWS CodePipeline to automate its release pipelines. The Development team is writing an AWS Lambda function that will send notifications for state changes of each of the actions in the stages. Which steps must be taken to associate the Lambda function with the event source?

1: Create a trigger that invokes the Lambda function from the Lambda console by selecting CodePipeline as the event source

2: Create an event trigger and specify the Lambda function from the CodePipeline console

3: Create an Amazon CloudWatch alarm that monitors status changes in CodePipeline and triggers the Lambda function

4: Create an Amazon CloudWatch Events rule that uses CodePipeline as an event source

Answer: 4

Explanation:

Amazon CloudWatch Events help you to respond to state changes in your AWS resources. When your resources change state, they automatically send events into an event stream. You can create rules that match selected events in the stream and route them to your AWS Lambda function to take action.

AWS CodePipeline can be configured as an event source in CloudWatch Events and can then send notifications using as service such as Amazon SNS. Therefore, the best answer is to create an Amazon CloudWatch Events rule that uses CodePipeline as an event source.

CORRECT: "Create an Amazon CloudWatch Events rule that uses CodePipeline as an event source" is the correct answer.

INCORRECT: "Create a trigger that invokes the Lambda function from the Lambda console by selecting CodePipeline as the event source" is incorrect as CodePipeline cannot be configured as a trigger for Lambda.

INCORRECT: "Create an event trigger and specify the Lambda function from the CodePipeline console" is incorrect as CodePipeline cannot be configured as a trigger for Lambda.

INCORRECT: "Create an Amazon CloudWatch alarm that monitors status changes in CodePipeline and triggers the Lambda function" is incorrect as CloudWatch Events is used for monitoring state changes.

52. Question

A Developer has made an update to an application. The application serves users around the world and uses Amazon CloudFront for caching content closer to users. It has been reported that after deploying the application updates, users are not able to see the latest changes. How can the Developer resolve this issue?

1: Remove the origin from the CloudFront configuration and add it again

2: Disable forwarding of query strings and request headers from the CloudFront distribution configuration

3: Invalidate all the application objects from the edge caches

4: Disable the CloudFront distribution and enable it again to update all the edge locations

Answer: 3

Explanation:

If you need to remove a file from CloudFront edge caches before it expires, you can do one of the following:

- Invalidate the file from edge caches. The next time a viewer requests the file, CloudFront returns to the origin to fetch the latest version of the file.
- Use file versioning to serve a different version of the file that has a different name. For more information, see Updating Existing Files Using Versioned File Names.

In this case, the best option available is to invalidate all the application objects from the edge caches. This will result in the new objects being cached next time a request is made for them.

CORRECT: "Invalidate all the application objects from the edge caches" is the correct answer.

INCORRECT: "Remove the origin from the CloudFront configuration and add it again" is incorrect as this is going to cause all objects to be removed and then recached which is overkill and will cost more.

INCORRECT: "Disable forwarding of query strings and request headers from the CloudFront distribution configuration" is incorrect as this is not a way to invalidate objects in Amazon CloudFront.

INCORRECT: "Disable the CloudFront distribution and enable it again to update all the edge locations" is incorrect as this will not cause the objects to expire, they will expire whenever their expiration date occurs and must be invalidated to make this happen sooner.

53. Question

A company has three different environments: Development, QA, and Production. The company wants to deploy its code first in the Development environment, then QA, and then Production. Which AWS service can be used to meet this requirement?

1: Use AWS CodeCommit to create multiple repositories to deploy the application

2: Use AWS CodeBuild to create, configure, and deploy multiple build application projects

3: Use AWS Data Pipeline to create multiple data pipeline provisions to deploy the application

4: Use AWS CodeDeploy to create multiple deployment groups

Answer: 4

Explanation:

You can specify one or more deployment groups for a CodeDeploy application. Each application deployment uses one of its deployment groups. The deployment group contains settings and configurations used during the deployment.

You can associate more than one deployment group with an application in CodeDeploy. This makes it possible to deploy an application revision to different sets of instances at different times. For example, you might use one deployment group to deploy an application revision to a set of instances tagged Test where you ensure the quality of the code.

Next, you deploy the same application revision to a deployment group with instances tagged Staging for additional verification. Finally, when you are ready to release the latest application to customers, you deploy to a deployment group that includes instances tagged Production.

Therefore, using AWS CodeDeploy to create multiple deployment groups can be used to meet the requirement

CORRECT: "Use AWS CodeDeploy to create multiple deployment groups" is the correct answer.

INCORRECT: "Use AWS CodeCommit to create multiple repositories to deploy the application" is incorrect as the requirement is to deploy the same code to separate environments in a staged manner. Therefore, having multiple code repositories is not useful.

INCORRECT: "Use AWS CodeBuild to create, configure, and deploy multiple build application projects" is incorrect as the requirement is not to build the application, it is to deploy the application.

INCORRECT: "Use AWS Data Pipeline to create multiple data pipeline provisions to deploy the application" is incorrect as Data Pipeline is a service used for data migration, not deploying updates to applications.

54. Question

A Developer has been tasked by a client to create an application. The client has provided the following requirements for the application:

- **Performance efficiency of seconds with up to a minute of latency**
- **Data storage requirements will be up to thousands of terabytes**
- **Per-message sizes may vary between 100 KB and 100 MB**
- **Data can be stored as key/value stores supporting eventual consistency**

What is the MOST cost-effective AWS service to meet these requirements?

1: Amazon DynamoDB

3: Amazon S3

3: Amazon RDS (with a MySQL engine)

4: Amazon ElastiCache

Answer: 2

Explanation:

The question is looking for a cost-effective solution. Multiple options can support the latency and scalability requirements. Amazon RDS is not a key/value store so that rules that option out. Of the remaining options ElastiCache would be expensive and DynamoDB only supports a maximum item size of 400 KB. Therefore, the best option is Amazon S3 which delivers all of the requirements.

CORRECT: "Amazon S3" is the correct answer.

INCORRECT: "Amazon DynamoDB" is incorrect as it supports a maximum item size of 400 KB and the messages will be up to 100 MB.

INCORRECT: "Amazon RDS (with a MySQL engine)" is incorrect as it is not a key/value store.

INCORRECT: "Amazon ElastiCache" is incorrect as it is an in-memory database and would be the most expensive solution.

55. Question

An application on-premises uses Linux servers and a relational database using PostgreSQL. The company will be migrating the application to AWS and require a managed service that will take care of capacity provisioning, load balancing, and auto-scaling. Which combination of services should the Developer use? (Select TWO)

1: AWS Elastic Beanstalk

2: Amazon EC2 with Auto Scaling

3: Amazon EC2 with PostgreSQL

4: Amazon RDS with PostrgreSQL

5: AWS Lambda with CloudWatch Events

Answer: 1,4

Explanation:

The company require a managed service therefore the Developer should choose to use Elastic Beanstalk for the compute layer and Amazon RDS with the PostgreSQL engine for the database layer.

AWS Elastic Beanstalk will handle all capacity provisioning, load balancing, and auto-scaling for the web front-end and Amazon RDS provides push-button scaling for the backend.

CORRECT: "AWS Elastic Beanstalk" is a correct answer.

CORRECT: "Amazon RDS with PostrgreSQL" is also a correct answer.

INCORRECT: "Amazon EC2 with Auto Scaling" is incorrect as though these services will be used to provide the automatic scalability required for the solution, they still need to be managed. The questions asks for a managed solution and Elastic Beanstalk will manage this for you. Also, there is no mention of a load balancer so connections cannot be distributed to instances.

INCORRECT: "Amazon EC2 with PostgreSQL" is incorrect as the question asks for a managed service and therefore the database should be run on Amazon RDS.

INCORRECT: "AWS Lambda with CloudWatch Events" is incorrect as there is no mention of refactoring application code to run on AWS Lambda.

56. Question

A company runs many microservices applications that use Docker containers. The company are planning to migrate the containers to Amazon ECS. The workloads are highly variable and therefore the company prefers to be charged per running task. Which solution is the BEST fit for the company's requirements?

1: Amazon ECS with the EC2 launch type

2: Amazon ECS with the Fargate launch type

3: An Amazon ECS Service with Auto Scaling

4: An Amazon ECS Cluster with Auto Scaling

Answer: 2

Explanation:

The key requirement is that the company should be charged per running task. Therefore, the best answer is to use Amazon ECS with the Fargate launch type as with this model AWS charge you for running tasks rather than running container instances.

The Fargate launch type allows you to run your containerized applications without the need to provision and manage the backend infrastructure. You just register your task definition and Fargate launches the container for you. The Fargate Launch Type is a serverless infrastructure managed by AWS.

CORRECT: "Amazon ECS with the Fargate launch type" is the correct answer.

INCORRECT: "Amazon ECS with the EC2 launch type" is incorrect as with this launch type you pay for running container instances (EC2 instances).

INCORRECT: "An Amazon ECS Service with Auto Scaling" is incorrect as this does not specify the launch type. You can run an ECS Service on the Fargate or EC2 launch types.

INCORRECT: "An Amazon ECS Cluster with Auto Scaling" is incorrect as this does not specify the launch type. You can run an ECS Cluster on the Fargate or EC2 launch types.

57. Question

A team of Developers require read-only access to an Amazon DynamoDB table. The Developers have been added to a group. What should an administrator do to provide the team with access whilst following the principal of least privilege?

1: Assign the AmazonDynamoDBReadOnlyAccess AWS managed policy to the group

2: Create a customer managed policy with read only access to DynamoDB and specify the ARN of the table for the "Resource" element. Attach the policy to the group

3: Assign the AWSLambdaDynamoDBExecutionRole AWS managed policy to the group

4: Create a customer managed policy with read/write access to DynamoDB for all resources. Attach the policy to the group

Answer: 2

Explanation:

The key requirement is to provide read-only access to the team for a specific DynamoDB table. Therefore, the AWS managed policy cannot be used as it will provide access to all DynamoDB tables in the account which does not follow the principal of least privilege.

Therefore, a customer managed policy should be created that provides read-only access and specifies the ARN of the table. For instance, the resource element might include the following ARN:

arn:aws:dynamodb:us-west-1:515148227241:table/exampletable

This will lock down access to the specific DynamoDB table, following the principal of least privilege.

CORRECT: "Create a customer managed policy with read only access to DynamoDB and specify the ARN of the table for the "Resource" element. Attach the policy to the group" is the correct answer.

INCORRECT: "Assign the AmazonDynamoDBReadOnlyAccess AWS managed policy to the group" is incorrect as this will provide read-only access to all DynamoDB tables in the account.

INCORRECT: "Assign the AWSLambdaDynamoDBExecutionRole AWS managed policy to the group" is incorrect as this is a role used with AWS Lambda.

INCORRECT: "Create a customer managed policy with read/write access to DynamoDB for all resources. Attach the policy to the group" is incorrect as read-only access should be provided, not read/write.

58. Question

A Developer is reviewing the permissions attached to an AWS Lambda function's execution role. What are the minimum permissions required for Lambda to create an Amazon CloudWatch Logs group and stream and write logs into the stream?

1: "logs:CreateLogGroup", "logs:CreateLogStream", "logs:PutLogEvents"

2: "logs:CreateLogGroup", "logs:CreateLogStream", "logs:PutDestination"

3: "logs:CreateExportTask", "logs:CreateLogStream", "logs:PutLogEvents"

4: "logs:GetLogEvents", "logs:GetLogRecord", "logs:PutLogEvents"

Answer: 1

Explanation:

The minimum permissions required are as follows:

- "logs:CreateLogGroup" - Creates a log group with the specified name.

- "logs:CreateLogStream" - Creates a log stream for the specified log group.
- "logs:PutLogEvents" - Uploads a batch of log events to the specified log stream.

CORRECT: ""logs:CreateLogGroup", "logs:CreateLogStream", "logs:PutLogEvents"" is the correct answer.

INCORRECT: ""logs:CreateLogGroup", "logs:CreateLogStream", "logs:PutDestination"" is incorrect as PutDestination creates or updates a destination.

INCORRECT: ""logs:CreateExportTask", "logs:CreateLogStream", "logs:PutLogEvents"" is incorrect as CreateExportTask creates an export task, which allows you to efficiently export data from a log group to an Amazon S3 bucket.

INCORRECT: ""logs:GetLogEvents", "logs:GetLogRecord", "logs:PutLogEvents"" is incorrect as all permissions are incorrect.

59. Question

An application needs to generate SMS text messages and emails for a large number of subscribers. Which AWS service can be used to send these messages to customers?

1: Amazon SES

2: Amazon SQS

3: Amazon SWF

4: Amazon SNS

Answer: 4

Explanation:

Amazon Simple Notification Service (Amazon SNS) is a web service that coordinates and manages the delivery or sending of messages to subscribing endpoints or clients. In Amazon SNS, there are two types of clients— publishers and subscribers—also referred to as producers and consumers.

Publishers communicate asynchronously with subscribers by producing and sending a message to a topic, which is a logical access point and communication channel.

Subscribers (that is, web servers, email addresses, Amazon SQS queues, AWS Lambda functions) consume or receive the message or notification over one of the supported protocols (that is, Amazon SQS, HTTP/S, email, SMS, Lambda) when they are subscribed to the topic.

CORRECT: "Amazon SNS" is the correct answer.

INCORRECT: "Amazon SES" is incorrect as this service only sends email, not SMS text messages.

INCORRECT: "Amazon SQS" is incorrect as this is a hosted message queue for decoupling application components.

INCORRECT: "Amazon SWF" is incorrect as the Simple Workflow Service is used for orchestrating multi-step workflows.

60. Question

A website is deployed in several AWS regions. A Developer needs to direct global users to the website that provides the best performance. How can the Developer achieve this?

1: Create Alias records in AWS Route 53 and direct the traffic to an Elastic Load Balancer

2: Create A records in AWS Route 53 and use a weighted routing policy

3: Create A records in AWS Route 53 and use a latency-based routing policy

4: Create CNAME records in AWS Route 53 and direct traffic to Amazon CloudFront

Answer: 3

Explanation:

If your application is hosted in multiple AWS Regions, you can improve performance for your users by serving their requests from the AWS Region that provides the lowest latency.

To use latency-based routing, you create latency records for your resources in multiple AWS Regions. When Route 53 receives a DNS query for your domain or subdomain (example.com or acme.example.com), it determines which AWS Regions you've created latency records for, determines which region gives the user the lowest latency, and then selects a latency record for that region. Route 53 responds with the value from the selected record, such as the IP address for a web server.

CORRECT: "Create A records in AWS Route 53 and use a latency-based routing policy" is the correct answer.

INCORRECT: "Create Alias records in AWS Route 53 and direct the traffic to an Elastic Load Balancer" is incorrect as an ELB is within a single region. In this case the Developer needs to direct traffic to different regions.

INCORRECT: "Create A records in AWS Route 53 and use a weighted routing policy" is incorrect as weighting is used to send more traffic to one region other another, not to direct for best performance.

INCORRECT: "Create CNAME records in AWS Route 53 and direct traffic to Amazon CloudFront" is incorrect as this does not direct traffic to different regions for best performance which is what the questions asks for.

61. Question

An IAM user is unable to assume an IAM role. The policy statement includes the "Effect": "Allow" and "Resource": "arn:aws:iam::*5123399432*:role/*MyCARole*" elements. Which other element MUST be included to allow the role to be assumed?

1: "Action": "ec2:AssumeRole

2: "Action": "sts:AssumeRole"

3: "Action": "sts:GetSessionToken"

4: "Action": "sts:GetAccessKeyInfo"

Answer: 2

Explanation:

The user needs to verify that the IAM policy grants permission to call sts:AssumeRole for the role that they want to assume. The Action element of an IAM policy must allow you to call the AssumeRole action. In addition, the Resource element of your IAM policy must specify the role that you want to assume.

For this situation the IAM policy would need to include a statement such as this:

"Effect": "Allow",

"Action": "sts:AssumeRole",

"Resource": "arn:aws:iam::5123399432:role/MyCARole"

CORRECT: ""Action": "sts:AssumeRole"" is the correct answer.

INCORRECT: ""Action": "ec2:AssumeRole"" is incorrect as the security token service (STS) is used for assuming roles.

INCORRECT: ""Action": "sts:GetSessionToken"" is incorrect as this API action returns a set of temporary credentials for an AWS account or IAM user.

INCORRECT: ""Action": "sts:GetAccessKeyInfo"" is incorrect as this API Action returns the account identifier for the specified access key ID.

62. Question

An existing IAM user needs access to AWS resources in another account from an insecure environment for a short-term need (around 15 minutes). What would be the MOST secure method to provide the required access?

1: Use the AssumeRoleWithWebIdentity API operation to assume a role in the other account that has the required permissions

2: Use the AssumeRole API operation to assume a role in the other account that has the required permissions

3: Use the GetFederationToken API operation to return a set of temporary security credentials

4: Use the GetSessionToken API operation to return a set of temporary security credentials and specify 900 seconds in the DurationSeconds parameter

Answer: 4

Explanation:

The GetSessionToken API operation returns a set of temporary security credentials to an existing IAM user. This is useful for providing enhanced security, such as allowing AWS requests only when MFA is enabled for the IAM user.

Because the credentials are temporary, they provide enhanced security when you have an IAM user who accesses your resources through a less secure environment. Examples of less secure environments include a mobile device or web browser.

By default, temporary security credentials for an IAM user are valid for a maximum of 12 hours. But you can request a duration as short as 15 minutes or as long as 36 hours using the DurationSeconds parameter.

GetSessionToken returns temporary security credentials consisting of a security token, an access key ID, and a secret access key.

CORRECT: "Use the GetSessionToken API operation to return a set of temporary security credentials and specify 900 seconds in the DurationSeconds parameter" is the correct answer.

INCORRECT: "Use the AssumeRoleWithWebIdentity API operation to assume a role in the other account that has the required permissions" is incorrect as this is used for federated users who are authenticated through a public identity provider.

INCORRECT: "Use the AssumeRole API operation to assume a role in the other account that has the required permissions" is incorrect as the without correct answer includes the DurationSeconds parameter which can be used to specify how long the credentials last. That is a more secure option and could also be used with AssumeRole but wasn't included with this option.

INCORRECT: "Use the GetFederationToken API operation to return a set of temporary security credentials" is incorrect.

63. Question

A Developer has created a task definition that includes the following JSON code:

```
"placementStrategy": [
  {
    "field": "attribute:ecs.availability-zone",
    "type": "spread"
  },
  {
    "field": "instanceId",
    "type": "spread"
  }
]
```

What is the effect of this task placement strategy?

1: It distributes tasks evenly across Availability Zones and then distributes tasks evenly across the instances within each Availability Zone

2: It distributes tasks evenly across Availability Zones and then bin packs tasks based on memory within each Availability Zone

3: It distributes tasks evenly across Availability Zones and then distributes tasks evenly across distinct instances within each Availability Zone

4: It distributes tasks evenly across Availability Zones and then distributes tasks randomly across instances within each Availability Zone

Answer: 1

Explanation:

A *task placement strategy* is an algorithm for selecting instances for task placement or tasks for termination. Task placement strategies can be specified when either running a task or creating a new service.

Amazon ECS supports the following task placement strategies:

binpack

Place tasks based on the least available amount of CPU or memory. This minimizes the number of instances in use.

random

Place tasks randomly.

spread

Place tasks evenly based on the specified value. Accepted values are instanceId (or host, which has the same effect), or any platform or custom attribute that is applied to a container instance, such as attribute:ecs.availability-zone.

You can specify task placement strategies with the following actions: CreateService, UpdateService, and RunTask. You can also use multiple strategies together as in the example JSON code provided with the question.

CORRECT: "It distributes tasks evenly across Availability Zones and then distributes tasks evenly across the instances within each Availability Zone" is the correct answer.

INCORRECT: "It distributes tasks evenly across Availability Zones and then bin packs tasks based on memory within each Availability Zone" is incorrect as it does not use the binpack strategy.

INCORRECT: "It distributes tasks evenly across Availability Zones and then distributes tasks evenly across distinct instances within each Availability Zone" is incorrect as it does not spread tasks across distinct instances (use a task placement constraint).

INCORRECT: "It distributes tasks evenly across Availability Zones and then distributes tasks randomly across instances within each Availability Zone" is incorrect as it does not use the random strategy.

64. Question

What is the most suitable storage solution for files up to 1 GB in size that must be stored for long periods of time that are accessed directly by applications with varying frequency?

1: Amazon S3 Glacier

2: Amazon DynamoDB

3: Amazon S3 Standard

4: Amazon RDS

Answer: 3

Explanation:

S3 Standard offers high durability, availability, and performance object storage for frequently accessed data.

Key Features:

- Low latency and high throughput performance
- Designed for durability of 99.999999999% of objects across multiple Availability Zones
- Resilient against events that impact an entire Availability Zone
- Designed for 99.99% availability over a given year
- Backed with the Amazon S3 Service Level Agreement for availability

- Supports SSL for data in transit and encryption of data at rest
- S3 Lifecycle management for automatic migration of objects to other S3 Storage Classes

Amazon S3 Standard is the best solution for this scenario as the data is accessed directly by applications with varying frequency. Therefore, the S3 Glacier storage class would not be suitable as it would archive the data and data must be restored before being accessible.

CORRECT: "Amazon S3 Standard" is the correct answer.

INCORRECT: "Amazon S3 Glacier" is incorrect as it would archive the data and data must be restored before being accessible

INCORRECT: "Amazon DynamoDB" is incorrect as this is a database and is not suitable for storing files of this size.

INCORRECT: "Amazon RDS" is incorrect as this a relational database and is not suitable for storing files.

65. Question

Users of an application using Amazon API Gateway, AWS Lambda and Amazon DynamoDB have reported errors when using the application. Which metrics should a Developer monitor in Amazon CloudWatch to determine the number of client-side and server-side errors?

1: 4XXError and 5XXError

2: CacheHitCount and CacheMissCount

3: IntegrationLatency and Latency

4: Errors

Answer: 1

Explanation:

To determine the number of client-side errors captured in a given period the Developer should look at the 4XXError metric. To determine the number of server-side errors captured in a given period the Developer should look at the 5XXError.

CORRECT: "4XXError and 5XXError" is the correct answer.

INCORRECT: "CacheHitCount and CacheMissCount" is incorrect as these count the number of requests served from the cache and the number of requests served from the backend.

INCORRECT: "IntegrationLatency and Latency" is incorrect as these measure the amount of time between when API Gateway relays a request to the backend and when it receives a response from the backend and the time between when API Gateway receives a request from a client and when it returns a response to the client.

INCORRECT: "Errors" is incorrect as this is not a metric related to Amazon API Gateway.

SET 2: PRACTICE QUESTIONS ONLY

For training purposes, go directly to Set 2: Practice Questions, Answers & Explanations

1. Question
A CloudFormation template is going to be used by a global team to deploy infrastructure in several regions around the world. Which section of the template file can be used to set values based on a region?

1: Metadata

2: Parameters

3: Conditions

4: Mappings

2. Question
An application searches a DynamoDB table to return items based on primary key attributes. A developer noticed some ProvisionedThroughputExceeded exceptions being generated by DynamoDB.

How can the application be optimized to reduce the load on DynamoDB and use the LEAST amount of RCU?

1: Modify the application to issue query API calls with eventual consistency reads

2: Modify the application to issue scan API calls with eventual consistency reads

3: Modify the application to issue query API calls with strong consistency reads

4: Modify the application to issue scan API calls with strong consistency reads

3. Question
A developer needs use the attribute of an Amazon S3 object that uniquely identifies the object in a bucket. Which of the following represents an Object Key?

1: s3://dctlabs/Development/Projects.xls

2: Development/Projects.xls

3: Project=Blue

4: arn:aws:s3:::dctlabs

4. Question
A developer has created an Amazon API Gateway with caching enabled in front of AWS Lambda. For some requests, it is necessary to ensure the latest data is received from the endpoint. How can the developer ensure the data is not stale?

1: Send requests with the Cache-Control: max-age=0 header

2: Modify the TTL on the cache to a lower number

3: The cache must be disabled

4: Send requests with the Cache-Delete: max-age=0 header

5. Question
A developer needs to add sign-up and sign-in capabilities for a mobile app. The solution should integrate with social identity providers (IdPs) and SAML IdPs. Which service should the developer use?

1: AWS Cognito user pool

2: AWS Cognito identity pool

3: API Gateway with a Lambda authorizer

4: AWS IAM and STS

6. Question

An Amazon EC2 instance is being deployed with an Elastic Load Balancer (ELB). A developer needs to run a script when the instance is being launched. What is the SIMPLEST method of running the script?

1: Place the code in the EC2 User Data

2: Using EC2 Run Command

3: Place the code in the EC2 Metadata

4: Using Amazon CloudWatch Events

7. Question

A call centre application is being refactored into a serverless architecture. The new application includes several AWS Lambda functions which are involved in the automation of support tickets.

What is the BEST way to coordinate the complex invocation logic for the Lambda functions?

1: Create a State Machine with AWS Step Functions

2: Include the invocation of other Lambda functions within the Lambda code

3: Create a Workflow using the Amazon Simple Workflow Service (SWF)

4: Use the AWS Serverless Application Model (SAM)

8. Question

An application is deployed using AWS Elastic Beanstalk and uses a Classic Load Balancer (CLB). A developer is performing a blue/green migration to change to an Application Load Balancer (ALB).

After deployment, the developer has noticed that customers connecting to the ALB need to re-authenticate every time they connect. Normally they would only authenticate once and then be able to reconnect without re-authenticating for several hours.

How can the developer resolve this issue?

1: Enable IAM authentication on the ALBs listener

2: Add a new SSL certificate to the ALBs listener

3: Change the load balancing algorithm on the target group to "least outstanding requests)

4: Enable Sticky Sessions on the target group

9. Question

A DynamoDB table is being used to store session information for users of an online game. A developer has noticed that the table size has increased considerably and much of the data is not required after a gaming session is completed.

What is the MOST cost-effective approach to reducing the size of the table?

1: Use the batch-write-item API to delete the data

2: Create an AWS Lambda function that purges stale items from the table daily

3: Enable a Time To Live (TTL) on the table and add a timestamp attribute on new items

4: Use the delete-item API to delete the data

10. Question

A decoupled application uses an Amazon SQS queue. The producers send messages to the queue every 30 seconds on average. What is the MOST efficient configuration for a message processor to poll the queue?

1: Set the queue attribute ReceiveMessageWaitTimeSeconds to 20

2: Set the queue attribute ReceiveMessageWaitTimeSeconds to 0

3: Set the Default Visibility Timeout to 0

4: Set the Delivery Delay to 20

11. Question

A developer needs to resolve an issue where orders are occasionally being processed twice. The application uses an Auto Scaling group of Amazon EC2 instances and an Amazon SQS queue. How can the developer resolve this issue most cost-effectively?

1: Use a FIFO queue and configure the producer to provide a message deduplication ID

2: Use a standard queue and configure the producer to provide a message deduplication ID

3: Use a FIFO queue and configure the consumer to provide a message deduplication ID

4: Use a standard queue and configure the consumer to provide a message deduplication ID

12. Question

A developer created an operational dashboard for a serverless application using Amazon API Gateway, AWS Lambda, Amazon S3, and Amazon DynamoDB. Users will connect to the dashboard from a variety of mobile applications, desktops and tablets.

The developer needs an authentication mechanism that can allow users to sign-in and will remember the devices users sign in from and suppress the second factor of authentication for remembered devices. Which AWS service should the developer use to support this scenario?

1: Amazon Cognito

2: AWS Directory Service

3: AWS KMS

4: Amazon IAM

13. Question

A developer is designing a web application that will run on Amazon EC2 Linux instances using an Auto Scaling Group. The application should scale based on a threshold for the number of users concurrently using the application.

How should the Auto Scaling Group be configured to scale out?

1: Create a custom Amazon CloudWatch metric for concurrent users

2: Use the Amazon CloudWatch metric "NetworkIn"

3: Use a target tracking scaling policy

4: Create a custom Amazon CloudWatch metric for memory usage

14. Question

An application needs to identify the public IPv4 address of the Amazon EC2 Linux instance on which it is running. How can a Developer configure the application to locate this information?

1: Locate the address within the instance metadata

2: Locate the address within the instance user data

3: Configure the application to run the ifconfig command to find the public IP address

4: Configure the application to run the ipconfig command to find the public IP address

15. Question

A Developer is creating an application and would like add AWS X-Ray to trace user requests end-to-end through the software stack. The Developer has implemented the changes and tested the application and the traces are successfully sent to X-Ray. The Developer then deployed the application on an Amazon EC2 instance, and noticed that the traces are not being sent to X-Ray.

What is the most likely cause of this issue? (Select TWO)

1: The X-Ray API is not installed on the EC2 instance

2: The instance's instance profile role does not have permission to upload trace data to X-Ray

3: The traces are reaching X-Ray, but the Developer does not have permission to view the records

4: The X-Ray daemon is not installed on the EC2 instance.

5: The X-Ray segments are being queued

16. Question

A Developer needs to manage AWS services from a local development server using the AWS CLI. How can the Developer ensure that the CLI uses their IAM permissions?

1: Create an IAM Role with the required permissions and attach it to the local server's instance profile

2: Put the Developer's IAM user account in an IAM group that has the necessary permissions

3: Save the Developer's IAM login credentials as environment variables and reference them when executing AWS CLI commands

4: Run the aws configure command and provide the Developer's IAM access key ID and secret access key

17. Question

A Developer is creating an application that will process some data and generate an image file from it. The application will use an AWS Lambda function which will require 150 MB of temporary storage while executing. The temporary files will not be needed after the function execution is completed.

What is the best location for the Developer to store the files?

1: Store the files in Amazon S3 and use a lifecycle policy to delete the files automatically

2: Store the files in the /tmp directory and delete the files when the execution completes

3: Store the files in an Amazon Instance Store and delete the files when the execution completes

4: Store the files in an Amazon EFS filesystem and delete the files when the execution completes

18. Question

AWS CodeBuild builds code for an application, creates the Docker image, pushes the image to Amazon Elastic Container Registry (Amazon ECR), and tags the image with a unique identifier.
If the Developers already have AWS CLI configured on their workstations, how can the Docker images be pulled to the workstations?

1: Run the following: docker pull REPOSITORY URI : TAG

2: Run the output of the following: aws ecr get-login and then run: docker pull REPOSITORY URI : TAG

3: Run the following: aws ecr get-login and then run: docker pull REPOSITORY URI : TAG

4: Run the output of the following: aws ecr get-download-url-for-layer and then run: docker pull REPOSITORY URI : TAG

19. Question

A company recently migrated a multi-tier application to AWS. The web tier runs on an Auto Scaling group of Amazon EC2 instances and the database tier uses Amazon DynamoDB. The database tier requires extremely high performance and most requests are repeated read requests.

What service can be used to scale the database tier for BEST performance?

1: Amazon CloudFront

2: Amazon ElastiCache

3: Amazon DynamoDB Accelerator (DAX)

4: Amazon SQS

20. Question

A company runs multiple microservices that each use their own Amazon DynamoDB table. The "customers" microservice needs data that originates in the "orders" microservice.

What approach represents the SIMPLEST method for the "customers" table to get near real-time updates from the "orders" table?

1: Enable Amazon DynamoDB streams on the "orders" table, configure the "customers" microservice to read records from the stream

2: Use Amazon CloudWatch Events to send notifications every time an item is added or modified in the "orders" table

3: Use Amazon Kinesis Firehose to deliver all changes in the "orders" table to the "customers" table

4: Enable DynamoDB streams for the "customers" table, trigger an AWS Lambda function to read records from the stream and write them to the "orders" table

21. Question

A company manages a web application that is deployed on AWS Elastic Beanstalk. A Developer has been instructed to update to a new version of the application code. There is no tolerance for downtime if the update fails and rollback should be fast.

What is the SAFEST deployment method to use?

1: All at once

2: Rolling

3: Rolling with Additional Batch

4: Immutable

22. Question

A Lambda function is taking a long time to complete. The Developer has discovered that inadequate compute capacity is being allocated to the function. How can the Developer ensure that more compute capacity is allocated to the function?

1: Allocate more memory to the function

2: Use an instance type with more CPU

3: Increase the maximum execution time

4: Increase the reserved concurrency

23. Question

A Developer is configuring an Amazon ECS Service with Auto Scaling. The tasks should scale based on user load in the previous 20 seconds. How can the Developer enable the scaling?

1: Create a high-resolution custom Amazon CloudWatch metric for user activity data, then publish data every 10 seconds

2: Create a high-resolution custom Amazon CloudWatch metric for user activity data, then publish data every 5 seconds

3: Create a standard-resolution custom Amazon CloudWatch metric for user activity data, then publish data every 30 seconds

4: Create a standard-resolution custom Amazon CloudWatch metric for user activity data, then publish data every 5 seconds

24. Question

An application exports documents to an Amazon S3 bucket. The data must be encrypted at rest and company policy mandates that encryption keys must be rotated annually. How can this be achieved automatically and with the LEAST effort?

1: Use AWS KMS keys with automatic rotation enabled

2: Import a custom key into AWS KMS and configure automatic rotation

3: Encrypt the data within the application before writing to S3

4: Configure automatic rotation with AWS Secrets Manager

25. Question

An application uses an Amazon SQS queue to decouple an online image processing application. The images can take up to 5 minutes to process. Which process below will result in successful processing of the message and remove it from the queue while MINIMIZING the chances of duplicate processing?

1: Retrieve the message with an increased visibility timeout, delete the message from the queue, process the message

2: Retrieve the message with increased DelaySeconds, process the message, delete the message from the queue

3: Retrieve the message with increased DelaySeconds, delete the message from the queue, process the message

4: Retrieve the message with an increased visibility timeout, process the message, delete the message from the queue

26. Question

A Development team are currently creating a new application that uses a microservices design pattern and runs on Docker containers. The team would like to run the platform on AWS using a managed platform. They want minimize management overhead for the platform. Which service should the Development team use?

1: Amazon ECS with EC2 launch type

2: Amazon ECS with Fargate launch type

3: Amazon Elastic Kubernetes Service (EKS)

4: AWS Lambda

27. Question

A company is using Amazon API Gateway to manage access to a set of microservices implemented as AWS Lambda functions. The company has made some minor changes to one of the APIs. The company wishes to give existing customers using the API up to 6 months to migrate from version 1 to version 2.

What approach should a Developer use to implement the change?

1: Update the underlying Lambda function and provide clients with the new Lambda invocation URL

2: Use API Gateway to automatically propagate the change to clients, specifying 180 days in the phased deployment parameter

3: Use API Gateway to deploy a new stage named v2 to the API and provide users with its URL

4: Update the underlying Lambda function, create an Amazon CloudFront distribution with the updated Lambda function as its origin

28. Question

A Developer has completed some code updates and needs to deploy the updates to an Amazon Elastic Beanstalk environment. The update must be deployed in the fastest possible time and application downtime is acceptable.

Which deployment policy should the Developer choose?

1: All at once

2: Rolling

3: Rolling with additional batch

4: Immutable

29. Question

A Developer is creating a DynamoDB table for storing transaction logs. The table has 10 write capacity units (WCUs). The Developer needs to configure the read capacity units (RCUs) for the table in order to MAXIMIZE the number of requests allowed per second. Which of the following configurations should the Developer use?

1: Eventually consistent reads of 5 RCUs reading items that are 4 KB in size

2: Strongly consistent reads of 5 RCUs reading items that are 4 KB in size

3: Eventually consistent reads of 15 RCUs reading items that are 1 KB in size

4: Strongly consistent reads of 15 RCUs reading items that are 1KB in size

30. Question

A Developer is attempting to call the Amazon CloudWatch API and is receiving HTTP 400: ThrottlingException errors intermittently. When a call fails, no data is retrieved.

What best practice should the Developer first attempt to resolve this issue?

1: Contact AWS Support for a limit increase

2: Use the AWS CLI to get the metrics

3: Analyze the applications and remove the API call

4: Retry the call with exponential backoff

31. Question

An application is processing data from an Amazon Kinesis Data Stream. The Data Stream has 12 shards with one KCL worker each. The volume of data has increased, and an additional 6 shards have been added to the stream.

What is the MAXIMUM number of EC2 instances required for optimum performance?

1: 18

2: 9

3: 36

4: 12

32. Question

A Developer has deployed an application that processes streaming big data. The application includes an Amazon Kinesis Stream and Amazon EC2 consumer instances. Each EC2 instance has exactly one KCL worker processing one Kinesis Data Stream which has 15 shards. To resolve performance issues the Developer has increased the number of shards to 25.

How many EC2 consumer instances are required to process the data from the stream with BEST performance?

1: 50

2: 25

3: 10

4: 30

33. Question

A Developer is using AWS SAM to create a template for deploying a serverless application. The Developer plans to leverage an application from the AWS Serverless Application Repository in the template as a nested application. Which resource type should the Developer specify?

1: AWS::Serverless::Application

2: AWS::Serverless:Function

3: AWS::Serverless:HttpApi

4: AWS::Serverless:SimpleTable

34. Question

A Developer needs to be notified by email for all new object creation events in a specific Amazon S3 bucket. Amazon SNS will be used for sending the messages. How can the Developer enable these notifications?

1: Create an event notification for all s3:ObjectCreated:Put API calls

2: Create an event notification for all s3:ObjectRemoved:Delete API calls

3: Create an event notification for all s3:ObjectRestore:Post API calls

4: Create an event notification for all s3:ObjectCreated:* API calls

35. Question

An application will be hosted on the AWS Cloud. Developers will be using an Agile software development methodology with regular updates deployed through a continuous integration and delivery (CI/CD) model. Which AWS service can assist the Developers with automating the build, test, and deploy phases of the release process every time there is a code change?

1: AWS CodeBuild

2: AWS CloudFormation

3: AWS Elastic Beanstalk

4: AWS CodePipeline

36. Question

A Developer is creating a design for an application that will include Docker containers on Amazon ECS with the EC2 launch type. The Developer needs to control the placement of tasks onto groups of container instances organized by availability zone and instance type.

Which Amazon ECS feature provides expressions that can be used to group container instances by the relevant attributes?

1: Cluster Query Language

2: Task Group

3: Task Placement Constraints

4: Task Placement Strategy

37. Question

An organization has an account for each environment: Production, Testing, Development. A Developer with an IAM user in the Development account needs to launch resources in the Production and Testing accounts. What is the MOST efficient way to provide access?

1: Create a role with the required permissions in the Production and Testing accounts and have the Developer assume that role

2: Create a separate IAM user in each account and have the Developer login separately to each account

3: Create an IAM group in the Production and Testing accounts and add the Developer's user from the Development account to the groups

4: Create an IAM permissions policy in the Production and Testing accounts and reference the IAM user in the Development account

38. Question

An application running on Amazon EC2 generates a large number of small files (1KB each) containing personally identifiable information that must be converted to ciphertext. The data will be stored on a proprietary network-attached file system. What is the SAFEST way to encrypt the data using AWS KMS?

1: Create a data encryption key from a customer master key and encrypt the data with the data encryption key

2: Encrypt the data directly with a customer managed customer master key

3: Create a data encryption key from a customer master key and encrypt the data with the customer master key

4: Encrypt the data directly with an AWS managed customer master key

39. Question

A new application will be deployed using AWS CodeDeploy to Amazon Elastic Container Service (ECS). What must be supplied to CodeDeploy to specify the ECS service to deploy?

1: The AppSpec file

2: The BuildSpec file

3: The Template file

4: The Policy file

40. Question

An application requires an in-memory caching engine. The cache should provide high availability as repopulating data is expensive. How can this requirement be met?

1: Use Amazon ElastiCache Redis with replicas

2: Use Amazon ElastiCache Memcached with partitions

3: Amazon RDS with a Read Replica

4: Amazon Aurora with a Global Database

41. Question

A new application will be hosted on the domain name dctlabs.com using an Amazon API Gateway REST API front end. The Developer needs to configure the API with a path to dctlabs.com/products that will be accessed using the HTTP GET verb. How MUST the Developer configure the API? (Select TWO)

1: Create a /products method

2: Create a /products resource

3: Create a GET resource

4: Create a GET method

5: Create a /GET method

42. Question

An application is hosted in AWS Elastic Beanstalk and is connected to a database running on Amazon RDS MySQL. A Developer needs to instrument the application to trace database queries and calls to downstream services using AWS X-Ray.

How can the Developer enable tracing for the application?

1: Enable active tracing in the Elastic Beanstalk console

2: Add a xray-daemon.config file to the root of the source code to enable the X-Ray deamon

3: Add a .ebextensions/xray-daemon.config file to the source code to enable the X-Ray daemon

4: Enable X-Ray tracing using an AWS Lambda function

43. Question

A Developer needs to delete some specific messages from a busy production Amazon SQS queue. There are over 200 hundred messages to delete. What is the most efficient way to accomplish this task?

1: Use the DeleteQueue and CreateQueue APIs to delete and then recreate the queue

2: Use the PurgeQueue API and specify the queue URL to fully purge all messages from the queue

3: Use the DeleteMessageBatch API and provide a list of message receipt handles corresponding to the messages that should be deleted

4: Use the ReceiveMessage API to retrieve the messages and then delete them from the queue with the DeleteMessage API

44. Question

A Developer implemented a static website hosted in Amazon S3 that makes web service requests hosted in Amazon API Gateway and AWS Lambda. The site is showing an error that reads:

"No 'Access-Control-Allow-Origin' header is present on the requested resource. Origin 'null' is therefore not allowed access."

What should the Developer do to resolve this issue?

1: Enable cross-origin resource sharing (CORS) on the S3 bucket

2: Enable cross-origin resource sharing (CORS) for the method in API Gateway

3: Add the Access-Control-Request-Method header to the request

4: Add the Access-Control-Request-Headers header to the request

45. Question

A company runs an e-commerce website that uses Amazon DynamoDB where pricing for items is dynamically updated in real time. At any given time, multiple updates may occur simultaneously for pricing

information on a particular product. This is causing the original editor's changes to be overwritten without a proper review process.

Which DynamoDB write option should be selected to prevent this overwriting?

1: Concurrent writes

2: Conditional writes

3: Atomic writes

4: Batch writes

46. Question

A company is using Amazon RDS MySQL instances for its application database tier and apache Tomcat servers for its web tier. Most of the database queries from web applications are repeated read requests.

A Developer plans to add an in-memory store to improve performance for repeated read requests. Which AWS service would BEST fit these requirements?

1: Amazon RDS Multi-AZ

2: Amazon SQS

3: Amazon ElastiCache

4: Amazon RDS read replica

47. Question

An application that runs on an Amazon EC2 instance needs to access and make API calls to multiple AWS services.

What is the MOST secure way to provide access to the AWS services with MINIMAL management overhead?

1: Use AWS KMS to store and retrieve credentials

2: Use EC2 instance profiles

3: Use AWS root user to make requests to the application

4: Store and retrieve credentials from AWS CodeCommit

48. Question

A company maintains a REST API service using Amazon API Gateway with native API key validation. The company recently launched a new registration page, which allows users to sign up for the service. The registration page creates a new API key using CreateApiKey and sends the new key to the user. When the user attempts to call the API using this key, the user receives a 403 Forbidden error. Existing users are unaffected and can still call the API.

What code updates will grant these new users' access to the API?

1: The createDeployment method must be called so the API can be redeployed to include the newly created API key

2: The updateAuthorizer method must be called to update the API's authorizer to include the newly created API key

3: The importApiKeys method must be called to import all newly created API keys into the current stage of the API

4: The createUsagePlanKey method must be called to associate the newly created API key with the correct usage plan

49. Question

A Developer has deployed an application that runs on an Auto Scaling group of Amazon EC2 instances. The application data is stored in an Amazon DynamoDB table and records are constantly updated by all instances. An instance sometimes retrieves old data. The Developer wants to correct this by making sure the reads are strongly consistent.

How can the Developer accomplish this?

1: Set ConsistentRead to true when calling GetItem

2: Create a new DynamoDB Accelerator (DAX) table

3: Set consistency to strong when calling UpdateTable

4: Use the GetShardIterator command

50. Question

A Developer created a new AWS account and must create a scalable AWS Lambda function that meets the following requirements for concurrent execution:

- **Average execution time of 100 seconds**
- **50 requests per second**

Which step must be taken prior to deployment to prevent errors?

1: Implement dead-letter queues to capture invocation errors

2: Add an event source from Amazon API Gateway to the Lambda function

3: Implement error handling within the application code

4: Contact AWS Support to increase the concurrent execution limits

51. Question

A company is developing a new online game that will run on top of Amazon ECS. Four distinct Amazon ECS services will be part of the architecture, each requiring specific permissions to various AWS services. The company wants to optimize the use of the underlying Amazon EC2 instances by bin packing the containers based on memory reservation.

Which configuration would allow the Development team to meet these requirements MOST securely?

1: Create a new Identity and Access Management (IAM) instance profile containing the required permissions for the various ECS services, then associate that instance role with the underlying EC2 instances

2: Create four distinct IAM roles, each containing the required permissions for the associated ECS services, then configure each ECS service to reference the associated IAM role

3: Create four distinct IAM roles, each containing the required permissions for the associated ECS services, then, create an IAM group and configure the ECS cluster to reference that group

4: Create four distinct IAM roles, each containing the required permissions for the associated ECS services, then configure each ECS task definition to reference the associated IAM role

52. Question

A utilities company needs to ensure that documents uploaded by customers through a web portal are securely stored in Amazon S3 with encryption at rest. The company does not want to manage the security infrastructure in-house. However, the company still needs maintain control over its encryption keys due to industry regulations.

Which encryption strategy should a Developer use to meet these requirements?

1: Server-side encryption with Amazon S3 managed keys (SSE-S3)

2: Server-side encryption with customer-provided encryption keys (SSE-C)

3: Server-side encryption with AWS KMS managed keys (SSE-KMS)

4: Client-side encryption

53. Question

A Developer is creating a REST service using Amazon API Gateway with AWS Lambda integration. The service adds data to a spreadsheet and the data is sent as query string parameters in the method request.

How should the Developer convert the query string parameters to arguments for the Lambda function?

1: Enable request validation

2: Include the Amazon Resource Name (ARN) of the Lambda function

3: Change the integration type

4: Create a mapping template

54. Question

A Development team would like to migrate their existing application code from a GitHub repository to AWS CodeCommit.

What needs to be created before they can migrate a cloned repository to CodeCommit over HTTPS?

1: A GitHub secure authentication token

2: A public and private SSH key file

3: A set of credentials generated from IAM

4: An Amazon EC2 IAM role with CodeCommit permissions

55. Question

A team of Developers need to deploy a website for a development environment. The team do not want to manage the infrastructure and just need to upload Node.js code to the instances.

Which AWS service should Developers do?

1: Create an AWS CloudFormation template

2: Create an AWS Elastic Beanstalk environment

3: Create an AWS Lambda package

4: Launch an Auto Scaling group of Amazon EC2 instances

56. Question

A Developer is launching an application on Amazon ECS. The application should scale tasks automatically based on load and incoming connections must be spread across the containers.

How should the Developer configure the ECS cluster?

1: Create an ECS Service with Auto Scaling and attach an Elastic Load Balancer

2: Create an ECS Task Definition that uses Auto Scaling and Elastic Load Balancing

3: Create a capacity provider and configure cluster auto scaling

4: Write statements using the Cluster Query Language to scale the Docker containers

57. Question

An Amazon DynamoDB table has been created using provisioned capacity. A manager needs to understand whether the DynamoDB table is cost-effective. How can the manager query how much provisioned capacity is actually being used?

1: Monitor the ConsumedReadCapacityUnits and ConsumedWriteCapacityUnits over a specified time period

2: Monitor the ReadThrottleEvents and WriteThrottleEvents metrics for the table

3: Use Amazon CloudTrail and monitor the DescribeLimits API action

4: Use AWS X-Ray to instrument the DynamoDB table and monitor subsegments

58. Question

A static website that serves a collection of images runs from an Amazon S3 bucket in the us-east-1 region. The website is gaining in popularity and a is now being viewed around the world. How can a Developer improve the performance of the website for global users?

1: Use cross region replication to replicate the bucket to several global regions

2: Use Amazon S3 Transfer Acceleration to improve the performance of the website

3: Use Amazon ElastiCache to cache the website content

4: Use Amazon CloudFront to cache the website content

59. Question

A customer requires a relational database for a transactional workload. Which type of AWS database is BEST suited to this requirement?

1: Amazon RDS

2: Amazon RedShift

3: Amazon DynamoDB

4: Amazon ElastiCache

60. Question

A Developer is developing a web application and will maintain separate sets of resources for the alpha, beta, and release stages. Each version runs on Amazon EC2 and uses an Elastic Load Balancer.

How can the Developer create a single page to view and manage all of the resources?

1: Create a resource group

2: Deploy all resources using a single Amazon CloudFormation stack

3: Create an AWS Elastic Beanstalk environment for each stage

4: Create a single AWS CodeDeploy deployment

61. Question

A temporary Developer needs to be provided with access to specific resources for a one week period. Which element of an IAM policy statement can be used to allow access only on or before a specific date?

1: Condition

2: NotResource

3: Action

4: Version

62. Question

A Developer has created an Amazon S3 bucket and uploaded some objects that will be used for a publicly available static website. What steps MUST be performed to configure the bucket as a static website? (Select TWO)

1: Upload an index and error document and enter the name of the index and error documents when enabling static website hosting

2: Upload an index document and enter the name of the index document when enabling static website hosting

3: Enable public access and grant everyone the s3:GetObject permissions

4: Create an object access control list (ACL) granting READ permissions to the AllUsers group

5: Upload a certificate from AWS Certificate Manager

63. Question

An application generates a message and requires a decoupled method to trigger multiple AWS Lambda functions with the payload of the message. How can this be achieved?

1: Publish a message to an Amazon SQS queue and subscribe the Lambda functions to the queue

2: Publish a message to an Amazon SNS topic and subscribe the Lambda functions to the topic

3: Use the AWS SDK to invoke the Lambda functions and pass the message payload as input to the function execution

4: Use the AWS CLI to invoke the Lambda functions and pass the message payload as input to the function execution

64. Question

There are multiple AWS accounts across multiple regions managed by a company. The operations team require a single operational dashboard that displays some key performance metrics from these accounts and regions. What is the SIMPLEST solution?

1: Create an Amazon CloudWatch cross-account cross-region dashboard

2: Create an Amazon CloudWatch dashboard in one account and region and import the data from the other accounts and regions

3: Create an AWS Lambda function that collects metrics from each account and region and pushes the metrics to the account where the dashboard has been created

4: Create an Amazon CloudTrail trail that applies to all regions and deliver the logs to a single Amazon S3 bucket. Create a dashboard using the data in the bucket

65. Question

Customers who use a REST API have reported performance issues. A Developer needs to measure the time between when API Gateway receives a request from a client and when it returns a response to the client.

Which metric should the Developer monitor?

1: IntegrationLatency

2: Latency

3: CacheHitCount

4: 5XXError

SET 2: PRACTICE QUESTIONS, ANSWERS & EXPLANATIONS

1. Question

A CloudFormation template is going to be used by a global team to deploy infrastructure in several regions around the world. Which section of the template file can be used to set values based on a region?

1: Metadata

2: Parameters

3: Conditions

4: Mappings

Answer: 4

Explanation:

The optional Mappings section matches a key to a corresponding set of named values. For example, if you want to set values based on a region, you can create a mapping that uses the region name as a key and contains the values you want to specify for each specific region. You use the Fn::FindInMap intrinsic function to retrieve values in a map.

The following example shows a Mappings section with a map RegionMap, which contains five keys that map to name-value pairs containing single string values. The keys are region names. Each name-value pair is the AMI ID for the HVM64 AMI in the region represented by the key.

CORRECT: "Mappings" is the correct answer.

INCORRECT: "Metadata" is incorrect. You can use the optional Metadata section to include arbitrary JSON or YAML objects that provide details about the template.

INCORRECT: "Parameters" is incorrect. Parameters enable you to input custom values to your template each time you create or update a stack.

INCORRECT: "Conditions" is incorrect. The optional Conditions section contains statements that define the circumstances under which entities are created or configured. For example, you can create a condition and then associate it with a resource or output so that AWS CloudFormation only creates the resource or output if the condition is true.

2. Question

An application searches a DynamoDB table to return items based on primary key attributes. A developer noticed some ProvisionedThroughputExceeded exceptions being generated by DynamoDB.

How can the application be optimized to reduce the load on DynamoDB and use the LEAST amount of RCU?

1: Modify the application to issue query API calls with eventual consistency reads

2: Modify the application to issue scan API calls with eventual consistency reads

3: Modify the application to issue query API calls with strong consistency reads

4: Modify the application to issue scan API calls with strong consistency reads

Answer: 1

Explanation:

In general, Scan operations are less efficient than other operations in DynamoDB. A Scan operation always scans the entire table or secondary index. It then filters out values to provide the result you want, essentially adding the extra step of removing data from the result set.

If possible, you should avoid using a Scan operation on a large table or index with a filter that removes many results. Also, as a table or index grows, the Scan operation slows. The Scan operation examines every item for the requested values and can use up the provisioned throughput for a large table or index in a single operation. For faster response times, design your tables and indexes so that your applications can use Query instead of Scan. (For tables, you can also consider using the GetItem and BatchGetItem APIs.)

Additionally, eventual consistency consumers fewer RCUs than strong consistency. Therefore, the application should be refactored to use scan APIs with eventual consistency.

CORRECT: "Modify the application to issue query API calls with eventual consistency reads" is the correct answer.

INCORRECT: "Modify the application to issue scan API calls with strong eventual reads" is incorrect as the Scan API is less efficient as it will return all items in the table.

INCORRECT: "Modify the application to issue query API calls with strong consistency reads" is incorrect as strong consistency reads will consume more RCUs.

INCORRECT: "Modify the application to issue scan API calls with strong consistency reads" is incorrect as the Scan API is less efficient as it will return all items in the table and strong consistency reads will use more RCUs.

3. Question

A developer needs use the attribute of an Amazon S3 object that uniquely identifies the object in a bucket. Which of the following represents an Object Key?

1: s3://dctlabs/Development/Projects.xls

2: Development/Projects.xls

3: Project=Blue

4: arn:aws:s3:::dctlabs

Answer: 2

Explanation:

When you create an object, you specify the key name, which uniquely identifies the object in the bucket. For example, in the Amazon S3 console, when you highlight a bucket, a list of objects in your bucket appears. These names are the object keys. The name for a key is a sequence of Unicode characters whose UTF-8 encoding is at most 1024 bytes long.

The Amazon S3 data model is a flat structure: you create a bucket, and the bucket stores objects. There is no hierarchy of subbuckets or subfolders. However, you can infer logical hierarchy using key name prefixes and delimiters as the Amazon S3 console does. The Amazon S3 console supports a concept of folders. Suppose that your bucket (admin-created) has four objects with the following object keys:

- Development/Projects.xls
- Finance/statement1.pdf
- Private/taxdocument.pdf
- s3-dg.pdf

The console uses the key name prefixes (Development/, Finance/, and Private/) and delimiter ('/') to present a folder structure as shown.

CORRECT: "Development/Projects.xls" is the correct answer.

INCORRECT: "s3://dctlabs/Development/Projects.xls" is incorrect as this is the full path to a file including the bucket name and object key.

INCORRECT: "Project=Blue" is incorrect as this is an example of an object tag. You can use object tagging to categorize storage. Each tag is a key-value pair.

INCORRECT: "arn:aws:s3:::dctlabs" is incorrect as this is the Amazon Resource Name (ARN) of a bucket.

4. Question

A developer has created an Amazon API Gateway with caching enabled in front of AWS Lambda. For some requests, it is necessary to ensure the latest data is received from the endpoint. How can the developer ensure the data is not stale?

1: Send requests with the Cache-Control: max-age=0 header

2: Modify the TTL on the cache to a lower number

3: The cache must be disabled

4: Send requests with the Cache-Delete: max-age=0 header

Answer: 1

Explanation:

You can invalidate an existing cache entry and reload it from the integration endpoint for individual requests. The request must contain the Cache-Control: max-age=0 header. The client receives the response directly from the integration endpoint instead of the cache, provided that the client is authorized to do so. This replaces the existing cache entry with the new response, which is fetched from the integration endpoint.

The following image shows a cache configuration in the settings for a stage:

Cache capacity	1.6GB ⬍
Encrypt cache data	⬜
Cache time-to-live (TTL)	300

Per-key cache invalidation

Require authorization	☑
Handle unauthorized requests	Ignore cache control header; Add a warning in response header ⬍

CORRECT: "Send requests with the Cache-Control: max-age=0 header" is the correct answer.

INCORRECT: "Modify the TTL on the cache to a lower number" is incorrect as that would expire all entries after the TTL expires. The question states that for some requests (not all requests) that latest data must be received, in this case the best way to ensure this is to use invalidate the cache entries using the header in the correct answer.

INCORRECT: "The cache must be disables" is incorrect as you can achieve this requirement using invalidation as detailed in the explanation above.

INCORRECT: "Send requests with the Cache-Delete: max-age=0 header " is incorrect as that is the wrong header to use. The Developer should use the Cache-Control: max-age=0 header instead.

5. Question

A developer needs to add sign-up and sign-in capabilities for a mobile app. The solution should integrate with social identity providers (IdPs) and SAML IdPs. Which service should the developer use?

1: AWS Cognito user pool

2: AWS Cognito identity pool

3: API Gateway with a Lambda authorizer

4: AWS IAM and STS

Answer: 1

Explanation:

User pools are for <u>authentication</u> (identify verification). With a user pool, your app users can sign in through the user pool or federate through a third-party identity provider (IdP).

Identity pools are for authorization (access control). You can use identity pools to create unique identities for users and give them access to other AWS services.

User pool use cases:

Use a user pool when you need to:

- Design sign-up and sign-in webpages for your app.
- Access and manage user data.
- Track user device, location, and IP address, and adapt to sign-in requests of different risk levels.
- Use a custom authentication flow for your app.

Identity pool use cases:

Use an identity pool when you need to:

- Give your users access to AWS resources, such as an Amazon Simple Storage Service (Amazon S3) bucket or an Amazon DynamoDB table.
- Generate temporary AWS credentials for unauthenticated users.

Therefore, a user pool is the correct service to use as in this case we are not granting access to AWS services, just providing sign-up and sign-in capabilities for a mobile app.

CORRECT: "AWS Cognito user pool" is the correct answer.

INCORRECT: "AWS Cognito identity pool" is incorrect as an identity pool is used when you need to provide access to AWS resources (see explanation above).

INCORRECT: "API Gateway with a Lambda authorizer" is incorrect as AWS Cognito is the best solution for providing sign-up and sign-in for mobile apps and also integrates with the 3rd party IdPs.

INCORRECT: "AWS IAM and STS" is incorrect as AWS Cognito is the best solution for providing sign-up and sign-in for mobile apps and also integrates with the 3rd party IdPs.

6. Question

An Amazon EC2 instance is being deployed with an Elastic Load Balancer (ELB). A developer needs to run a script when the instance is being launched. What is the SIMPLEST method of running the script?

1: Place the code in the EC2 User Data

2: Using EC2 Run Command

3: Place the code in the EC2 Metadata

4: Using Amazon CloudWatch Events

Answer: 1

Explanation:

When you launch an instance in Amazon EC2, you have the option of passing user data to the instance that can be used to perform common automated configuration tasks and even run scripts after the instance starts. You can pass two types of user data to Amazon EC2: shell scripts and cloud-init directives. You can also pass this data into the launch wizard as plain text, as a file (this is useful for launching instances using the command line tools), or as base64-encoded text (for API calls).

Using user data is definitely the simplest method of achieving this requirement. If using an Auto Scaling Group, you would also only have to place the data in the user data field once for the launch configuration.

CORRECT: "Place the code in the EC2 User Data" is the correct answer.

INCORRECT: "Using EC2 Run Command" is incorrect. Run command does allow the running of scripts on EC2 instances at scale. However, this is not the simplest method of achieving this objective as we're only dealing with a single instance.

INCORRECT: "Place the code in the EC2 Metadata" is incorrect. Instance metadata is data about your instance that you can use to configure or manage the running instance.

INCORRECT: "Using Amazon CloudWatch Events" is incorrect as this service alerts you to events happening in your AWS resources, it does not allow you to run scripts on EC2 instances.

7. Question

A call centre application is being refactored into a serverless architecture. The new application includes several AWS Lambda functions which are involved in the automation of support tickets.

What is the BEST way to coordinate the complex invocation logic for the Lambda functions?

1: Create a State Machine with AWS Step Functions

2: Include the invocation of other Lambda functions within the Lambda code

3: Create a Workflow using the Amazon Simple Workflow Service (SWF)

4: Use the AWS Serverless Application Model (SAM)

Answer: 1

Explanation:

AWS Step Functions makes it easy to coordinate the components of distributed applications as a series of steps in a visual workflow. You can quickly build and run state machines to execute the steps of your application in a reliable and scalable fashion.

AWS Step Functions is built on Lambda and is and orchestration service that lets you easily coordinate multiple Lambda functions into flexible workflows that are easy to debug and easy to change.

CORRECT: "Create a State Machine with AWS Step Functions" is the correct answer.

INCORRECT: "Include the invocation of other Lambda functions within the Lambda code" is incorrect as this would be complex and cumbersome to manage. It would be preferable to use Step Functions as this will provide a visual view of the complex invocation logic and will be easier to troubleshoot and manage.

INCORRECT: "Create a Workflow using the Amazon Simple Workflow Service (SWF)" is incorrect as Step Functions should be used for serverless applications.

INCORRECT: "Use the AWS Serverless Application Model (SAM)" is incorrect as this is used to package and deploy serverless applications, it is not used for orchestrating Lambda invocations.

8. Question

An application is deployed using AWS Elastic Beanstalk and uses a Classic Load Balancer (CLB). A developer is performing a blue/green migration to change to an Application Load Balancer (ALB).

After deployment, the developer has noticed that customers connecting to the ALB need to re-authenticate every time they connect. Normally they would only authenticate once and then be able to reconnect without re-authenticating for several hours.

How can the developer resolve this issue?

1: Enable IAM authentication on the ALBs listener

2: Add a new SSL certificate to the ALBs listener

3: Change the load balancing algorithm on the target group to "least outstanding requests)

4: Enable Sticky Sessions on the target group

Answer: 4

Explanation:

Sticky sessions are a mechanism to route requests to the same target in a target group. This is useful for servers that maintain state information in order to provide a continuous experience to clients. To use sticky sessions, the clients must support cookies.

In this case, it is likely that the clients authenticate to the back-end instance and when they are reconnecting without sticky sessions enabled they may be load balanced to a different instance and need to authenticate again.

The most obvious first step in troubleshooting this issue is to enable sticky sessions on the target group.

CORRECT: "Enable Sticky Sessions on the target group" is the correct answer.

INCORRECT: "Enable IAM authentication on the ALBs listener" is incorrect as you cannot enable "IAM authentication" on a listener.

INCORRECT: "Add a new SSL certificate to the ALBs listener" is incorrect as this is not related to authentication.

INCORRECT: "Change the load balancing algorithm on the target group to "least outstanding requests)" is incorrect as this does not prevent the customer from being load balanced to a different instance, which is what is most likely to resolve this issue.

9. Question

A DynamoDB table is being used to store session information for users of an online game. A developer has noticed that the table size has increased considerably and much of the data is not required after a gaming session is completed.

What is the MOST cost-effective approach to reducing the size of the table?

1: Use the batch-write-item API to delete the data

2: Create an AWS Lambda function that purges stale items from the table daily

3: Enable a Time To Live (TTL) on the table and add a timestamp attribute on new items

4: Use the delete-item API to delete the data

Answer: 3

Explanation:

Time to Live (TTL) for Amazon DynamoDB lets you define when items in a table expire so that they can be automatically deleted from the database. With TTL enabled on a table, you can set a timestamp for deletion on a per-item basis, allowing you to limit storage usage to only those records that are relevant.

TTL is useful if you have continuously accumulating data that loses relevance after a specific time period (for example, session data, event logs, usage patterns, and other temporary data). If you have sensitive data that must be retained only for a certain amount of time according to contractual or regulatory obligations, TTL helps you ensure that it is removed promptly and as scheduled.

Therefore, using a TTL is the best solution as it will automatically purge items after their useful lifetime.

CORRECT: "Enable a Time To Live (TTL) on the table and add a timestamp attribute on new items" is the correct answer.

INCORRECT: "Use the batch-write-item API to delete the data" is incorrect as this would use RCUs and WCUs to remove the data.

INCORRECT: "Create an AWS Lambda function that purges stale items from the table daily" is incorrect as this would also require reading/writing to the table so it would require RCUs/WCUs.

INCORRECT: "Use the delete-item API to delete the data" is incorrect is incorrect as this would use RCUs and WCUs to remove the data.

10. Question

A decoupled application uses an Amazon SQS queue. The producers send messages to the queue every 30 seconds on average. What is the MOST efficient configuration for a message processor to poll the queue?

1: Set the queue attribute ReceiveMessageWaitTimeSeconds to 20

2: Set the queue attribute ReceiveMessageWaitTimeSeconds to 0

3: Set the Default Visibility Timeout to 0

4: Set the Delivery Delay to 20

Answer: 1

Explanation:

The process of consuming messages from a queue depends on whether you use short or long polling. By default, Amazon SQS uses *short polling*, querying only a subset of its servers (based on a weighted random distribution) to determine whether any messages are available for a response. You can use *long polling* to reduce your costs while allowing your consumers to receive messages as soon as they arrive in the queue.

When the wait time for the ReceiveMessage API action is greater than 0, *long polling* is in effect. The maximum long polling wait time is 20 seconds. Long polling helps reduce the cost of using Amazon SQS by eliminating the number of empty responses (when there are no messages available for a ReceiveMessage request) and false empty responses (when messages are available but aren't included in a response).

Therefore, setting the queue attribute ReceiveMessageWaitTimeSeconds to 20 will result in fewer attempts to poll the queue which is more efficient and will reduce cost.

CORRECT: "Set the queue attribute ReceiveMessageWaitTimeSeconds to 20" is the correct answer.

INCORRECT: "Set the queue attribute ReceiveMessageWaitTimeSeconds to 0" is incorrect as this would enable short polling.

INCORRECT: "Set the Default Visibility Timeout to 0" is incorrect as this does not affect polling, it affect the invisibility timeout.

INCORRECT: "Set the Delivery Delay to 20" is incorrect as this is used to delay delivery of a message to the queue.

11. Question

A developer needs to resolve an issue where orders are occasionally being processed twice. The application uses an Auto Scaling group of Amazon EC2 instances and an Amazon SQS queue. How can the developer resolve this issue most cost-effectively?

1: Use a FIFO queue and configure the producer to provide a message deduplication ID

2: Use a standard queue and configure the producer to provide a message deduplication ID

3: Use a FIFO queue and configure the consumer to provide a message deduplication ID

4: Use a standard queue and configure the consumer to provide a message deduplication ID

Answer: 1

Explanation:

The message deduplication ID is the token used for deduplication of sent messages. If a message with a particular message deduplication ID is sent successfully, any messages sent with the same message deduplication ID are accepted successfully but aren't delivered during the 5-minute deduplication interval.

The message deduplication ID is used with FIFO queues which also provide exactly-once processing (unlike standard queues which only provide "at least once delivery"). The producer should provide message deduplication ID values for each message.

Therefore, the best answer is to use a FIFO queue and configure the producer to provide a message deduplication ID.

CORRECT: "Use a FIFO queue and configure the producer to provide a message deduplication ID" is the correct answer.

INCORRECT: "Use a standard queue and configure the producer to provide a message deduplication ID" is incorrect as standard queues do not support message deduplication IDs or exactly-once processing.

INCORRECT: "Use a FIFO queue and configure the consumer to provide a message deduplication ID" is incorrect as the producer, not the consumer must provide the message deduplication ID.

INCORRECT: "Use a standard queue and configure the consumer to provide a message deduplication ID" is incorrect as standard queues do not support message deduplication IDs or exactly-once processing and the producer, not the consumer must provide the message deduplication ID.

12. Question

A developer created an operational dashboard for a serverless application using Amazon API Gateway, AWS Lambda, Amazon S3, and Amazon DynamoDB. Users will connect to the dashboard from a variety of mobile applications, desktops and tablets.

The developer needs an authentication mechanism that can allow users to sign-in and will remember the devices users sign in from and suppress the second factor of authentication for remembered devices. Which AWS service should the developer use to support this scenario?

1: Amazon Cognito

2: AWS Directory Service

3: AWS KMS

4: Amazon IAM

Answer: 1

Explanation:

Amazon Cognito lets you add user sign-up, sign-in, and access control to your web and mobile apps quickly and easily. Cognito supports multiple devices types including mobile applications, desktops and tablets.

You can enable device remembering for Amazon Cognito user pools. A remembered device can serve in place of the security code delivered via SMS as a second factor of authentication. This suppresses the second authentication challenge from remembered devices and thus reduces the friction users experience with multi-factor authentication (MFA).

Therefore, Amazon Cognito is the best answer and will support all of the requirements in the scenario.

CORRECT: "Amazon Cognito" is the correct answer.

INCORRECT: "AWS Directory Service" is incorrect as this service enables directory-aware workloads and AWS resources to use managed Active Directory in the AWS Cloud.

INCORRECT: "AWS KMS" is incorrect as KMS is used to manage encryption keys; it does not enable authentication from mobile devices.

INCORRECT: "Amazon IAM" is incorrect as IAM is not the best authentication solution for mobile users. It also does not support device remembering or any ability to suppress MFA when it is enabled.

13. Question

A developer is designing a web application that will run on Amazon EC2 Linux instances using an Auto Scaling Group. The application should scale based on a threshold for the number of users concurrently using the application.

How should the Auto Scaling Group be configured to scale out?

1: Create a custom Amazon CloudWatch metric for concurrent users

2: Use the Amazon CloudWatch metric "NetworkIn"

3: Use a target tracking scaling policy

4: Create a custom Amazon CloudWatch metric for memory usage

Answer: 1

Explanation:

You can create a custom CloudWatch metric for your EC2 Linux instance statistics by creating a script through the AWS Command Line Interface (AWS CLI). Then, you can monitor that metric by pushing it to CloudWatch. In this scenario you could then monitor the number of users currently logged in.

CORRECT: "Create a custom Amazon CloudWatch metric for concurrent users" is the correct answer.

INCORRECT: "Use the Amazon CloudWatch metric "NetworkIn"" is incorrect as this will only shows statistics for the number of inbound connections, not the number of concurrent users.

INCORRECT: "Use a target tracking scaling policy" is incorrect as this is used to maintain a certain number of instances based on a target utilization.

INCORRECT: "Create a custom Amazon CloudWatch metric for memory usage" is incorrect as memory usage does not tell us how many users are logged in.

14. Question

An application needs to identify the public IPv4 address of the Amazon EC2 Linux instance on which it is running. How can a Developer configure the application to locate this information?

1: Locate the address within the instance metadata

2: Locate the address within the instance user data

3: Configure the application to run the ifconfig command to find the public IP address

4: Configure the application to run the ipconfig command to find the public IP address

Answer: 1

Explanation:

You can use the Amazon EC2 console to determine the private IPv4 addresses, public IPv4 addresses, and Elastic IP addresses of your instances. You can also determine the public IPv4 and private IPv4 addresses of your instance from within your instance by using instance metadata.

You can access the instance metadata by using the following URL: http://169.254.169.254/latest/meta-data/

CORRECT: "Locate the address within the instance metadata " is the correct answer.

INCORRECT: "Locate the address within the instance user data" is incorrect. Instance user data is used to run scripts at instance launch.

INCORRECT: "Configure the application to run the ifconfig command to find the public IP address" is incorrect as you cannot see the public IPv4 address when you run ifconfig as the address is not locally attached, it is mapped externally from an Elastic Network Interface (ENI) to the private IP of the instance.

INCORRECT: "Configure the application to run the ipconfig command to find the public IP address" is incorrect as this command is used for Windows systems. As with the previous answer this would also not reveal the public IPv4 address, only the private address.

15. Question

A Developer is creating an application and would like add AWS X-Ray to trace user requests end-to-end through the software stack. The Developer has implemented the changes and tested the application and the traces are successfully sent to X-Ray. The Developer then deployed the application on an Amazon EC2 instance, and noticed that the traces are not being sent to X-Ray.

What is the most likely cause of this issue? (Select TWO)

1: The X-Ray API is not installed on the EC2 instance

2: The instance's instance profile role does not have permission to upload trace data to X-Ray

3: The traces are reaching X-Ray, but the Developer does not have permission to view the records

4: The X-Ray daemon is not installed on the EC2 instance.

5: The X-Ray segments are being queued

Answer: 2,4

Explanation:

AWS X-Ray is a service that collects data about requests that your application serves, and provides tools you can use to view, filter, and gain insights into that data to identify issues and opportunities for optimization. For any traced request to your application, you can see detailed information not only about the request and response, but also about calls that your application makes to downstream AWS resources, microservices, databases and HTTP web APIs.

You can run the X-Ray daemon on the following operating systems on Amazon EC2:

- Amazon Linux
- Ubuntu
- Windows Server (2012 R2 and newer)

The X-Ray daemon must be running on the EC2 instance in order to collect data. You can use a user data script to run the daemon automatically when you launch the instance. The X-Ray daemon uses the AWS SDK to upload trace data to X-Ray, and it needs AWS credentials with permission to do that.

On Amazon EC2, the daemon uses the instance's instance profile role automatically. The IAM role or user that the daemon's credentials belong to must have permission to write data to the service on your behalf.

- To use the daemon on Amazon EC2, create a new instance profile role or add the managed policy to an existing one.
- To use the daemon on Elastic Beanstalk, add the managed policy to the Elastic Beanstalk default instance profile role.
- To run the daemon locally, create an IAM user and save its access keys on your computer.

Therefore, the most likely cause of the issues being experienced in this scenario is that the instance's instance profile role does not have permission to upload trace data to X-Ray or the X-Ray daemon is not running on the EC2 instance.

CORRECT: "The instance's instance profile role does not have permission to upload trace data to X-Ray" is the correct answer.

CORRECT: "The X-Ray daemon is not installed on the EC2 instance." is also a correct answer.

INCORRECT: "The X-Ray API is not installed on the EC2 instance " is incorrect as you do not install the X-Ray API, you run the X-Ray daemon. The API will always be accessible using the X-Ray endpoint.

INCORRECT: "The traces are reaching X-Ray, but the Developer does not have permission to view the records" is incorrect as the developer previously viewed data in X-Ray so clearly has permissions.

INCORRECT: "The X-Ray segments are being queued" is incorrect. The X-Ray daemon is responsible for relaying trace data to X-Ray. However, it will not queue data for an extended period of time so this is unlikely to be a cause of this issue.

16. Question

A Developer needs to manage AWS services from a local development server using the AWS CLI. How can the Developer ensure that the CLI uses their IAM permissions?

1: Create an IAM Role with the required permissions and attach it to the local server's instance profile

2: Put the Developer's IAM user account in an IAM group that has the necessary permissions

3: Save the Developer's IAM login credentials as environment variables and reference them when executing AWS CLI commands

4: Run the aws configure command and provide the Developer's IAM access key ID and secret access key

Answer: 4

Explanation:

For general use, the aws configure command is the fastest way to set up your AWS CLI installation. The following example shows sample values:

```
$ aws configure
AWS Access Key ID [None]: AKIAIOSFODNN7EXAMPLE
AWS Secret Access Key [None]: wJalrXUtnFEMI/K7MDENG/bPxRfiCYEXAMPLEKEY
Default region name [None]: us-west-2
Default output format [None]: json
```

You can configure the AWS CLI on Linux, MacOS, and Windows. Computers can be located anywhere as long as they can connect to the AWS API.

For this scenario, the best solution is to run aws configure and use the IAM user's access key ID and secret access key. This will mean that commands run using the AWS CLI will use the user's IAM permissions as required.

CORRECT: "Run the aws configure command and provide the Developer's IAM access key ID and secret access key" is the correct answer.

INCORRECT: "Create an IAM Role with the required permissions and attach it to the local server's instance profile" is incorrect as this is not an Amazon EC2 instance so you cannot attach an IAM role.

INCORRECT: "Put the Developer's IAM user account in an IAM group that has the necessary permissions" is incorrect as this does not assist with configuring the AWS CLI.

INCORRECT: "Save the Developer's IAM login credentials as environment variables and reference them when executing AWS CLI commands" is incorrect as the IAM login credentials cannot be used with the AWS CLI. You need to use an access key ID and secret access key with the AWS CLI and these are configured for use by running aws configure.

17. Question

A Developer is creating an application that will process some data and generate an image file from it. The application will use an AWS Lambda function which will require 150 MB of temporary storage while executing. The temporary files will not be needed after the function execution is completed.

What is the best location for the Developer to store the files?

1: Store the files in Amazon S3 and use a lifecycle policy to delete the files automatically

2: Store the files in the /tmp directory and delete the files when the execution completes

3: Store the files in an Amazon Instance Store and delete the files when the execution completes

4: Store the files in an Amazon EFS filesystem and delete the files when the execution completes

Answer: 2

Explanation:

The /tmp directory can be used for storing temporary files within the execution context. This can be used for storing static assets that can be used by subsequent invocations of the function. If the assets must be deleted before the function is invoked again the function code should take care of deleting them.

There is a limit of 512 MB storage space in the /tmp directory, but this is more than adequate for this scenario.

CORRECT: "Store the files in the /tmp directory and delete the files when the execution completes" is the correct answer.

INCORRECT: "Store the files in Amazon S3 and use a lifecycle policy to delete the files automatically" is incorrect. The /tmp directory within the execution context has enough space for these files and this will reduce latency, cost, and execution time.

INCORRECT: "Store the files in an Amazon Instance Store and delete the files when the execution completes" is incorrect. Instance stores are ephemeral storage attached to Ec2 instances, they cannot be used except by EC2 instances for temporary storage.

INCORRECT: "Store the files in an Amazon EFS filesystem and delete the files when the execution completes" is incorrect. This is another option that would increase cost, complexity and latency. It is better to use the /tmp directory.

18. Question

AWS CodeBuild builds code for an application, creates the Docker image, pushes the image to Amazon Elastic Container Registry (Amazon ECR), and tags the image with a unique identifier.
If the Developers already have AWS CLI configured on their workstations, how can the Docker images be pulled to the workstations?

1: Run the following: docker pull REPOSITORY URI : TAG

2: Run the output of the following: aws ecr get-login and then run: docker pull REPOSITORY URI : TAG

3: Run the following: aws ecr get-login and then run: docker pull REPOSITORY URI : TAG

4: Run the output of the following: aws ecr get-download-url-for-layer and then run: docker pull REPOSITORY URI : TAG

Answer: 2

Explanation:

If you would like to run a Docker image that is available in Amazon ECR, you can pull it to your local environment with the docker pull command. You can do this from either your default registry or from a registry associated with another AWS account.

Docker CLI does not support standard AWS authentication methods, so client authentication must be handled so that ECR knows who is requesting to push or pull an image. To do this you can issue the aws ecr get-login or aws ecr get-login-password (AWS CLI v2) and then use the output to login using docker login and then issue a docker pull command specifying the repository and image with the REPOSITORY URI : TAG format.

CORRECT: "Run the output of the following: aws ecr get-login and then run: docker pull REPOSITORY URI : TAG" is the correct answer.

INCORRECT: "Run the following: docker pull REPOSITORY URI : TAG" is incorrect as you need to authenticate first.

INCORRECT: "Run the following: aws ecr get-login and then run: docker pull REPOSITORY URI : TAG" is incorrect as you need to run the output of the "aws ecr get-login" command before you can issue a "docker pull" command.

INCORRECT: "Run the output of the following: aws ecr get-download-url-for-layer and then run: docker pull REPOSITORY URI : TAG" is incorrect as the first command is incorrect. You need to run the output of the "aws ecr -get-login" command instead.

19. Question

A company recently migrated a multi-tier application to AWS. The web tier runs on an Auto Scaling group of Amazon EC2 instances and the database tier uses Amazon DynamoDB. The database tier requires extremely high performance and most requests are repeated read requests.

What service can be used to scale the database tier for BEST performance?

1: Amazon CloudFront

2: Amazon ElastiCache

3: Amazon DynamoDB Accelerator (DAX)

4: Amazon SQS

Answer: 3

Explanation:

Amazon DynamoDB Accelerator (DAX) is a fully managed, highly available, in-memory cache for DynamoDB that delivers up to a 10x performance improvement – from milliseconds to microseconds – even at millions of requests per second. DAX does all the heavy lifting required to add in-memory acceleration to your DynamoDB tables, without requiring developers to manage cache invalidation, data population, or cluster management.

How it works:

- DAX is a write-through caching service – this means the data is written to the cache as well as the back end store at the same time.
- Allows you to point your DynamoDB API calls at the DAX cluster and if the item is in the cache (cache hit), DAX returns the result to the application.
- If the item requested is not in the cache (cache miss) then DAX performs an Eventually Consistent GetItem operations against DynamoDB
- Retrieval of data from DAX reduces the read load on DynamoDB tables.
- This may result in being able to reduce the provisioned read capacity on the table.

DynamoDB DAX is the correct solution for best performance for a read-heavy workload.

CORRECT: "Amazon DynamoDB Accelerator (DAX)" is the correct answer.

INCORRECT: "Amazon CloudFront" is incorrect. CloudFront is a content delivery network (CDN) that is used for serving static assets from a cache around the globe. It is used to get content closer to end users for better performance. However, it cannot cache DynamoDB read requests.

INCORRECT: "Amazon ElastiCache" is incorrect. ElastiCache is an in-memory database that can be used for caching read requests to a backend database. However, ElastiCache is not the correct choice to put in front of DynamoDB (better for RDS), you should choose DAX instead.

INCORRECT: "Amazon SQS" is incorrect. An SQS queue is used for decoupling application components, this will not assist with improving the performance of the DynamoDB database.

20. Question

A company runs multiple microservices that each use their own Amazon DynamoDB table. The "customers" microservice needs data that originates in the "orders" microservice.

What approach represents the SIMPLEST method for the "customers" table to get near real-time updates from the "orders" table?

1: Enable Amazon DynamoDB streams on the "orders" table, configure the "customers" microservice to read records from the stream

2: Use Amazon CloudWatch Events to send notifications every time an item is added or modified in the "orders" table

3: Use Amazon Kinesis Firehose to deliver all changes in the "orders" table to the "customers" table

4: Enable DynamoDB streams for the "customers" table, trigger an AWS Lambda function to read records from the stream and write them to the "orders" table

Answer: 1

Explanation:

DynamoDB Streams captures a time-ordered sequence of item-level modifications in any DynamoDB table and stores this information in a log for up to 24 hours. Applications can access this log and view the data items as they appeared before and after they were modified, in near-real time.

Whenever an application creates, updates, or deletes items in the table, DynamoDB Streams writes a stream record with the primary key attributes of the items that were modified. A stream record contains information about a data modification to a single item in a DynamoDB table. You can configure the stream so that the stream records capture additional information, such as the "before" and "after" images of modified items.

For this scenario, we can enable a DynamoDB stream on the "orders" table and the configure the "customers" microservice to read records from the stream and then write those records, or relevant attributes of those records, to the "customers' table.

CORRECT: "Enable Amazon DynamoDB streams on the "orders" table, configure the "customers" microservice to read records from the stream" is the correct answer.

INCORRECT: "Enable DynamoDB streams for the "customers" table, trigger an AWS Lambda function to read records from the stream and write them to the "orders" table" is incorrect. This could be a good solution if it wasn't backward. We can trigger a Lambda function to then process the records from the stream. However, we should be enabling the stream on the "orders" table, not the "customers" table, and then writing the records to the "customers" table, not the "orders" table.

INCORRECT: "Use Amazon CloudWatch Events to send notifications every time an item is added or modified in the "orders" table" is incorrect. CloudWatch Events is used to respond to changes in the state of specific AWS services. It does not support DynamoDB.

INCORRECT: "Use Amazon Kinesis Firehose to deliver all changes in the "orders" table to the "customers" table" is incorrect. Kinesis Firehose cannot be configured to ingest data from a DynamoDB table, nor is DynamoDB a supported destination.

21. Question

A company manages a web application that is deployed on AWS Elastic Beanstalk. A Developer has been instructed to update to a new version of the application code. There is no tolerance for downtime if the update fails and rollback should be fast.

What is the SAFEST deployment method to use?

1: All at once

2: Rolling

3: Rolling with Additional Batch

4: Immutable

Answer: 4

Explanation:

AWS Elastic Beanstalk provides several options for how deployments are processed, including deployment policies (**All at once**, **Rolling**, **Rolling with additional batch**, and **Immutable**) and options that let you configure batch size and health check behavior during deployments.

For this scenario we need to ensure that no downtime occurs if the update fails and there is a quick way to rollback.

All policies except for Immutable and Blue/Green require manual redeployment of the previous version of the code which will take time and result in downtime. The blue/green option is not actually an Elastic Beanstalk policy but it is a method you can use, however it is not offered as an answer choice

Therefore, the best deployment policy to use for this scenario is the **Immutable** deployment policy.

CORRECT: "Immutable" is the correct answer.

INCORRECT: "All at once" is incorrect as it causes complete downtime and manual redeployment in the case of failure.

INCORRECT: "Rolling" is incorrect because it requires manual redeployment in the case of failure.

INCORRECT: "Rolling with Additional Batch" is incorrect because it requires manual redeployment in the case of failure.

22. Question

A Lambda function is taking a long time to complete. The Developer has discovered that inadequate compute capacity is being allocated to the function. How can the Developer ensure that more compute capacity is allocated to the function?

1: Allocate more memory to the function

2: Use an instance type with more CPU

3: Increase the maximum execution time

4: Increase the reserved concurrency

Answer: 1

Explanation:

You can allocate memory between 128 MB and 3,008 MB in 64-MB increments. AWS Lambda allocates CPU power linearly in proportion to the amount of memory configured. At 1,792 MB, a function has the equivalent of one full vCPU (one vCPU-second of credits per second).

Therefore, the way provide more compute capacity to this function is to allocate more memory.

CORRECT: "Allocate more memory to the function" is the correct answer.

INCORRECT: "Use an instance type with more CPU" is incorrect as Lambda is a serverless service and you cannot choose an instance type for your function.

INCORRECT: "Increase the maximum execution time" is incorrect as the function is not timing out, it's just taking longer than expected due to having insufficient compute allocated.

INCORRECT: "Increase the reserved concurrency" is incorrect as this would enable more invocations to run in parallel but would not add more CPU to each function execution.

23. Question

A Developer is configuring an Amazon ECS Service with Auto Scaling. The tasks should scale based on user load in the previous 20 seconds. How can the Developer enable the scaling?

1: Create a high-resolution custom Amazon CloudWatch metric for user activity data, then publish data every 10 seconds

2: Create a high-resolution custom Amazon CloudWatch metric for user activity data, then publish data every 5 seconds

3: Create a standard-resolution custom Amazon CloudWatch metric for user activity data, then publish data every 30 seconds

4: Create a standard-resolution custom Amazon CloudWatch metric for user activity data, then publish data every 5 seconds

Answer: 1

Explanation:

Metrics produced by AWS services are standard resolution by default. When you publish a custom metric, you can define it as either standard resolution or high resolution. When you publish a high-resolution metric, CloudWatch stores it with a resolution of 1 second, and you can read and retrieve it with a period of 1 second, 5 seconds, 10 seconds, 30 seconds, or any multiple of 60 seconds.

User activity is not a standard CloudWatch metric and as stated above for the resolution we need in this scenario a custom CloudWatch metric is required anyway. Therefore, for this scenario the Developer should create a high-resolution custom Amazon CloudWatch metric for user activity data and publish the data every 10 seconds.

CORRECT: "Create a high-resolution custom Amazon CloudWatch metric for user activity data, then publish data every 10 seconds" is the correct answer.

INCORRECT: "Create a high-resolution custom Amazon CloudWatch metric for user activity data, then publish data every 5 seconds" is incorrect as the resolution is higher than required which will cost more. We need the resolution to be 20 seconds so that means publishing in 10 second intervals with 2 data points. At 5 second intervals there would be 4 data points which will incur additional costs.

INCORRECT: "Create a standard-resolution custom Amazon CloudWatch metric for user activity data, then publish data every 30 seconds" is incorrect as standard resolution metrics have a granularity of one minute.

INCORRECT: "Create a standard-resolution custom Amazon CloudWatch metric for user activity data, then publish data every 5 seconds" is incorrect as standard resolution metrics have a granularity of one minute.

24. Question

An application exports documents to an Amazon S3 bucket. The data must be encrypted at rest and company policy mandates that encryption keys must be rotated annually. How can this be achieved automatically and with the LEAST effort?

1: Use AWS KMS keys with automatic rotation enabled

2: Import a custom key into AWS KMS and configure automatic rotation

3: Encrypt the data within the application before writing to S3

4: Configure automatic rotation with AWS Secrets Manager

Answer: 1

Explanation:

With AWS KMS you can choose to have AWS KMS automatically rotate CMKs every year, provided that those keys were generated within AWS KMS HSMs. Automatic key rotation is not supported for imported keys, asymmetric keys, or keys generated in an AWS CloudHSM cluster using the AWS KMS custom key store feature.

If you choose to import keys to AWS KMS or asymmetric keys or use a custom key store, you can manually rotate them by creating a new CMK and mapping an existing key alias from the old CMK to the new CMK.

If you choose to have AWS KMS automatically rotate keys, you don't have to re-encrypt your data. AWS KMS automatically keeps previous versions of keys to use for decryption of data encrypted under an old version of a key. All new encryption requests against a key in AWS KMS are encrypted under the newest version of the key.

CORRECT: "Use AWS KMS keys with automatic rotation enabled" is the correct answer.

INCORRECT: "Import a custom key into AWS KMS and configure automatic rotation" is incorrect as per the explanation above KMS will not automatically rotate imported encryption keys (it can automatically rotate imported CMKs though).

INCORRECT: "Encrypt the data within the application before writing to S3" is incorrect as this is both an incomplete solution (where would the encryption keys come from) and would also likely require more maintenance and management overhead.

INCORRECT: "Configure automatic rotation with AWS Secrets Manager" is incorrect as Secrets Manager is used for rotating credentials, not encryption keys.

25. Question

An application uses an Amazon SQS queue to decouple an online image processing application. The images can take up to 5 minutes to process. Which process below will result in successful processing of the message and remove it from the queue while MINIMIZING the chances of duplicate processing?

1: Retrieve the message with an increased visibility timeout, delete the message from the queue, process the message

2: Retrieve the message with increased DelaySeconds, process the message, delete the message from the queue

3: Retrieve the message with increased DelaySeconds, delete the message from the queue, process the message

4: Retrieve the message with an increased visibility timeout, process the message, delete the message from the queue

Answer: 4

Explanation:

When a consumer receives and processes a message from a queue, the message remains in the queue. Amazon SQS doesn't automatically delete the message. Because Amazon SQS is a distributed system, there's no guarantee that the consumer actually receives the message (for example, due to a connectivity issue, or due to an issue in the consumer application). Thus, the consumer must delete the message from the queue after receiving and processing it.

Immediately after a message is received, it remains in the queue. To prevent other consumers from processing the message again, Amazon SQS sets a *visibility timeout*, a period of time during which Amazon SQS prevents other consumers from receiving and processing the message. The default visibility timeout for a message is 30 seconds. The minimum is 0 seconds. The maximum is 12 hours.

For this scenario, the best way to minimize the chances of duplicate processing, the Developer should configure the visibility timeout to be at least 5 minutes to allow time for processing of the message. This will prevent the message from becoming visible while it is still being processed (which could result in another consumer processing it).

CORRECT: "Retrieve the message with an increased visibility timeout, process the message, delete the message from the queue" is the correct answer.

INCORRECT: "Retrieve the message with an increased visibility timeout, delete the message from the queue, process the message" is incorrect as the message should be processed before it is deleted. This protects against the consumer failing. If the consumer fails during processing another consumer can pick up the message after the expiration of the visibility timeout (when the message becomes visible again).

INCORRECT: "Retrieve the message with increased DelaySeconds, process the message, delete the message from the queue" is incorrect as DelaySeconds relates to delay queues which postpone the delivery of new messages to a queue for a number of seconds.

INCORRECT: "Retrieve the message with increased DelaySeconds, delete the message from the queue, process the message" is incorrect as DelaySeconds relates to delay queues which postpone the delivery of new messages to a queue for a number of seconds.

26. Question

A Development team are currently creating a new application that uses a microservices design pattern and runs on Docker containers. The team would like to run the platform on AWS using a managed platform. They want minimize management overhead for the platform. Which service should the Development team use?

1: Amazon ECS with EC2 launch type

2: Amazon ECS with Fargate launch type

3: Amazon Elastic Kubernetes Service (EKS)

4: AWS Lambda

Answer: 2

Explanation:

AWS Fargate is a serverless compute engine for containers that works with both Amazon Elastic Container Service (ECS) and Amazon Elastic Kubernetes Service (EKS). Fargate makes it easy for you to focus on building your applications. Fargate removes the need to provision and manage servers, lets you specify and pay for resources per application, and improves security through application isolation by design.

There are two launch types with Amazon ECS. With the EC2 launch type you must manage the infrastructure layer (Amazon EC2 instances), whereas with Amazon Fargate you do not. Therefore, for this scenario the Fargate launch type should be used.

CORRECT: "Amazon ECS with Fargate launch type" is the correct answer.

INCORRECT: "Amazon ECS with EC2 launch type" is incorrect as the EC2 launch type requires more platform overhead as you must manage Amazon EC2 instances.

INCORRECT: "Amazon Elastic Kubernetes Service (EKS)" is incorrect as this would require more management overhead (unless used with Fargate).

INCORRECT: "AWS Lambda" is incorrect as this is not a service that can be used to run Docker containers.

27. Question

A company is using Amazon API Gateway to manage access to a set of microservices implemented as AWS Lambda functions. The company has made some minor changes to one of the APIs. The company wishes to give existing customers using the API up to 6 months to migrate from version 1 to version 2.

What approach should a Developer use to implement the change?

1: Update the underlying Lambda function and provide clients with the new Lambda invocation URL

2: Use API Gateway to automatically propagate the change to clients, specifying 180 days in the phased deployment parameter

3: Use API Gateway to deploy a new stage named v2 to the API and provide users with its URL

4: Update the underlying Lambda function, create an Amazon CloudFront distribution with the updated Lambda function as its origin

Answer: 3

Amazon API Gateway is an AWS service for creating, publishing, maintaining, monitoring, and securing REST and WebSocket APIs at any scale. API developers can create APIs that access AWS or other web services as well as data stored in the AWS Cloud.

A stage is a named reference to a deployment, which is a snapshot of the API. You use a Stage to manage and optimize a particular deployment. For example, you can set up stage settings to enable caching, customize request throttling, configure logging, define stage variables or attach a canary release for testing.

You deploy your API to a stage and it is given a unique URL that contains the stage name. This URL can be used to direct customers to your URL based on the stage (or version) you'd like them to use.

The following invocation URLs can be used to direct customers to version 1 or version 2 of an API:

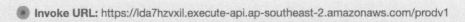

Invoke URL: https://lda7hzvxil.execute-api.ap-southeast-2.amazonaws.com/prodv1

Invoke URL: https://lda7hzvxil.execute-api.ap-southeast-2.amazonaws.com/prodv2

Therefore, the best approach is to use API Gateway to deploy a new stage named v2 to the API and provide users with its URL.

CORRECT: "Use API Gateway to deploy a new stage named v2 to the API and provide users with its URL" is the correct answer.

INCORRECT: "Update the underlying Lambda function and provide clients with the new Lambda invocation URL" is incorrect as the API has been updated, not the Lambda function. We deploy API updates to stages, so we need to deploy a new stage.

INCORRECT: "Use API Gateway to automatically propagate the change to clients, specifying 180 days in the phased deployment parameter" is incorrect as this is not a valid method of migrating users from one stage in API Gateway to another.

INCORRECT: "Update the underlying Lambda function, create an Amazon CloudFront distribution with the updated Lambda function as its origin" is incorrect as the API has been updated, not the Lambda function.

28. Question

A Developer has completed some code updates and needs to deploy the updates to an Amazon Elastic Beanstalk environment. The update must be deployed in the fastest possible time and application downtime is acceptable.

Which deployment policy should the Developer choose?

1: All at once

2: Rolling

3: Rolling with additional batch

4: Immutable

Answer: 1

Explanation:

AWS Elastic Beanstalk provides several options for how deployments are processed, including deployment policies and options that let you configure batch size and health check behavior during deployments.

Each deployment policy has advantages and disadvantages and it's important to select the best policy to use for each situation.

The "all at once" policy will deploy the update in the fastest time but will incur downtime.

All at once:

- Deploys the new version to all instances simultaneously.
- All of your instances are out of service while the deployment takes place.
- Fastest deployment.
- Good for quick iterations in development environment.
- You will experience an outage while the deployment is taking place – not ideal for mission-critical systems.
- If the update fails, you need to roll back the changes by re-deploying the original version to all of your instances.
- No additional cost.

For this scenario downtime is acceptable and deploying in the fastest possible time is required so the "all at once" policy is the best choice.

CORRECT: "All at once" is the correct answer.

INCORRECT: "Rolling" is incorrect as this takes longer than "all at once". This is a better choice if speed is required but downtime is not acceptable.

INCORRECT: "Rolling with additional batch" is incorrect if you require no reduction in capacity as it adds an additional batch of instances to the deployment.

INCORRECT: "Immutable" is incorrect as this takes a long time to complete. This is good if you cannot sustain application downtime and need to be able to quickly and easily roll back if issues occur.

29. Question

A Developer is creating a DynamoDB table for storing transaction logs. The table has 10 write capacity units (WCUs). The Developer needs to configure the read capacity units (RCUs) for the table in order to MAXIMIZE the number of requests allowed per second. Which of the following configurations should the Developer use?

1: Eventually consistent reads of 5 RCUs reading items that are 4 KB in size

2: Strongly consistent reads of 5 RCUs reading items that are 4 KB in size

3: Eventually consistent reads of 15 RCUs reading items that are 1 KB in size

4: Strongly consistent reads of 15 RCUs reading items that are 1KB in size

Answer: 3

Explanation:

A *read capacity unit* represents one strongly consistent read per second, or two eventually consistent reads per second, for an item up to 4 KB in size. For example, suppose that you create a table with 10 provisioned read capacity units. This allows you to perform 10 strongly consistent reads per second, or 20 eventually consistent reads per second, for items up to 4 KB.

Reading an item larger than 4 KB consumes more read capacity units. For example, a strongly consistent read of an item that is 8 KB (4 KB × 2) consumes 2 read capacity units. An eventually consistent read on that same item consumes only 1 read capacity unit.

Item sizes for reads are rounded up to the next 4 KB multiple. For example, reading a 3,500-byte item consumes the same throughput as reading a 4 KB item. Therefore, the smaller (1 KB) items in this scenario would consume the same number of RCUs as the 4 KB items. Also, we know that eventually consistent reads consume half the RCUs of strongly consistent reads.

The following bullets provide the read throughput for each configuration:

- Eventually consistent, 15 RCUs, 1 KB item = 30 items read per second.
- Strongly consistent, 15 RCUs, 1 KB item = 15 items read per second.
- Eventually consistent, 5 RCUs, 4 KB item = 10 items read per second.
- Strongly consistent, 5 RCUs, 4 KB item = 5 items read per second.

Therefore, the Developer should choose the option to enable eventually consistent reads of 15 RCUs reading items that are 1 KB in size as this will result in the highest number of items read per second.

CORRECT: "Eventually consistent reads of 15 RCUs reading items that are 1 KB in size" is the correct answer.

INCORRECT: "Eventually consistent reads of 5 RCUs reading items that are 4 KB in size" is incorrect as described above.

INCORRECT: "Strongly consistent reads of 5 RCUs reading items that are 4 KB in size" is incorrect as described above.

INCORRECT: "Strongly consistent reads of 15 RCUs reading items that are 1KB in size" is incorrect as described above.

30. Question

A Developer is attempting to call the Amazon CloudWatch API and is receiving HTTP 400: ThrottlingException errors intermittently. When a call fails, no data is retrieved.

What best practice should the Developer first attempt to resolve this issue?

1: Contact AWS Support for a limit increase

2: Use the AWS CLI to get the metrics

3: Analyze the applications and remove the API call

4: Retry the call with exponential backoff

Answer: 4

Explanation:

Occasionally ,you may receive the 400 ThrottlingException error for PutMetricData API calls in Amazon CloudWatch with a detailed response.

CloudWatch requests are throttled for each Amazon Web Services (AWS) account on a per-Region basis to help service performance. For current PutMetricData API request limits, see CloudWatch Limits.

All calls to the PutMetricData API in an AWS Region count towards the maximum allowed request rate. This number includes calls from any custom or third-party application, such as calls from the CloudWatch Agent, the AWS Command Line Interface (AWS CLI), or the AWS Management Console.

Resolutions: It's a best practice to use the following methods to reduce your call rate and avoid API throttling:

- Distribute your API calls evenly over time rather than making several API calls in a short time span. If you require data to be available with a one-minute resolution, you have an entire minute to emit that metric. Use jitter (randomized delay) to send data points at various times.

- Combine as many metrics as possible into a single API call. For example, a single PutMetricData call can include 20 metrics and 150 data points. You can also use pre-aggregated data sets, such as StatisticSet, to publish aggregated data points, thus reducing the number of PutMetricData calls per second.

- Retry your call with exponential backoff and jitter.

Following attempting the above resolutions AWS suggest the following: "If you still require a higher limit, you can request a limit increase. Increasing the rate limit can have a high financial impact on your AWS bill."

Therefore, the first thing the Developer should do, from the list of options presented, is to retry the call with exponential backoff.

CORRECT: "Retry the call with exponential backoff" is the correct answer.

INCORRECT: "Contact AWS Support for a limit increase" is incorrect. As mentioned above, there are other resolutions the Developer should attempt before contacting support to raise the limit.

INCORRECT: "Use the AWS CLI to get the metrics" is incorrect as this will still make the same API calls.

INCORRECT: "Analyze the applications and remove the API call" is incorrect as this is not a good resolution to the issue as this may mean that important monitoring and logging data is not recorded for the application.

31. Question

An application is processing data from an Amazon Kinesis Data Stream. The Data Stream has 12 shards with one KCL worker each. The volume of data has increased, and an additional 6 shards have been added to the stream.

What is the MAXIMUM number of EC2 instances required for optimum performance?

1: 18

2: 9

3: 36

4: 12

Answer: 1

Explanation:

Resharding enables you to increase or decrease the number of shards in a stream in order to adapt to changes in the rate of data flowing through the stream. Resharding is typically performed by an administrative application that monitors shard data-handling metrics. Although the KCL itself doesn't initiate resharding operations, it is designed to adapt to changes in the number of shards that result from resharding.

Typically, when you use the KCL, you should ensure that the number of instances does not exceed the number of shards (except for failure standby purposes). Each shard is processed by exactly one KCL worker and has exactly one corresponding record processor, so you never need multiple instances to process one shard. However, one worker can process any number of shards, so it's fine if the number of shards exceeds the number of instances.

To scale up processing in your application, you should test a combination of these approaches:

- Increasing the instance size (because all record processors run in parallel within a process)

- Increasing the number of instances up to the maximum number of open shards (because shards can be processed independently)

- Increasing the number of shards (which increases the level of parallelism)

Therefore, the optimum number of EC2 instances required for this scenario is 18 (equal to the number of shards).

CORRECT: "18" is the correct answer.

INCORRECT: "9" is incorrect as each shard is processed by exactly one KCL worker so there would be too few workers.

INCORRECT: "36" is incorrect as the optimum ratio is 1:1 between KCL workers and shards.

INCORRECT: "12" is incorrect as the optimum ratio is 1:1 between KCL workers and shards.

32. Question

A Developer has deployed an application that processes streaming big data. The application includes an Amazon Kinesis Stream and Amazon EC2 consumer instances. Each EC2 instance has exactly one KCL worker processing one Kinesis Data Stream which has 15 shards. To resolve performance issues the Developer has increased the number of shards to 25.

How many EC2 consumer instances are required to process the data from the stream with BEST performance?

1: 50

2: 25

3: 10

4: 30

Answer: 2

Explanation:

Resharding enables you to increase or decrease the number of shards in a stream in order to adapt to changes in the rate of data flowing through the stream. Resharding is typically performed by an administrative application that monitors shard data-handling metrics. Although the KCL itself doesn't initiate resharding operations, it is designed to adapt to changes in the number of shards that result from resharding.

Typically, when you use the KCL, you should ensure that the number of instances does not exceed the number of shards (except for failure standby purposes). Each shard is processed by exactly one KCL worker and has exactly one corresponding record processor, so you never need multiple instances to process one shard. However, one worker can process any number of shards, so it's fine if the number of shards exceeds the number of instances.

To scale up processing in your application, you should test a combination of these approaches:

- Increasing the instance size (because all record processors run in parallel within a process)
- Increasing the number of instances up to the maximum number of open shards (because shards can be processed independently)
- Increasing the number of shards (which increases the level of parallelism)

Therefore, the optimum number of EC2 instances required for this scenario is 25 (equal to the number of shards).

CORRECT: "25" is the correct answer.

INCORRECT: "50" is incorrect as each shard is processed by exactly one KCL worker and has exactly one corresponding record processor, so you never need multiple instances to process one shard.

INCORRECT: "10" is incorrect as the optimum ratio is 1:1 between KCL workers and shards.

INCORRECT: "30" is incorrect as each shard is processed by exactly one KCL worker and has exactly one corresponding record processor, so you never need multiple instances to process one shard.

33. Question

A Developer is using AWS SAM to create a template for deploying a serverless application. The Developer plans to leverage an application from the AWS Serverless Application Repository in the template as a nested application. Which resource type should the Developer specify?

1: AWS::Serverless::Application

2: AWS::Serverless:Function

3: AWS::Serverless:HttpApi

4: AWS::Serverless:SimpleTable

Answer: 1

Explanation:

A serverless application can include one or more **nested applications**. You can deploy a nested application as a stand-alone artifact or as a component of a larger application.

As serverless architectures grow, common patterns emerge in which the same components are defined in multiple application templates. You can now separate out common patterns as dedicated applications, and then nest them as part of new or existing application templates. With nested applications, you can stay more focused on the business logic that's unique to your application.

To define a nested application in your serverless application, use the AWS::Serverless::Application resource type.

CORRECT: "AWS::Serverless::Application" is the correct answer.

INCORRECT: "AWS::Serverless:Function" is incorrect as this is used to define a serverless Lamdba function.

INCORRECT: "AWS::Serverless:HttpApi" is incorrect as this is used to define an API Gateway HTTP API.

INCORRECT: "AWS::Serverless:SimpleTable" is incorrect as this is used to define a DynamoDB table.

34. Question

A Developer needs to be notified by email for all new object creation events in a specific Amazon S3 bucket. Amazon SNS will be used for sending the messages. How can the Developer enable these notifications?

1: Create an event notification for all s3:ObjectCreated:Put API calls

2: Create an event notification for all s3:ObjectRemoved:Delete API calls

3: Create an event notification for all s3:ObjectRestore:Post API calls

4: Create an event notification for all s3:ObjectCreated:* API calls

Answer: 4

Explanation:

The Amazon S3 notification feature enables you to receive notifications when certain events happen in your bucket. To enable notifications, you must first add a notification configuration that identifies the events you want Amazon S3 to publish and the destinations where you want Amazon S3 to send the notifications. You store this configuration in the *notification* subresource that is associated with a bucket.

Currently, Amazon S3 can publish notifications for the following events:

- **New object created events** — Amazon S3 supports multiple APIs to create objects. You can request notification when only a specific API is used (for example, s3:ObjectCreated:Put), or you can use a wildcard (for example, s3:ObjectCreated:*) to request notification when an object is created regardless of the API used.

- **Object removal events** — Amazon S3 supports deletes of versioned and unversioned objects. For information about object versioning, see Object Versioning and Using Versioning.

- **Restore object events** — Amazon S3 supports the restoration of objects archived to the S3 Glacier storage class. You request to be notified of object restoration completion by using s3:ObjectRestore:Completed. You use s3:ObjectRestore:Post to request notification of the initiation of a restore.

- **Reduced Redundancy Storage (RRS) object lost events** — Amazon S3 sends a notification message when it detects that an object of the RRS storage class has been lost.

- **Replication events** — Amazon S3 sends event notifications for replication configurations that have S3 Replication Time Control (S3 RTC) enabled. It sends these notifications when an object fails replication, when an object exceeds the 15-minute threshold, when an object is replicated after the 15-minute threshold, and when an object is no longer tracked by replication metrics. It publishes a second event when that object replicates to the destination Region.

Therefore, the Developer should create an event notification for all s3:ObjectCreated:* API calls as this will capture all new object creation events.

CORRECT: "Create an event notification for all s3:ObjectCreated:* API calls" is the correct answer.

INCORRECT: "Create an event notification for all s3:ObjectCreated:Put API calls" is incorrect as this will not capture all new object creation events (e.g. POST or COPY). The wildcard should be used instead.

INCORRECT: "Create an event notification for all s3:ObjectRemoved:Delete API calls" is incorrect as this is used for object deletions.

INCORRECT: "Create an event notification for all s3:ObjectRestore:Post API calls" is incorrect as this is used for restore events from Amazon S3 Glacier archives.

35. Question

An application will be hosted on the AWS Cloud. Developers will be using an Agile software development methodology with regular updates deployed through a continuous integration and delivery (CI/CD) model. Which AWS service can assist the Developers with automating the build, test, and deploy phases of the release process every time there is a code change?

1: AWS CodeBuild

2: AWS CloudFormation

3: AWS Elastic Beanstalk

4: AWS CodePipeline

Answer: 4

Explanation:

AWS CodePipeline is a continuous delivery service you can use to model, visualize, and automate the steps required to release your software. You can quickly model and configure the different stages of a software release process. CodePipeline automates the steps required to release your software changes continuously.

Specifically, you can:

- **Automate your release processes**: CodePipeline fully automates your release process from end to end, starting from your source repository through build, test, and deployment. You can prevent changes from moving through a pipeline by including a manual approval action in any stage except a Source stage. You can release when you want, in the way you want, on the systems of your choice, across one instance or multiple instances.

- **Establish a consistent release process**: Define a consistent set of steps for every code change. CodePipeline runs each stage of your release according to your criteria.

- **Speed up delivery while improving quality**: You can automate your release process to allow your developers to test and release code incrementally and speed up the release of new features to your customers.

- **Use your favorite tools**: You can incorporate your existing source, build, and deployment tools into your pipeline.

- **View progress at a glance**: You can review real-time status of your pipelines, check the details of any alerts, retry failed actions, view details about the source revisions used in the latest pipeline execution in each stage, and manually rerun any pipeline.
- **View pipeline history details**: You can view details about executions of a pipeline, including start and end times, run duration, and execution IDs.

Therefore, AWS CodePipeline is the perfect tool for the Developer's requirements.

CORRECT: "AWS CodePipeline" is the correct answer.

INCORRECT: "AWS CloudFormation" is incorrect as CloudFormation is not triggered by changes in a source code repository. You must create change sets for deploying updates.

INCORRECT: "AWS Elastic Beanstalk" is incorrect as this is a platform service that can be used to deploy code to managed runtimes such as Nodejs. It does not update automatically based on changes to source code. You must update that environment when you need to release new code.

INCORRECT: "AWS CodeBuild" is incorrect as CodeBuild is used for compiling code, running unit tests and creating the deployment package. It does not manage the deployment of the code.

36. Question

A Developer is creating a design for an application that will include Docker containers on Amazon ECS with the EC2 launch type. The Developer needs to control the placement of tasks onto groups of container instances organized by availability zone and instance type.

Which Amazon ECS feature provides expressions that can be used to group container instances by the relevant attributes?

1: Cluster Query Language

2: Task Group

3: Task Placement Constraints

4: Task Placement Strategy

Answer: 1

Explanation:

Cluster queries are expressions that enable you to group objects. For example, you can group container instances by attributes such as Availability Zone, instance type, or custom metadata.

After you have defined a group of container instances, you can customize Amazon ECS to place tasks on container instances based on group. You can also apply a group filter when listing container instances.

As an example, the following cluster query expressions selects instances with the specified instance type:

attribute:ecs.instance-type == t2.small

The following cluster query expressions selects instances in the us-east-1a or us-east-1b availability zones:

attribute:ecs.availability-zone in [us-east-1a, us-east-1b]

The Developer should therefore use the cluster query language to generate expressions that can group the container instances by instance type and availability zone.

CORRECT: "Cluster Query Language" is the correct answer.

INCORRECT: "Task Group" is incorrect as this is just a set of related tasks with the same task group name.

INCORRECT: "Task Placement Constraints" is incorrect. A *task placement constraint* is a rule that is considered during task placement. Task placement constraints can be specified when either running a task or creating a new service.

INCORRECT: "Task Placement Strategy" is incorrect. A *task placement strategy* is an algorithm for selecting instances for task placement or tasks for termination. Task placement strategies can be specified when either running a task or creating a new service.

37. Question

An organization has an account for each environment: Production, Testing, Development. A Developer with an IAM user in the Development account needs to launch resources in the Production and Testing accounts. What is the MOST efficient way to provide access?

1: Create a role with the required permissions in the Production and Testing accounts and have the Developer assume that role

2: Create a separate IAM user in each account and have the Developer login separately to each account

3: Create an IAM group in the Production and Testing accounts and add the Developer's user from the Development account to the groups

4: Create an IAM permissions policy in the Production and Testing accounts and reference the IAM user in the Development account

Answer: 1

Explanation:

You can grant your IAM users' permission to switch to roles within your AWS account or to roles defined in other AWS accounts that you own. This is known as cross-account access.

The user is able to assume the role in the Production account and access the S3 bucket. This is more efficient than providing the user with multiple accounts. In this scenario the user requests to switch to the role through either the console or the API/CLI.

CORRECT: "Create a role with the required permissions in the Production and Testing accounts and have the Developer assume that role" is the correct answer.

INCORRECT: "Create a separate IAM user in each account and have the Developer login separately to each account" is incorrect as this is not the most efficient method of providing access. Cross-account access is preferred .

INCORRECT: "Create an IAM group in the Production and Testing accounts and add the Developer's user from the Development account to the groups" is incorrect as you cannot add an IAM user from another AWS account to a group.

INCORRECT: "Create an IAM permissions policy in the Production and Testing accounts and reference the IAM user in the Development account" is incorrect as you cannot reference an IAM user from another AWS account in a permissions policy.

38. Question

An application running on Amazon EC2 generates a large number of small files (1KB each) containing personally identifiable information that must be converted to ciphertext. The data will be stored on a proprietary network-attached file system. What is the SAFEST way to encrypt the data using AWS KMS?

1: Create a data encryption key from a customer master key and encrypt the data with the data encryption key

2: Encrypt the data directly with a customer managed customer master key

3: Create a data encryption key from a customer master key and encrypt the data with the customer master key

4: Encrypt the data directly with an AWS managed customer master key

Answer: 2

Explanation:

With AWS KMS you can encrypt files directly with a customer master key (CMK). A CMK can encrypt up to 4KB (4096 bytes) of data in a single encrypt, decrypt, or reencrypt operation. As CMKs cannot be exported from KMS this is a very safe way to encrypt small amounts of data.

Customer managed CMKs are CMKs in your AWS account that you create, own, and manage. You have full control over these CMKs, including establishing and maintaining their <u>key policies, IAM policies, and</u>

grants, <u>enabling and disabling</u> them, <u>rotating their cryptographic material</u>, <u>adding tags</u>, <u>creating aliases</u> that refer to the CMK, and <u>scheduling the CMKs for deletion</u>.

AWS managed CMKs are CMKs in your account that are created, managed, and used on your behalf by an AWS service that is integrated with AWS KMS. Some AWS services support only an AWS managed CMK. In this example the Amazon EC2 instance is saving files on a proprietary network-attached file system and this will not have support for AWS managed CMKs.

Data keys are encryption keys that you can use to encrypt data, including large amounts of data and other data encryption keys. You can use AWS KMS CMKs to generate, encrypt, and decrypt data keys. However, AWS KMS does not store, manage, or track your data keys, or perform cryptographic operations with data keys. You must use and manage data keys outside of AWS KMS – this is potentially less secure as you need to manage the security of these keys.

CORRECT: "Encrypt the data directly with a customer managed customer master key" is the correct answer.

INCORRECT: "Create a data encryption key from a customer master key and encrypt the data with the data encryption key" is incorrect as this is not the most secure option here as you need to secure the data encryption key outside of KMS. It is also unwarranted as you can use a CMK directly to encrypt files up to 4KB in size.

INCORRECT: "Create a data encryption key from a customer master key and encrypt the data with the customer master key" is incorrect as the creation of the data encryption key is of no use here. It does not necessarily pose a security risk as the data key hasn't been used (and you can use the CMK to encrypt the data), however this is not the correct process to follow.

INCORRECT: "Encrypt the data directly with an AWS managed customer master key" is incorrect as the network-attached file system is proprietary and therefore will not be supported by AWS managed CMKs.

39. Question

A new application will be deployed using AWS CodeDeploy to Amazon Elastic Container Service (ECS). What must be supplied to CodeDeploy to specify the ECS service to deploy?

1: The AppSpec file

2: The BuildSpec file

3: The Template file

4: The Policy file

Answer: 1

Explanation:

The application specification file (AppSpec file) is a <u>YAML</u>-formatted or JSON-formatted file used by CodeDeploy to manage a deployment.

If your application uses the Amazon ECS compute platform, the AppSpec file is named appspec.yaml. It is used by CodeDeploy to determine:

- Your Amazon ECS task definition file. This is specified with its ARN in the TaskDefinition instruction in the AppSpec file.

- The container and port in your replacement task set where your Application Load Balancer or Network Load Balancer reroutes traffic during a deployment. This is specified with the LoadBalancerInfo instruction in the AppSpec file.

- Optional information about your Amazon ECS service, such the platform version on which it runs, its subnets, and its security groups.

- Optional Lambda functions to run during hooks that correspond with lifecycle events during an Amazon ECS deployment. For more information, see <u>AppSpec 'hooks' Section for an Amazon ECS Deployment</u>.

CORRECT: "The AppSpec file" is the correct answer.

INCORRECT: "The BuildSpec file" is incorrect as this is a file type that is used with AWS CodeBuild.

INCORRECT: "The Template file" is incorrect as this is something that is used with AWS CloudFormation and AWS SAM.

INCORRECT: "The Policy file" is incorrect as a policy is typically referring to an IAM permissions policy document.

40. Question

An application requires an in-memory caching engine. The cache should provide high availability as repopulating data is expensive. How can this requirement be met?

1: Use Amazon ElastiCache Redis with replicas

2: Use Amazon ElastiCache Memcached with partitions

3: Amazon RDS with a Read Replica

4: Amazon Aurora with a Global Database

Answer: 1

Explanation:

Single-node Amazon ElastiCache Redis clusters are in-memory entities with limited data protection services (AOF). If your cluster fails for any reason, you lose all the cluster's data.

However, if you're running the Redis engine, you can group 2 to 6 nodes into a cluster with replicas where 1 to 5 read-only nodes contain replicate data of the group's single read/write primary node.

In this scenario, if one node fails for any reason, you do not lose all your data since it is replicated in one or more other nodes. Due to replication latency, some data may be lost if it is the primary read/write node that fails. Therefore, the best solution is to use ElastiCache Redis with replicas.

CORRECT: "Use Amazon ElastiCache Redis with replicas" is the correct answer.

INCORRECT: "Use Amazon ElastiCache Memcached with partitions" is incorrect as partitions are not copies of data so if you lose a partition you lose the data contained within it (no high availability).

INCORRECT: "Amazon RDS with a Read Replica" is incorrect as this is not an in-memory database and is read-only.

INCORRECT: "Amazon Aurora with a Global Database" is incorrect as this is not an in-memory database and this configuration is for scaling a database globally.

41. Question

A new application will be hosted on the domain name dctlabs.com using an Amazon API Gateway REST API front end. The Developer needs to configure the API with a path to dctlabs.com/products that will be accessed using the HTTP GET verb. How MUST the Developer configure the API? (Select TWO)

1: Create a /products method

2: Create a /products resource

3: Create a GET resource

4: Create a GET method

5: Create a /GET method

Answer: 2,4

Explanation:

An API Gateway REST API is a collection of HTTP resources and methods that are integrated with backend HTTP endpoints, Lambda functions, or other AWS services. You can deploy this collection in one or more stages. Typically, API resources are organized in a resource tree according to the application logic. Each API resource can expose one or more API methods that have unique HTTP verbs supported by API Gateway.

The Developer would need to create a resource which in this case would be /products. The Developer would then create a GET method within the resource.

CORRECT: "Create a /products resource" is a correct answer.

CORRECT: "Create a GET method" is a correct answer.

INCORRECT: "Create a /products method" is incorrect as a resource should be created.

INCORRECT: "Create a GET resource" is incorrect as a method should be created.

INCORRECT: "Create a /GET method" is incorrect as a method is not preceded by a slash.

42. Question

An application is hosted in AWS Elastic Beanstalk and is connected to a database running on Amazon RDS MySQL. A Developer needs to instrument the application to trace database queries and calls to downstream services using AWS X-Ray.

How can the Developer enable tracing for the application?

1: Enable active tracing in the Elastic Beanstalk console

2: Add a xray-daemon.config file to the root of the source code to enable the X-Ray deamon

3: Add a .ebextensions/xray-daemon.config file to the source code to enable the X-Ray daemon

4: Enable X-Ray tracing using an AWS Lambda function

Answer: 3

Explanation:

To relay trace data from your application to AWS X-Ray, you can run the X-Ray daemon on your Elastic Beanstalk environment's Amazon EC2 instances.

Elastic Beanstalk platforms provide a configuration option that you can set to run the daemon automatically. You can enable the daemon in a configuration file in your source code or by choosing an option in the Elastic Beanstalk console. When you enable the configuration option, the daemon is installed on the instance and runs as a service.

The following example code can be placed in the .ebextensions/xray-daemon.config file in your source code:

```
option_settings:
  aws:elasticbeanstalk:xray:
    XRayEnabled: true
```

The above code will ensure the X-Ray daemon starts and the Developer can enable tracing for the application as required.

CORRECT: "Add a .ebextensions/xray-daemon.config file to the source code to enable the X-Ray daemon" is the correct answer.

INCORRECT: "Add a xray-daemon.config file to the root of the source code to enable the X-Ray deamon" is incorrect as all .config files must be stored in the .ebextensions folder in the source code.

INCORRECT: "Enable active tracing in the Elastic Beanstalk console" is incorrect as you cannot enable active tracing through the console for Elastic Beanstalk. This is available for AWS Lambda and API Gateway.

INCORRECT: "Enable X-Ray tracing using an AWS Lambda function" is incorrect as there is no need to add a Lambda function to the application to add tracing support. The developer can enable tracing by enabling the X-Ray daemon.

43. Question

A Developer needs to delete some specific messages from a busy production Amazon SQS queue. There are over 200 hundred messages to delete. What is the most efficient way to accomplish this task?

1: Use the DeleteQueue and CreateQueue APIs to delete and then recreate the queue

2: Use the PurgeQueue API and specify the queue URL to fully purge all messages from the queue

3: Use the DeleteMessageBatch API and provide a list of message receipt handles corresponding to the messages that should be deleted

4: Use the ReceiveMessage API to retrieve the messages and then delete them from the queue with the DeleteMessage API

Answer: 3

Explanation:

The DeleteMessageBatch API deletes the specified message from the specified queue. To select the message to delete, use the ReceiptHandle of the message (*not* the MessageId which you receive when you send the message). Amazon SQS can delete a message from a queue even if a visibility timeout setting causes the message to be locked by another consumer. Amazon SQS automatically deletes messages left in a queue longer than the retention period configured for the queue.

The DeleteMessageBatch API deletes up to ten messages from the specified queue. This is a batch version of <u>DeleteMessage</u>. The result of the action on each message is reported individually in the response.

In this scenario the Developer has some specific messages that must be deleted. Therefore, we can assume the Developer is able to identify which messages need to be deleted by receipt handle. Using this information, the Developer can issue an API call with DeleteMessageBatch and specify up to 10 messages to delete per API call. This is the most efficient option available.

CORRECT: "Use the DeleteMessageBatch API and provide a list of message receipt handles corresponding to the messages that should be deleted" is the correct answer.

INCORRECT: "Use the DeleteQueue and CreateQueue APIs to delete and then recreate the queue" is incorrect as this is a busy production queue and deleting the queue will mean losing all messages (including those sent during the process) and the recreated queue will have a new URL.

INCORRECT: "Use the PurgeQueue API and specify the queue URL to fully purge all messages from the queue" is incorrect as this will purge all messages. The question states that specific message should be deleted and it's a production queue so the Developer cannot delete any other messages.

INCORRECT: "Use the ReceiveMessage API to retrieve the messages and then delete them from the queue with the DeleteMessage API" is incorrect as there is no reason to receive the message first (inefficient) as they do not need to be processed and the DeleteMessage API is less efficient compared to DeleteMessageBatch.

44. Question

A Developer implemented a static website hosted in Amazon S3 that makes web service requests hosted in Amazon API Gateway and AWS Lambda. The site is showing an error that reads:

"No 'Access-Control-Allow-Origin' header is present on the requested resource. Origin 'null' is therefore not allowed access."

What should the Developer do to resolve this issue?

1: Enable cross-origin resource sharing (CORS) on the S3 bucket

2: Enable cross-origin resource sharing (CORS) for the method in API Gateway

3: Add the Access-Control-Request-Method header to the request

4: Add the Access-Control-Request-Headers header to the request

Answer: 1

Explanation:

Cross-origin resource sharing (CORS) defines a way for client web applications that are loaded in one domain to interact with resources in a different domain. With CORS support, you can build rich client-side web applications with Amazon S3 and selectively allow cross-origin access to your Amazon S3 resources.

To configure your bucket to allow cross-origin requests, you create a CORS configuration, which is an XML document with rules that identify the origins that you will allow to access your bucket, the operations (HTTP methods) that will support for each origin, and other operation-specific information.

CORRECT: "Enable cross-origin resource sharing (CORS) on the S3 bucket" is the correct answer.

INCORRECT: "Enable cross-origin resource sharing (CORS) for the method in API Gateway" is incorrect as CORS is enabled on the API Gateway resource.

INCORRECT: "Add the Access-Control-Request-Method header to the request" is incorrect as this is a request header value that asks permission to use a specific HTTP method.

INCORRECT: "Add the Access-Control-Request-Headers header to the request" is incorrect as this notifies a server what headers will be sent in a request.

45. Question

A company runs an e-commerce website that uses Amazon DynamoDB where pricing for items is dynamically updated in real time. At any given time, multiple updates may occur simultaneously for pricing information on a particular product. This is causing the original editor's changes to be overwritten without a proper review process.

Which DynamoDB write option should be selected to prevent this overwriting?

1: Concurrent writes

2: Conditional writes

3: Atomic writes

4: Batch writes

Answer: 2

Explanation:

By default, the DynamoDB write operations (PutItem, UpdateItem, DeleteItem) are *unconditional*: Each operation overwrites an existing item that has the specified primary key.

DynamoDB optionally supports conditional writes for these operations. A conditional write succeeds only if the item attributes meet one or more expected conditions. Otherwise, it returns an error. Conditional writes are helpful in many situations. For example, you might want a PutItem operation to succeed only if there is not already an item with the same primary key. Or you could prevent an UpdateItem operation from modifying an item if one of its attributes has a certain value.

Conditional writes are helpful in cases where multiple users attempt to modify the same item.

Therefore, conditional writes are should be used to prevent the overwriting that has been occurring.

CORRECT: "Conditional writes" is the correct answer.

INCORRECT: "Concurrent writes" is incorrect is not a feature of DynamoDB. If concurrent writes occur this could lead to the very issues that conditional writes can be used to resolve.

INCORRECT: "Atomic writes" is incorrect. Atomic reads and writes are something that can be performed using DynamoDB transactions using conditional writes.

INCORRECT: "Batch writes" is incorrect as this is just a way of making multiple put or delete API operations in a single batch operation.

46. Question

A company is using Amazon RDS MySQL instances for its application database tier and apache Tomcat servers for its web tier. Most of the database queries from web applications are repeated read requests.

A Developer plans to add an in-memory store to improve performance for repeated read requests. Which AWS service would BEST fit these requirements?

1: Amazon RDS Multi-AZ

2: Amazon SQS

3: Amazon ElastiCache

4: Amazon RDS read replica

Answer: 3

Explanation:

There are two options that can assist with improving performance for read requests: Amazon RDS read replicas, and Amazon ElastiCache. Both of these solutions will provide horizontal scaling for read requests to reduce the impact on the main database.

However, only Amazon ElastiCache is an in-memory database so the best solution is for the Developer to use Amazon ElastiCache to improve performance for repeated read requests.

CORRECT: "Amazon ElastiCache" is the correct answer.

INCORRECT: "Amazon RDS Multi-AZ" is incorrect as multi-AZ is used for fault-tolerance and disaster recovery, not improving read performance.

INCORRECT: "Amazon SQS" is incorrect as SQS is a hosted message queue use for decoupling.

INCORRECT: "Amazon RDS read replica" is incorrect as this is not an in-memory store.

47. Question

An application that runs on an Amazon EC2 instance needs to access and make API calls to multiple AWS services.

What is the MOST secure way to provide access to the AWS services with MINIMAL management overhead?

1: Use AWS KMS to store and retrieve credentials

2: Use EC2 instance profiles

3: Use AWS root user to make requests to the application

4: Store and retrieve credentials from AWS CodeCommit

Answer: 2

Explanation:

An instance profile is a container for an IAM role that you can use to pass role information to an EC2 instance when the instance starts. This is a secure way to authorize and EC2 instance to access AWS services.

Instance profiles are created automatically if you use the console to add a role to an instance. You can also create instance profiles using the AWS CLI or API and assign roles to them.

CORRECT: "Use EC2 instance profiles" is the correct answer.

INCORRECT: "Use AWS KMS to store and retrieve credentials" is incorrect as KMS is used for encrypting data, not storing credentials.

INCORRECT: "Use AWS root user to make requests to the application " is incorrect as this is not a secure way to access services as the root user has full privileges to the AWS account.

INCORRECT: "Store and retrieve credentials from AWS CodeCommit" is incorrect as this is not a suitable solution for storing this data as CodeCommit is used for storing source code.

48. Question

A company maintains a REST API service using Amazon API Gateway with native API key validation. The company recently launched a new registration page, which allows users to sign up for the service. The

registration page creates a new API key using CreateApiKey and sends the new key to the user. When the user attempts to call the API using this key, the user receives a 403 Forbidden error. Existing users are unaffected and can still call the API.

What code updates will grant these new users' access to the API?

1: The createDeployment method must be called so the API can be redeployed to include the newly created API key

2: The updateAuthorizer method must be called to update the API's authorizer to include the newly created API key

3: The importApiKeys method must be called to import all newly created API keys into the current stage of the API

4: The createUsagePlanKey method must be called to associate the newly created API key with the correct usage plan

Answer: 4

Explanation:

A *usage plan* specifies who can access one or more deployed API stages and methods—and also how much and how fast they can access them. The plan uses API keys to identify API clients and meters access to the associated API stages for each key. It also lets you configure throttling limits and quota limits that are enforced on individual client API keys.

API keys are alphanumeric string values that you distribute to application developer customers to grant access to your API. You can use API keys together with usage plans or Lambda authorizers to control access to your APIs. API Gateway can generate API keys on your behalf, or you can import them from a CSV file. You can generate an API key in API Gateway, or import it into API Gateway from an external source.

To associate the newly created key with a usage plan the CreatUsagePlanKey API can be called. This creates a usage plan key for adding an existing API key to a usage plan.

CORRECT: "The createUsagePlanKey method must be called to associate the newly created API key with the correct usage plan" is the correct answer.

INCORRECT: "The createDeployment method must be called so the API can be redeployed to include the newly created API key" is incorrect as you do not need to redeploy an API to a stage in order to associate an API key.

INCORRECT: "The updateAuthorizer method must be called to update the API's authorizer to include the newly created API key" is incorrect as this updates and authorizer resource, not an API key.

INCORRECT: "The importApiKeys method must be called to import all newly created API keys into the current stage of the API" is incorrect as this imports API keys to API Gateway from an external source such as a CSV file which is not relevant to this scenario.

49. Question

A Developer has deployed an application that runs on an Auto Scaling group of Amazon EC2 instances. The application data is stored in an Amazon DynamoDB table and records are constantly updated by all instances. An instance sometimes retrieves old data. The Developer wants to correct this by making sure the reads are strongly consistent.

How can the Developer accomplish this?

1: Set ConsistentRead to true when calling GetItem

2: Create a new DynamoDB Accelerator (DAX) table

3: Set consistency to strong when calling UpdateTable

4: Use the GetShardIterator command

Answer: 1

Explanation:

When you request a strongly consistent read, DynamoDB returns a response with the most up-to-date data, reflecting the updates from all prior write operations that were successful.

The GetItem operation returns a set of attributes for the item with the given primary key. If there is no matching item, GetItem does not return any data and there will be no Item element in the response.

GetItem provides an eventually consistent read by default. If your application requires a strongly consistent read, set ConsistentRead to true. Although a strongly consistent read might take more time than an eventually consistent read, it always returns the last updated value.

Therefore, the Developer should set ConsistentRead to true when calling GetItem.

CORRECT: "Set ConsistentRead to true when calling GetItem" is the correct answer.

INCORRECT: "Create a new DynamoDB Accelerator (DAX) table" is incorrect as DAX is not used to enable strongly consistent reads. DAX is used for improving read performance as it caches data in an in-memory cache.

INCORRECT: "Set consistency to strong when calling UpdateTable" is incorrect as you cannot use this API action to configure consistency at a table level.

INCORRECT: "Use the GetShardIterator command" is incorrect as this is not related to DynamoDB, it is related to Amazon Kinesis.

50. Question

A Developer created a new AWS account and must create a scalable AWS Lambda function that meets the following requirements for concurrent execution:

- **Average execution time of 100 seconds**
- **50 requests per second**

Which step must be taken prior to deployment to prevent errors?

1: Implement dead-letter queues to capture invocation errors

2: Add an event source from Amazon API Gateway to the Lambda function

3: Implement error handling within the application code

4: Contact AWS Support to increase the concurrent execution limits

Answer: 4

Explanation:

Concurrency is the number of requests that your function is serving at any given time. When your function is invoked, Lambda allocates an instance of it to process the event. When the function code finishes running, it can handle another request. If the function is invoked again while a request is still being processed, another instance is allocated, which increases the function's concurrency.

In this scenario, the average execution time is 100 seconds and 50 requests are received per second. This means the concurrency requirement is 100 x 50 = 5,000. As 5,000 is well above the default allowed concurrency of 1,000 executions a second. Therefore, the Developer will need to contact AWS Support to increase the concurrent execution limits.

CORRECT: "Contact AWS Support to increase the concurrent execution limits" is the correct answer.

INCORRECT: "Implement dead-letter queues to capture invocation errors" is incorrect as this is a method of capturing information for later analysis. The Developer first needs to ensure the Lambda can scale to its expected load.

INCORRECT: "Add an event source from Amazon API Gateway to the Lambda function " is incorrect as this is not necessary and will not ensure Lambda can scale to handle the load.

INCORRECT: "Implement error handling within the application code" is incorrect as there's little point relying on error handling when you know the function will not be able to scale to expected load.

51. Question

A company is developing a new online game that will run on top of Amazon ECS. Four distinct Amazon ECS services will be part of the architecture, each requiring specific permissions to various AWS services. The company wants to optimize the use of the underlying Amazon EC2 instances by bin packing the containers based on memory reservation.

Which configuration would allow the Development team to meet these requirements MOST securely?

1: Create a new Identity and Access Management (IAM) instance profile containing the required permissions for the various ECS services, then associate that instance role with the underlying EC2 instances

2: Create four distinct IAM roles, each containing the required permissions for the associated ECS services, then configure each ECS service to reference the associated IAM role

3: Create four distinct IAM roles, each containing the required permissions for the associated ECS services, then, create an IAM group and configure the ECS cluster to reference that group

4: Create four distinct IAM roles, each containing the required permissions for the associated ECS services, then configure each ECS task definition to reference the associated IAM role

Answer: 4

Explanation:

With IAM roles for Amazon ECS tasks, you can specify an IAM role that can be used by the containers in a task. Applications must sign their AWS API requests with AWS credentials, and this feature provides a strategy for managing credentials for your applications to use, similar to the way that Amazon EC2 instance profiles provide credentials to EC2 instances.

Instead of creating and distributing your AWS credentials to the containers or using the EC2 instance's role, you can associate an IAM role with an ECS task definition or RunTask API operation. The applications in the task's containers can then use the AWS SDK or CLI to make API requests to authorized AWS services.

In this case each service requires access to different AWS services so following the principal of least privilege it is best to assign as a separate role to each task definition.

CORRECT: "Create four distinct IAM roles, each containing the required permissions for the associated ECS services, then configure each ECS task definition to reference the associated IAM role" is the correct answer.

INCORRECT: "Create a new Identity and Access Management (IAM) instance profile containing the required permissions for the various ECS services, then associate that instance role with the underlying EC2 instances" is incorrect. It is a best practice to use IAM roles for tasks instead of assigning the roles to the container instances.

INCORRECT: "Create four distinct IAM roles, each containing the required permissions for the associated ECS services, then configure each ECS service to reference the associated IAM role" is incorrect as the reference should be made within the task definition.

INCORRECT: "Create four distinct IAM roles, each containing the required permissions for the associated ECS services, then, create an IAM group and configure the ECS cluster to reference that group" is incorrect as the reference should be made within the task definition.

52. Question

A utilities company needs to ensure that documents uploaded by customers through a web portal are securely stored in Amazon S3 with encryption at rest. The company does not want to manage the security infrastructure in-house. However, the company still needs maintain control over its encryption keys due to industry regulations.

Which encryption strategy should a Developer use to meet these requirements?

1: Server-side encryption with Amazon S3 managed keys (SSE-S3)

2: Server-side encryption with customer-provided encryption keys (SSE-C)

3: Server-side encryption with AWS KMS managed keys (SSE-KMS)

4: Client-side encryption

Answer: 2

Explanation:

Server-side encryption is about protecting data at rest. Server-side encryption encrypts only the object data, not object metadata. Using server-side encryption with customer-provided encryption keys (SSE-C) allows you to set your own encryption keys.

With the encryption key you provide as part of your request, Amazon S3 manages the encryption as it writes to disks and decryption when you access your objects. Therefore, you don't need to maintain any code to perform data encryption and decryption. The only thing you do is manage the encryption keys you provide.

Therefore, SSE-C is the best choice as AWS will manage all encryption and decryption operations whilst the company get to supply keys that they can manage.

CORRECT: "Server-side encryption with customer-provided encryption keys (SSE-C)" is the correct answer.

INCORRECT: "Server-side encryption with Amazon S3 managed keys (SSE-S3)" is incorrect as with this option AWS manage the keys in S3.

INCORRECT: "Server-side encryption with AWS KMS managed keys (SSE-KMS)" is incorrect as with this option the keys are managed by AWS KMS.

INCORRECT: "Client-side encryption" is incorrect as with this option all encryption and decryption is handled by the company (client) which is not desired in this scenario.

53. Question

A Developer is creating a REST service using Amazon API Gateway with AWS Lambda integration. The service adds data to a spreadsheet and the data is sent as query string parameters in the method request.

How should the Developer convert the query string parameters to arguments for the Lambda function?

1: Enable request validation

2: Include the Amazon Resource Name (ARN) of the Lambda function

3: Change the integration type

4: Create a mapping template

Answer: 4

Explanation:

Standard API Gateway parameter and response code mapping templates allow you to map parameters one-to-one and map a family of integration response status codes (matched by a regular expression) to a single response status code.

Mapping template overrides provides you with the flexibility to perform many-to-one parameter mappings; override parameters after standard API Gateway mappings have been applied; conditionally map parameters based on body content or other parameter values; programmatically create new parameters on the fly; and override status codes returned by your integration endpoint.

Any type of request parameter, response header, or response status code may be overridden.

Following are example uses for a mapping template override:

- To create a new header (or overwrite an existing header) as a concatenation of two parameters
- To override the response code to a success or failure code based on the contents of the body
- To conditionally remap a parameter based on its contents or the contents of some other parameter
- To iterate over the contents of a json body and remap key value pairs to headers or query strings

Therefore, the Developer can convert the query string parameters by creating a mapping template.

CORRECT: "Create a mapping template" is the correct answer.

INCORRECT: "Enable request validation" is incorrect as this is used to configure API Gateway to perform basic validation of an API request before proceeding with the integration request.

INCORRECT: "Include the Amazon Resource Name (ARN) of the Lambda function" is incorrect as that doesn't assist with converting the query string parameters.

INCORRECT: "Change the integration type" is incorrect as to perform a conversion the Lambda integration does not need to have a different integration type such as Lambda proxy.

54. Question

A Development team would like to migrate their existing application code from a GitHub repository to AWS CodeCommit.

What needs to be created before they can migrate a cloned repository to CodeCommit over HTTPS?

1: A GitHub secure authentication token

2: A public and private SSH key file

3: A set of credentials generated from IAM

4: An Amazon EC2 IAM role with CodeCommit permissions

Answer: 3

Explanation:

The simplest way to set up connections to AWS CodeCommit repositories is to configure Git credentials for CodeCommit in the IAM console, and then use those credentials for HTTPS connections.

You can also use these same credentials with any third-party tool or individual development environment (IDE) that supports HTTPS authentication using a static user name and password. For examples, see For Connections from Development Tools.

CORRECT: "A set of credentials generated from IAM" is the correct answer.

INCORRECT: "A GitHub secure authentication token" is incorrect as this is not how you authenticated to CodeCommit.

INCORRECT: "A public and private SSH key file" is incorrect as that is required for accessing CodeCommit using SSH.

INCORRECT: "An Amazon EC2 IAM role with CodeCommit permissions" is incorrect as that would be used to provide access to administer CodeCommit. However, the question is asking how to authenticate a Git client to CodeCommit using HTTPS.

55. Question

A team of Developers need to deploy a website for a development environment. The team do not want to manage the infrastructure and just need to upload Node.js code to the instances.

Which AWS service should Developers do?

1: Create an AWS CloudFormation template

2: Create an AWS Elastic Beanstalk environment

3: Create an AWS Lambda package

4: Launch an Auto Scaling group of Amazon EC2 instances

Answer: 2

Explanation:

The Developers do not want to manage the infrastructure so the best AWS service for them to use to create a website for a development environment is AWS Elastic Beanstalk. This will allow the Developers to simply upload their Node.js code to Elastic Beanstalk and it will handle the provisioning and management of the underlying infrastructure.

AWS Elastic Beanstalk can be used to quickly deploy and manage applications in the AWS Cloud. Developers upload applications and Elastic Beanstalk handles the deployment details of capacity provisioning, load balancing, auto-scaling, and application health monitoring. AWS Elastic Beanstalk leverages Elastic Load Balancing and Auto Scaling to automatically scale your application in and out based on your application's specific needs.

CORRECT: "Create an AWS Elastic Beanstalk environment" is the correct answer.

INCORRECT: "Create an AWS CloudFormation template" is incorrect as though you can use CloudFormation to deploy the infrastructure, it will not be managed for you.

INCORRECT: "Create an AWS Lambda package" is incorrect as the Developers are deploying a website and Lambda is not a website. It is possible to use a Lambda function for a website however this would require a front-end component such as REST API.

INCORRECT: "Launch an Auto Scaling group of Amazon EC2 instances" is incorrect as this would not provide a managed solution.

56. Question

A Developer is launching an application on Amazon ECS. The application should scale tasks automatically based on load and incoming connections must be spread across the containers.

How should the Developer configure the ECS cluster?

1: Create an ECS Service with Auto Scaling and attach an Elastic Load Balancer

2: Create an ECS Task Definition that uses Auto Scaling and Elastic Load Balancing

3: Create a capacity provider and configure cluster auto scaling

4: Write statements using the Cluster Query Language to scale the Docker containers

Answer: 1

Explanation:

Automatic scaling is the ability to increase or decrease the desired count of tasks in your Amazon ECS service automatically. Amazon ECS leverages the Application Auto Scaling service to provide this functionality.

Amazon ECS publishes CloudWatch metrics with your service's average CPU and memory usage. You can use these and other CloudWatch metrics to scale out your service (add more tasks) to deal with high demand at peak times, and to scale in your service (run fewer tasks) to reduce costs during periods of low utilization.

Amazon ECS services support the Application Load Balancer, Network Load Balancer, and Classic Load Balancer load balancer types. Application Load Balancers are used to route HTTP/HTTPS (or Layer 7) traffic. Network Load Balancers and Classic Load Balancers are used to route TCP (or Layer 4) traffic.

Therefore, the Developer should create an ECS Service with Auto Scaling and attach an Elastic Load Balancer.

CORRECT: "Create an ECS Service with Auto Scaling and attach an Elastic Load Balancer" is the correct answer.

INCORRECT: "Create an ECS Task Definition that uses Auto Scaling and Elastic Load Balancing" is incorrect as the Developer needs to configure auto scaling and load balancing in a service, not a task definition.

INCORRECT: "Create a capacity provider and configure cluster auto scaling " is incorrect as this is used to scale the cluster container instances, not the number of tasks.

INCORRECT: "Write statements using the Cluster Query Language to scale the Docker containers" is incorrect as cluster queries are expressions that enable you to group objects.

57. Question

An Amazon DynamoDB table has been created using provisioned capacity. A manager needs to understand whether the DynamoDB table is cost-effective. How can the manager query how much provisioned capacity is actually being used?

1: Monitor the ConsumedReadCapacityUnits and ConsumedWriteCapacityUnits over a specified time period

2: Monitor the ReadThrottleEvents and WriteThrottleEvents metrics for the table

3: Use Amazon CloudTrail and monitor the DescribeLimits API action

4: Use AWS X-Ray to instrument the DynamoDB table and monitor subsegments

Answer: 1

Explanation:

You can monitor Amazon DynamoDB using CloudWatch, which collects and processes raw data from DynamoDB into readable, near real-time metrics. These statistics are retained for a period of time, so that you can access historical information for a better perspective on how your web application or service is performing. By default, DynamoDB metric data is sent to CloudWatch automatically.

To determine how much of the provisioned capacity is being used you can monitor ConsumedReadCapacityUnits or ConsumedWriteCapacityUnits over the specified time period.

CORRECT: "Monitor the ConsumedReadCapacityUnits and ConsumedWriteCapacityUnits over a specified time period" is the correct answer.

INCORRECT: "Monitor the ReadThrottleEvents and WriteThrottleEvents metrics for the table" is incorrect as these metrics are used to determine which requests exceed the provisioned throughput limits of a table.

INCORRECT: "Use Amazon CloudTrail and monitor the DescribeLimits API action" is incorrect as CloudTrail records API actions, not performance metrics.

INCORRECT: "Use AWS X-Ray to instrument the DynamoDB table and monitor subsegments" is incorrect. DynamoDB does not directly integrate with X-Ray but you can record information in subsegments for downstream requests. This is not, however, a method for monitoring provisioned capacity utilization.

58. Question

A static website that serves a collection of images runs from an Amazon S3 bucket in the us-east-1 region. The website is gaining in popularity and a is now being viewed around the world. How can a Developer improve the performance of the website for global users?

1: Use cross region replication to replicate the bucket to several global regions

2: Use Amazon S3 Transfer Acceleration to improve the performance of the website

3: Use Amazon ElastiCache to cache the website content

4: Use Amazon CloudFront to cache the website content

Answer: 4

Explanation:

CloudFront is a web service that gives businesses and web application developers an easy and cost-effective way to distribute content with low latency and high data transfer speeds. CloudFront is a good choice for distribution of frequently accessed static content that benefits from edge delivery—like popular website images, videos, media files or software downloads.

CORRECT: "Use Amazon CloudFront to cache the website content" is the correct answer.

INCORRECT: "Use Amazon ElastiCache to cache the website content" is incorrect as ElastiCache is used for caching the contents of databases, not S3 buckets.

INCORRECT: "Use cross region replication to replicate the bucket to several global regions" is incorrect as though this would get the content closer to users it would not provide a mechanism for connecting to those copies. This could be achieved using Route 53 latency based routing however it would be easier to use CloudFront.

INCORRECT: "Use Amazon S3 Transfer Acceleration to improve the performance of the website" is incorrect as this service is used for improving the performance of uploads to Amazon S3.

59. Question

A customer requires a relational database for a transactional workload. Which type of AWS database is BEST suited to this requirement?

1: Amazon RDS

2: Amazon RedShift

3: Amazon DynamoDB

4: Amazon ElastiCache

Answer: 1

Explanation:

Amazon Relational Database Service (Amazon RDS) is a managed service that makes it easy to set up, operate, and scale a relational database in the cloud. RDS is an Online Transaction Processing (OLTP) type of database. The primary use case is a transactional database (rather than analytical) and it is best for structured, relational data store requirements.

CORRECT: "Amazon RDS" is the correct answer.

INCORRECT: "Amazon RedShift" is incorrect as though this is a relational database it is best suited for analytics workloads rather than transactional workloads.

INCORRECT: "Amazon DynamoDB" is incorrect as this is non-relational database.

INCORRECT: "Amazon ElastiCache" is incorrect as this is a key/value database used for caching databases (including Amazon RDS).

60. Question

A Developer is developing a web application and will maintain separate sets of resources for the alpha, beta, and release stages. Each version runs on Amazon EC2 and uses an Elastic Load Balancer.

How can the Developer create a single page to view and manage all of the resources?

1: Create a resource group

2: Deploy all resources using a single Amazon CloudFormation stack

3: Create an AWS Elastic Beanstalk environment for each stage

4: Create a single AWS CodeDeploy deployment

Answer: 1

Explanation:

In AWS, a *resource* is an entity that you can work with. Examples include an Amazon EC2 instance, an AWS CloudFormation stack, or an Amazon S3 bucket. If you work with multiple resources, you might find it useful to manage them as a group rather than move from one AWS service to another for each task.

By default, the AWS Management Console is organized by AWS service. But with Resource Groups, you can create a custom console that organizes and consolidates information based on criteria specified in tags, or the resources in an AWS CloudFormation stack. The following list describes some of the cases in which resource grouping can help organize your resources.

- An application that has different phases, such as development, staging, and production.
- Projects managed by multiple departments or individuals.
- A set of AWS resources that you use together for a common project or that you want to manage or monitor as a group.
- A set of resources related to applications that run on a specific platform, such as Android or iOS.

CORRECT: "Create a resource group" is the correct answer.

INCORRECT: "Deploy all resources using a single Amazon CloudFormation stack" is incorrect as this would not be a best practice as it is better to create separate stacks to manage deployment separately.

INCORRECT: "Create an AWS Elastic Beanstalk environment for each stage" is incorrect. It's fine to create separate environments for each stage, however this won't create a single view to view and manage all resources.

INCORRECT: "Create a single AWS CodeDeploy deployment" is incorrect as each stage should be created in a separate deployment.

61. Question

A temporary Developer needs to be provided with access to specific resources for a one week period. Which element of an IAM policy statement can be used to allow access only on or before a specific date?

1: Condition

2: NotResource

3: Action

4: Version

Answer: 1

Explanation:

The Condition element (or Condition *block*) lets you specify conditions for when a policy is in effect.
The Condition element is optional. In the Condition element, you build expressions in which you use <u>condition operators</u> (equal, less than, etc.) to match the condition keys and values in the policy against keys and values in the request context.

INCORRECT: "NotResource" is incorrect. NotResource is an advanced policy element that explicitly matches every resource except those specified.

INCORRECT: "Action" is incorrect. The Action element describes the specific action or actions that will be allowed or denied.

INCORRECT: "Version" is incorrect. The Version policy element is used within a policy and defines the version of the policy language.

62. Question

A Developer has created an Amazon S3 bucket and uploaded some objects that will be used for a publicly available static website. What steps MUST be performed to configure the bucket as a static website? (Select TWO)

1: Upload an index and error document and enter the name of the index and error documents when enabling static website hosting

2: Upload an index document and enter the name of the index document when enabling static website hosting

3: Enable public access and grant everyone the s3:GetObject permissions

4: Create an object access control list (ACL) granting READ permissions to the AllUsers group

5: Upload a certificate from AWS Certificate Manager

Answer: 2,3

Explanation:

You can use Amazon S3 to host a static website. On a *static* website, individual webpages include static content. They might also contain client-side scripts.

To host a static website on Amazon S3, you configure an Amazon S3 bucket for website hosting and then upload your website content to the bucket. When you configure a bucket as a static website, you enable static website hosting, set permissions, and add an index document.

When you enable static website hosting for your bucket, you enter the name of the index document (for example, index.html). After you enable static website hosting for your bucket, you upload an HTML file with the index document name to your bucket. Note that an error document is optional.

To provide permissions, it is necessary to disable "block public access" settings and then create a bucket policy that grants everyone the s3:GetObject permission. For example:

```
{
    "Version": "2012-10-17",
    "Statement": [
        {
            "Sid": "PublicReadGetObject",
            "Effect": "Allow",
            "Principal": "*",
            "Action": [
                "s3:GetObject"
            ],
            "Resource": [
                "arn:aws:s3:::example.com/*"
            ]
        }
    ]
}
```

CORRECT: "Upload an index document and enter the name of the index document when enabling static website hosting" is a correct answer.

CORRECT: "Enable public access and grant everyone the s3:GetObject permissions" is also a correct answer.

INCORRECT: "Upload an index and error document and enter the name of the index and error documents when enabling static website hosting" is incorrect as the error document is optional and the question specifically asks for the steps that MUST be completed.

INCORRECT: "Create an object access control list (ACL) granting READ permissions to the AllUsers group" is incorrect. This may be necessary if the bucket objects are not owned by the bucket owner but the question states that the Developer created the bucket and uploaded the objects and so must be the object owner.

INCORRECT: "Upload a certificate from AWS Certificate Manager" is incorrect as this is not supported or necessary for static websites on Amazon S3.

63. Question

An application generates a message and requires a decoupled method to trigger multiple AWS Lambda functions with the payload of the message. How can this be achieved?

1: Publish a message to an Amazon SQS queue and subscribe the Lambda functions to the queue

2: Publish a message to an Amazon SNS topic and subscribe the Lambda functions to the topic

3: Use the AWS SDK to invoke the Lambda functions and pass the message payload as input to the function execution

4: Use the AWS CLI to invoke the Lambda functions and pass the message payload as input to the function execution

Answer: 2

Explanation:

Amazon SNS and AWS Lambda are integrated so you can invoke Lambda functions with Amazon SNS notifications. When a message is published to an SNS topic that has a Lambda function subscribed to it, the Lambda function is invoked with the payload of the published message.

The Lambda function receives the message payload as an input parameter and can manipulate the information in the message, publish the message to other SNS topics, or send the message to other AWS services.

Therefore, the message can be published to an Amazon SNS topic and the Lambda functions can be subscribed to the topic.

CORRECT: "Publish a message to an Amazon SNS topic and subscribe the Lambda functions to the topic" is the correct answer.

INCORRECT: "Publish a message to an Amazon SQS queue and subscribe the Lambda functions to the queue" is incorrect as you cannot subscribe a Lambda function to an SQS queue. You can configure Lambda to receive messages from a queue but this is not a publisher/subscriber model (SQS is pull not push) and not suitable for multiple functions to pick up the same message.

INCORRECT: "Use the AWS SDK to invoke the Lambda functions and pass the message payload as input to the function execution" is incorrect as this is not a decoupled method. This is directly invoking each function and would require coding connectivity to each function into the application.

INCORRECT: "Use the AWS CLI to invoke the Lambda functions and pass the message payload as input to the function execution" is incorrect as this is also not a decoupled method.

64. Question

There are multiple AWS accounts across multiple regions managed by a company. The operations team require a single operational dashboard that displays some key performance metrics from these accounts and regions. What is the SIMPLEST solution?

1: Create an Amazon CloudWatch cross-account cross-region dashboard

2: Create an Amazon CloudWatch dashboard in one account and region and import the data from the other accounts and regions

3: Create an AWS Lambda function that collects metrics from each account and region and pushes the metrics to the account where the dashboard has been created

4: Create an Amazon CloudTrail trail that applies to all regions and deliver the logs to a single Amazon S3 bucket. Create a dashboard using the data in the bucket

Answer: 1

Explanation:

You can create *cross-account cross-Region dashboards*, which summarize your CloudWatch data from multiple AWS accounts and multiple Regions into one dashboard. From this high-level dashboard you can get a view of your entire application, and also drill down into more specific dashboards without having to log in and out of accounts or switch Regions.

You can create cross-account cross-Region dashboards in the AWS Management Console and programmatically.

CORRECT: "Create an Amazon CloudWatch cross-account cross-region dashboard" is the correct answer.

INCORRECT: "Create an Amazon CloudWatch dashboard in one account and region and import the data from the other accounts and regions" is incorrect as this is more complex and unnecessary.

INCORRECT: "Create an AWS Lambda function that collects metrics from each account and region and pushes the metrics to the account where the dashboard has been created" is incorrect as this is not a simple solution.

INCORRECT: "Create an Amazon CloudTrail trail that applies to all regions and deliver the logs to a single Amazon S3 bucket. Create a dashboard using the data in the bucket" is incorrect as CloudTrail logs API activity, not performance metrics.

65. Question

Customers who use a REST API have reported performance issues. A Developer needs to measure the time between when API Gateway receives a request from a client and when it returns a response to the client.

Which metric should the Developer monitor?

1: IntegrationLatency

2: Latency

3: CacheHitCount

4: 5XXError

Answer: 2

Explanation:

The Latency metric measures the time between when API Gateway receives a request from a client and when it returns a response to the client. The latency includes the integration latency and other API Gateway overhead.

CORRECT: "Latency" is the correct answer.

INCORRECT: "IntegrationLatency" is incorrect. This measures the time between when API Gateway relays a request to the backend and when it receives a response from the backend.

INCORRECT: "CacheHitCount" is incorrect. This measures the number of requests served from the API cache in a given period.

INCORRECT: "5XXError" is incorrect. This measures the number of server-side errors captured in a given period.

SET 3: PRACTICE QUESTIONS ONLY

For training purposes, go directly to Set 3: Practice Questions, Answers & Explanations

1. Question
An AWS Lambda function has been connected to a VPC to access an application running a private subnet. The Lambda function also pulls data from an Internet-based service and is no longer able to connect to the Internet. How can this be rectified?

1: Connect the Lambda function to an Internet Gateway

2: Add a NAT Gateway to a public subnet and specify a route in the private subnet

3: Connect an AWS VPN to Lambda to connect to the Internet

4: Add an Elastic IP to the Lambda function

2. Question
A batch job runs every 24 hours and writes around 1 million items into a DynamoDB table each day. The batch job completes quickly, and the items are processed within 2 hours and are no longer needed. What's the MOST efficient way to provide an empty table each day?

1: Use the BatchUpdateItem API with expressions

2: Issue an AWS CLI aws dynamodb delete-item command with a wildcard

3: Delete the entire table and recreate it each day

4: Use the BatchWriteItem API with a DeleteRequest

3. Question
A development team is migrating data from various file shares to AWS from on-premises. The data will be migrated into a single Amazon S3 bucket. What is the SIMPLEST method to ensure the data is encrypted at rest in the S3 bucket?

1: Use SSL to transmit the data over the Internet

2: Ensure all requests use the x-amz-server-side-encryption-customer-key header

3: Ensure all requests use the x-amz-server-side-encryption header

4: Enable default encryption when creating the bucket

4. Question
A company needs to provide additional security for their APIs deployed on Amazon API Gateway. They would like to be able to authenticate their customers with a token. What is the SAFEST way to do this?

1: Setup usage plans and distribute API keys to the customers

2: Create an Amazon Cognito identity pool

3: Create an API Gateway Lambda authorizer

4: Use AWS Single Sign-on to authenticate the customers

5. Question
A developer is making updates to the code for a Lambda function. The developer is keen to test the code updates by directing a small amount of traffic to a new version. How can this BEST be achieved?

1: Create two versions of the function code. Configure the application to direct a subset of requests to the new version

2: Create an alias that points to both the new and previous versions of the function code and assign a weighting for sending a portion of traffic to the new version

3: Create an API using API Gateway and use stage variables to point to different versions of the Lambda function

4: Create a new function using the new code and update the application to split requests between the new functions

6. Question

A company runs a popular online game on premises. The application stores players' results in an in-memory database. The application is being migrated to AWS and the company needs to ensure there is no reduction in performance. Which database would be MOST suitable?

1: Amazon RDS

2: Amazon ElastiCache

3: Amazon DynamoDB

4: Amazon Elastic Beanstalk

7. Question

An Amazon RDS database that stores product information for an online eCommerce marketplace is experiencing heavy demand. An increase in read requests is causing the database performance to be impacted and is affecting database writes. What is the best way to offload the read traffic from the database with MINIMAL code changes and cost?

1: Change the RDS database instance type to an instance with more CPU/RAM

2: Create an RDS Multi AZ DB and modify the application to send read requests to the standby DB

3: Create an ElastiCache Memcached cluster and modify the application to send read requests to the cluster

4: Create an RDS Read Replica and modify the application to send read requests to the replica

8. Question

A developer has deployed a serverless application with AWS Lambda. The function must make remote calls to external endpoints. Which configuration element in Lambda can be used store the connection strings related to the external endpoints?

1: Aliases

2: Tags

3: Environment variables

4: Versions

9. Question

A developer is building a web application that will be hosted on Amazon EC2 instances. The EC2 instances will store configuration data in an Amazon S3 bucket. What is the SAFEST way to allow the EC2 instances to access the S3 bucket?

1: Store an access key and secret ID that has the necessary permissions on the EC2 instances

2: Create an IAM Role with a customer-managed policy attached that has the necessary permissions and attach the role to the EC2 instances

3: Create an IAM Role with an AWS managed policy attached that has the necessary permissions and attach the role to the EC2 instances

4: Use the AWS SDK and authenticate with a user account that has the necessary permissions on the EC2 instances

10. Question

An AWS Lambda functions downloads a 50MB from an object storage system each time it is invoked. The download delays the function completion and causes intermittent timeouts which is slowing down the application.

How can the application be refactored to resolve the timeout?

1: Increase the memory allocation of the function

2: Increase the timeout of the function

3: Increase the concurrency allocation of the function

4: Store the file in the /tmp directory of the execution context and reuse it on subsequent invocations

11. Question

The development team is working on an API that will be served from Amazon API Gateway. The API will serve three environments PROD, DEV, and TEST and requires a cache size of 250GB. What is the MOST cost-efficient deployment strategy?

1: Create three API Gateways, one for each environment and enable the cache for the DEV and TEST environments only when required

2: Create a single API Gateway with three stages and enable the cache for the DEV and TEST environments only when required

3: Create a single API Gateway with three stages and enable the cache for all environments

4: Create a single API Gateway with three deployments and configure a global cache of 250GB

12. Question

A developer is creating an Auto Scaling group of Amazon EC2 instances. The developer needs to publish a custom metric to Amazon CloudWatch. Which method would be the MOST secure way to authenticate a CloudWatch PUT request?

1: Modify the CloudWatch metric policies to allow the PutMetricData permission to instances from the Auto Scaling group

2: Create an IAM role with the PutMetricData permission and create a new Auto Scaling launch configuration to launch instances using that role

3: Create an IAM user with the PutMetricData permission and modify the Auto Scaling launch configuration to inject the user credentials into the instance user data

4: Create an IAM role with the PutMetricData permission and modify the Amazon EC2 instances to use that role

13. Question

An application includes several producer services that send data to an Amazon SQS queue. The messages are then processed by a consumer component that must ensure that each producer's messages are processed in the order they are received. How can a Developer ensure the messages are processed in the correct order?

1: Configure each message with a unique MessageGroupId

2: Enable the MessageDeduplicationId on the SQS queue

3: Configure each producer with a unique MessageGroupId

4: Enable ContentBasedDeduplication on the SQS queue

14. Question

An application is being deployed at a media company. The application will receive data from applications at many new outlets around the country. The application will ingest the data, process it with AWS Lambda and then store the data in an Amazon S3 bucket. Which AWS service would be BEST suited to these requirements?

1: Amazon SQS

2: Amazon SNS

3: Amazon CloudFront

4: Amazon Kinesis Firehose

15. Question

A company uses an Amazon S3 bucket to store a large number of sensitive files relating to eCommerce transactions. The company has a policy that states that all data written to the S3 bucket must be encrypted. How can a Developer ensure compliance with this policy?

1: Create a bucket policy that denies the S3 PutObject request with the attribute x-amz-acl having values public-read, public-read-write, or authenticated-read

2: Create an S3 bucket policy that denies any S3 Put request that does not include the x-amz-server-side-encryption

3: Enable Server-Side Encryption with Amazon S3-Managed Keys (SSE-S3) on the Amazon S3 bucket

4: Create an Amazon CloudWatch alarm that notifies an administrator if unencrypted objects are uploaded to the S3 bucket

16. Question

An application uses Amazon API Gateway, an AWS Lambda function and a DynamoDB table. The developer requires that another Lambda function is triggered when an item lifecycle activity occurs in the DynamoDB table. How can this be achieved?

1: Configure an Amazon CloudWatch alarm that sends an Amazon SNS notification. Trigger the Lambda function asynchronously from the SNS notification

2: Enable a DynamoDB stream and trigger the Lambda function synchronously from the stream

3: Enable a DynamoDB stream and trigger the Lambda function asynchronously from the stream

4: Configure an Amazon CloudTrail API alarm that sends a message to an Amazon SQS queue. Configure the Lambda function to poll the queue and invoke the function synchronously

17. Question

An application is using Amazon DynamoDB as its data store and needs to be able to read 100 items per second as strongly consistent reads. Each item is 5 KB in size. What value should be set for the table's provisioned throughput for reads?

1: 50 Read Capacity Units

2: 200 Read Capacity Units

3: 250 Read Capacity Units

18. Question

A company runs an application on a fleet of web servers running on Amazon EC2 instances. The web servers are behind an Elastic Load Balancer (ELB) and use an Amazon DynamoDB table for storing session state. A Developer has been asked to implement a mechanism for automatically deleting session state data that is older than 24 hours. What is the SIMPLEST solution to this requirement?

1: Add an attribute with the expiration time; enable the Time To Live feature based on that attribute

2: Each day, create a new table to hold session data; delete the previous day's table

3: Write a script that deletes old records; schedule the scripts as a cron job on an Amazon EC2 instance

4: Add an attribute with the expiration time; name the attribute ItemExpiration

19. Question

A gaming company is building an application to track the scores for their games using an Amazon DynamoDB table. Each item in the table is identified by a partition key
(user_id) and a sort key (game_name). The table also includes the attribute "TopScore". The table design is shown below:

A Developer has been asked to write a leaderboard application to display the highest achieved scores for each game (game_name), based on the score identified in the "TopScore" attribute.
What process will allow the Developer to extract results MOST efficiently from the DynamoDB table?

1: Create a local secondary index with a primary key of "game_name" and a sort key of "TopScore" and get the results based on the score attribute

2: Create a global secondary index with a primary key of "game_name" and a sort key of "TopScore" and get the results based on the score attribute

3: Use a DynamoDB scan operation to retrieve the scores for "game_name" using the "TopScore" attribute, and order the results based on the score attribute

4: Create a global secondary index with a primary key of "user_id" and a sort key of "game_name" and get the results based on the "TopScore" attribute

20. Question

A company is running a web application on Amazon EC2 behind an Elastic Load Balancer (ELB). The company is concerned about the security of the web application and would like to secure the application with SSL certificates. The solution should not have any performance impact on the EC2 instances. What steps should be taken to secure the web application? (Select TWO)

1: Configure the Elastic Load Balancer with SSL passthrough

2: Add an SSL certificate to the Elastic Load Balancer

3: Install SSL certificates on the EC2 instances

4: Configure the Elastic Load Balancer for SSL termination

5: Configure Server-Side Encryption with KMS managed keys

21. Question

An application is running on an Amazon EC2 Linux instance. The instance needs to make AWS API calls to several AWS services. What is the MOST secure way to provide access to the AWS services with MINIMAL management overhead?

1: Use AWS KMS to store and retrieve credentials

2: Use EC2 instance profiles

3: Store the credentials in AWS CloudHSM

4: Store the credentials in the ~/.aws/credentials file

22. Question

A Developer is creating a serverless application that includes Amazon API Gateway, Amazon DynamoDB and AWS Lambda. The Developer will use AWS CloudFormation to deploy the application and is creating a template. Which tool should the Developer use to define simplified syntax for expressing serverless resources?

1: AWS Step Functions State Machine

2: OpenAPI Swagger Specification

3: AWS Serverless Application Model

4: A CloudFormation Serverless Plugin

23. Question

A Developer has added a Global Secondary Index (GSI) to an existing Amazon DynamoDB table. The GSI is used mainly for read operations whereas the primary table is extremely write-intensive. Recently, the Developer has noticed throttling occurring under heavy write activity on the primary table. However, the write capacity units on the primary table are not fully utilized. What is the best explanation for why the writes are being throttled on the primary table?

1: There are insufficient read capacity units on the primary table

2: The Developer should have added an LSI instead of a GSI

3: There are insufficient write capacity units on the primary table

4: The write capacity units on the GSI are under provisioned

24. Question

A development team manage a high-traffic e-Commerce site with dynamic pricing that is updated in real-time. There have been incidents where multiple updates occur simultaneously and cause an original editor's updates to be overwritten. How can the developers ensure that overwriting does not occur?

1: Use concurrent writes

2: Use atomic counters

3: Use conditional writes

4: Use batch operations

25. Question

A Development team are creating a new REST API that uses Amazon API Gateway and AWS Lambda. To support testing there need to be different versions of the service. What is the BEST way to provide multiple versions of the REST API?

1: Create an API Gateway resource policy to isolate versions and provide context to the Lambda functions

2: Deploy the API versions as unique stages with unique endpoints and use stage variables to provide further context

3: Create an AWS Lambda authorizer to route API clients to the correct API version

4: Deploy an HTTP Proxy integration and configure the proxy with API versions

26. Question

A Developer is creating an AWS Lambda function that will process data from an Amazon Kinesis data stream. The function is expected to be invoked 50 times per second and take 100 seconds to complete each request. What MUST the Developer do to ensure the functions runs without errors?

1: Contact AWS and request to increase the limit for concurrent executions

2: No action is required as AWS Lambda can easily accommodate this requirement

3: Increase the concurrency limit for the function

4: Implement exponential backoff in the function code

27. Question

An AWS Lambda application writes data to an Amazon S3 bucket. The application sometimes needs to overwrite an object, and then immediately read the object. In some cases, the application retrieves the old version of the object. What is the MOST likely explanation for this?

1: Amazon S3 overwrite PUTS are eventually consistent, so the application may read the old object

2: The function has cached the old version of the object and retrieved it from the cache

3: All Amazon S3 PUTS are eventually consistent, so the application may read the old object

4: The application did not explicitly specify the latest version when retrieving the object

28. Question

A legacy service has an XML-based SOAP interface. The Developer wants to expose the functionality of the service to external clients with the Amazon API Gateway. Which technique will accomplish this?

1: Create a RESTful API with the API Gateway; transform the incoming JSON into a valid XML message for the SOAP interface using mapping templates

2: Create a RESTful API with the API Gateway; pass the incoming JSON to the SOAP interface through an Application Load Balancer

3: Create a RESTful API with the API Gateway; pass the incoming XML to the SOAP interface through an Application Load Balancer

4: Create a RESTful API with the API Gateway; transform the incoming XML into a valid message for the SOAP interface using mapping templates

29. Question

A Developer has completed some code updates and needs to deploy the updates to an Amazon Elastic Beanstalk environment. The environment includes twelve Amazon EC2 instances and there can be no reduction in application performance and availability during the update. Which deployment policy is the most cost-effective choice so suit these requirements?

1: All at once

2: Rolling

3: Rolling with additional batch

4: Immutable

30. Question

A Developer is creating a DynamoDB table for storing application logs. The table has 5 write capacity units (WCUs). The Developer needs to configure the read capacity units (RCUs) for the table. Which of the following configurations represents the most efficient use of throughput?

1: Eventually consistent reads of 5 RCUs reading items that are 4 KB in size

2: Strongly consistent reads of 5 RCUs reading items that are 4 KB in size

3: Eventually consistent reads of 15 RCUs reading items that are 1 KB in size

4: Strongly consistent reads of 15 RCUs reading items that are 1KB in size

31. Question

The source code for an application is stored in a file named index.js that is in a folder along with a template file that includes the following code:

AWSTemplateFormatVersion: '2010-09-09'

Transform: 'AWS::Serverless-2016-10-31'

Resources:

  LambdaFunctionWithAPI:

   Type: AWS::Serverless::Function

   Properties:

    Handler: index.handler

    Runtime: nodejs12.x

What does a Developer need to do to prepare the template so it can be deployed using an AWS CLI command?

1: Run the aws cloudformation compile command to base64 encode and embed the source file into a modified CloudFormation template

2: Run the aws cloudformation package command to upload the source code to an Amazon S3 bucket and produce a modified CloudFormation template

3: Run the aws lambda zip command to package the source file together with the CloudFormation template and deploy the resulting zip archive

4: Run the aws serverless create-package command to embed the source file directly into the existing CloudFormation template

32. Question

A customer service provider runs a real-time dashboard for monitoring customer request activity. The dashboard relies on an Amazon Kinesis Data Stream and a fleet of Amazon EC2 instances that process the data. Performance metrics have highlighted a number of "cold" shards. What course of action should the company take to minimize the cost of the Kinesis Data Stream?

1: Split the cold shards to increase the capacity of the stream

2: Merge the cold shards to decrease the capacity of the stream

3: Replace the shards with fewer, higher-capacity shards

4: Reduce the number of EC2 instances

33. Question

A Developer is creating an application that will include decoupled components. A service is required to receive incoming data from a set of EC2 instances and store it for later processing by another set of EC2 instances. The decoupling service must dynamically scale and provide strict ordering of messages. Which AWS service should the Developer use?

1: Amazon Kinesis Data Streams

2: AWS Step Functions

3: Amazon Simple Queue Service (SQS) with a FIFO queue

4: Amazon Simple Storage Service (S3)

34. Question

A Developer is using AWS SAM to create a template for deploying a serverless application. The Developer plans deploy an AWS Lambda function and an Amazon DynamoDB table using the template. Which resource types should the Developer specify? (Select TWO)

1: AWS::Serverless::Application

2: AWS::Serverless:Function

3: AWS::Serverless:LayerVersion

4: AWS::Serverless:API

5: AWS::Serverless::SimpleTable

35. Question

An application is being migrated into the cloud. The application is stateless and will run on a fleet of Amazon EC2 instances. The application should scale elastically. How can a Developer ensure that the number of instances available is sufficient for current demand?

1: Create a launch configuration and use Amazon CodeDeploy

2: Create a task definition and use an Amazon ECS cluster

3: Create a launch configuration and use Amazon EC2 Auto Scaling

4: Create a task definition and use an AWS Fargate cluster

36. Question

An application uses an Auto Scaling group of Amazon EC2 instances, an Application Load Balancer (ALB), and an Amazon Simple Queue Service (SQS) queue. An Amazon CloudFront distribution caches content for global users. A Developer needs to add in-transit encryption to the data by configuring end-to-end SSL between the CloudFront Origin and the end users. How can the Developer meet this requirement? (Select TWO)

1: Configure the Origin Protocol Policy

2: Create an Origin Access Identity (OAI)

3: Add a certificate to the Auto Scaling Group

4: Configure the Viewer Protocol Policy

5: Create an encrypted distribution

37. Question

A Developer is creating a microservices architecture for a modern application. The application will run on Docker containers. The Developer requires a serverless service. Which AWS service is MOST suitable?

1: Amazon ECS

2: AWS Elastic Beanstalk

3: AWS Lambda

4: AWS Fargate

38. Question

A Developer needs to create an instance profile for an Amazon EC2 instance using the AWS CLI. How can this be achieved? (Select THREE)

1: Run the aws iam create-instance-profile command

2: Run the CreateInstanceProfile API

3: Run the aws iam add-role-to-instance-profile command

4: Run the AddRoleToInstanceProfile API

5: Run the aws ec2 associate-instance-profile command

6: Run the AssignInstanceProfile API

39. Question

An application will use AWS Lambda and an Amazon RDS database. The Developer needs to secure the database connection string and enable automatic rotation every 30 days. What is the SIMPLEST way to achieve this requirement?

1: Store a SecureString in Systems Manager Parameter Store and enable automatic rotation every 30 days

2: Store the connection string as an encrypted environment variable in Lambda and create a separate function that rotates the connection string every 30 days

3: Store a secret in AWS Secrets Manager and enable automatic rotation every 30 days

4: Store the connection string in an encrypted Amazon S3 bucket and use a scheduled CloudWatch Event to update the connection string every 30 days

40. Question

A Developer needs to choose the best data store for a new application. The application requires a data store that supports key/value pairs and optimistic locking. Which of the following would provide the MOST suitable solution?

1: Amazon RDS

2: Amazon RedShift

3: Amazon DynamoDB

4: Amazon S3

41. Question

A financial application is hosted on an Auto Scaling group of EC2 instance with an Elastic Load Balancer. A Developer needs to capture information about the IP traffic going to and from network interfaces in the VPC. How can the Developer capture this information?

1: Capture the information directly into Amazon CloudWatch Logs

2: Create a flow log in the VPC and publish data to Amazon S3

3: Capture the information using a Network ACL

4: Create a flow log in the VPC and publish data to Amazon CloudTrail

42. Question

A Developer is designing a cloud native application. The application will use several AWS Lambda functions that will process items that the functions read from an event source. Which AWS services are supported for Lambda event source mappings? (Select THREE)

1: Amazon Kinesis

2: Amazon Simple Notification Service (SNS)

3: Amazon DynamoDB

4: Amazon Simple Queue Service (SQS)

5: Amazon Simple Storage Service (S3)

6: Another Lambda function

43. Question

An application is instrumented to generate traces using AWS X-Ray and generates a large amount of trace data. A Developer would like to use filter expressions to filter the results to specific key-value pairs added to custom subsegments. How should the Developer add the key-value pairs to the custom subsegments?

1: Add metadata to the custom subsegments

2: Add annotations to the custom subsegments

3: Add the key-value pairs to the Trace ID

4: Setup sampling for the custom subsegments

44. Question

A website is running on a single Amazon EC2 instance. A Developer wants to publish the website on the Internet and is creating an A record on Amazon Route 53 for the website's public DNS name. What type of IP address MUST be assigned to the EC2 instance and used in the A record to ensure ongoing connectivity?

1: Public IP address

2: Dynamic IP address

3: Elastic IP address

4: Private IP address

45. Question

A company needs a version control system for collaborative software development. The solution must include support for batches of changes across multiple files and parallel branching. Which AWS service will meet these requirements?

1: AWS CodePipeline

2: Amazon S3

3: AWS CodeBuild

4: AWS CodeCommit

46. Question

To include objects defined by the AWS Serverless Application Model (SAM) in an AWS CloudFormation template, in addition to Resources, what section MUST be included in the document root?

1: Conditions

2: Globals

3: Transform

47. Question

A company is creating an application that will require users to access AWS services and allow them to reset their own passwords. Which of the following would allow the company to manage users and authorization while allowing users to reset their own passwords?

1: Amazon Cognito identity pools and AWS STS

2: Amazon Cognito identity pools and AWS IAM

3: Amazon Cognito user pools and AWS KMS

4: Amazon Cognito user pools and identity pools

48. Question

An application writes items to an Amazon DynamoDB table. As the application scales to thousands of instances, calls to the DynamoDB API generate occasional ThrottlingException errors. The application is coded in a language incompatible with the AWS SDK. How should the error be handled?

1: Add exponential backoff to the application logic

2: Use Amazon SQS as an API message bus

3: Pass API calls through Amazon API Gateway

4: Send the items to DynamoDB through Amazon Kinesis Data Firehose

49. Question

A Development team has deployed several applications running on an Auto Scaling fleet of Amazon EC2 instances. The Operations team have asked for a display that shows a key performance metric for each application on a single screen for monitoring purposes. What steps should a Developer take to deliver this capability using Amazon CloudWatch?

1: Create a custom namespace with a unique metric name for each application

2: Create a custom dimension with a unique metric name for each application

3: Create a custom event with a unique metric name for each application

4: Create a custom alarm with a unique metric name for each application

50. Question

A Developer is storing sensitive documents in Amazon S3. The documents must be encrypted at rest and company policy mandates that the encryption keys must be rotated annually. What is the EASIEST way to achieve this?

1: Encrypt the data before sending it to Amazon S3

2: Import a custom key into AWS KMS with annual rotation enabled

3: Use AWS KMS with automatic key rotation

4: Export a key from AWS KMS to encrypt the data

51. Question

A Developer is designing a fault-tolerant environment where client sessions will be saved. How can the Developer ensure that no sessions are lost if an Amazon EC2 instance fails?

1: Use sticky sessions with an Elastic Load Balancer target group

2: Use Amazon SQS to save session data

3: Use Amazon DynamoDB to perform scalable session handling

4: Use Elastic Load Balancer connection draining to stop sending requests to failing instances

52. Question

A company wants to implement authentication for its new REST service using Amazon API Gateway. To authenticate the calls, each request must include HTTP headers with a client ID and user ID. These credentials must be compared to authentication data in an Amazon DynamoDB table. What MUST the company do to implement this authentication in API Gateway?

1: Implement an AWS Lambda authorizer that references the DynamoDB authentication table

2: Create a model that requires the credentials, then grant API Gateway access to the authentication table

3: Modify the integration requests to require the credentials, then grant API Gateway access to the authentication table

4: Implement an Amazon Cognito authorizer that references the DynamoDB authentication table

53. Question

AWS CodeBuild builds code for an application, creates a Docker image, pushes the image to Amazon Elastic Container Registry (ECR), and tags the image with a unique identifier. If the Developers already have AWS CLI configured on their workstations, how can the Docker images be pulled to the workstations?

1: Run the following: docker pull REPOSITORY URI : TAG

2: Run the output of the following: aws ecr get-login, and then run docker pull REPOSITORY URI : TAG

3: Run the following: aws ecr get-login, and then run: docker pull REPOSITORY URI : TAG

4: Run the output of the following: aws ecr get-download-url-for-layer, and then run docker pull REPOSITORY URI : TAG

54. Question

A company needs to ingest several terabytes of data every hour from a large number of distributed sources. The messages are delivered continually 24 hrs a day. Messages must be delivered in real time for security analysis and live operational dashboards. Which approach will meet these requirements?

1: Send the messages to an Amazon SQS queue, then process the messages by using a fleet of Amazon EC2 instances

2: Use the Amazon S3 API to write messages to an S3 bucket, then process the messages by using Amazon RedShift

3: Use AWS Data Pipeline to automate the movement and transformation of data

4: Use Amazon Kinesis Data Streams with Kinesis Client Library to ingest and deliver messages

55. Question

A Developer wants to debug an application by searching and filtering log data. The application logs are stored in Amazon CloudWatch Logs. The Developer creates a new metric filter to count exceptions in the application logs. However, no results are returned from the logs. What is the reason that no filtered results are being returned?

1: A setup of the Amazon CloudWatch interface VPC endpoint is required for filtering the CloudWatch Logs in the VPC

2: CloudWatch Logs only publishes metric data for events that happen after the filter is created

3: The log group for CloudWatch Logs should be first streamed to Amazon Elasticsearch Service before filtering returns the results

4: Metric data points to logs groups can be filtered only after they are exported to an Amazon S3 bucket

56. Question
A serverless application requires a storage location for log files. Which storage solution is the BEST fit?

1: Amazon EBS

2: Amazon EFS

3: Amazon S3

4: Amazon EC2 instance store

57. Question
Fault tolerance needs to be increased for a stateless application that runs on Amazon EC2 instances. The application runs in an Auto Scaling group of EC2 instances in a single subnet behind an Application Load Balancer. How can the application be made more fault tolerant?

1: Add a subnet in another AZ to the ASG and add the same subnet to the ALB

2: Add a subnet in another region to the ASG and add the same subnet to the ALB

3: Add an Elastic IP to each instance and use Amazon Route 53 Alias records to distribute incoming connections

4: Add a subnet in another VPC to the ASG and add the same subnet to the ALB

58. Question
A customer-facing web application runs on Amazon EC2 with an Application Load Balancer and an Amazon RDS database back end. Recently, the security team noticed some SQL injection attacks and cross-site scripting attacks targeting the web application. Which service can a Developer use to protect against future attacks?

1: Security Groups

2: Network ACLs

3: AWS WAF

4: AWS KMS

59. Question
A developer is planning the deployment of a new version of an application to AWS Elastic Beanstalk. The new version of the application should be deployed only to new EC2 instances. Which deployment methods will meet these requirements? (Select TWO)

1: Rolling with additional batch

2: Immutable

3: Rolling

4: All at once

5: Blue/green

60. Question
A customer requires a schema-less, key/value database that can be used for storing customer orders. Which type of AWS database is BEST suited to this requirement?

1: Amazon DynamoDB

2: Amazon RDS

3: Amazon ElastiCache

4: Amazon S3

61. Question

A highly secured AWS environment has strict policies for granting access to Developers. A Developer requires the ability to use the API to call ec2:StartInstances and ec2:StopInstances. Which element of an IAM policy statement should be used to specify which APIs can be called?

1: Action

2: Effect

3: Resource

4: Condition

62. Question

A team of Developers are building a continuous integration and delivery pipeline using AWS Developer Tools. Which services should they use for running tests against source code and installing compiled code on their AWS resources? (Select TWO)

1: AWS CodeBuild for running tests against source code

2: AWS CodeDeploy for installing compiled code on their AWS resources

3: AWS CodePipeline for running tests against source code

4: AWS CodeCommit for installing compiled code on their AWS resources

5: AWS Cloud9 for running tests against source code

63. Question

Messages produced by an application must be pushed to multiple Amazon SQS queues. What is the BEST solution for this requirement?

1: Create an Amazon SWF workflow that receives the messages and pushes them to multiple SQS queues

2: Create and AWS Step Functions state machine that uses multiple Lambda functions to process and push the messages into multiple SQS queues

3: Publish the messages to an Amazon SNS topic and subscribe each SQS queue to the topic

4: Publish the messages to an Amazon SQS queue and configure an AWS Lambda function to duplicate the message into multiple queues

64. Question

An application has been instrumented to use the AWS X-Ray SDK to collect data about the requests the application serves. The Developer has set the user field on segments to a string that identifies the user who sent the request. How can the Developer search for segments associated with specific users?

1: Use a filter expression to search for the user field in the segment metadata

2: By using the GetTraceSummaries API with a filter expression

3: By using the GetTraceGraph API with a filter expression

4: Use a filter expression to search for the user field in the segment annotations

65. Question

The following permissions policy is applied to an IAM user account:

```
{
  "Version": "2012-10-17",
  "Statement": [{
    "Effect": "Allow",
    "Action": "sqs:*",
    "Resource": "arn:aws:sqs:*:513246782345:staging-queue*"
  }]
}
```

Due to this policy, what Amazon SQS actions will the user be able to perform?

1: The user will be able to use all Amazon SQS actions, but only for queues with names begin with the string "staging-queue"

2: The user will be able to create a queue named "staging-queue"

3: The user will be able to apply a resource-based policy to the Amazon SQS queue named "staging-queue"

4: The user will be granted cross-account access from account number "513246782345" to queue "staging-queue"

SET 3: PRACTICE QUESTIONS, ANSWERS & EXPLANATIONS

1. Question

An AWS Lambda function has been connected to a VPC to access an application running a private subnet. The Lambda function also pulls data from an Internet-based service and is no longer able to connect to the Internet. How can this be rectified?

1: Connect the Lambda function to an Internet Gateway

2: Add a NAT Gateway to a public subnet and specify a route in the private subnet

3: Connect an AWS VPN to Lambda to connect to the Internet

4: Add an Elastic IP to the Lambda function

Answer: 2

Explanation:

To enable connectivity to an application in a private subnet and the Internet you must first allow the function to connect to the private subnet (which has already been done).

Lambda needs the following VPC configuration information so that it can connect to the VPC:

- Private subnet ID.
- Security Group ID (with required access).

Lambda uses this information to setup an Elastic Network Interface (ENI) using an available IP address from your private subnet. Next you need to add a NAT Gateway for Internet access (no public IP).

The NAT Gateway should be connected to a public subnet and a route needs to be added to the private subnet.

CORRECT: "Add a NAT Gateway to the private subnet" is the correct answer.

INCORRECT: "Connect the Lambda function to an Internet Gateway" is incorrect. Though by using a NAT Gateway you are effectively establishing routing to an Internet Gateway, you cannot actually connect Lambda to an Internet Gateway.

INCORRECT: "Connect an AWS VPN to Lambda to connect to the Internet" is incorrect as you cannot connect an AWS VPN to a Lambda function.

INCORRECT: "Add an Elastic IP to the Lambda function" is incorrect as you cannot add an Elastic IP to a Lambda function.

2. Question

A batch job runs every 24 hours and writes around 1 million items into a DynamoDB table each day. The batch job completes quickly, and the items are processed within 2 hours and are no longer needed. What's the MOST efficient way to provide an empty table each day?

1: Use the BatchUpdateItem API with expressions

2: Issue an AWS CLI aws dynamodb delete-item command with a wildcard

3: Delete the entire table and recreate it each day

4: Use the BatchWriteItem API with a DeleteRequest

Answer: 3

Explanation:

With this scenario we have a table that has a large number of items quickly written to it on a recurring schedule. These items are no longer of use after they have been processed (within 2 hours) so from that point on until the next job the table is not being used. The items need to be deleted and we need to choose the most efficient (think cost as well as operations) way of doing this.

Any delete operation will consume RCUs to scan/query the table and WCUs to delete the items. It will be much cheaper and simpler to just delete the table and recreate it again ahead of the next batch job. This can easily be automated through the API.

CORRECT: "Delete the entire table and recreate it each day" is the correct answer.

INCORRECT: "Use the BatchUpdateItem API with expressions" is incorrect as this API does not exist.

INCORRECT: "Issue an AWS CLI aws dynamodb delete-item command with a wildcard" is incorrect as this operation deletes data from a table one item at a time, which is highly inefficient. You also must specify the item's primary key values; you cannot use a wildcard.

INCORRECT: "Use the BatchWriteItem API with a DeleteRequest" is incorrect as this is an inefficient way to solve this challenge.

3. Question

A development team is migrating data from various file shares to AWS from on-premises. The data will be migrated into a single Amazon S3 bucket. What is the SIMPLEST method to ensure the data is encrypted at rest in the S3 bucket?

1: Use SSL to transmit the data over the Internet

2: Ensure all requests use the x-amz-server-side-encryption-customer-key header

3: Ensure all requests use the x-amz-server-side-encryption header

4: Enable default encryption when creating the bucket

Answer: 4

Explanation:

Amazon S3 default encryption provides a way to set the default encryption behavior for an S3 bucket. You can set default encryption on a bucket so that all new objects are encrypted when they are stored in the bucket. The objects are encrypted using server-side encryption with either Amazon S3-managed keys (SSE-S3) or customer master keys (CMKs) stored in AWS Key Management Service (AWS KMS).

CORRECT: "Enable default encryption when creating the bucket" is the correct answer.

INCORRECT: "Use SSL to transmit the data over the Internet" is incorrect as this only deals with encrypting the data whilst it is being transmitted, it does not provide encryption at rest.

INCORRECT: "Ensure all requests use the x-amz-server-side-encryption-customer-key header" is incorrect as it is unnecessary to use customer-provided keys. This is used with client-side encryption which is more complex to manage and is not required in this scenario.

INCORRECT: "Ensure all requests use the x-amz-server-side-encryption header" is incorrect as though this has the required effect of ensuring all data is encrypted, it is not the simplest method. In this scenario there is a team migrating data from different file shares which increases the risk of human error where a team member may neglect to add the header to the API call. Using default encryption on the bucket is a simpler solution.

4. Question

A company needs to provide additional security for their APIs deployed on Amazon API Gateway. They would like to be able to authenticate their customers with a token. What is the SAFEST way to do this?

1: Setup usage plans and distribute API keys to the customers

2: Create an Amazon Cognito identity pool

3: Create an API Gateway Lambda authorizer

4: Use AWS Single Sign-on to authenticate the customers

Answer: 3

Explanation:

A *Lambda authorizer* (formerly known as a *custom authorizer*) is an API Gateway feature that uses a Lambda function to control access to your API.

A Lambda authorizer is useful if you want to implement a custom authorization scheme that uses a bearer token authentication strategy such as OAuth or SAML, or that uses request parameters to determine the caller's identity.

When a client makes a request to one of your API's methods, API Gateway calls your Lambda authorizer, which takes the caller's identity as input and returns an IAM policy as output.

There are two types of Lambda authorizers:

- A *token-based* Lambda authorizer (also called a TOKEN authorizer) receives the caller's identity in a bearer token, such as a JSON Web Token (JWT) or an OAuth token.

- A *request parameter-based* Lambda authorizer (also called a REQUEST authorizer) receives the caller's identity in a combination of headers, query string parameters, stageVariables, and $context variables.

For this scenario, a Lambda authorizer is the most secure method available. It can also be used with usage plans and AWS recommend that you don't rely only on API keys, so a Lambda authorizer is a better solution.

CORRECT: "Create an API Gateway Lambda authorizer" is the correct answer.

INCORRECT: "Setup usage plans and distribute API keys to the customers" is incorrect as this is not the most secure (safest) option. AWS recommend that you don't rely on API keys as your only means of authentication and authorization for your APIs.

INCORRECT: "Create an Amazon Cognito identity pool" is incorrect. You can create an authorizer in API Gateway that uses Cognito user pools, but not identity pools.

INCORRECT: "Use AWS Single Sign-on to authenticate the customers" is incorrect. This is used to centrally access multiple AWS accounts and business applications from one place.

5. Question

A developer is making updates to the code for a Lambda function. The developer is keen to test the code updates by directing a small amount of traffic to a new version. How can this BEST be achieved?

1: Create two versions of the function code. Configure the application to direct a subset of requests to the new version

2: Create an alias that points to both the new and previous versions of the function code and assign a weighting for sending a portion of traffic to the new version

3: Create an API using API Gateway and use stage variables to point to different versions of the Lambda function

4: Create a new function using the new code and update the application to split requests between the new functions

Answer: 2

Explanation:

You can create one or more aliases for your AWS Lambda function. A Lambda alias is like a pointer to a specific Lambda function version. Users can access the function version using the alias ARN.

You can point an alias to multiple versions of your function code and then assign a weighting to direct certain amounts of traffic to each version. This enables a blue/green style of deployment and means it's easy to roll back to the older version by simply updating the weighting if issues occur.

CORRECT: "Create an alias that points to both the new and previous versions of the function code and assign a weighting for sending a portion of traffic to the new version" is the correct answer.

INCORRECT: "Create two versions of the function code. Configure the application to direct a subset of requests to the new version" is incorrect as this would entail using application logic to direct traffic to the different versions. This is not the best way to solve this problem as Lambda aliases are a better solution.

INCORRECT: "Create an API using API Gateway and use stage variables to point to different versions of the Lambda function" is incorrect. Stage variables are name-value pairs that you can define as configuration attributes associated with a deployment stage of a REST API. They act like environment variables and can be used in your API setup and mapping templates. You can use stage variables to point to different Lambda ARNs and associate these with different stages of your API, however this is not a good solution for this scenario.

INCORRECT: "Create a new function using the new code and update the application to split requests between the new functions" is incorrect as this would entail using application logic to direct traffic to the different versions. This is not the best way to solve this problem as Lambda aliases are a better solution.

6. Question

A company runs a popular online game on premises. The application stores players' results in an in-memory database. The application is being migrated to AWS and the company needs to ensure there is no reduction in performance. Which database would be MOST suitable?

1: Amazon RDS

2: Amazon ElastiCache

3: Amazon DynamoDB

4: Amazon Elastic Beanstalk

Answer: 2

Explanation:

ElastiCache is a fully managed, low latency, in-memory data store that supports either Memcached or Redis. With ElastiCache, management tasks such as provisioning, setup, patching, configuration, monitoring, backup, and failure recovery are taken care of, so you can focus on application development.

Amazon ElastiCache is a popular choice for real-time use cases like Caching, Session Stores, Gaming, Geospatial Services, Real-Time Analytics, and Queuing. For this scenario, the company is currently running an in-memory database and needs to ensure similar performance, so this is an ideal use case for ElastiCache.

CORRECT: "Amazon ElastiCache" is the correct answer.

INCORRECT: "Amazon RDS" is incorrect as RDS is not an in-memory database so the performance may not be as good as ElastiCache.

INCORRECT: "Amazon DynamoDB" is incorrect as this is not an in-memory database. DynamoDB does offer great performance but if you need an in-memory cache you must use DynamoDB Accelerator (DAX).

INCORRECT: "Amazon Elastic Beanstalk" is incorrect as this is not a database service at all. You can launch databases such as RDS through Elastic Beanstalk, however EB itself is a platform service responsible for launching and managing the resources.

7. Question

An Amazon RDS database that stores product information for an online eCommerce marketplace is experiencing heavy demand. An increase in read requests is causing the database performance to be

impacted and is affecting database writes. What is the best way to offload the read traffic from the database with MINIMAL code changes and cost?

1: Change the RDS database instance type to an instance with more CPU/RAM

2: Create an RDS Multi AZ DB and modify the application to send read requests to the standby DB

3: Create an ElastiCache Memcached cluster and modify the application to send read requests to the cluster

4: Create an RDS Read Replica and modify the application to send read requests to the replica

Answer: 4

Explanation:

Amazon RDS read replicas are used for offloading reads from the primary database instance. Read replicas provide a read-only copy of the database. In this scenario this represents the simplest way of achieving the required outcome. The application will need to be modified to point to the read replica for all read requests. This requires some code changes, but they are minimal.

CORRECT: "Create an RDS Read Replica and modify the application to send read requests to the replica" is the correct answer.

INCORRECT: "Change the RDS database instance type to an instance with more CPU/RAM" is incorrect as this is not a way of "offloading the read traffic from the database". This is an example of scaling vertically, rather than scaling horizontally.

INCORRECT: "Create an RDS Multi AZ DB and modify the application to send read requests to the standby DB" is incorrect as we are trying to simply offload read traffic which is a use case for a read replica. However, it is possible for some database engines (MySQL and MariaDB) to combine multi-AZ and read replicas.

INCORRECT: "Create an ElastiCache Memcached cluster and modify the application to send read requests to the cluster" is incorrect as this would require more code changes and higher cost. For this use case an RDS read replica will be simpler and cheaper.

8. Question

A developer has deployed a serverless application with AWS Lambda. The function must make remote calls to external endpoints. Which configuration element in Lambda can be used store the connection strings related to the external endpoints?

1: Aliases

2: Tags

3: Environment variables

4: Versions

Answer: 3

Explanation:

Use environment variables to pass environment-specific settings to your code. For example, you can have two functions with the same code but different configuration. One function connects to a test database, and the other connects to a production database. In this situation, you use environment variables to tell the function the hostname and other connection details for the database. You might also set an environment variable to configure your test environment to use more verbose logging or more detailed tracing.

Therefore, using environment variables is the correct place to store the connection strings associated with the external endpoints.

CORRECT: "Environment variables" is the correct answer.

INCORRECT: "Aliases" is incorrect. A Lambda alias is like a pointer to a specific Lambda function version. Users can access the function version using the alias ARN.

INCORRECT: "Tags" is incorrect. Tags are key-value pairs that you attach to AWS resources to better organize them.

INCORRECT: "Versions" is incorrect. You can use versions to manage the deployment of your AWS Lambda functions.

9. Question

A developer is building a web application that will be hosted on Amazon EC2 instances. The EC2 instances will store configuration data in an Amazon S3 bucket. What is the SAFEST way to allow the EC2 instances to access the S3 bucket?

1: Store an access key and secret ID that has the necessary permissions on the EC2 instances

2: Create an IAM Role with a customer-managed policy attached that has the necessary permissions and attach the role to the EC2 instances

3: Create an IAM Role with an AWS managed policy attached that has the necessary permissions and attach the role to the EC2 instances

4: Use the AWS SDK and authenticate with a user account that has the necessary permissions on the EC2 instances

Answer: 2

Explanation:

Applications that run on an EC2 instance must include AWS credentials in their AWS API requests. You could have your developers store AWS credentials directly within the EC2 instance and allow applications in that instance to use those credentials. But developers would then have to manage the credentials and ensure that they securely pass the credentials to each instance and update each EC2 instance when it's time to rotate the credentials. That's a lot of additional work.

Instead, you can and should use an IAM role to manage *temporary* credentials for applications that run on an EC2 instance. When you use a role, you don't have to distribute long-term credentials (such as a user name and password or access keys) to an EC2 instance. Instead, the role supplies temporary permissions that applications can use when they make calls to other AWS resources. When you launch an EC2 instance, you specify an IAM role to associate with the instance. Applications that run on the instance can then use the role-supplied temporary credentials to sign API requests.

There are two answers that would work in this scenario. In one a customer-managed policy is used and in the other an AWS managed policy is used. The customer-managed policy is more secure in this situation as it can be locked down with more granularity to ensure the EC2 instances can only read and write to the specific bucket.

With an AWS managed policy, you must choose from read only or full access and full access would provide more access than is required.

CORRECT: "Create an IAM Role with a customer-managed policy attached that has the necessary permissions and attach the role to the EC2 instances" is the correct answer.

INCORRECT: "Store an access key and secret ID that has the necessary permissions on the EC2 instances" is incorrect as storing access keys on the EC2 instances is insecure and cumbersome to manage.

INCORRECT: "Create an IAM Role with an AWS managed policy attached that has the necessary permissions and attach the role to the EC2 instances" is incorrect as the AWS managed policy would provide more privileges than required.

INCORRECT: "Use the AWS SDK and authenticate with a user account that has the necessary permissions on the EC2 instances " is incorrect as you cannot authenticate through the AWS SDK using a user account on an EC2 instance.

10. Question

An AWS Lambda functions downloads a 50MB from an object storage system each time it is invoked. The download delays the function completion and causes intermittent timeouts which is slowing down the application.

How can the application be refactored to resolve the timeout?

1: Increase the memory allocation of the function

2: Increase the timeout of the function

3: Increase the concurrency allocation of the function

4: Store the file in the /tmp directory of the execution context and reuse it on subsequent invocations

Answer: 4

Explanation:

You can use the /tmp directory if the function needs to download a large file or disk space for operations. The maximum size is 512 MB. The content is frozen within the execution context so multiple invocations can use the data.

Therefore, the download will occur once, and then subsequent invocations will use the file from the /tmp directory. This requires minimal refactoring and is the best way of resolving these issues.

CORRECT: "Store the file in the /tmp directory of the execution context and reuse it on subsequent invocations" is the correct answer.

INCORRECT: "Increase the memory allocation of the function" is incorrect as this will not resolve the issue of needing to download the file for each invocation. Adding memory results in more CPU being allocated which can reduce processing time but the problem still remains.

INCORRECT: "Increase the timeout of the function" is incorrect as this does not resolve the main issue. The download will still need to occur for each invocation and therefore the application will continue to be affected by poor performance.

INCORRECT: "Increase the concurrency allocation of the function" is incorrect as concurrency is not the issue here. The issue that needs to be resolved is to remove the requirement to download the large file for each invocation.

11. Question

The development team is working on an API that will be served from Amazon API Gateway. The API will serve three environments PROD, DEV, and TEST and requires a cache size of 250GB. What is the MOST cost-efficient deployment strategy?

1: Create three API Gateways, one for each environment and enable the cache for the DEV and TEST environments only when required

2: Create a single API Gateway with three stages and enable the cache for the DEV and TEST environments only when required

3: Create a single API Gateway with three stages and enable the cache for all environments

4: Create a single API Gateway with three deployments and configure a global cache of 250GB

Answer: 2

Explanation:

You can enable API caching in Amazon API Gateway to cache your endpoint's responses. With caching, you can reduce the number of calls made to your endpoint and also improve the latency of requests to your API.

Caching is enabled for a stage. When you enable caching for a stage, API Gateway caches responses from your endpoint for a specified time-to-live (TTL) period, in seconds. API Gateway then responds to the request by looking up the endpoint response from the cache instead of making a request to your endpoint.

The default TTL value for API caching is 300 seconds. The maximum TTL value is 3600 seconds. TTL=0 means caching is disabled.

In this scenario we are asked to choose the most cost-efficient solution. Therefore, the best answer is to use a single API Gateway with three stages and, as caching is enabled per stage, we can choose to save cost by only enabling the cache on DEV and TEST when we need to perform tests relating to that functionality.

CORRECT: "Create a single API Gateway with three stages and enable the cache for the DEV and TEST environments only when required" is the correct answer.

INCORRECT: "Create three API Gateways, one for each environment and enable the cache for the DEV and TEST environments only when required" is incorrect. It is unnecessary to create separate API Gateways. This will increase complexity. Instead we can choose to use stages for the different environments.

INCORRECT: "Create a single API Gateway with three stages and enable the cache for all environments" is incorrect as this would not be the most cost-efficient option.

INCORRECT: "Create a single API Gateway with three deployments and configure a global cache of 250GB" is incorrect. When you deploy you API, you do so to a stage. Caching is enabled at the stage level, not globally.

12. Question

A developer is creating an Auto Scaling group of Amazon EC2 instances. The developer needs to publish a custom metric to Amazon CloudWatch. Which method would be the MOST secure way to authenticate a CloudWatch PUT request?

1: Modify the CloudWatch metric policies to allow the PutMetricData permission to instances from the Auto Scaling group

2: Create an IAM role with the PutMetricData permission and create a new Auto Scaling launch configuration to launch instances using that role

3: Create an IAM user with the PutMetricData permission and modify the Auto Scaling launch configuration to inject the user credentials into the instance user data

4: Create an IAM role with the PutMetricData permission and modify the Amazon EC2 instances to use that role

Answer: 2

Explanation:

The most secure configuration to authenticate the request is to create an IAM role with a permissions policy that only provides the minimum permissions requires (least privilege). This IAM role should have a customer-managed permissions policy applied with the PutMetricData allowed.

The PutMetricData API publishes metric data points to Amazon CloudWatch. CloudWatch associates the data points with the specified metric. If the specified metric does not exist, CloudWatch creates the metric. When CloudWatch creates a metric, it can take up to fifteen minutes for the metric to appear in calls to ListMetrics.

CORRECT: "Create an IAM role with the PutMetricData permission and create a new Auto Scaling launch configuration to launch instances using that role" is the correct answer

INCORRECT: "Modify the CloudWatch metric policies to allow the PutMetricData permission to instances from the Auto Scaling group" is incorrect as this is not possible. You should instead grant the permissions through a permissions policy and attach that to a role that the EC2 instances can assume.

INCORRECT: "Create an IAM user with the PutMetricData permission and modify the Auto Scaling launch configuration to inject the user credentials into the instance user data" is incorrect. You cannot "inject user credentials" using a launch configuration. Instead, you can attach an IAM role which allows the instance to assume the role and take on the privileges allowed through any permissions policies that are associated with that role.

INCORRECT: "Create an IAM role with the PutMetricData permission and modify the Amazon EC2 instances to use that role" is incorrect as you should create a new launch configuration for the Auto Scaling group rather than updating the instances manually.

13. Question

An application includes several producer services that send data to an Amazon SQS queue. The messages are then processed by a consumer component that must ensure that each producer's messages are processed in the order they are received. How can a Developer ensure the messages are processed in the correct order?

1: Configure each message with a unique MessageGroupId

2: Enable the MessageDeduplicationId on the SQS queue

3: Configure each producer with a unique MessageGroupId

4: Enable ContentBasedDeduplication on the SQS queue

Answer: 3

Explanation:

The MessageDeduplicationId is available in an Amazon SQS FIFO queue. With a FIFO queue, the order in which messages are sent and received is strictly preserved and a message is delivered once and remains available until a consumer processes and deletes it.

Duplicates are not introduced into the queue. FIFO queues also support message groups that allow multiple ordered message groups within a single queue.

Deduplication with FIFO queues:

- Provide a MessageDeduplicationId with the message.
- The de-duplication interval is 5 minutes.
- Content based duplication – the MessageDeduplicationId is generated as the SHA-256 with the message body.

Sequencing with FIFO queues:

- To ensure strict ordering between messages, specify a MessageGroupId.
- Messages with a different Group ID may be received out of order.
- Messages with the same Group ID are delivered to one consumer at a time.

In this case, we need to ensure the messages from a specific producer are processed in order. Therefore, we need to configure each producer to send messages with a unique MessageGroupId.

CORRECT: "Configure each producer with a unique MessageGroupId" is the correct answer.

INCORRECT: "Configure each message with a unique MessageGroupId" is incorrect as the MessageGroupId should be applied to all messages that need to be ordered. You should not use a unique ID with each message.

INCORRECT: "Enable the MessageDeduplicationId on the SQS queue" is incorrect. The message deduplication ID is the token used for deduplication of sent messages. If a message with a particular message deduplication ID is sent successfully, any messages sent with the same message deduplication ID are accepted successfully but aren't delivered during the 5-minute deduplication interval.

INCORRECT: "Enable ContentBasedDeduplication on the SQS queue" is incorrect.
When ContentBasedDeduplication is in effect, messages with identical content sent within the deduplication interval are treated as duplicates and only one copy of the message is delivered. This is not what we need to achieve here, we need to ensure the order of our messages not deduplicate them.

14. Question

An application is being deployed at a media company. The application will receive data from applications at many new outlets around the country. The application will ingest the data, process it with AWS Lambda and then store the data in an Amazon S3 bucket. Which AWS service would be BEST suited to these requirements?

1: Amazon SQS

2: Amazon SNS

3: Amazon CloudFront

4: Amazon Kinesis Firehose

Answer: 4

Explanation:

Amazon Kinesis Data Firehose is the easiest way to reliably load streaming data into data lakes, data stores and analytics tools. It can capture, transform, and load streaming data into Amazon S3, Amazon Redshift, Amazon Elasticsearch Service, and Splunk, enabling near real-time analytics with existing business intelligence tools and dashboards you're already using today.

You can configure Amazon Kinesis Data Firehose to prepare your streaming data before it is loaded to data stores. Simply select an AWS Lambda function from the Amazon Kinesis Data Firehose delivery stream configuration tab in the AWS Management console. Amazon Kinesis Data Firehose will automatically apply that function to every input data record and load the transformed data to destinations.

Therefore, the best solution for these requirements is to use Amazon Kinesis Firehose with AWS Lambda for the transformation/processing of data. Kinesis Firehose can then load the data to Amazon S3.

CORRECT: "Amazon Kinesis Firehose" is the correct answer.

INCORRECT: "Amazon CloudFront" is incorrect. CloudFront is a good solution for getting content closer to users for performance. However, in this use case we need a solution for ingesting streaming data and then loading it into a datastore with processing of the data happening as well. This is a good use case for Kinesis Firehose.

INCORRECT: "Amazon SQS" is incorrect as Amazon SQS is a message bus that is used for decoupling application components. Though you could have the applications place the data in an SQS queue and then have a consumer layer picking up those records and passing them to Lambda, there are conditions with SQS queues for message size that could complicate this solution. Also, Kinesis Firehose is ideal and designed specifically for this type of use case, so the better solution is to use Firehose instead.

INCORRECT: "Amazon SNS" is incorrect as the SNS service is involved with sending notifications not ingesting, processing and then loading data into a data store.

15. Question

A company uses an Amazon S3 bucket to store a large number of sensitive files relating to eCommerce transactions. The company has a policy that states that all data written to the S3 bucket must be encrypted. How can a Developer ensure compliance with this policy?

1: Create a bucket policy that denies the S3 PutObject request with the attribute x-amz-acl having values public-read, public-read-write, or authenticated-read

2: Create an S3 bucket policy that denies any S3 Put request that does not include the x-amz-server-side-encryption

3: Enable Server-Side Encryption with Amazon S3-Managed Keys (SSE-S3) on the Amazon S3 bucket

4: Create an Amazon CloudWatch alarm that notifies an administrator if unencrypted objects are uploaded to the S3 bucket

Answer: 2

Explanation:

To encrypt an object at the time of upload, you need to add a header called x-amz-server-side-encryption to the request to tell S3 to encrypt the object using SSE-C, SSE-S3, or SSE-KMS.

Enabling encryption on an S3 bucket does not enforce encryption however, so it is still necessary to take extra steps to force compliance with the policy. Bucket policies are applied before encryption settings so PUT requests without encryption information can be rejected by a bucket policy.

Therefore, we need to create an S3 bucket policy that denies any S3 Put request that do not include the x-amz-server-side-encryption header. There are two possible values for the x-amz-server-side-encryption header: AES256, which tells S3 to use S3-managed keys, and aws:kms, which tells S3 to use AWS KMS–managed keys.

CORRECT: "Create an S3 bucket policy that denies any S3 Put request that does not include the x-amz-server-side-encryption" is the correct answer.

INCORRECT: "Create a bucket policy that denies the S3 PutObject request with the attribute x-amz-acl having values public-read, public-read-write, or authenticated-read" is incorrect. This policy means that authenticated users cannot upload objects to the bucket if the objects have public permissions.

INCORRECT: "Enable Server-Side Encryption with Amazon S3-Managed Keys (SSE-S3) on the Amazon S3 bucket" is incorrect as this will enable default encryption but will not enforce encryption on the S3 bucket. You do still need to enable default encryption on the bucket, but this alone will not enforce encryption.

INCORRECT: "Create an Amazon CloudWatch alarm that notifies an administrator if unencrypted objects are uploaded to the S3 bucket" is incorrect. This is operationally difficult to manage and only notifies, it does not prevent.

16. Question

An application uses Amazon API Gateway, an AWS Lambda function and a DynamoDB table. The developer requires that another Lambda function is triggered when an item lifecycle activity occurs in the DynamoDB table. How can this be achieved?

1: Configure an Amazon CloudWatch alarm that sends an Amazon SNS notification. Trigger the Lambda function asynchronously from the SNS notification

2: Enable a DynamoDB stream and trigger the Lambda function synchronously from the stream

3: Enable a DynamoDB stream and trigger the Lambda function asynchronously from the stream

4: Configure an Amazon CloudTrail API alarm that sends a message to an Amazon SQS queue. Configure the Lambda function to poll the queue and invoke the function synchronously

Answer: 2

Explanation:

Amazon DynamoDB is integrated with AWS Lambda so that you can create *triggers*—pieces of code that automatically respond to events in DynamoDB Streams. With triggers, you can build applications that react to data modifications in DynamoDB tables.

If you enable DynamoDB Streams on a table, you can associate the stream Amazon Resource Name (ARN) with an AWS Lambda function that you write. Immediately after an item in the table is modified, a new record appears in the table's stream. AWS Lambda polls the stream and invokes your Lambda function synchronously when it detects new stream records.

CORRECT: "Enable a DynamoDB stream and trigger the Lambda function synchronously from the stream" is the correct answer.

INCORRECT: "Enable a DynamoDB stream and trigger the Lambda function asynchronously from the stream" is incorrect as the invocation should be synchronous.

INCORRECT: "Configure an Amazon CloudWatch alarm that sends an Amazon SNS notification. Trigger the Lambda function asynchronously from the SNS notification" is incorrect as you cannot configure a CloudWatch alarm that notifies based on item lifecycle events. It is better to use DynamoDB streams and integrate Lambda.

INCORRECT: "Configure an Amazon CloudTrail API alarm that sends a message to an Amazon SQS queue. Configure the Lambda function to poll the queue and invoke the function synchronously" is incorrect. There is no such alarm that notifies from Amazon CloudTrail relating to item lifecycle events.

17. Question

An application is using Amazon DynamoDB as its data store and needs to be able to read 100 items per second as strongly consistent reads. Each item is 5 KB in size. What value should be set for the table's provisioned throughput for reads?

1: 50 Read Capacity Units

2: 200 Read Capacity Units

3: 250 Read Capacity Units

4: 500 Read Capacity Units

Answer: 2

Explanation:

With provisioned capacity mode, you specify the number of data reads and writes per second that you require for your application.

Read capacity unit (RCU):

- Each API call to read data from your table is a read request.
- Read requests can be strongly consistent, eventually consistent, or transactional.
- For items up to 4 KB in size, one RCU can perform one *strongly consistent* read request per second.
- Items larger than 4 KB require additional RCUs.
- For items up to 4 KB in size, one RCU can perform two *eventually consistent* read requests per second.
- *Transactional* read requests require two RCUs to perform one read per second for items up to 4 KB.
- For example, a strongly consistent read of an 8 KB item would require two RCUs, an eventually consistent read of an 8 KB item would require one RCU, and a transactional read of an 8 KB item would require four RCUs.

Write capacity unit (WCU):

- Each API call to write data to your table is a write request.
- For items up to 1 KB in size, one WCU can perform one *standard* write request per second.
- Items larger than 1 KB require additional WCUs.
- *Transactional* write requests require two WCUs to perform one write per second for items up to 1 KB.

- For example, a standard write request of a 1 KB item would require one WCU, a standard write request of a 3 KB item would require three WCUs, and a transactional write request of a 3 KB item would require six WCUs.

To determine the number of RCUs required to handle 100 strongly consistent reads per/second with an average item size of 5KB, perform the following steps:

- **Determine the average item size by rounding up the next multiple of 4KB (5KB rounds up to 8KB).**
- **Determine the RCU per item by dividing the item size by 4KB (8KB/4KB = 2).**
- **Multiply the value from step 2 with the number of reads required per second (2x100 = 200).**

CORRECT: "200 Read Capacity Units" is the correct answer.

INCORRECT: "50 Read Capacity Units" is incorrect.

INCORRECT: "250 Read Capacity Units" is incorrect.

INCORRECT: "500 Read Capacity Units" is incorrect.

18. Question

A company runs an application on a fleet of web servers running on Amazon EC2 instances. The web servers are behind an Elastic Load Balancer (ELB) and use an Amazon DynamoDB table for storing session state. A Developer has been asked to implement a mechanism for automatically deleting session state data that is older than 24 hours. What is the SIMPLEST solution to this requirement?

1: Add an attribute with the expiration time; enable the Time To Live feature based on that attribute

2: Each day, create a new table to hold session data; delete the previous day's table

3: Write a script that deletes old records; schedule the scripts as a cron job on an Amazon EC2 instance

4: Add an attribute with the expiration time; name the attribute ItemExpiration

Answer: 1

Explanation:

Time to Live (TTL) for Amazon DynamoDB lets you define when items in a table expire so that they can be automatically deleted from the database. With TTL enabled on a table, you can set a timestamp for deletion on a per-item basis, allowing you to limit storage usage to only those records that are relevant.

TTL is useful if you have continuously accumulating data that loses relevance after a specific time period (for example, session data, event logs, usage patterns, and other temporary data). If you have sensitive data that must be retained only for a certain amount of time according to contractual or regulatory obligations, TTL helps you ensure that it is removed promptly and as scheduled.

When Time to Live (TTL) is enabled on a table in Amazon DynamoDB, a background job checks the TTL attribute of items to determine whether they are expired.

DynamoDB compares the current time, in epoch time format, to the value stored in the user-defined Number attribute of an item. If the attribute's value is in the epoch time format, is less than the current time, and is not older than 5 years, the item is deleted.

Processing takes place automatically, in the background, and doesn't affect read or write traffic to the table. In addition, deletes performed via TTL are not counted towards capacity units or request units. TTL deletes are available at no additional cost.

For this requirement, the Developer must add an attribute to each item with the expiration time in epoch format and then enable the Time To Live (TTL) feature based on that attribute.

CORRECT: "Add an attribute with the expiration time; enable the Time To Live feature based on that attribute" is the correct answer.

INCORRECT: "Each day, create a new table to hold session data; delete the previous day's table" is incorrect. This solution would delete some data that is not 24 hours old as it would have to run at a specific time.

INCORRECT: "Write a script that deletes old records; schedule the scripts as a cron job on an Amazon EC2 instance" is incorrect. This is not an elegant solution and would also cost more as it requires RCUs/WCUs to delete the items.

INCORRECT: "Add an attribute with the expiration time; name the attribute ItemExpiration" is incorrect as this is not a complete solution. You also need to enable the TTL feature on the table.

19. Question

A gaming company is building an application to track the scores for their games using an Amazon DynamoDB table. Each item in the table is identified by a partition key (user_id) and a sort key (game_name). The table also includes the attribute "TopScore". The table design is shown below:

Primary key*   Partition key

| user_id | String ⇕ ⓘ |

☑ Add sort key

| game_name | String ⇕ ⓘ |

A Developer has been asked to write a leaderboard application to display the highest achieved scores for each game (game_name), based on the score identified in the "TopScore" attribute.
What process will allow the Developer to extract results MOST efficiently from the DynamoDB table?

1: Create a local secondary index with a primary key of "game_name" and a sort key of "TopScore" and get the results based on the score attribute

2: Create a global secondary index with a primary key of "game_name" and a sort key of "TopScore" and get the results based on the score attribute

3: Use a DynamoDB scan operation to retrieve the scores for "game_name" using the "TopScore" attribute, and order the results based on the score attribute

4: Create a global secondary index with a primary key of "user_id" and a sort key of "game_name" and get the results based on the "TopScore" attribute

Answer: 2

Explanation:

In an Amazon DynamoDB table, the primary key that uniquely identifies each item in the table can be composed not only of a partition key, but also of a sort key.

Well-designed sort keys have two key benefits:

- They gather related information together in one place where it can be queried efficiently. Careful design of the sort key lets you retrieve commonly needed groups of related items using range queries with operators such as begins_with, between, >, <, and so on.

- Composite sort keys let you define hierarchical (one-to-many) relationships in your data that you can query at any level of the hierarchy.

To speed up queries on non-key attributes, you can create a global secondary index. A global secondary index contains a selection of attributes from the base table, but they are organized by a primary key that is different from that of the table. The index key does not need to have any of the key attributes from the table. It doesn't even need to have the same key schema as a table.

For this scenario we need to identify the top achieved score for each game. The most efficient way to do this is to create a global secondary index using "game_name" as the partition key and "TopScore" as the sort key. We can then efficiently query the global secondary index to find the top achieved score for each game.

CORRECT: "Create a global secondary index with a primary key of "game_name" and a sort key of "TopScore" and get the results based on the score attribute" is the correct answer.

INCORRECT: "Create a local secondary index with a primary key of "game_name" and a sort key of "TopScore" and get the results based on the score attribute" is incorrect. With a local secondary index you can have a different sort key but the partition key is the same.

INCORRECT: "Use a DynamoDB scan operation to retrieve the scores for "game_name" using the "TopScore" attribute, and order the results based on the score attribute" is incorrect. This would be inefficient as it scans the whole table. First, we should create a global secondary index, and then use a query to efficiently retrieve the data.

INCORRECT: "Create a global secondary index with a primary key of "user_id" and a sort key of "game_name" and get the results based on the score attribute" is incorrect as with a global secondary index you have a different partition key and sort key. Also, we don't need "user_id", we need "game_name" and "TopScore".

20. Question

A company is running a web application on Amazon EC2 behind an Elastic Load Balancer (ELB). The company is concerned about the security of the web application and would like to secure the application with SSL certificates. The solution should not have any performance impact on the EC2 instances. What steps should be taken to secure the web application? (Select TWO)

1: Configure the Elastic Load Balancer with SSL passthrough

2: Add an SSL certificate to the Elastic Load Balancer

3: Install SSL certificates on the EC2 instances

4: Configure the Elastic Load Balancer for SSL termination

5: Configure Server-Side Encryption with KMS managed keys

Answer: 2,4

Explanation:

The requirements clearly state that we cannot impact the performance of the EC2 instances at all. Therefore, we will not be able to add certificates to the EC2 instances as that would place a burden on the CPU when encrypting and decrypting data.

We are therefore left with configuring SSL on the Elastic Load Balancer itself. For this we need to add an SSL certificate to the ELB and then configure the ELB for SSL termination.

You can create an HTTPS listener, which uses encrypted connections (also known as *SSL offload*). This feature enables traffic encryption between your load balancer and the clients that initiate SSL or TLS sessions.

To use an HTTPS listener, you must deploy at least one SSL/TLS server certificate on your load balancer. The load balancer uses a server certificate to terminate the front-end connection and then decrypt requests from clients before sending them to the targets.

This is the most secure solution we can created without adding any performance impact to the EC2 instances.

CORRECT: "Add an SSL certificate to the Elastic Load Balancer" is a correct answer.

CORRECT: "Configure the Elastic Load Balancer for SSL termination" is also a correct answer.

INCORRECT: "Configure the Elastic Load Balancer with SSL passthrough" is incorrect as this would be used to forward encrypted packets directly to the EC2 instance for termination but we do not want to add SSL certificates to the EC2 instances due to the extra processing required.

INCORRECT: "Install SSL certificates on the EC2 instances" is incorrect as we do not want to add SSL certificates to the EC2 instances due to the extra processing required.

INCORRECT: "Configure Server-Side Encryption with KMS managed keys" is incorrect as this applies to Amazon S3, not ELB.

21. Question

An application is running on an Amazon EC2 Linux instance. The instance needs to make AWS API calls to several AWS services. What is the MOST secure way to provide access to the AWS services with MINIMAL management overhead?

1: Use AWS KMS to store and retrieve credentials

2: Use EC2 instance profiles

3: Store the credentials in AWS CloudHSM

4: Store the credentials in the ~/.aws/credentials file

Answer: 2

Explanation:

An instance profile is a container for an IAM role that you can use to pass role information to an EC2 instance when the instance starts. Using an instance profile you can attach an IAM Role to an EC2 instance that the instance can then assume in order to gain access to AWS services.

CORRECT: "Use EC2 instance profiles" is the correct answer.

INCORRECT: "Use AWS KMS to store and retrieve credentials" is incorrect as KMS is used to manage encryption keys.

INCORRECT: "Store the credentials in AWS CloudHSM" is incorrect as CloudHSM is also used to manage encryption keys. It is similar to KMS but uses a dedicated hardware device that is not multi-tenant.

INCORRECT: "Store the credentials in the ~/.aws/credentials file" is incorrect as this is not the most secure option. The credentials file is associated with the AWS CLI and used for passing credentials in the form of an access key ID and secret access key when making programmatic requests from the command line.

22. Question

A Developer is creating a serverless application that includes Amazon API Gateway, Amazon DynamoDB and AWS Lambda. The Developer will use AWS CloudFormation to deploy the application and is creating a template. Which tool should the Developer use to define simplified syntax for expressing serverless resources?

1: AWS Step Functions State Machine

2: OpenAPI Swagger Specification

3: AWS Serverless Application Model

4: A CloudFormation Serverless Plugin

Answer: 3

Explanation:

The AWS Serverless Application Model (AWS SAM) is an open-source framework that you can use to build serverless applications on AWS. A serverless application is a combination of Lambda functions, event sources, and other resources that work together to perform tasks.

Note: A serverless application is more than just a Lambda function—it can include additional resources such as APIs, databases, and event source mappings.

You can use AWS SAM to define your serverless applications. AWS SAM consists of the following components:

- **AWS SAM template specification**. You use this specification to define your serverless application. It provides you with a simple and clean syntax to describe the functions, APIs, permissions, configurations, and events that make up a serverless application.

- **AWS SAM command line interface (AWS SAM CLI)**. You use this tool to build serverless applications that are defined by AWS SAM templates.

CORRECT: "AWS Serverless Application Model" is the correct answer.

INCORRECT: "AWS Step Functions State Machine" is incorrect. AWS Step Functions is a web service that enables you to coordinate the components of distributed applications and microservices using visual workflows. It does not provide a simplified syntax for expressing serverless resources in a CloudFormation template.

INCORRECT: "OpenAPI Swagger Specification" is incorrect. Swagger is an open-source software framework backed by a large ecosystem of tools that helps developers design, build, document, and consume RESTful web services.

INCORRECT: "A CloudFormation Serverless Plugin" is incorrect as this does not exist.

23. Question

A Developer has added a Global Secondary Index (GSI) to an existing Amazon DynamoDB table. The GSI is used mainly for read operations whereas the primary table is extremely write-intensive. Recently, the Developer has noticed throttling occurring under heavy write activity on the primary table. However, the write capacity units on the primary table are not fully utilized. What is the best explanation for why the writes are being throttled on the primary table?

1: There are insufficient read capacity units on the primary table

2: The Developer should have added an LSI instead of a GSI

3: There are insufficient write capacity units on the primary table

4: The write capacity units on the GSI are under provisioned

Answer: 4

Explanation:

Some applications might need to perform many kinds of queries, using a variety of different attributes as query criteria. To support these requirements, you can create one or more global secondary indexes and issue Query requests against these indexes in Amazon DynamoDB.

When items from a primary table are written to the GSI they consume write capacity units. It is essential to ensure the GSI has sufficient WCUs (typically, at least as many as the primary table). If writes are throttled on the GSI, the main table will be throttled (even if there's enough WCUs on the main table). LSIs do not cause any special throttling considerations.

In this scenario, it is likely that the Developer assumed that the GSI would need fewer WCUs as it is more read-intensive and neglected to factor in the WCUs required for writing data into the GSI. Therefore, the most likely explanation is that the write capacity units on the GSI are under provisioned

CORRECT: "The write capacity units on the GSI are under provisioned" is the correct answer.

INCORRECT: "There are insufficient read capacity units on the primary table" is incorrect as the table is being throttled due to writes, not reads.

INCORRECT: "The Developer should have added an LSI instead of a GSI" is incorrect as a GSI has specific advantages and there was likely good reason for adding a GSI. Also, you cannot add an LSI to an existing table.

INCORRECT: "There are insufficient write capacity units on the primary table" is incorrect as the question states that the WCUs are underutilized.

24. Question

A development team manage a high-traffic e-Commerce site with dynamic pricing that is updated in real-time. There have been incidents where multiple updates occur simultaneously and cause an original editor's updates to be overwritten. How can the developers ensure that overwriting does not occur?

1: Use concurrent writes

2: Use atomic counters

3: Use conditional writes

4: Use batch operations

Answer: 3

Explanation:

By default, the DynamoDB write operations (PutItem, UpdateItem, DeleteItem) are *unconditional*: Each operation overwrites an existing item that has the specified primary key.

DynamoDB optionally supports conditional writes for these operations. A conditional write succeeds only if the item attributes meet one or more expected conditions. Otherwise, it returns an error. Conditional writes are helpful in many situations. For example, you might want a PutItem operation to succeed only if there is not already an item with the same primary key. Or you could prevent an UpdateItem operation from modifying an item if one of its attributes has a certain value.

Conditional writes can be ***idempotent*** if the conditional check is on the same attribute that is being updated. This means that DynamoDB performs a given write request only if certain attribute values in the item match what you expect them to be at the time of the request.

For example, suppose that you issue an UpdateItem request to increase the Price of an item by 3, but only if the Price is currently 20. After you send the request, but before you get the results back, a network error occurs, and you don't know whether the request was successful. Because this conditional write is idempotent, you can retry the same UpdateItem request, and DynamoDB updates the item only if the Price is currently 20.

The following example shows how to use the condition-expression parameter to achieve a conditional write with idempotence:

*aws dynamodb update-item *

* --table-name ProductCatalog *

* --key '{"Id":{"N":"1"}}' *

* --update-expression "SET Price = :newval" *

* --condition-expression "Price = :currval" *

* --expression-attribute-values file://expression-attribute-values.json*

For this scenario, conditional writes with idempotence will mean that each writer can check the current price and update the price only if the price matches that price. If the price is updated by another writer before the write is made, it will fail as the item price has changed and will not reflect the expected price.

CORRECT: "Use conditional writes" is the correct answer.

INCORRECT: "Use concurrent writes" is incorrect as writing concurrently to the same items is exactly what we want to avoid.

INCORRECT: "Use atomic counters" is incorrect. An atomic counter is a numeric attribute that is incremented, unconditionally, without interfering with other write requests. This is used for cases such as tracking visitors to a website. This does not prevent recent updated from being overwritten.

INCORRECT: "Use batch operations" is incorrect. Batch operations can reduce the number of network round trips from your application to DynamoDB. However, this does not solve the problem of preventing recent updates from being overwritten.

25. Question

A Development team are creating a new REST API that uses Amazon API Gateway and AWS Lambda. To support testing there need to be different versions of the service. What is the BEST way to provide multiple versions of the REST API?

1: Create an API Gateway resource policy to isolate versions and provide context to the Lambda functions

2: Deploy the API versions as unique stages with unique endpoints and use stage variables to provide further context

3: Create an AWS Lambda authorizer to route API clients to the correct API version

4: Deploy an HTTP Proxy integration and configure the proxy with API versions

Answer: 2

Explanation:

A stage is a named reference to a deployment, which is a snapshot of the API. You use a Stage to manage and optimize a particular deployment. For example, you can set up stage settings to enable caching, customize request throttling, configure logging, define stage variables or attach a canary release for testing. APIs are deployed to stages.

Stage variables are name-value pairs that you can define as configuration attributes associated with a deployment stage of a REST API. They act like environment variables and can be used in your API setup and mapping templates.

With deployment stages in API Gateway, you can manage multiple release stages for each API, such as alpha, beta, and production. Using stage variables you can configure an API deployment stage to interact with different backend endpoints. For example, your API can pass a GET request as an HTTP proxy to the backend web host (for example, http://example.com).

In this case, the backend web host is configured in a stage variable so that when developers call your production endpoint, API Gateway calls example.com. When you call your beta endpoint, API Gateway uses the value configured in the stage variable for the beta stage, and calls a different web host (for example, beta.example.com). Similarly, stage variables can be used to specify a different AWS Lambda function name for each stage in your API.

Therefore, for this scenario the Developers can deploy the API versions as unique stages with unique endpoints and use stage variables to provide further context such as connections to different backend services.

CORRECT: "Deploy the API versions as unique stages with unique endpoints and use stage variables to provide further context" is the correct answer.

INCORRECT: "Create an API Gateway resource policy to isolate versions and provide context to the Lambda functions" is incorrect. API Gateway resource policies are JSON policy documents that you attach to an API to control whether a specified principal (typically, an IAM user or role) can invoke the API.

INCORRECT: "Create an AWS Lambda authorizer to route API clients to the correct API version" is incorrect. A *Lambda authorizer* (formerly known as a *custom authorizer*) is an API Gateway feature that uses a Lambda function to control access to your API. This is not used for routing API clients to different versions.

INCORRECT: "Deploy an HTTP Proxy integration and configure the proxy with API versions" is incorrect. The HTTP proxy integration allows a client to access the backend HTTP endpoints with a streamlined integration setup on a single API method. This is not used for providing multiple versions of the API, use stages and stage variables instead.

26. Question

A Developer is creating an AWS Lambda function that will process data from an Amazon Kinesis data stream. The function is expected to be invoked 50 times per second and take 100 seconds to complete each request. What MUST the Developer do to ensure the functions runs without errors?

1: Contact AWS and request to increase the limit for concurrent executions

2: No action is required as AWS Lambda can easily accommodate this requirement

3: Increase the concurrency limit for the function

4: Implement exponential backoff in the function code

Answer: 1

Explanation:

Concurrency is the number of requests that your function is serving at any given time. When your function is invoked, Lambda allocates an instance of it to process the event. When the function code finishes running, it can handle another request. If the function is invoked again while a request is still being processed, another instance is allocated, which increases the function's concurrency.

Concurrency is subject to a Regional limit that is shared by all functions in a Region. For an initial burst of traffic, your functions' cumulative concurrency in a Region can reach an initial level of between 500 and 3000, which varies per Region:

- **3000** – US West (Oregon), US East (N. Virginia), Europe (Ireland)
- **1000** – Asia Pacific (Tokyo), Europe (Frankfurt)
- **500** – Other Regions

After the initial burst, your functions' concurrency can scale by an additional 500 instances each minute. This continues until there are enough instances to serve all requests, or until a concurrency limit is reached. When requests come in faster than your function can scale, or when your function is at maximum concurrency, additional requests fail with a throttling error (429 status code).

The function continues to scale until the account's concurrency limit for the function's Region is reached. The function catches up to demand, requests subside, and unused instances of the function are stopped after being idle for some time. Unused instances are frozen while they're waiting for requests and don't incur any charges.

The regional concurrency limit starts at 1,000. You can increase the limit by submitting a request in the Support Center console.

Calculating concurrency requirements for this scenario

To calculate the concurrency requirements for this scenario, simply multiply the invocation requests per second (50) with the average execution time in seconds (100). This calculation is 50 x 100 = 5,000.

Therefore, 5,000 concurrent executions is over the default limit and the Developer will need to request in the AWS Support Center console.

CORRECT: "Contact AWS and request to increase the limit for concurrent executions" is the correct answer.

INCORRECT: "No action is required as AWS Lambda can easily accommodate this requirement" is incorrect as by default the AWS account will be limited. Lambda can easily scale to this level of demand however the account limits must first be increased.

INCORRECT: "Increase the concurrency limit for the function" is incorrect as the default account limit of 1,000 concurrent executions will mean you can only assign up to 900 executions to the function (100 must be left unreserved). This is insufficient for this requirement to the account limit must be increased.

INCORRECT: "Implement exponential backoff in the function code" is incorrect. Exponential backoff means configuring the application to wait longer between API calls, slowing the demand. However, this is not a good resolution to this issue as it will have negative effects on the application. The correct choice is to raise the account limits so the function can concurrently execute according to its requirements.

27. Question

An AWS Lambda application writes data to an Amazon S3 bucket. The application sometimes needs to overwrite an object, and then immediately read the object. In some cases, the application retrieves the old version of the object. What is the MOST likely explanation for this?

1: Amazon S3 overwrite PUTS are eventually consistent, so the application may read the old object

2: The function has cached the old version of the object and retrieved it from the cache

3: All Amazon S3 PUTS are eventually consistent, so the application may read the old object

4: The application did not explicitly specify the latest version when retrieving the object

Answer: 1

Explanation:

Amazon S3 provides read-after-write consistency for PUTS of new objects in your S3 bucket in all Regions with one caveat. The caveat is that if you make a HEAD or GET request to a key name before the object is created, then create the object shortly after that, a subsequent GET might not return the object due to eventual consistency.

Amazon S3 offers eventual consistency for overwrite PUTS and DELETES in all Regions. Therefore, the most likely explanation for this issue is that the old object version was retrieved due to Amazon's eventual consistency model for overwrite PUTS.

CORRECT: "Amazon S3 overwrite PUTS are eventually consistent, so the application may read the old object" is the correct answer.

INCORRECT: "The function has cached the old version of the object and retrieved it from the cache" is incorrect

INCORRECT: "All Amazon S3 PUTS are eventually consistent, so the application may read the old object" is incorrect

INCORRECT: "The application did not explicitly specify the latest version when retrieving the object" is incorrect

28. Question

A legacy service has an XML-based SOAP interface. The Developer wants to expose the functionality of the service to external clients with the Amazon API Gateway. Which technique will accomplish this?

1: Create a RESTful API with the API Gateway; transform the incoming JSON into a valid XML message for the SOAP interface using mapping templates

2: Create a RESTful API with the API Gateway; pass the incoming JSON to the SOAP interface through an Application Load Balancer

3: Create a RESTful API with the API Gateway; pass the incoming XML to the SOAP interface through an Application Load Balancer

4: Create a RESTful API with the API Gateway; transform the incoming XML into a valid message for the SOAP interface using mapping templates

Answer: 1

Explanation:

Amazon API Gateway is an AWS service for creating, publishing, maintaining, monitoring, and securing REST and WebSocket APIs at any scale. API developers can create APIs that access AWS or other web services as well as data stored in the AWS Cloud.

In API Gateway, an API's method request can take a payload in a different format from the corresponding integration request payload, as required in the backend. Similarly, the backend may return an integration response payload different from the method response payload, as expected by the frontend.

API Gateway lets you use mapping templates to map the payload from a method request to the corresponding integration request and from an integration response to the corresponding method response.

If an existing legacy service returns XML-style data, you can use the API Gateway to transform the output to JSON as part of your modernization effort. The API Gateway can be configured to transform the output of legacy services from XML to JSON, allowing them to make a move that is seamless and non-disruptive. The transformation is specified using JSON-Schema.

Therefore, the technique the Developer should use is to create a RESTful API with the API Gateway and transform the incoming JSON into a valid XML message for the SOAP interface using mapping templates.

CORRECT: "Create a RESTful API with the API Gateway; transform the incoming JSON into a valid XML message for the SOAP interface using mapping templates" is the correct answer.

INCORRECT: "Create a RESTful API with the API Gateway; pass the incoming JSON to the SOAP interface through an Application Load Balancer" is incorrect as we don't need an ALB to do this, we can use a mapping template within the API Gateway which will be more cost-efficient.

INCORRECT: "Create a RESTful API with the API Gateway; pass the incoming XML to the SOAP interface through an Application Load Balancer" is incorrect as the incoming data will be JSON, not XML as the Developer needs to publish a modern application interface. A mapping template should also be used in place of the ALB.

INCORRECT: "Create a RESTful API with the API Gateway; transform the incoming XML into a valid message for the SOAP interface using mapping templates" is incorrect as the incoming data will be JSON, not XML as the Developer needs to publish a modern application interface.

29. Question

A Developer has completed some code updates and needs to deploy the updates to an Amazon Elastic Beanstalk environment. The environment includes twelve Amazon EC2 instances and there can be no reduction in application performance and availability during the update. Which deployment policy is the most cost-effective choice so suit these requirements?

1: All at once

2: Rolling

3: Rolling with additional batch

4: Immutable

Answer: 3

Explanation:

AWS Elastic Beanstalk provides several options for how deployments are processed, including deployment policies and options that let you configure batch size and health check behavior during deployments.

Each deployment policy has advantages and disadvantages and it's important to select the best policy to use for each situation.

The "rolling with additional batch" policy will add an additional batch of instances, updates those instances, then move onto the next batch.

Rolling with additional batch:

- Like Rolling but launches new instances in a batch ensuring that there is full availability.
- Application is running at capacity.
- Can set the bucket size.
- Application is running both versions simultaneously.
- Small additional cost.
- Additional batch is removed at the end of the deployment.
- Longer deployment.
- Good for production environments.

For this scenario there can be no reduction in application performance and availability during the update. The question also asks for the most cost-effective choice.

Therefore, the "rolling with additional batch" is the best choice as it will ensure fully availability of the application but minimize cost as the additional batch size can be kept small.

CORRECT: "Rolling with additional batch" is the correct answer.

INCORRECT: "Rolling" is incorrect as this will result in a reduction in capacity as there is no additional batch of instances introduced to the environment. This is a better choice if speed is required and a reduction in capacity of a batch size is acceptable.

INCORRECT: "All at once" is incorrect as this will take the application down and cause a complete outage of the application during the update.

INCORRECT: "Immutable" is incorrect as this is the most expensive option as it doubles capacity with a whole new set of instances attached to a new ASG.

30. Question

A Developer is creating a DynamoDB table for storing application logs. The table has 5 write capacity units (WCUs). The Developer needs to configure the read capacity units (RCUs) for the table. Which of the following configurations represents the most efficient use of throughput?

1: Eventually consistent reads of 5 RCUs reading items that are 4 KB in size

2: Strongly consistent reads of 5 RCUs reading items that are 4 KB in size

3: Eventually consistent reads of 15 RCUs reading items that are 1 KB in size

4: Strongly consistent reads of 15 RCUs reading items that are 1KB in size

Answer: 1

Explanation:

In this scenario the Developer needs to maximize efficiency of RCUs. Therefore, the Developer will need to consider the item size and consistency model to determine the most efficient usage of RCUs.

Item size/consistency model: we know that both 1 KB items and 4 KB items consume the same number of RCUs as a *read capacity unit* represents one strongly consistent read per second, or two eventually consistent reads per second, for an item up to 4 KB in size.

The following bullets provide the read throughput for each configuration:

- Eventually consistent, 15 RCUs, 1 KB item = 30 items/s = 2 items per RCU
- Strongly consistent, 15 RCUs, 1 KB item = 15 items/s = 1 item per RCU
- Eventually consistent, 5 RCUs, 4 KB item = 10 items/s = 2 items per RCU
- Strongly consistent, 5 RCUs, 4 KB item = 5 items/s = 1 item per RCU

From the above we can see that 4 KB items with eventually consistent reads is the most efficient option. Therefore, the Developer should choose the option "Eventually consistent reads of 5 RCUs reading items that are 4 KB in size". This will achieve 2x 4 KB items per RCU.

CORRECT: "Eventually consistent reads of 5 RCUs reading items that are 4 KB in size" is the correct answer.

INCORRECT: "Eventually consistent reads of 15 RCUs reading items that are 1 KB in size" is incorrect as described above.

INCORRECT: "Strongly consistent reads of 5 RCUs reading items that are 4 KB in size" is incorrect as described above.

INCORRECT: "Strongly consistent reads of 15 RCUs reading items that are 1KB in size" is incorrect as described above.

31. Question

The source code for an application is stored in a file named index.js that is in a folder along with a template file that includes the following code:

AWSTemplateFormatVersion: '2010-09-09'

Transform: 'AWS::Serverless-2016-10-31'

Resources:

  LambdaFunctionWithAPI:

   Type: AWS::Serverless::Function

   Properties:

    Handler: index.handler

    Runtime: nodejs12.x

What does a Developer need to do to prepare the template so it can be deployed using an AWS CLI command?

1: Run the aws cloudformation compile command to base64 encode and embed the source file into a modified CloudFormation template

2: Run the aws cloudformation package command to upload the source code to an Amazon S3 bucket and produce a modified CloudFormation template

3: Run the aws lambda zip command to package the source file together with the CloudFormation template and deploy the resulting zip archive

4: Run the aws serverless create-package command to embed the source file directly into the existing CloudFormation template

Answer: 2

Explanation:

The template shown is an AWS SAM template for deploying a serverless application. This can be identified by the template header: *Transform: 'AWS::Serverless-2016-10-31'*

The Developer will need to package and then deploy the template. To do this the source code must be available in the same directory or referenced using the "codeuri" parameter. Then, the Developer can use the "aws cloudformation package" or "sam package" commands to prepare the local artifacts (local paths) that your AWS CloudFormation template references.

The command uploads local artifacts, such as source code for an AWS Lambda function or a Swagger file for an AWS API Gateway REST API, to an S3 bucket. The command returns a copy of your template, replacing references to local artifacts with the S3 location where the command uploaded the artifacts.

Once that is complete the template can be deployed using the "aws cloudformation deploy" or "sam deploy" commands. Therefore, the next step in this scenario is for the Developer to run the "aws cloudformation" package command to upload the source code to an Amazon S3 bucket and produce a modified CloudFormation template. An example of this command is provided below:

aws cloudformation package --template-file /path_to_template/template.json --s3-bucket bucket-name --output-template-file packaged-template.json

CORRECT: "Run the aws cloudformation package command to upload the source code to an Amazon S3 bucket and produce a modified CloudFormation template" is the correct answer.

INCORRECT: "Run the aws cloudformation compile command to base64 encode and embed the source file into a modified CloudFormation template" is incorrect as the Developer should run the "aws cloudformation package" command.

INCORRECT: "Run the aws lambda zip command to package the source file together with the CloudFormation template and deploy the resulting zip archive" is incorrect as the Developer should run the "aws cloudformation package" command which will automatically copy the relevant files to Amazon S3.

INCORRECT: "Run the aws serverless create-package command to embed the source file directly into the existing CloudFormation template" is incorrect as the Developer has the choice to run either "aws cloudformation package" or "sam package", but not "aws serverless create-package".

32. Question

A customer service provider runs a real-time dashboard for monitoring customer request activity. The dashboard relies on an Amazon Kinesis Data Stream and a fleet of Amazon EC2 instances that process the data. Performance metrics have highlighted a number of "cold" shards. What course of action should the company take to minimize the cost of the Kinesis Data Stream?

1: Split the cold shards to increase the capacity of the stream

2: Merge the cold shards to decrease the capacity of the stream

3: Replace the shards with fewer, higher-capacity shards

4: Reduce the number of EC2 instances

Answer: 2

Explanation:

The purpose of resharding in Amazon Kinesis Data Streams is to enable your stream to adapt to changes in the rate of data flow. You split shards to increase the capacity (and cost) of your stream. You merge shards to reduce the cost (and capacity) of your stream.

One approach to resharding could be to split every shard in the stream—which would double the stream's capacity. However, this might provide more additional capacity than you actually need and therefore create unnecessary cost.

You can also use metrics to determine which are your "hot" or "cold" shards, that is, shards that are receiving much more data, or much less data, than expected. You could then selectively split the hot shards to increase capacity for the hash keys that target those shards. Similarly, you could merge cold shards to make better use of their unused capacity.

You can obtain some performance data for your stream from the Amazon CloudWatch metrics that Kinesis Data Streams publishes. However, you can also collect some of your own metrics for your streams. One approach would be to log the hash key values generated by the partition keys for your data records.

For this scenario, the company has identified that there are shards which are underutilized, therefore the best approach to minimizing the cost of the Kinesis Data Stream is to merge the "cold" shards. This will reduce cost as you pay for each shard.

CORRECT: "Merge the cold shards to decrease the capacity of the stream" is the correct answer.

INCORRECT: "Split the cold shards to increase the capacity of the stream" is incorrect as this would increase the cost of the stream as you are charged on a per-shard basis.

INCORRECT: "Replace the shards with fewer, higher-capacity shards" is incorrect you cannot change the capacity of shards. However, it is wise to reduce the number of shards in this scenario.

INCORRECT: "Reduce the number of EC2 instances" is incorrect as this will not reduce the cost of the Kinesis Data Stream (consumers are EC2 instances that process the data). In this case we need to decrease the number of shards as they are underutilized. We also don't know from the question how many EC2 instances there are, the optimum number is equal to the number of shards so decreasing below this ratio would result in not having enough consumers to process the data in the shards.

33. Question

A Developer is creating an application that will include decoupled components. A service is required to receive incoming data from a set of EC2 instances and store it for later processing by another set of EC2 instances. The decoupling service must dynamically scale and provide strict ordering of messages. Which AWS service should the Developer use?

1: Amazon Kinesis Data Streams

2: AWS Step Functions

3: Amazon Simple Queue Service (SQS) with a FIFO queue

4: Amazon Simple Storage Service (S3)

Answer: 3

Explanation:

Amazon Simple Queue Service (Amazon SQS) offers a secure, durable, and available hosted queue that lets you integrate and decouple distributed software systems and components. Amazon SQS can process each buffered request independently, scaling transparently to handle any load increases or spikes without any provisioning instructions.

There are two different types of queue: standard queues and FIFO queues. Standard queues offer best-effort ordering whereas first-in-first-out (FIFO) queues offer strict preservation of the message order.

Therefore, Amazon SQS with a FIFO queue is a perfect solution for this scenario as it will provide a decoupling service that scales dynamically and provides strict preservation of the message order.

CORRECT: "Amazon Simple Queue Service (SQS) with a FIFO queue" is the correct answer.

INCORRECT: "Amazon Kinesis Data Streams" is incorrect as though you can use Kinesis Data Streams for decoupling, and it does provide ordering at the shard level, it does not scale dynamically (you must add shards).

INCORRECT: "AWS Step Functions" is incorrect as this is a service that is used for coordinating serverless workflows.

INCORRECT: "Amazon Simple Storage Service (S3)" is incorrect as though you could create a decoupled and scalable solution for messages between application components using S3, it does not offer any capability in S3 itself for preserving the order of messages. Therefore, you would need to add logic to your application.

34. Question

A Developer is using AWS SAM to create a template for deploying a serverless application. The Developer plans deploy an AWS Lambda function and an Amazon DynamoDB table using the template. Which resource types should the Developer specify? (Select TWO)

1: AWS::Serverless::Application

2: AWS::Serverless:Function

3: AWS::Serverless:LayerVersion

4: AWS::Serverless:API

5: AWS::Serverless::SimpleTable

Answer: 2,5

Explanation:

A **serverless application** is a combination of Lambda functions, event sources, and other resources that work together to perform tasks. Note that a serverless application is more than just a Lambda function—it can include additional resources such as APIs, databases, and event source mappings.

AWS SAM templates are an extension of AWS CloudFormation templates, with some additional components that make them easier to work with.

To create a Lambda function using an AWS SAM template the Developer can use the AWS::Serverless::Function resource type. The AWS::Serverless::Function resource type can be used to Create a Lambda function, IAM execution role, and event source mappings that trigger the function.

To create a DynamoDB table using an AWS SAM template the Developer can use the AWS::Serverless::SimpleTable resource type which creates a DynamoDB table with a single attribute primary key. It is useful when data only needs to be accessed via a primary key.

CORRECT: "AWS::Serverless:Function" is a correct answer.

CORRECT: "AWS::Serverless:SimpleTable" is also a correct answer.

INCORRECT: "AWS::Serverless::Application" is incorrect as this embeds a serverless application from the AWS Serverless Application Repository or from an Amazon S3 bucket as a nested application.

INCORRECT: "AWS::Serverless:LayerVersion" is incorrect as this creates a Lambda LayerVersion that contains library or runtime code needed by a Lambda Function.

INCORRECT: "AWS::Serverless:API" is incorrect as this creates a collection of Amazon API Gateway resources and methods that can be invoked through HTTPS endpoints.

35. Question

An application is being migrated into the cloud. The application is stateless and will run on a fleet of Amazon EC2 instances. The application should scale elastically. How can a Developer ensure that the number of instances available is sufficient for current demand?

1: Create a launch configuration and use Amazon CodeDeploy

2: Create a task definition and use an Amazon ECS cluster

3: Create a launch configuration and use Amazon EC2 Auto Scaling

4: Create a task definition and use an AWS Fargate cluster

Answer: 3

Explanation:

Amazon EC2 Auto Scaling helps you maintain application availability and allows you to automatically add or remove EC2 instances according to conditions you define. You can use the fleet management features of EC2 Auto Scaling to maintain the health and availability of your fleet.

You can also use the dynamic and predictive scaling features of EC2 Auto Scaling to add or remove EC2 instances. Dynamic scaling responds to changing demand and predictive scaling automatically schedules the right number of EC2 instances based on predicted demand. Dynamic scaling and predictive scaling can be used together to scale faster.

A *launch configuration* is an instance configuration template that an Auto Scaling group uses to launch EC2 instances. When you create a launch configuration, you specify information for the instances. Include the ID of the Amazon Machine Image (AMI), the instance type, a key pair, one or more security groups, and a block device mapping. If you've launched an EC2 instance before, you specified the same information in order to launch the instance.

You can specify your launch configuration with multiple Auto Scaling groups. However, you can only specify one launch configuration for an Auto Scaling group at a time, and you can't modify a launch configuration after you've created it. To change the launch configuration for an Auto Scaling group, you must create a launch configuration and then update your Auto Scaling group with it.

Therefore, the Developer should create a launch configuration and use Amazon EC2 Auto Scaling.

CORRECT: "Create a launch configuration and use Amazon EC2 Auto Scaling" is the correct answer.

INCORRECT: "Create a launch configuration and use Amazon CodeDeploy" is incorrect as CodeDeploy is not used for auto scaling of Amazon EC2 instances.

INCORRECT: "Create a task definition and use an Amazon ECS cluster" is incorrect as the migrated application will be running on Amazon EC2 instances, not containers.

INCORRECT: "Create a task definition and use an AWS Fargate cluster" is incorrect as the migrated application will be running on Amazon EC2 instances, not containers.

36. Question

An application uses an Auto Scaling group of Amazon EC2 instances, an Application Load Balancer (ALB), and an Amazon Simple Queue Service (SQS) queue. An Amazon CloudFront distribution caches content for global users. A Developer needs to add in-transit encryption to the data by configuring end-to-end SSL between the CloudFront Origin and the end users. How can the Developer meet this requirement? (Select TWO)

1: Configure the Origin Protocol Policy

2: Create an Origin Access Identity (OAI)

3: Add a certificate to the Auto Scaling Group

4: Configure the Viewer Protocol Policy

5: Create an encrypted distribution

Answer: 1,4

Explanation:

For web distributions, you can configure CloudFront to require that viewers use HTTPS to request your objects, so that connections are encrypted when CloudFront communicates with viewers. You also can configure CloudFront to use HTTPS to get objects from your origin, so that connections are encrypted when CloudFront communicates with your origin.

If you configure CloudFront to require HTTPS both to communicate with viewers and to communicate with your origin, here's what happens when CloudFront receives a request for an object:

1. A viewer submits an HTTPS request to CloudFront. There's some SSL/TLS negotiation here between the viewer and CloudFront. In the end, the viewer submits the request in an encrypted format.

2. If the object is in the CloudFront edge cache, CloudFront encrypts the response and returns it to the viewer, and the viewer decrypts it.

3. If the object is not in the CloudFront cache, CloudFront performs SSL/TLS negotiation with your origin and, when the negotiation is complete, forwards the request to your origin in an encrypted format.

4. Your origin decrypts the request, encrypts the requested object, and returns the object to CloudFront.

5. CloudFront decrypts the response, re-encrypts it, and forwards the object to the viewer. CloudFront also saves the object in the edge cache so that the object is available the next time it's requested.

6. The viewer decrypts the response.

To enable SSL between the origin and the distribution the Developer can configure the Origin Protocol Policy. Depending on the domain name used (CloudFront default or custom), the steps are different. To enable SSL between the end-user and CloudFront the Viewer Protocol Policy should be configured.

CORRECT: "Configure the Origin Protocol Policy" is a correct answer.

CORRECT: "Configure the Viewer Protocol Policy" is also a correct answer.

INCORRECT: "Create an Origin Access Identity (OAI)" is incorrect as this is a special user used for securing objects in Amazon S3 origins.

INCORRECT: "Add a certificate to the Auto Scaling Group" is incorrect as you do not add certificates to an ASG. The certificate should be located on the ALB listener in this scenario.

INCORRECT: "Create an encrypted distribution" is incorrect as there's no such thing as an encrypted distribution

37. Question

A Developer is creating a microservices architecture for a modern application. The application will run on Docker containers. The Developer requires a serverless service. Which AWS service is MOST suitable?

1: Amazon ECS

2: AWS Elastic Beanstalk

3: AWS Lambda

4: AWS Fargate

Answer: 4

Explanation:

AWS Fargate is a serverless compute engine for Docker containers that works with both Amazon Elastic Container Service (ECS) and Amazon Elastic Kubernetes Service (EKS). Fargate makes it easy for you to focus on building your applications. Fargate removes the need to provision and manage servers, lets you specify and pay for resources per application, and improves security through application isolation by design.

AWS Fargate is serverless, however, the EC2 launch type requires the management of EC2 instances. Therefore, the most suitable service for the Developer's requirements is AWS Fargate.

CORRECT: "AWS Fargate" is the correct answer.

INCORRECT: "Amazon ECS" is incorrect as this is not a serverless service, it requires the launching and management of EC2 instances.

INCORRECT: "AWS Elastic Beanstalk" is incorrect as this is also not a serverless service. It uses EC2 instances that are partially managed for you but must be scaled.

INCORRECT: "AWS Lambda" is incorrect as though this is a serverless service, it is not used for running Docker containers.

38. Question

A Developer needs to create an instance profile for an Amazon EC2 instance using the AWS CLI. How can this be achieved? (Select THREE)

1: Run the aws iam create-instance-profile command

2: Run the CreateInstanceProfile API

3: Run the aws iam add-role-to-instance-profile command

4: Run the AddRoleToInstanceProfile API

5: Run the aws ec2 associate-instance-profile command

6: Run the AssignInstanceProfile API

Answer: 1,3,5

Explanation:

To add a role to an Amazon EC2 instance using the AWS CLI you must first create an instance profile. Then you need to add the role to the instance profile and finally assign the instance profile to the Amazon EC2 instance.

The following example commands would achieve this outcome:

1. aws iam create-instance-profile --instance-profile-name EXAMPLEPROFILENAME
2. aws iam add-role-to-instance-profile --instance-profile-name EXAMPLEPROFILENAME --role-name EXAMPLEROLENAME
3. aws ec2 associate-iam-instance-profile --iam-instance-profile Name=EXAMPLEPROFILENAME --instance-id i-012345678910abcde

CORRECT: "Run the aws iam create-instance-profile command" is a correct answer.

CORRECT: "Run the aws iam add-role-to-instance-profile command" is a correct answer.

CORRECT: "Run the aws ec2 associate-instance-profile command" is a correct answer.

INCORRECT: "Run the CreateInstanceProfile API" is incorrect as this is an API action, not an AWS CLI command.

INCORRECT: "Run the AddRoleToInstanceProfile API" is incorrect as this is an API action, not an AWS CLI command.

INCORRECT: "Run the AssignInstanceProfile API" is incorrect as this is an API action, not an AWS CLI command.

39. Question

An application will use AWS Lambda and an Amazon RDS database. The Developer needs to secure the database connection string and enable automatic rotation every 30 days. What is the SIMPLEST way to achieve this requirement?

1: Store a SecureString in Systems Manager Parameter Store and enable automatic rotation every 30 days

2: Store the connection string as an encrypted environment variable in Lambda and create a separate function that rotates the connection string every 30 days

3: Store a secret in AWS Secrets Manager and enable automatic rotation every 30 days

4: Store the connection string in an encrypted Amazon S3 bucket and use a scheduled CloudWatch Event to update the connection string every 30 days

Answer: 3

Explanation:

AWS Secrets Manager encrypts secrets at rest using encryption keys that you own and store in AWS Key Management Service (KMS). When you retrieve a secret, Secrets Manager decrypts the secret and transmits it securely over TLS to your local environment.

With AWS Secrets Manager, you can rotate secrets on a schedule or on demand by using the Secrets Manager console, AWS SDK, or AWS CLI.

For example, to rotate a database password, you provide the database type, rotation frequency, and master database credentials when storing the password in Secrets Manager. Secrets Manager natively supports rotating credentials for databases hosted on Amazon RDS and Amazon DocumentDB and clusters hosted on Amazon Redshift.

CORRECT: "Store a secret in AWS Secrets Manager and enable automatic rotation every 30 days" is the correct answer.

INCORRECT: "Store a SecureString in Systems Manager Parameter Store and enable automatic rotation every 30 days" is incorrect as SSM Parameter Store does not support automatic key rotation.

INCORRECT: "Store the connection string as an encrypted environment variable in Lambda and create a separate function that rotates the connection string every 30 days" is incorrect as this is not the simplest solution. In this scenario using AWS Secrets Manager would be easier to implement as it provides native features for rotating the secret.

INCORRECT: "Store the connection string in an encrypted Amazon S3 bucket and use a scheduled CloudWatch Event to update the connection string every 30 days" is incorrect. There is no native capability of CloudWatch to update connection strings so you would need some other service such as a Lambda function to execute and rotate the connection string which is missing from this answer.

40. Question

A Developer needs to choose the best data store for a new application. The application requires a data store that supports key/value pairs and optimistic locking. Which of the following would provide the MOST suitable solution?

1: Amazon RDS

2: Amazon RedShift

3: Amazon DynamoDB

4: Amazon S3

Answer: 3

Explanation:

Amazon DynamoDB is a key-value and document database that delivers single-digit millisecond performance at any scale. *Optimistic locking* is a strategy to ensure that the client-side item that you are updating (or deleting) is the same as the item in Amazon DynamoDB. If you use this strategy, your database writes are protected from being overwritten by the writes of others, and vice versa.

With optimistic locking, each item has an attribute that acts as a version number. If you retrieve an item from a table, the application records the version number of that item. You can update the item, but only if the version number on the server side has not changed. If there is a version mismatch, it means that someone else has modified the item before you did.

In the diagram below, the application on the left updates an item and increments the version number. Then, the application on the right attempts to update the item but only if the version number is 1.

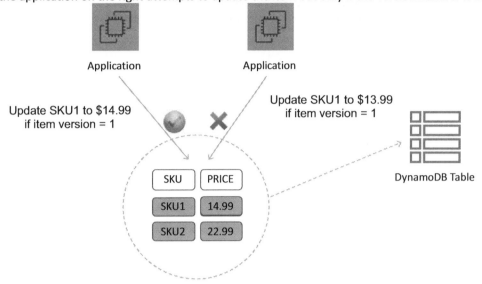

The update attempt fails, because the application has a stale version of the item. Optimistic locking prevents you from accidentally overwriting changes that were made by others. It also prevents others from accidentally overwriting your changes.

CORRECT: "Amazon DynamoDB" is the correct answer.

INCORRECT: "Amazon RDS" is incorrect as RDS is not a key/value database, nor does it support optimistic locking.

INCORRECT: "Amazon RedShift" is incorrect as RedShift is not a key/value database, nor does it support optimistic locking.

INCORRECT: "Amazon S3" is incorrect as though it does store objects as key/value pairs it does not support optimistic locking.

41. Question

A financial application is hosted on an Auto Scaling group of EC2 instance with an Elastic Load Balancer. A Developer needs to capture information about the IP traffic going to and from network interfaces in the VPC. How can the Developer capture this information?

1: Capture the information directly into Amazon CloudWatch Logs

2: Create a flow log in the VPC and publish data to Amazon S3

3: Capture the information using a Network ACL

4: Create a flow log in the VPC and publish data to Amazon CloudTrail

Answer: 2

Explanation:

VPC Flow Logs is a feature that enables you to capture information about the IP traffic going to and from network interfaces in your VPC. Flow log data can be published to Amazon CloudWatch Logs or Amazon S3. After you've created a flow log, you can retrieve and view its data in the chosen destination.

Flow logs can help you with a number of tasks, such as:

- Diagnosing overly restrictive security group rules

- Monitoring the traffic that is reaching your instance

- Determining the direction of the traffic to and from the network interfaces

As you can see in the image below, you can create a flow log for a VPC, a subnet, or a network interface. If you create a flow log for a subnet or VPC, each network interface in that subnet or VPC is monitored.

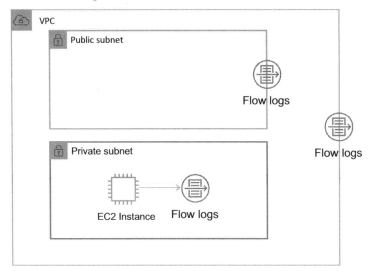

Therefore, the Developer should create a flow log in the VPC and publish data to Amazon S3. The Developer could also choose CloudWatch Logs as a destination for publishing the data, but this is not presented as an option.

CORRECT: "Create a flow log in the VPC and publish data to Amazon S3" is the correct answer.

INCORRECT: "Capture the information directly into Amazon CloudWatch Logs" is incorrect as you cannot capture this information directly into CloudWatch Logs. You would need to capture with a flow log and then publish to CloudWatch Logs.

INCORRECT: "Capture the information using a Network ACL" is incorrect as you cannot capture data using a Network ACL as it is a subnet-level firewall.

INCORRECT: "Create a flow log in the VPC and publish data to Amazon CloudTrail" is incorrect as you cannot publish data from a flow log to CloudTrail. Amazon CloudTrail captures information about API calls.

42. Question

A Developer is designing a cloud native application. The application will use several AWS Lambda functions that will process items that the functions read from an event source. Which AWS services are supported for Lambda event source mappings? (Select THREE)

1: Amazon Kinesis

2: Amazon Simple Notification Service (SNS)

3: Amazon DynamoDB

4: Amazon Simple Queue Service (SQS)

5: Amazon Simple Storage Service (S3)

6: Another Lambda function

Answer: 1,3,4

Explanation:

An event source mapping is an AWS Lambda resource that reads from an event source and invokes a Lambda function. You can use event source mappings to process items from a stream or queue in services that don't invoke Lambda functions directly. Lambda provides event source mappings for the following services.

Services That Lambda Reads Events From

- Amazon Kinesis
- Amazon DynamoDB
- Amazon Simple Queue Service

An event source mapping uses permissions in the function's execution role to read and manage items in the event source. Permissions, event structure, settings, and polling behavior vary by event source.

CORRECT: "Amazon Kinesis, Amazon DynamoDB, and Amazon Simple Queue Service (SQS)" are the correct answers.

INCORRECT: "Amazon Simple Notification Service (SNS)" is incorrect as SNS should be used as destination for asynchronous invocation.

INCORRECT: "Amazon Simple Storage Service (S3)" is incorrect as Lambda does not read from Amazon S3, you must configure the event notification on the S3 side.

INCORRECT: "Another Lambda function" is incorrect as another function should be invoked asynchronously.

43. Question

An application is instrumented to generate traces using AWS X-Ray and generates a large amount of trace data. A Developer would like to use filter expressions to filter the results to specific key-value pairs added to custom subsegments. How should the Developer add the key-value pairs to the custom subsegments?

1: Add metadata to the custom subsegments

2: Add annotations to the custom subsegments

3: Add the key-value pairs to the Trace ID

4: Setup sampling for the custom subsegments

Answer: 2

Explanation:

You can record additional information about requests, the environment, or your application with annotations and metadata. You can add annotations and metadata to the segments that the X-Ray SDK creates, or to custom subsegments that you create.

Annotations are key-value pairs with string, number, or Boolean values. Annotations are indexed for use with filter expressions. Use annotations to record data that you want to use to group traces in the console, or when calling the GetTraceSummaries API.

Metadata are key-value pairs that can have values of any type, including objects and lists, but are not indexed for use with filter expressions. Use metadata to record additional data that you want stored in the trace but don't need to use with search.

Annotations can be used with filter expressions, so this is the best solution for this requirement. The Developer can add annotations to the custom subsegments and will then be able to use filter expressions to filter the results in AWS X-Ray.

CORRECT: "Add annotations to the custom subsegments" is the correct answer.

INCORRECT: "Add metadata to the custom subsegments" is incorrect as though you can add metadata to custom subsegments it is not indexed and cannot be used with filters.

INCORRECT: "Add the key-value pairs to the Trace ID" is incorrect as this is not something you can do.

INCORRECT: "Setup sampling for the custom subsegments " is incorrect as this is a mechanism used by X-Ray to send only statistically significant data samples to the API.

44. Question

A website is running on a single Amazon EC2 instance. A Developer wants to publish the website on the Internet and is creating an A record on Amazon Route 53 for the website's public DNS name. What type of IP address MUST be assigned to the EC2 instance and used in the A record to ensure ongoing connectivity?

1: Public IP address

2: Dynamic IP address

3: Elastic IP address

4: Private IP address

Answer: 3

Explanation:

In Amazon Route 53 when you create an A record you must supply an IP address for the resource to connect to. For a public hosted zone this must be a public IP address.

There are three types of IP address that can be assigned to an Amazon EC2 instance:

- Public – public address that is assigned automatically to instances in public subnets and reassigned if instance is stopped/started.
- Private – private address assigned automatically to all instances.
- Elastic IP – public address that is static.

To ensure ongoing connectivity the Developer needs to use an Elastic IP address for the EC2 instance and DNS A record as this is the only type of static, public IP address you can assign to an Amazon EC2 instance.

CORRECT: "Elastic IP address" is the correct answer.

INCORRECT: "Public IP address" is incorrect as though this is a public IP address, it is not static and will change every time the EC2 instance restarts. Therefore, connectivity would be lost until you update the Route 53 A record.

INCORRECT: "Dynamic IP address" is incorrect as a dynamic IP address is an IP address that will change over time. For this scenario a static, public address is required.

INCORRECT: "Private IP address" is incorrect as a public IP address is required for the public DNS A record.

45. Question

A company needs a version control system for collaborative software development. The solution must include support for batches of changes across multiple files and parallel branching. Which AWS service will meet these requirements?

1: AWS CodePipeline

2: Amazon S3

3: AWS CodeBuild

4: AWS CodeCommit

Answer: 4

Explanation:

AWS CodeCommit is a version control service hosted by Amazon Web Services that you can use to privately store and manage assets (such as documents, source code, and binary files) in the cloud.

CodeCommit is optimized for team software development. It manages batches of changes across multiple files, which can occur in parallel with changes made by other developers.

CORRECT: "AWS CodeCommit" is the correct answer.

INCORRECT: "AWS CodeBuild" is incorrect as it is a fully managed continuous integration service that compiles source code, runs tests, and produces software packages that are ready to deploy.

INCORRECT: "AWS CodePipeline" is incorrect as it is a fully managed <u>continuous delivery</u> service that helps you automate your release pipelines for fast and reliable application and infrastructure updates.

INCORRECT: "Amazon S3" is incorrect. Amazon S3 versioning supports the recovery of past versions of files, but it's not focused on collaborative file tracking features that software development teams need.

46. Question

To include objects defined by the AWS Serverless Application Model (SAM) in an AWS CloudFormation template, in addition to Resources, what section MUST be included in the document root?

1: Conditions

2: Globals

3: Transform

4: Properties

Answer: 3

Explanation:

The primary differences between AWS SAM templates and AWS CloudFormation templates are the following:

- **Transform declaration.** The declaration Transform: AWS::Serverless-2016-10-31 is required for AWS SAM templates. This declaration identifies an AWS CloudFormation template as an AWS SAM template.

- **Globals section.** The Globals section is unique to AWS SAM. It defines properties that are common to all your serverless functions and APIs. All the AWS::Serverless::Function, AWS::Serverless::Api, and AWS::Serverless::SimpleTable resources inherit the properties that are defined in the Globals section.

- **Resources section.** In AWS SAM templates the Resources section can contain a combination of AWS CloudFormation resources and AWS SAM resources.

Of these three sections, only the Transform section and Resources sections are required; the Globals section is optional.

CORRECT: "Transform" is the correct answer.

INCORRECT: "Globals" is incorrect as this is not a required section.

INCORRECT: "Conditions" is incorrect as this is an optional section.

INCORRECT: "Properties" is incorrect as this is not a section in a template, it is used within a resource.

47. Question

A company is creating an application that will require users to access AWS services and allow them to reset their own passwords. Which of the following would allow the company to manage users and authorization while allowing users to reset their own passwords?

1: Amazon Cognito identity pools and AWS STS

2: Amazon Cognito identity pools and AWS IAM

3: Amazon Cognito user pools and AWS KMS

4: Amazon Cognito user pools and identity pools

Answer: 4

Explanation:

There are two key requirements in this scenario. Firstly the company wants to manage user accounts using a system that allows users to reset their own passwords. The company also wants to authorize users to access AWS services.

The first requirement is provided by an Amazon Cognito User Pool. With a Cognito user pool you can add sign-up and sign-in to mobile and web apps and it also offers a user directory so user accounts can be created directly within the user pool. Users also have the ability to reset their passwords.

To access AWS services you need a Cognito Identity Pool. An identity pool can be used with a user pool and enables a user to obtain temporary limited-privilege credentials to access AWS services.

Therefore, the best answer is to use Amazon Cognito user pools and identity pools.

CORRECT: "Amazon Cognito user pools and identity pools" is the correct answer.

INCORRECT: "Amazon Cognito identity pools and AWS STS" is incorrect as there is no user directory in this solution. A Cognito user pool is required.

INCORRECT: "Amazon Cognito identity pools and AWS IAM" is incorrect as a Cognito user pool should be used as the directory source for creating and managing users. IAM is used for accounts that are used to administer AWS services, not for application user access.

INCORRECT: "Amazon Cognito user pools and AWS KMS" is incorrect as KMS is used for encryption, not for authentication to AWS services.

48. Question

An application writes items to an Amazon DynamoDB table. As the application scales to thousands of instances, calls to the DynamoDB API generate occasional ThrottlingException errors. The application is coded in a language incompatible with the AWS SDK. How should the error be handled?

1: Add exponential backoff to the application logic

2: Use Amazon SQS as an API message bus

3: Pass API calls through Amazon API Gateway

4: Send the items to DynamoDB through Amazon Kinesis Data Firehose

Answer: 1

Explanation:

Exponential backoff can improve an application's reliability by using progressively longer waits between retries. When using the AWS SDK, this logic is built-in. However, in this case the application is incompatible with the AWS SDK so it is necessary to manually implement exponential backoff.

CORRECT: "Add exponential backoff to the application logic" is the correct answer.

INCORRECT: "Use Amazon SQS as an API message bus" is incorrect as SQS requires instances or functions to pick up and process the messages and put them in the DynamoDB table. This is unnecessary cost and complexity and will not improve performance.

INCORRECT: "Pass API calls through Amazon API Gateway" is incorrect as this is not a suitable method of throttling the application. Exponential backoff logic in the application is a better solution.

INCORRECT: "Send the items to DynamoDB through Amazon Kinesis Data Firehose" is incorrect as DynamoDB is not a destination for Kinesis Data Firehose.

49. Question

A Development team has deployed several applications running on an Auto Scaling fleet of Amazon EC2 instances. The Operations team have asked for a display that shows a key performance metric for each

application on a single screen for monitoring purposes. What steps should a Developer take to deliver this capability using Amazon CloudWatch?

1: Create a custom namespace with a unique metric name for each application

2: Create a custom dimension with a unique metric name for each application

3: Create a custom event with a unique metric name for each application

4: Create a custom alarm with a unique metric name for each application

Answer: 1

Explanation:

A *namespace* is a container for CloudWatch metrics. Metrics in different namespaces are isolated from each other, so that metrics from different applications are not mistakenly aggregated into the same statistics.

Therefore, the Developer should create a custom namespace with a unique metric name for each application. This namespace will then allow the metrics for each individual application to be shown in a single view through CloudWatch.

CORRECT: "Create a custom namespace with a unique metric name for each application" is the correct answer.

INCORRECT: "Create a custom dimension with a unique metric name for each application" is incorrect as a dimension further clarifies what a metric is and what data it stores.

INCORRECT: "Create a custom event with a unique metric name for each application" is incorrect as an event is not used to organize metrics for display.

INCORRECT: "Create a custom alarm with a unique metric name for each application" is incorrect as alarms are used to trigger actions when a threshold is reached, this is not relevant to organizing metrics for display.

50. Question

A Developer is storing sensitive documents in Amazon S3. The documents must be encrypted at rest and company policy mandates that the encryption keys must be rotated annually. What is the EASIEST way to achieve this?

1: Encrypt the data before sending it to Amazon S3

2: Import a custom key into AWS KMS with annual rotation enabled

3: Use AWS KMS with automatic key rotation

4: Export a key from AWS KMS to encrypt the data

Answer: 3

Explanation:

Cryptographic best practices discourage extensive reuse of encryption keys. To create new cryptographic material for your AWS Key Management Service (AWS KMS) customer master keys (CMKs), you can create new CMKs, and then change your applications or aliases to use the new CMKs. Or, you can enable automatic key rotation for an existing customer managed CMK.

When you enable *automatic key rotation* for a customer managed CMK, AWS KMS generates new cryptographic material for the CMK every year. AWS KMS also saves the CMK's older cryptographic material in perpetuity so it can be used to decrypt data that it encrypted. AWS KMS does not delete any rotated key material until you delete the CMK.

Key rotation changes only the CMK's *backing key*, which is the cryptographic material that is used in encryption operations. The CMK is the same logical resource, regardless of whether or how many times its backing key changes. The properties of the CMK do not change.

Therefore, the easiest way to meet this requirement is to use AWS KMS with automatic key rotation.

CORRECT: "Use AWS KMS with automatic key rotation" is the correct answer.

INCORRECT: "Encrypt the data before sending it to Amazon S3" is incorrect as that requires managing your own encryption infrastructure which is not the easiest way to achieve the requirements.

INCORRECT: "Import a custom key into AWS KMS with annual rotation enabled" is incorrect as when you import key material into AWS KMS you are still responsible for the key material while allowing KMS to use a copy of it. Therefore, this is not the easiest solution as you must manage the key materials.

INCORRECT: "Export a key from AWS KMS to encrypt the data" is incorrect as when you export a data encryption key you are then responsible for using it and managing it.

51. Question

A Developer is designing a fault-tolerant environment where client sessions will be saved. How can the Developer ensure that no sessions are lost if an Amazon EC2 instance fails?

1: Use sticky sessions with an Elastic Load Balancer target group

2: Use Amazon SQS to save session data

3: Use Amazon DynamoDB to perform scalable session handling

4: Use Elastic Load Balancer connection draining to stop sending requests to failing instances

Answer: 3

Explanation:

The **DynamoDB Session Handler** is a custom session handler for PHP that allows developers to use Amazon DynamoDB as a session store. Using DynamoDB for session storage alleviates issues that occur with session handling in a distributed web application by moving sessions off of the local file system and into a shared location. DynamoDB is fast, scalable, easy to setup, and handles replication of your data automatically.

CORRECT: "Use Amazon DynamoDB to perform scalable session handling" is the correct answer.

INCORRECT: "Use sticky sessions with an Elastic Load Balancer target group" is incorrect as this involves maintaining session state data on the EC2 instances which means that data is lost if an instance fails.

INCORRECT: "Use Amazon SQS to save session data" is incorrect as SQS is not used for session data, it is used for application component decoupling.

INCORRECT: "Use Elastic Load Balancer connection draining to stop sending requests to failing instances" is incorrect as this does not solve the problem of ensuring the session data is available, the data will be on the failing instance and will be lost.

52. Question

A company wants to implement authentication for its new REST service using Amazon API Gateway. To authenticate the calls, each request must include HTTP headers with a client ID and user ID. These credentials must be compared to authentication data in an Amazon DynamoDB table. What MUST the company do to implement this authentication in API Gateway?

1: Implement an AWS Lambda authorizer that references the DynamoDB authentication table

2: Create a model that requires the credentials, then grant API Gateway access to the authentication table

3: Modify the integration requests to require the credentials, then grant API Gateway access to the authentication table

4: Implement an Amazon Cognito authorizer that references the DynamoDB authentication table

Answer: 1

Explanation:

A *Lambda authorizer* (formerly known as a *custom authorizer*) is an API Gateway feature that uses a Lambda function to control access to your API.

A Lambda authorizer is useful if you want to implement a custom authorization scheme that uses a bearer token authentication strategy such as OAuth or SAML, or that uses request parameters to determine the caller's identity.

When a client makes a request to one of your API's methods, API Gateway calls your Lambda authorizer, which takes the caller's identity as input and returns an IAM policy as output.

There are two types of Lambda authorizers:

- A *token-based* Lambda authorizer (also called a TOKEN authorizer) receives the caller's identity in a bearer token, such as a JSON Web Token (JWT) or an OAuth token.

- A *request parameter-based* Lambda authorizer (also called a REQUEST authorizer) receives the caller's identity in a combination of headers, query string parameters, stageVariables, and $context variables.

- For WebSocket APIs, only request parameter-based authorizers are supported.

In this scenario, the authentication is using headers in the request and therefore the request parameter-based Lambda authorizer should be used.

CORRECT: "Implement an AWS Lambda authorizer that references the DynamoDB authentication table" is the correct answer.

INCORRECT: "Create a model that requires the credentials, then grant API Gateway access to the authentication table" is incorrect as a model defines the structure of the incoming payload using the JSON Schema.

INCORRECT: "Modify the integration requests to require the credentials, then grant API Gateway access to the authentication table" is incorrect as API Gateway will not authorize directly using the table information, an authorizer should be used.

INCORRECT: "Implement an Amazon Cognito authorizer that references the DynamoDB authentication table" is incorrect as a Lambda authorizer should be used in this example as the authentication data is being passed in request headers.

53. Question

AWS CodeBuild builds code for an application, creates a Docker image, pushes the image to Amazon Elastic Container Registry (ECR), and tags the image with a unique identifier. If the Developers already have AWS CLI configured on their workstations, how can the Docker images be pulled to the workstations?

1: Run the following: docker pull REPOSITORY URI : TAG

2: Run the output of the following: aws ecr get-login, and then run docker pull REPOSITORY URI : TAG

3: Run the following: aws ecr get-login, and then run: docker pull REPOSITORY URI : TAG

4: Run the output of the following: aws ecr get-download-url-for-layer, and then run docker pull REPOSITORY URI : TAG

Answer: 2

Explanation:

If you would like to run a Docker image that is available in Amazon ECR, you can pull it to your local environment with the docker pull command. You can do this from either your default registry or from a registry associated with another AWS account.

Docker CLI does not support standard AWS authentication methods, so client authentication must be handled so that ECR knows who is requesting to push or pull an image. To do this you can issue the aws ec2 get-login or aws ec2 get-login-password (AWS CLI v2) and then use the output to login using docker login and then issue a docker pull command specifying the image name using registry/repository[:tag].

CORRECT: "Run the output of the following: aws ecr get-login, and then run docker pull REPOSITORY URI : TAG" is the correct answer.

INCORRECT: "Run the following: docker pull REPOSITORY URI : TAG" is incorrect as the Developers first need to authenticate before they can pull the image.

INCORRECT: "Run the following: aws ecr get-login, and then run: docker pull REPOSITORY URI : TAG" is incorrect. The Developers need to not just run the login command but run the output of the login command which contains the authentication token required to log in.

INCORRECT: "Run the output of the following: aws ecr get-download-url-for-layer, and then run docker pull REPOSITORY URI : TAG" is incorrect as this command retrieves a pre-signed Amazon S3 download URL corresponding to an image layer.

54. Question

A company needs to ingest several terabytes of data every hour from a large number of distributed sources. The messages are delivered continually 24 hrs a day. Messages must be delivered in real time for security analysis and live operational dashboards. Which approach will meet these requirements?

1: Send the messages to an Amazon SQS queue, then process the messages by using a fleet of Amazon EC2 instances

2: Use the Amazon S3 API to write messages to an S3 bucket, then process the messages by using Amazon RedShift

3: Use AWS Data Pipeline to automate the movement and transformation of data

4: Use Amazon Kinesis Data Streams with Kinesis Client Library to ingest and deliver messages

Answer: 4

Explanation:

You can use Amazon Kinesis Data Streams to collect and process large streams of data records in real time. You can create data-processing applications, known as *Kinesis Data Streams applications*. A typical Kinesis Data Streams application reads data from a *data stream* as data records.

These applications can use the Kinesis Client Library, and they can run on Amazon EC2 instances. You can send the processed records to dashboards, use them to generate alerts, dynamically change pricing and advertising strategies, or send data to a variety of other AWS services.

This scenario is an ideal use case for Kinesis Data Streams as large volumes of real time streaming data are being ingested. Therefore, the best approach is to use Amazon Kinesis Data Streams with Kinesis Client Library to ingest and deliver messages

CORRECT: "Use Amazon Kinesis Data Streams with Kinesis Client Library to ingest and deliver messages" is the correct answer.

INCORRECT: "Send the messages to an Amazon SQS queue, then process the messages by using a fleet of Amazon EC2 instances" is incorrect as this is not an ideal use case for SQS because SQS is used for decoupling application components, not for ingesting streaming data. It would require more cost (lots of instances to process data) and introduce latency. Also, the message size limitations could be an issue.

INCORRECT: "Use the Amazon S3 API to write messages to an S3 bucket, then process the messages by using Amazon RedShift" is incorrect as RedShift does not process messages from S3. RedShift is a data warehouse which is used for analytics.

INCORRECT: "Use AWS Data Pipeline to automate the movement and transformation of data" is incorrect as the question is not asking for transformation of data. The scenario calls for a solution for ingesting and processing the real time streaming data for analytics and feeding some data into a system that generates an operational dashboard.

55. Question

A Developer wants to debug an application by searching and filtering log data. The application logs are stored in Amazon CloudWatch Logs. The Developer creates a new metric filter to count exceptions in the application logs. However, no results are returned from the logs. What is the reason that no filtered results are being returned?

1: A setup of the Amazon CloudWatch interface VPC endpoint is required for filtering the CloudWatch Logs in the VPC

2: CloudWatch Logs only publishes metric data for events that happen after the filter is created

3: The log group for CloudWatch Logs should be first streamed to Amazon Elasticsearch Service before filtering returns the results

4: Metric data points to logs groups can be filtered only after they are exported to an Amazon S3 bucket

Answer: 2

Explanation:

After the CloudWatch Logs agent begins publishing log data to Amazon CloudWatch, you can begin searching and filtering the log data by creating one or more metric filters. Metric filters define the terms and patterns to look for in log data as it is sent to CloudWatch Logs.

CloudWatch Logs uses these metric filters to turn log data into numerical CloudWatch metrics that you can graph or set an alarm on. You can use any type of CloudWatch statistic, including percentile statistics, when viewing these metrics or setting alarms.

Filters do not retroactively filter data. Filters only publish the metric data points for events that happen after the filter was created. Filtered results return the first 50 lines, which will not be displayed if the timestamp on the filtered results is earlier than the metric creation time.

Therefore, the filtered results are not being returned as CloudWatch Logs only publishes metric data for events that happen after the filter is created.

CORRECT: "CloudWatch Logs only publishes metric data for events that happen after the filter is created" is the correct answer.

INCORRECT: "A setup of the Amazon CloudWatch interface VPC endpoint is required for filtering the CloudWatch Logs in the VPC" is incorrect as a VPC endpoint is not required.

INCORRECT: "The log group for CloudWatch Logs should be first streamed to Amazon Elasticsearch Service before filtering returns the results" is incorrect as you do not need to stream the results to Elasticsearch.

INCORRECT: "Metric data points to logs groups can be filtered only after they are exported to an Amazon S3 bucket" is incorrect as it is not necessary to export the logs to an S3 bucket.

56. Question

A serverless application requires a storage location for log files. Which storage solution is the BEST fit?

1: Amazon EBS

2: Amazon EFS

3: Amazon S3

4: Amazon EC2 instance store

Answer: 3

Explanation:

Amazon S3 is an object-based storage system. The serverless application can use the REST API or AWS SDK to write data to an S3 bucket. This is a suitable solution for storing log files from a serverless app at low cost.

CORRECT: "Amazon S3" is the correct answer.

INCORRECT: "Amazon EBS " is incorrect as this is a block-based storage solution in which volumes are attached to EC2 instances so it is not suitable for a serverless application.

INCORRECT: "Amazon EFS" is incorrect as this is file-based storage solution that is mounted from EC2 instances using the NFS protocol. This is not suitable for a serverless application.

INCORRECT: "Amazon EC2 instance store" is incorrect as this is an ephemeral storage volume that is locally attached to EC2 instances from the same physical hardware. It is not suitable for a serverless application.

57. Question

Fault tolerance needs to be increased for a stateless application that runs on Amazon EC2 instances. The application runs in an Auto Scaling group of EC2 instances in a single subnet behind an Application Load Balancer. How can the application be made more fault tolerant?

1: Add a subnet in another AZ to the ASG and add the same subnet to the ALB

2: Add a subnet in another region to the ASG and add the same subnet to the ALB

3: Add an Elastic IP to each instance and use Amazon Route 53 Alias records to distribute incoming connections

4: Add a subnet in another VPC to the ASG and add the same subnet to the ALB

Answer: 1

Explanation:

The application currently resides in a single subnet and that is within a single availability zone. To increase fault tolerance the application instances should be split across subnets that are in different availability zones. This will protect against any faults that occur within a single AZ.

To do this, a subnet in another AZ can be added to both the ASG and the ALB. The ASG will automatically launch instances in the new subnet and try and balance the number of instances between these subnets. The ALB will distribute connections across both subnets/AZs.

CORRECT: "Add a subnet in another AZ to the ASG and add the same subnet to the ALB" is the correct answer.

INCORRECT: "Add a subnet in another region to the ASG and add the same subnet to the ALB" is incorrect as it is not possible to add subnets in different regions to an ASG or ALB.

INCORRECT: "Add an Elastic IP to each instance and use Amazon Route 53 Alias records to distribute incoming connections" is incorrect as this will not increase fault tolerance. The instances would still be in a single subnet/AZ.

INCORRECT: "Add a subnet in another VPC to the ASG and add the same subnet to the ALB" is incorrect as you cannot add a subnet in another VPC to an ASG or ALB.

58. Question

A customer-facing web application runs on Amazon EC2 with an Application Load Balancer and an Amazon RDS database back end. Recently, the security team noticed some SQL injection attacks and cross-site scripting attacks targeting the web application. Which service can a Developer use to protect against future attacks?

1: Security Groups

2: Network ACLs

3: AWS WAF

4: AWS KMS

Answer: 3

Explanation:

AWS WAF is a web application firewall that helps protect your web applications or APIs against common web exploits that may affect availability, compromise security, or consume excessive resources.

AWS WAF gives you control over how traffic reaches your applications by enabling you to create security rules that block common attack patterns, such as SQL injection or cross-site scripting, and rules that filter out specific traffic patterns you define.

CORRECT: "AWS WAF" is the correct answer.

INCORRECT: "AWS KMS" is incorrect as this service is used for creating and managing encryption keys.

INCORRECT: "Security Groups" is incorrect as they are an instance-level firewall. They do not have the ability to prevent SQL injection or cross-site scripting attacks.

INCORRECT: "Network ACLs" is incorrect as this is a subnet-level firewall. It doesn't not have the ability to prevent SQL injection or cross-site scripting attacks.

59. Question

A developer is planning the deployment of a new version of an application to AWS Elastic Beanstalk. The new version of the application should be deployed only to new EC2 instances. Which deployment methods will meet these requirements? (Select TWO)

1: Rolling with additional batch

2: Immutable

3: Rolling

4: All at once

5: Blue/green

Answer: 2,5

Explanation:

AWS Elastic Beanstalk provides several options for how deployments are processed, including deployment policies and options that let you configure batch size and health check behavior during deployments.

All at once:

- Deploys the new version to all instances simultaneously.

Rolling:

- Update a few instances at a time (bucket), and then move onto the next bucket once the first bucket is healthy (downtime for 1 bucket at a time).

Rolling with additional batch:

- Like Rolling but launches new instances in a batch ensuring that there is full availability.

Immutable:

- Launches new instances in a new ASG and deploys the version update to these instances before swapping traffic to these instances once healthy.

- Zero downtime.

Blue / Green deployment:

- Zero downtime and release facility.

- Create a new "stage" environment and deploy updates there.

The immutable and blue/green options both provide zero downtime as they will deploy the new version to a new version of the application. These are also the only two options that will ONLY deploy the updates to new EC2 instances.

CORRECT: "Immutable" is the correct answer.

CORRECT: "Blue/green" is the correct answer.

INCORRECT: "All-at-once" is incorrect as this will deploy the updates to existing instances.

INCORRECT: "Rolling" is incorrect as this will deploy the updates to existing instances.

INCORRECT: "Rolling with additional batch" is incorrect as this will launch new instances but will also update the existing instances as well (which is not allowed according to the requirements).

60. Question

A customer requires a schema-less, key/value database that can be used for storing customer orders. Which type of AWS database is BEST suited to this requirement?

1: Amazon DynamoDB

2: Amazon RDS

3: Amazon ElastiCache

4: Amazon S3

Answer: 1

Explanation:

Amazon DynamoDB is a fully managed NoSQL database service that provides fast and predictable performance with seamless scalability. It is a non-relational (schema-less), key-value type of database. This is the most suitable solution for this requirement.

CORRECT: "Amazon DynamoDB" is the correct answer.

INCORRECT: "Amazon RDS" is incorrect as this a relational database that has a schema.

INCORRECT: "Amazon ElastiCache" is incorrect as this is a key/value database but it is used to cache the contents of other databases (including DynamoDB and RDS) for better performance for reads.

INCORRECT: "Amazon S3" is incorrect as this is an object-based storage system not a database. It is a key/value store but DynamoDB is a better fit for a customer order database.

61. Question

A highly secured AWS environment has strict policies for granting access to Developers. A Developer requires the ability to use the API to call ec2:StartInstances and ec2:StopInstances. Which element of an IAM policy statement should be used to specify which APIs can be called?

1: Action

2: Effect

3: Resource

4: Condition

Answer: 1

Explanation:

The Action element describes the specific action or actions that will be allowed or denied. Statements must include either an Action or NotAction element. Each AWS service has its own set of actions that describe tasks that you can perform with that service.

For this scenario, the Action element might include the following JSON"

```
"Action": [ "ec2:StartInstances", "ec2:StopInstances" ]
```

CORRECT: "Action" is the correct answer.

INCORRECT: "Effect" is incorrect. The Effect element is required and specifies whether the statement results in an allow or an explicit deny.

INCORRECT: "Resource" is incorrect. The Resource element specifies the object or objects that the statement covers.

INCORRECT: "Condition" is incorrect. The Condition element (or Condition *block*) lets you specify conditions for when a policy is in effect.

62. Question

A team of Developers are building a continuous integration and delivery pipeline using AWS Developer Tools. Which services should they use for running tests against source code and installing compiled code on their AWS resources? (Select TWO)

1: AWS CodeBuild for running tests against source code

2: AWS CodeDeploy for installing compiled code on their AWS resources

3: AWS CodePipeline for running tests against source code

4: AWS CodeCommit for installing compiled code on their AWS resources

5: AWS Cloud9 for running tests against source code

Answer: 1,2

Explanation:

AWS CodeBuild is a fully managed build service in the cloud. CodeBuild compiles your source code, runs unit tests, and produces artifacts that are ready to deploy. CodeBuild eliminates the need to provision, manage, and scale your own build servers. It provides pre-packaged build environments for popular programming languages and build tools such as Apache Maven, Gradle, and more.

CodeDeploy is a deployment service that automates application deployments to Amazon EC2 instances, on-premises instances, serverless Lambda functions, or Amazon ECS services.

CORRECT: "AWS CodeBuild for running tests against source code" is a correct answer.

CORRECT: "AWS CodeBuild for running tests against source code" is also a correct answer.

INCORRECT: "AWS CodePipeline for running tests against source code" is incorrect. AWS CodePipeline is a fully managed continuous delivery service that helps you automate your release pipelines for fast and reliable application and infrastructure updates. This service works with the other Developer Tools to create a pipeline.

INCORRECT: "AWS CodeCommit for installing compiled code on their AWS resources" is incorrect as AWS CodeCommit is a fully-managed source control service that hosts secure Git-based repositories.

INCORRECT: "AWS Cloud9 for running tests against source code" is incorrect as AWS Cloud9 is a cloud-based integrated development environment (IDE) that lets you write, run, and debug your code with just a browser.

63. Question

Messages produced by an application must be pushed to multiple Amazon SQS queues. What is the BEST solution for this requirement?

1: Create an Amazon SWF workflow that receives the messages and pushes them to multiple SQS queues

2: Create and AWS Step Functions state machine that uses multiple Lambda functions to process and push the messages into multiple SQS queues

3: Publish the messages to an Amazon SNS topic and subscribe each SQS queue to the topic

4: Publish the messages to an Amazon SQS queue and configure an AWS Lambda function to duplicate the message into multiple queues

Answer: 3

Explanation:

Amazon SNS works closely with Amazon Simple Queue Service (Amazon SQS). Both services provide different benefits for developers. Amazon SNS allows applications to send time-critical messages to multiple subscribers through a "push" mechanism, eliminating the need to periodically check or "poll" for updates.

When you subscribe an Amazon SQS queue to an Amazon SNS topic, you can publish a message to the topic and Amazon SNS sends an Amazon SQS message to the subscribed queue. The Amazon SQS message contains the subject and message that were published to the topic along with metadata about the message in a JSON document.

CORRECT: "Publish the messages to an Amazon SNS topic and subscribe each SQS queue to the topic" is the correct answer.

INCORRECT: "Publish the messages to an Amazon SQS queue and configure an AWS Lambda function to duplicate the message into multiple queues" is incorrect as this seems like an inefficient solution. By using SNS we can eliminate the initial queue and Lambda function.

INCORRECT: "Create an Amazon SWF workflow that receives the messages and pushes them to multiple SQS queues" is incorrect as this is not a workable solution. Amazon SWF is not suitable for pushing messages to SQS queues.

INCORRECT: Create and AWS Step Functions state machine that uses multiple Lambda functions to process and push the messages into multiple SQS queues"" is incorrect as this is an inefficient solution and there is not mention on how the functions will be invoked with the message data

64. Question

An application has been instrumented to use the AWS X-Ray SDK to collect data about the requests the application serves. The Developer has set the user field on segments to a string that identifies the user who sent the request. How can the Developer search for segments associated with specific users?

1: Use a filter expression to search for the user field in the segment metadata

2: By using the GetTraceSummaries API with a filter expression

3: By using the GetTraceGraph API with a filter expression

4: Use a filter expression to search for the user field in the segment annotations

Answer: 2

Explanation:

A **segment document** conveys information about a segment to X-Ray. A segment document can be up to 64 kB and contain a whole segment with subsegments, a fragment of a segment that indicates that a request is in progress, or a single subsegment that is sent separately. You can send segment documents directly to X-Ray by using the PutTraceSegments API.

Example minimally complete segment:

```
{
 "name" : "example.com",
 "id" : "70de5b6f19ff9a0a",
 "start_time" : 1.478293361271E9,
 "trace_id" : "1-581cf771-a006649127e371903a2de979",
 "end_time" : 1.478293361449E9
}
```

A subset of segment fields are indexed by X-Ray for use with filter expressions. For example, if you set the user field on a segment to a unique identifier, you can search for segments associated with specific users in the X-Ray console or by using the GetTraceSummaries API.

CORRECT: "By using the GetTraceSummaries API with a filter expression" is the correct answer.

INCORRECT: "By using the GetTraceGraph API with a filter expression" is incorrect as this API action retrieves a service graph for one or more specific trace IDs.

INCORRECT: "Use a filter expression to search for the user field in the segment metadata" is incorrect as the user field is not part of the segment metadata and metadata is not is not indexed for search.

INCORRECT: "Use a filter expression to search for the user field in the segment annotations" is incorrect as the user field is not part of the segment annotations.

65. Question

The following permissions policy is applied to an IAM user account:

```
{
  "Version": "2012-10-17",
  "Statement": [{
    "Effect": "Allow",
    "Action": "sqs:*",
    "Resource": "arn:aws:sqs:*:513246782345:staging-queue*"
  }]
}
```

Due to this policy, what Amazon SQS actions will the user be able to perform?

1: The user will be able to use all Amazon SQS actions, but only for queues with names begin with the string "staging-queue"

2: The user will be able to create a queue named "staging-queue"

3: The user will be able to apply a resource-based policy to the Amazon SQS queue named "staging-queue"

4: The user will be granted cross-account access from account number "513246782345" to queue "staging-queue"

Answer: 1

Explanation:

The policy allows the user to use all Amazon SQS actions, but only with queues whose names are prefixed with the literal string "staging-queue". This policy is useful to provide a queue creator the ability to use Amazon SQS actions. Any user who has permissions to create a queue must also have permissions to use other Amazon SQS actions in order to do anything with the created queues.

CORRECT: "The user will be able to use all Amazon SQS actions, but only for queues with names begin with the string "staging-queue"" is the correct answer.

INCORRECT: "The user will be able to create a queue named "staging-queue"" is incorrect as this policy provides the permissions to perform SQS actions on an existing queue.

INCORRECT: "The user will be able to apply a resource-based policy to the Amazon SQS queue named "staging-queue"" is incorrect as this is a single operation and the permissions policy allows all SQS actions.

INCORRECT: "The user will be granted cross-account access from account number "513246782345" to queue "staging-queue"" is incorrect as this is not a policy for granting cross-account access. The account number and queue relate to the same account.

SET 4: PRACTICE QUESTIONS ONLY

For training purposes, go directly to Set 4: Practice Questions, Answers & Explanations

1. Question

A developer is completing the configuration for an Amazon ECS cluster. Which task placement strategy will MINIMIZE the number of instances in use?

1: binpack

2: random

3: spread

4: Canary

2. Question

A company is using AWS Lambda for processing small images that are uploaded to Amazon S3. This was working well until a large number of small files (several thousand) were recently uploaded and an error was generated by AWS Lambda (status code 429). What is the MOST likely cause?

1: The concurrency execution limit for the account has been exceeded

2: Amazon S3 could not handle the sudden burst in traffic

3: Lambda cannot process multiple files simultaneously

4: The event source mapping has not been configured

3. Question

A developer is creating a serverless application that will use a DynamoDB table. The average item size is 7KB. The application will make 3 strongly consistent reads/sec, and 1 standard write/sec. How many RCUs/WCUs are required?

1: 3 RCU and 7 WCU

2: 6 RCU and 7 WCU

3: 6 RCU and 14 WCU

4: 12 RCU and 14 WCU

4. Question

A developer is building a multi-tier web application that accesses an Amazon RDS MySQL database. The application must use a credentials to connect and these need to be stored securely. The application will take care of secret rotation. Which AWS service represents the LOWEST cost solution for storing credentials?

1: AWS IAM with the Security Token Service (STS)

2: AWS Secrets Manager

3: AWS Systems Manager Parameter Store

4: AWS Key Management Service (KMS)

5. Question

A mobile application is being developed that will use AWS Lambda, Amazon API Gateway and Amazon DynamoDB. A developer would like to securely authenticate the users of the mobile application and then grant them access to the API. What is the BEST way to achieve this?

1: Create a Lambda authorizer in API Gateway

2: Create a COGNITO_USER_POOLS authorizer in API Gateway

3: Create a COGNITO_IDENTITY_POOLS authorizer in API Gateway

4: Create an IAM authorizer in API Gateway

6. Question
A developer is preparing the resources for creating a multicontainer Docker environment on AWS Elastic Beanstalk. How can the developer define the Docker containers?

1: Define the containers in the Dockerrun.aws.json file in JSON format and save at the root of the source directory

2: Create a Docker.config file and save it in the .ebextensions folder at the root of the source directory

3: Define the containers in the Dockerrun.aws.json file in YAML format and save at the root of the source directory

4: Create a buildspec.yml file and save it at the root of the source directory

7. Question
A developer is planning to launch as serverless application composed of AWS Lambda, Amazon API Gateway, and Amazon DynamoDB. What is the EASIEST way to deploy the application using simple syntax?

1: Use AWS CloudFormation

2: Use AWS Elastic Beanstalk

3: Use the Serverless Application Model

4: Use the Serverless Application Repository

8. Question
A web application has been deployed on AWS. A developer is concerned about exposure to common exploits that could affect application availability or compromise security. Which AWS service can protect from these threats?

1: AWS Web Application Firewall (WAF)

2: AWS CloudFront

3: Amazon Cognito

4: AWS CloudHSM

9. Question
A team of developers are adding an API layer to a multicontainer Docker environment running on AWS Elastic Beanstalk. The client-submitted method requests should be passed directly to the backend, without modification. Which integration type is MOST suitable for this solution?

1: AWS

2: HTTP

3: HTTP_PROXY

4: AWS_PROXY

10. Question

A company runs a booking system for a medical practice. The AWS SDK is used to communicate with between several AWS services. Due to compliance requirements, the security department has requested that a record is made of all API calls. How can this requirement be met?

1: Use Amazon CloudWatch logs to keep a history of API calls

2: Use AWS X-Ray to trace the API calls and keep a record

3: Use an AWS Lambda to function to continually monitor API calls and log them to an Amazon S3 bucket

4: Use Amazon CloudTrail to keep a history of API calls

11. Question

A company is in the process of migrating an application from a monolithic architecture to a microservices-based architecture. The developers need to refactor the application so that the many microservices can asynchronously communicate with each other in a decoupled manner. Which AWS services can be used for asynchronous message passing? (Select TWO)

1: Amazon SQS

2: Amazon Kinesis

3: Amazon ECS

4: AWS Lambda

5: Amazon SNS

12. Question

A developer needs to implement a caching layer in front of an Amazon RDS database. If the caching layer fails, it is time consuming to repopulate cached data so the solution should be designed for maximum uptime. Which solution is best for this scenario?

1: Implement Amazon ElastiCache Memcached

2: Migrate the database to Amazon RedShift

3: Implement Amazon DynamoDB DAX

4: Implement Amazon ElastiCache Redis

13. Question

An application running on a fleet of EC2 instances use the AWS SDK for Java to copy files into several AWS buckets using access keys stored in environment variables. A Developer has modified the instances to use an assumed IAM role with a more restrictive policy that allows access to only one bucket. However, after applying the change the Developer logs into one of the instances and is still able to write to all buckets. What is the MOST likely explanation for this situation?

1: An IAM inline policy is being used on the IAM role

2: An IAM managed policy is being used on the IAM role

3: The AWS CLI is corrupt and needs to be reinstalled

4: The AWS credential provider looks for instance profile credentials last

14. Question

A static website is hosted on Amazon S3 using the bucket name of dctlabs.com. Some HTML pages on the site use JavaScript to download images that are located in the bucket https://dctlabsimages.s3.amazonaws.com/. Users have reported that the images are not being displayed. What is the MOST likely cause?

1: Cross Origin Resource Sharing is not enabled on the dctlabsimages bucket

2: The dctlabsimages bucket is not in the same region as the dctlabs.com bucket

3: Amazon S3 Transfer Acceleration should be enabled on the dctlabs.com bucket

4: Cross Origin Resource Sharing is not enabled on the dctlabs.com bucket

15. Question

A Developer received the following error when attempting to launch an Amazon EC2 instance using the AWS CLI.

An error occurred (UnauthorizedOperation) when calling the RunInstances operation: You are not authorized to perform this operation. Encoded authorization failure message:

VNVaHFdCohROkbyT_rIXoRyNTp7vXFJCqnGiwPuyKnsSVf-
WSSGK_06H3vKnrkUa3qx5D40hqj9HEG8kznr04Acmi6lvc8m51tfqtsomFSDylK15x96ZrxMW7MjDJLrMkM0BasP
vy8ixo1wi6X2b0C-J1ThyWU9IcrGd7WbaRDOiGbBhJtKs1z01WSn2rVa5_7sr5PwEK-
ARrC9y5Pl54pmeF6wh7QhSv2pFO0y39WVBajL2GmByFmQ4p8s-
6Lcgxy23b4NJdJwWOF4QGxK9HcKof1VTVZ2oIpsl-dH6_0t2Dl0BTwaIgmaT7ldontl1p7OGz-
3wPgXm67x2NVNgaK63zPxjYNbpl32QuXLKUKNIB9DdkSdoLvsuFlvf-
lQOXLPHnZKCWMqrkI87eqKHYpYKyV5c11TIZTAJ3MntTGO_TJ4U9ySYvTzU2LgswYOtKF_O76-
13fryGG5dhgOW5NxwCWBj6WT2NSJvqOeLykAFjR_ET4lM6Dl1XYfQlTWCqlzlvlQdLmHJ1jqjp4gW56VcQCdqozLv
2UAg8IdrZIXd0OJ047RQcvvN1IyZN0ElL7dR6RzAAQrftoKMRhZQng6THZs8PZM6wep6-
ylnzwfg8J5_FW6G_PwYqO-4VunVtJSTzM_F_8kojGlRmzqy7eCk5or__blisUoslw

What action should the Developer perform to make this error more human-readable?

1: Make a call to AWS KMS to decode the message

2: Use the AWS STS decode-authorization-message API to decode the message

3: Use an open source decoding library to decode the message

4: Use the AWS IAM decode-authorization-message API to decode this message

16. Question

A company is developing a game for the Android and iOS platforms. The mobile game will securely store user game history and other data locally on the device. The company would like users to be able to use multiple mobile devices and synchronize data between devices. Which service can be used to synchronize the data across mobile devices without the need to create a backend application?

1: AWS Lambda

2: Amazon API Gateway

3: Amazon DynamoDB

4: Amazon Cognito

17. Question

An application is using Amazon DynamoDB as its data store and needs to be able to read 200 items per second as eventually consistent reads. Each item is 12 KB in size.
What value should be set for the table's provisioned throughput for reads?

1: 300 Read Capacity Units

2: 600 Read Capacity Units

3: 1200 Read Capacity Units

4: 150 Read Capacity Units

18. Question

An application uses AWS Lambda to process many files. The Lambda function takes approximately 3 minutes to process each file and does not return any important data. A Developer has written a script that will invoke the function using the AWS CLI. What is the FASTEST way to process all the files?

1: Invoke the Lambda function synchronously with the invocation type Event and process the files in parallel

2: Invoke the Lambda function synchronously with the invocation type RequestResponse and process the files sequentially

3: Invoke the Lambda function asynchronously with the invocation type Event and process the files in parallel

4: Invoke the Lambda function asynchronously with the invocation type RequestResponse and process the files sequentially

19. Question

A development team are creating a mobile application that customers will use to receive notifications and special offers. Users will not be required to log in. What is the MOST efficient method to grant users access to AWS resources?

1: Use an IAM SAML 2.0 identity provider to establish trust

2: Use Amazon Cognito Federated Identities and setup authentication using a Cognito User Pool

3: Use Amazon Cognito to associate unauthenticated users with an IAM role that has limited access to resources

4: Embed access keys in the application that have limited access to resources

20. Question

A serverless application is used to process customer information and outputs a JSON file to an Amazon S3 bucket. AWS Lambda is used for processing the data. The data is sensitive and should be encrypted. How can a Developer modify the Lambda function to ensure the data is encrypted before it is uploaded to the S3 bucket?

1: Use the GenerateDataKey API, then use the data key to encrypt the file using the Lambda code

2: Enable server-side encryption on the S3 bucket and create a policy to enforce encryption

3: Use the S3 managed key and call the GenerateDataKey API to encrypt the file

4: Use the default KMS key for S3 and encrypt the file using the Lambda code

21. Question

A Developer is troubleshooting an issue with a DynamoDB table. The table is used to store order information for a busy online store and uses the order date as the partition key. During busy periods writes to the table are being throttled despite the consumed throughput being well below the provisioned throughput. According to AWS best practices, how can the Developer resolve the issue at the LOWEST cost?

1: Increase the read and write capacity units for the table

2: Add a random number suffix to the partition key values

3: Add a global secondary index to the table

4: Use an Amazon SQS queue to buffer the incoming writes

22. Question

A company is migrating a stateful web service into the AWS cloud. The objective is to refactor the application to realize the benefits of cloud computing. How can the Developer leading the project refactor the application to enable more elasticity? (Select TWO)

1: Use Amazon CloudFormation and the Serverless Application Model

2: Use Amazon CloudFront with a Web Application Firewall

3: Store the session state in an Amazon RDS database

4: Use an Elastic Load Balancer and Auto Scaling Group

5: Store the session state in an Amazon DynamoDB table

23. Question

A company uses continuous integration and continuous delivery (CI/CD) systems. A Developer needs to automate the deployment of a software package to Amazon EC2 instances as on-premises virtual servers. Which AWS service can be used for the software deployment?

1: AWS CodePipeline

2: AWS CloudBuild

3: AWS Elastic Beanstalk

4: AWS CodeDeploy

24. Question

A company uses Amazon SQS to decouple an online application that generates memes. The SQS consumers poll the queue regularly to keep throughput high and this is proving to be costly and resource intensive. A Developer has been asked to review the system and propose changes that can reduce costs and the number of empty responses. What would be the BEST approach to MINIMIZING cost?

1: Set the imaging queue visibility Timeout attribute to 20 seconds

2: Set the Imaging queue ReceiveMessageWaitTimeSeconds attribute to 20 seconds

3: Set the imaging queue MessageRetentionPeriod attribute to 20 seconds

4: Set the DelaySeconds parameter of a message to 20 seconds

25. Question

A Developer has updated an AWS Lambda function and published a new version. To ensure the code is working as expected the Developer needs to initially direct a percentage of traffic to the new version and gradually increase this over time. It is important to be able to rollback if there are any issues reported. What is the BEST way the Developer can implement the migration to the new version SAFELY?

1: Create an Alias, assign the current and new versions and use traffic shifting to assign a percentage of traffic to the new version

2: Create an Amazon Route 53 weighted routing policy pointing to the current and new versions, assign a lower weight to the new version

3: Use an immutable update with a new ASG to deploy the new version in parallel, following testing cutover to the new version

4: Use an Amazon Elastic Load Balancer to direct a percentage of traffic to each target group containing the Lambda function versions

26. Question

A Development team is creating a microservices application running on Amazon ECS. The release process workflow of the application requires a manual approval step before the code is deployed into the production environment. What is the BEST way to achieve this using AWS CodePipeline?

1: Use an Amazon SNS notification from the deployment stage

2: Use an approval action in a stage before deployment

3: Disable the stage transition to allow manual approval

4: Disable a stage just prior the deployment stage

27. Question

A web application is using Amazon Kinesis Data Streams for ingesting IoT data that is then stored before processing for up to 24 hours. How can the Developer implement encryption at rest for data stored in Amazon Kinesis Data Streams?

1: Add a certificate and enable SSL/TLS connections to Kinesis Data Streams

2: Use the Amazon Kinesis Consumer Library (KCL) to encrypt the data

3: Encrypt the data once it is at rest with an AWS Lambda function

4: Enable server-side encryption on Kinesis Data Streams with an AWS KMS CMK

28. Question

A Developer has completed some code updates and needs to deploy the updates to an Amazon Elastic Beanstalk environment. Due to the criticality of the application, the ability to quickly roll back must be prioritized of any other considerations. Which deployment policy should the Developer choose?

1: All at once

2: Rolling

3: Rolling with additional batch

4: Immutable

29. Question

A Developer needs to configure an Elastic Load Balancer that is deployed through AWS Elastic Beanstalk. Where should the Developer place the load-balancer.config file in the application source bundle?

1: In the root of the source code

2: In the bin folder

3: In the load-balancer.config.root

4: In the .ebextensions folder

30. Question

A Developer has created the code for a Lambda function saved the code in a file named lambda_function.py. He has also created a template that named template.yaml. The following code is included in the template file:

AWSTemplateFormatVersion: '2010-09-09'

Transform: 'AWS::Serverless-2016-10-31'

Resources:

  microservicehttpendpointpython3:

Type: 'AWS::Serverless::Function'

Properties:

 Handler: lambda_function.lambda_handler

 CodeUri: .

What commands can the Developer use to prepare and then deploy this template? (Select TWO)

1: Run aws cloudformation package and then aws cloudformation deploy

2: Run sam package and then sam deploy

3: Run aws cloudformation compile and then aws cloudformation deploy

4: Run sam build and then sam package

5: Run aws serverless package and then aws serverless deploy

31. Question

A Developer manages a monitoring service for a fleet of IoT sensors in a major city. The monitoring application uses an Amazon Kinesis Data Stream with a group of EC2 instances processing the data. Amazon CloudWatch custom metrics show that the instances a reaching maximum processing capacity and there are insufficient shards in the Data Stream to handle the rate of data flow. What course of action should the Developer take to resolve the performance issues?

1: Increase the number of EC2 instances to match the number of shards

2: Increase the EC2 instance size and add shards to the stream

3: Increase the EC2 instance size

4: Increase the number of open shards

32. Question

A company uses an Amazon Simple Storage Service (SQS) Standard queue for an application. An issue has been identified where applications are picking up messages from the queue that are still being processed causing duplication. What can a Developer do to resolve this issue?

1: Increase the DelaySeconds API action on the queue

2: Increase the VisibilityTimeout API action on the queue

3: Increase the ReceiveMessageWaitTimeSeconds API action on the queue

4: Create a RedrivePolicy for the queue

33. Question

A Developer is using AWS SAM to create a template for deploying a serverless application. The Developer plans deploy a Lambda function using the template. Which resource type should the Developer specify?

1: AWS::Serverless::Application

2: AWS::Serverless:Function

3: AWS::Serverless:LayerVersion

4: AWS::Serverless:API

34. Question

A team of Developers have been assigned to a new project. The team will be collaborating on the development and delivery of a new application and need a centralized private repository for managing source code. The repository should support updates from multiple sources. Which AWS service should the development team use?

1: AWS CodeCommit

2: AWS CodeBuild

3: AWS CodeDeploy

4: AWS CodePipeline

35. Question

A development team have deployed a new application and users have reported some performance issues. The developers need to enable monitoring for specific metrics with a data granularity of one second. How can this be achieved?

1: Do nothing, CloudWatch uses standard resolution metrics by default

2: Create custom metrics and configure them as standard resolution

3: Create custom metrics and enable detailed monitoring

4: Create custom metrics and configure them as high resolution

36. Question

A Developer is deploying an application using Docker containers on Amazon ECS. One of the containers runs a database and should be placed on instances in the "databases" task group. What should the Developer use to control the placement of the database task?

1: Cluster Query Language

2: Task Placement Constraint

3: IAM Group

4: ECS Container Agent

37. Question

An organization has a new AWS account and is setting up IAM users and policies. According to AWS best practices, which of the following strategies should be followed? (Select TWO.)

1: Use groups to assign permissions to users

2: Create standalone policies instead of using inline policies

3: Use user accounts to delegate permissions

4: Create user accounts that can be shared for efficiency

5: Always use customer managed policies instead of AWS managed policies

38. Question

A Developer is deploying an update to a serverless application that includes AWS Lambda using the AWS Serverless Application Model (SAM). The traffic needs to move from the old Lambda version to the new Lambda version gradually, within the shortest period of time. Which deployment configuration is MOST suitable for these requirements?

1: CodeDeployDefault.LambdaCanary10Percent5Minutes

2: CodeDeployDefault.HalfAtATime

3: CodeDeployDefault.LambdaLinear10PercentEvery1Minute

4: CodeDeployDefault.LambdaLinear10PercentEvery2Minutes

39. Question

A Developer recently created an Amazon DynamoDB table. The table has the following configuration:

Table details
_____

Table name	table1
Primary partition key	userid (String)
Primary sort key	-

The Developer attempted to add two items for userid "user0001" with unique timestamps and received an error for the second item stating: "The conditional request failed". What MUST the Developer do to resolve the issue?

1: Use the SDK to add the items

2: Update the table with a primary sort key for the timestamp attribute

3: Recreate the table with a composite key consisting of userid and timestamp

4: Add a local secondary index (LSI) for the timestamp attribute

40. Question

A Developer has deployed an AWS Lambda function and an Amazon DynamoDB table. The function code returns data from the DynamoDB table when it receives a request. The Developer needs to implement a front end that can receive HTTP GET requests and proxy the request information to the Lambda function. What is the SIMPLEST and most COST-EFFECTIVE solution?

1: Implement an API Gateway API with Lambda proxy integration

2: Implement an API Gateway API with a POST method

3: Implement an Elastic Load Balancer with a Lambda function target

4: Implement an Amazon Cognito User Pool with a Lambda proxy integration

41. Question

A Developer needs to write some code to invoke an AWS Lambda function using the AWS Command Line Interface (CLI). Which option must be specified to cause the function to be invoked asynchronously?

1: Set the –invocation-type option to Event

2: Set the –invocation-type option to Invoke

3: Set the –payload option to Asynchronous

4: Set the –qualifier option to Asynchronous

42. Question

A serverless application uses Amazon API Gateway an AWS Lambda function and a Lambda authorizer function. There is a failure with the application and a developer needs to trace and analyze user requests that pass through API Gateway through to the back end services. Which AWS service is MOST suitable for this purpose?

1: Amazon CloudWatch

2: Amazon Inspector

3: VPC Flow Logs

43. Question

A website is being delivered using Amazon CloudFront and a Developer recently modified some images that are displayed on website pages. Upon testing the changes, the Developer noticed that the new versions of the images are not displaying. What should the Developer do to force the new images to be displayed?

1: Delete the images from the origin and then save the new version on the origin

2: Invalidate the old versions of the images on the edge caches

3: Invalidate the old versions of the images on the origin

4: Force an update of the cache

44. Question

A company is using Amazon CloudFront to provide low-latency access to a web application to its global users. The organization must encrypt all traffic between users and CloudFront, and all traffic between CloudFront and the web application. How can these requirements be met? (Select TWO)

1: Use AWS KMS to encrypt traffic between CloudFront and the web application

2: Set the Origin Protocol Policy to "HTTPS Only"

3: Set the Origin's HTTP Port to 443

4: Set the Viewer Protocol Policy to "HTTPS Only" or "Redirect HTTP to HTTPS"

5: Enable the CloudFront option Restrict Viewer Access

45. Question

A Developer is working on an AWS Lambda function that accesses Amazon DynamoDB. The Lambda function must retrieve an item and update some of its attributes or create the item if it does not exist. The Lambda function has access to the primary key. Which IAM permission should the Developer request for the Lambda function to achieve this functionality?

1: "dynamodb:DeleteItem", "dynamodb:GetItem", and "dynamodb:PutItem"

2: "dynamodb:UpdateItem", "dynamodb:GetItem", and "dynamodb:DescribeTable"

3: "dynamodb:GetRecords", "dynamodb:PutItem", and "dynamodb:UpdateTable"

4: "dynamodb:UpdateItem", "dynamodb:GetItem", and "dynamodb:PutItem"

46. Question

A Developer is trying to make API calls using AWS SDK. The IAM user credentials used by the application require multi-factor authentication for all API calls. Which method should the Developer use to access the multi-factor authentication protected API?

1: GetFederationToken

2: GetCallerIdentity

3: GetSessionToken

4: DecodeAuthorizationMessage

47. Question

A company is creating a REST service using an Amazon API Gateway with AWS Lambda integration. The service must run different versions for testing purposes. What would be the BEST way to accomplish this?

1: Use an X-Version header to denote which version is being called and pass that header to the Lambda function(s)

2: Create an API Gateway Lambda authorizer to route API clients to the correct API version

3: Create an API Gateway resource policy to isolate versions and provide context to the Lambda function(s)

4: Deploy the API version as unique stages with unique endpoints and use stage variables to provide further context

48. Question

A set of APIs are exposed to customers using Amazon API Gateway. These APIs have caching enabled on the API Gateway. Customers have asked for an option to invalidate this cache for each of the APIs. What action can be taken to allow API customers to invalidate the API Cache?

1: Ask customers to use AWS credentials to call the InvalidateCache API

2: Ask customers to invoke an AWS API endpoint which invalidates the cache

3: Ask customers to pass an HTTP header called Cache-Control:max-age=0

4: Ask customers to add a query string parameter called INVALIDATE_CACHE" when making an API call

49. Question

A Developer is writing a web application that allows users to view images from an Amazon S3 bucket. The users will log in with their Amazon login, as well as Facebook and/or Google accounts. How can the Developer provide this authentication capability?

1: Use Amazon Cognito with web identity federation

2: Use Amazon Cognito with SAML-based identity federation

3: Use AWS IAM Access/Secret keys in the application code to allow Get* on the S3 bucket

4: Use AWS STS AssumeRole in the application code and assume a role with Get* permissions on the S3 bucket

50. Question

A mobile application has hundreds of users. Each user may use multiple devices to access the application. The Developer wants to assign unique identifiers to these users regardless of the device they use. Which of the following methods should be used to obtain unique identifiers?

1: Create a user table in Amazon DynamoDB as key-value pairs of users and their devices. Use these keys as unique identifiers

2: Use IAM-generated access key IDs for the users as the unique identifier, but do not store secret keys

3: Implement developer-authenticated identities by using Amazon Cognito, and get credentials for these identities

4: Assign IAM users and roles to the users. Use the unique IAM resource ID as the unique identifier

51. Question

A gaming application stores scores for players in an Amazon DynamoDB table that has four attributes: user_id, user_name, user_score, and user_rank. The users are allowed to update their names only. A user is authenticated by web identity federation. Which set of conditions should be added in the policy attached to the role for the dynamodb:PutItem API call?

1.

```json
"Condition": {
  "ForAllValues:StringEquals": {
    "dynamodb:LeadingKeys": [
      "${www.amazon.com:user_id}"
    ],
    "dynamodb:Attributes": [
      "user_name"
    ]
  }
}
```

2.

```json
"Condition": {
  "ForAllValues:StringEquals": {
    "dynamodb:LeadingKeys": [
      "${www.amazon.com:user_name}"
    ],
    "dynamodb:Attributes": [
      "user_id"
    ]
  }
}
```

3.

```json
"Condition": {
  "ForAllValues:StringEquals": {
    "dynamodb:LeadingKeys": [
      "${www.amazon.com:user_id}"
    ],
    "dynamodb:Attributes": [
      "user_name", "user_id"
    ]
  }
}
```

4.

```json
"Condition": {
  "ForAllValues:StringEquals": {
    "dynamodb:LeadingKeys": [
      "${www.amazon.com:user_name}"
    ],
    "dynamodb:Attributes": [
      "user_name", "user_id"
```

52. Question

A company is running an order processing system on AWS. Amazon SQS is used to queue orders and an AWS Lambda function processes them. The company recently started noticing a lot of orders are failing to process. How can a Developer MOST effectively manage these failures to debug the failed orders later and reprocess them, as necessary?

1: Implement dead-letter queues for failed orders from the order queue

2: Publish failed orders from the order queue to an Amazon SNS topic

3: Log the failed orders from the order queue using Amazon CloudWatch Logs

4: Send failed orders from the order queue to AWS CloudTrail logs

53. Question

A Developer must deploy a new AWS Lambda function using an AWS CloudFormation template. Which procedures will deploy a Lambda function? (Select TWO.)

1: Upload the code to an AWS CodeCommit repository, then add a reference to it in an AWS::Lambda::Function resource in the template

2: Create an AWS::Lambda::Function resource in the template, then write the code directly inside the CloudFormation template

3: Upload a ZIP file containing the function code to Amazon S3, then add a reference to it in an AWS::Lambda::Function resource in the template

4: Upload a ZIP file to AWS CloudFormation containing the function code, then add a reference to it in an AWS::Lambda::Function resource in the template

5: Upload the function code to a private Git repository, then add a reference to it in an AWS::Lambda::Function resource in the template

54. Question

A company is running an application built on AWS Lambda functions. One Lambda function has performance issues when it has to download a 50 MB file from the internet every execution. This function is called multiple times a second. What solution would give the BEST performance increase?

1: Cache the file in the /tmp directory

2: Increase the Lambda maximum execution time

3: Put an Elastic Load Balancer in front of the Lambda function

4: Cache the file in Amazon S3

55. Question

A company is migrating several applications to the AWS cloud. The security team has strict security requirements and mandate that a log of all API calls to AWS resources must be maintained. Which AWS service should be used to record this information for the security team?

1: Amazon CloudWatch

2: AWS CloudTrail

3: Amazon CloudWatch Logs

4: AWS X-Ray

56. Question

A Developer has written some code that will connect and pull information from several hundred websites. The code needs to run on a daily schedule and execution time will be less than 60 seconds. Which AWS service will be most suitable and cost-effective?

1: Amazon ECS Fargate

2: Amazon EC2

3: AWS Lambda

4: Amazon API Gateway

57. Question

A team of Developers require access to an AWS account that is a member account in AWS Organizations. The administrator of the master account needs to restrict the AWS services, resources, and API actions that can be accessed by the users in the account. What should the administrator create?

1: A Service Control Policy (SCP)

2: A Tag Policy

3: An Organizational Unit

4: A Consolidated Billing account

58. Question

A three tier web application has been deployed on Amazon EC2 instances using Amazon EC2 Auto Scaling. The EC2 instances in the web tier sometimes receive bursts of traffic and the application tier cannot scale fast enough to keep up with messages sometimes resulting in message loss. How can a Developer decouple the application to prevent loss of messages?

1: Add an Amazon SQS queue between the application tier and the database tier

2: Configure the web tier to publish messages to an SNS topic and subscribe the application tier to the SNS topic

3: Add an Amazon SQS queue between the web tier and the application tier

4: Migrate the database tier to Amazon DynamoDB and enable scalable session handling

59. Question

A security officer has requested that a Developer enable logging for API actions for all AWS regions to a single Amazon S3 bucket. What is the EASIEST way for the Developer to achieve this requirement?

1: Create an AWS CloudTrail trail and apply it to all regions, configure logging to a single S3 bucket

2: Create an AWS CloudTrail trail in each region, configure logging to a single S3 bucket

3: Create an AWS CloudTrail trail in each region, configure logging to a local bucket, and then use cross-region replication to replicate all logs to a single S3 bucket

4: Create an AWS CloudTrail trail and apply it to all regions, configure logging to a local bucket, and then use cross-region replication to replicate all logs to a single S3 bucket

60. Question

A small team of Developers require access to an Amazon S3 bucket. An admin has created a resource-based policy. Which element of the policy should be used to specify the ARNs of the user accounts that will be granted access?

1: Sid

2: Condition

3: Principal

4: Id

61. Question

An Amazon DynamoDB table will store authentication credentials for a mobile app. The table must be secured so only a small group of Developers are able to access it. How can table access be secured according to this requirement and following AWS best practice?

1: Attach a permissions policy to an IAM group containing the Developer's IAM user accounts that grants access to the table

2: Attach a resource-based policy to the table and add an IAM group containing the Developer's IAM user accounts as a Principal in the policy

3: Create an AWS KMS resource-based policy to a CMK and grant the developer's user accounts the permissions to decrypt data in the table using the CMK

4: Create a shared user account and attach a permissions policy granting access to the table. Instruct the Developer's to login with the user account

62. Question

Based on the following AWS CLI command the resulting output, what has happened here?

$ aws lambda invoke --function-name MyFunction --invocation-type Event --payload
ewogICJrZXkxIjogInZhbHVlMSIsCiAgImtleTIiOiAidmFsdWUyIiwKICAia2V5MyI6ICJ2YWx1ZTMiCn0=
response.json

```
{
    "StatusCode": 202
}
```

1: An AWS Lambda function has been invoked synchronously and has completed successfully

2: An AWS Lambda function has been invoked synchronously and has not completed successfully

3: An AWS Lambda function has been invoked asynchronously and has completed successfully

4: An AWS Lambda function has been invoked asynchronously and has not completed successfully

63. Question

A Developer is creating a service on Amazon ECS and needs to ensure that each task is placed on a different container instance. How can this be achieved?

1: Use a task placement strategy

2: Use a task placement constraint

3: Create a service on Fargate

4: Create a cluster with multiple container instances

64. Question

An application exports files which must be saved for future use but are not frequently accessed. Compliance requirements necessitate redundant retention of data across AWS regions. Which solution is the MOST cost-effective for these requirements?

1: Amazon S3 with Same-Region Replication (CRR)

2: Amazon DynamoDB with Global Tables

3: AWS Storage Gateway with a replicated file gateway

4: Amazon S3 with Cross-Region Replication (CRR)

65. Question

An AWS Lambda function requires several environment variables with secret values. The secret values should be obscured in the Lambda console and API output even for users who have permission to use the key. What is the best way to achieve this outcome and MINIMIZE complexity and latency?

1: Encrypt the secret values client-side using encryption helpers

2: Encrypt the secret values with a customer-managed CMK

3: Store the encrypted values in an encrypted Amazon S3 bucket and reference them from within the code

4: Use an external encryption infrastructure to encrypt the values and add them as environment variables

SET 4: PRACTICE QUESTIONS, ANSWERS & EXPLANATIONS

1. Question

A developer is completing the configuration for an Amazon ECS cluster. Which task placement strategy will MINIMIZE the number of instances in use?

1: binpack

2: random

3: spread

4: Canary

Answer: 1

Explanation:

A *task placement strategy* is an algorithm for selecting instances for task placement or tasks for termination. Task placement strategies can be specified when either running a task or creating a new service.

Amazon ECS supports the following task placement strategies:

binpack - place tasks based on the least available amount of CPU or memory. This minimizes the number of instances in use.

random - place tasks randomly.

spread - place tasks evenly based on the specified value. Accepted values are instanceId (or host, which has the same effect), or any platform or custom attribute that is applied to a container instance, such as attribute:ecs.availability-zone. Service tasks are spread based on the tasks from that service. Standalone tasks are spread based on the tasks from the same task group.

To minimize the number of instances in use, the binpack placement strategy is the best choice for this scenario.

CORRECT: "binpack" is the correct answer.

INCORRECT: "random" is incorrect as random places tasks randomly so this will not minimize the number of instances in use.

INCORRECT: "spread" is incorrect as this places tasks evenly.

INCORRECT: "Canary" is incorrect as this is a traffic shifting strategy associated with Elastic Beanstalk

2. Question

A company is using AWS Lambda for processing small images that are uploaded to Amazon S3. This was working well until a large number of small files (several thousand) were recently uploaded and an error was generated by AWS Lambda (status code 429). What is the MOST likely cause?

1: The concurrency execution limit for the account has been exceeded

2: Amazon S3 could not handle the sudden burst in traffic

3: Lambda cannot process multiple files simultaneously

4: The event source mapping has not been configured

Answer: 1

Explanation:

The first time you invoke your function, AWS Lambda creates an instance of the function and runs its handler method to process the event. When the function returns a response, it stays active and waits to process additional events. If you invoke the function again while the first event is being processed, Lambda initializes another instance, and the function processes the two events concurrently.

Your functions' concurrency is the number of instances that serve requests at a given time. For an initial burst of traffic, your functions' cumulative concurrency in a Region can reach an initial level of between 500 and 3000, which varies per Region.

Burst Concurrency Limits:

- 3000 – US West (Oregon), US East (N. Virginia), Europe (Ireland).

- 1000 – Asia Pacific (Tokyo), Europe (Frankfurt).

- 500 – Other Regions.

After the initial burst, your functions' concurrency can scale by an additional 500 instances each minute. This continues until there are enough instances to serve all requests, or until a concurrency limit is reached.

The default account limit is up to 1000 executions per second, per region (can be increased). It is therefore most likely that the concurrency execution limit for the account was exceeded.

CORRECT: "The concurrency execution limit for the account has been exceeded" is the correct answer.

INCORRECT: "Amazon S3 could not handle the sudden burst in traffic" is incorrect as S3 can easily achieve thousands of transactions per second and automatically scales to high request rates.

INCORRECT: "Lambda cannot process multiple files simultaneously" is incorrect as Lambda can run multiple executions concurrently as explained above.

INCORRECT: "The event source mapping has not been configured" is incorrect as the solution was working well until that large number of files were uploaded. If the event source mapping was not configured it would not have worked at all.

3. Question

A developer is creating a serverless application that will use a DynamoDB table. The average item size is 7KB. The application will make 3 strongly consistent reads/sec, and 1 standard write/sec. How many RCUs/WCUs are required?

1: 3 RCU and 7 WCU

2: 6 RCU and 7 WCU

3: 6 RCU and 14 WCU

4: 12 RCU and 14 WCU

Answer: 2

Explanation:

With provisioned capacity mode, you specify the number of data reads and writes per second that you require for your application.

Read capacity unit (RCU):

- Each API call to read data from your table is a read request.
- Read requests can be strongly consistent, eventually consistent, or transactional.
- For items up to 4 KB in size, one RCU can perform one *strongly consistent* read request per second.
- Items larger than 4 KB require additional RCUs.
- For items up to 4 KB in size, one RCU can perform two *eventually consistent* read requests per second.
- *Transactional* read requests require two RCUs to perform one read per second for items up to 4 KB.

- For example, a strongly consistent read of an 8 KB item would require two RCUs, an eventually consistent read of an 8 KB item would require one RCU, and a transactional read of an 8 KB item would require four RCUs.

Write capacity unit (WCU):

- Each API call to write data to your table is a write request.
- For items up to 1 KB in size, one WCU can perform one *standard* write request per second.
- Items larger than 1 KB require additional WCUs.
- *Transactional* write requests require two WCUs to perform one write per second for items up to 1 KB.
- For example, a standard write request of a 1 KB item would require one WCU, a standard write request of a 3 KB item would require three WCUs, and a transactional write request of a 3 KB item would require six WCUs.

To determine the number of RCUs required to handle 3 strongly consistent reads per/second with an average item size of 7KB, perform the following steps:

- Determine the average item size by rounding up the next multiple of 4KB (7KB rounds up to 8KB).
- Determine the RCU per item by dividing the item size by 4KB (8KB/4KB = 2).
- Multiply the value from step 2 with the number of reads required per second (2x3 = 6).

To determine the number of WCUs required to handle 1 standard write per/second, simply multiply the average item size by the number of writes required (7x1=7).

CORRECT: "6 RCU and 7 WCU" is the correct answer.

INCORRECT: "3 RCU and 7 WCU" is incorrect. This would be the correct answer for eventual consistent reads and standard writes.

INCORRECT: "6 RCU and 14 WCU" is incorrect. This would be the correct answer for strongly consistent reads and transactional writes.

INCORRECT: "12 RCU and 14 WCU" is incorrect. This would be the correct answer for transactional reads and transactional writes

4. Question

A developer is building a multi-tier web application that accesses an Amazon RDS MySQL database. The application must use a credentials to connect and these need to be stored securely. The application will take care of secret rotation. Which AWS service represents the LOWEST cost solution for storing credentials?

1: AWS IAM with the Security Token Service (STS)

2: AWS Secrets Manager

3: AWS Systems Manager Parameter Store

4: AWS Key Management Service (KMS)

Answer: 3

Explanation:

AWS Systems Manager Parameter Store provides secure, hierarchical storage for configuration data management and secrets management. You can store data such as passwords, database strings, and license codes as parameter values. It is highly scalable, available, and durable.

You can store values as plaintext (unencrypted data) or ciphertext (encrypted data). You can then reference values by using the unique name that you specified when you created the parameter.

There are no additional charges for using SSM Parameter Store. However, there are limit of 10,000 parameters per account

CORRECT: "AWS Systems Manager Parameter Store" is the correct answer.

INCORRECT: "AWS IAM with the Security Token Service (STS)" is incorrect as the application is using credentials to connect, it is not using IAM.

INCORRECT: "AWS Secrets Manager" is incorrect as it is not the lowest cost solution as it is a chargeable service. Secrets Manager performs native key rotation; however, this isn't required in this scenario as the application is handling credential rotation.

INCORRECT: "AWS Key Management Service (KMS)" is incorrect as this service is involved with encryption keys, it is not used for storing credentials. You can however encrypt you credentials in SSM using KMS.

5. Question

A mobile application is being developed that will use AWS Lambda, Amazon API Gateway and Amazon DynamoDB. A developer would like to securely authenticate the users of the mobile application and then grant them access to the API. What is the BEST way to achieve this?

1: Create a Lambda authorizer in API Gateway

2: Create a COGNITO_USER_POOLS authorizer in API Gateway

3: Create a COGNITO_IDENTITY_POOLS authorizer in API Gateway

4: Create an IAM authorizer in API Gateway

Answer: 2

Explanation:

A user pool is a user directory in Amazon Cognito. With a user pool, your users can sign into your web or mobile app through Amazon Cognito. Your users can also sign in through social identity providers like Google, Facebook, Amazon, or Apple, and through SAML identity providers. Whether your users sign in directly or through a third party, all members of the user pool have a directory profile that you can access through a Software Development Kit (SDK).

As an alternative to using IAM roles and policies or Lambda authorizers (formerly known as custom authorizers), you can use an Amazon Cognito user pool to control who can access your API in Amazon API Gateway.

To use an Amazon Cognito user pool with your API, you must first create an authorizer of the COGNITO_USER_POOLS type and then configure an API method to use that authorizer. After the API is deployed, the client must first sign the user in to the user pool, obtain an identity or access token for the user, and then call the API method with one of the tokens, which are typically set to the request's Authorization header. The API call succeeds only if the required token is supplied and the supplied token is valid, otherwise, the client isn't authorized to make the call because the client did not have credentials that could be authorized.

CORRECT: "Create a COGNITO_USER_POOLS authorizer in API Gateway" is the correct answer.

INCORRECT: "Create a COGNITO_IDENTITY_POOLS authorizer in API Gateway" is incorrect as you should use a Cognito user pool for creating an authorizer in API Gateway.

INCORRECT: "Create a Lambda authorizer in API Gateway" is incorrect as this is a mobile application and so the best solution is to use Cognito which is designed for this purpose.

INCORRECT: "Create an IAM authorizer in API Gateway" is incorrect as there's no such thing as an IAM authorizer. You can use IAM roles and policies but then you would need your users to have accounts in IAM. For a mobile application your users are better located in a Cognito user pool.

6. Question

A developer is preparing the resources for creating a multicontainer Docker environment on AWS Elastic Beanstalk. How can the developer define the Docker containers?

1: Define the containers in the Dockerrun.aws.json file in JSON format and save at the root of the source directory

2: Create a Docker.config file and save it in the .ebextensions folder at the root of the source directory

3: Define the containers in the Dockerrun.aws.json file in YAML format and save at the root of the source directory

4: Create a buildspec.yml file and save it at the root of the source directory

Answer: 1

Explanation:

You can launch a cluster of multicontainer instances in a single-instance or autoscaling Elastic Beanstalk environment using the Elastic Beanstalk console. The single container and multicontainer Docker platforms for Elastic Beanstalk support the use of Docker images stored in a public or private online image repository.

You specify images by name in the Dockerrun.aws.json file and save it in the root of your source directory.

CORRECT: "Define the containers in the Dockerrun.aws.json file in JSON format and save at the root of the source directory" is the correct answer.

INCORRECT: "Create a Docker.config file and save it in the .ebextensions folder at the root of the source directory" is incorrect as the you need to create a Dockerrun.aws.json file, not a Dokcer.config file and it should be saved at the root of the source directory not in the .ebextensions folder.

INCORRECT: "Define the containers in the Dockerrun.aws.json file in YAML format and save at the root of the source directory" is incorrect because the contents of the file should be in JSON format, not YAML format.

INCORRECT: "Create a buildspec.yml file and save it at the root of the source directory" is incorrect as the buildspec.yml file is used with AWS CodeBuild, not Elastic Beanstalk.

7. Question

A developer is planning to launch as serverless application composed of AWS Lambda, Amazon API Gateway, and Amazon DynamoDB. What is the EASIEST way to deploy the application using simple syntax?

1: Use AWS CloudFormation

2: Use AWS Elastic Beanstalk

3: Use the Serverless Application Model

4: Use the Serverless Application Repository

Answer: 3

Explanation:

The AWS Serverless Application Model (SAM) is an open-source framework for building serverless applications. It provides shorthand syntax to express functions, APIs, databases, and event source mappings. With just a few lines per resource, you can define the application you want and model it using YAML. During deployment, SAM transforms and expands the SAM syntax into AWS CloudFormation syntax, enabling you to build serverless applications faster.

To get started with building SAM-based applications, use the AWS SAM CLI. SAM CLI provides a Lambda-like execution environment that lets you locally build, test, and debug applications defined by SAM templates. You can also use the SAM CLI to deploy your applications to AWS.

With the SAM CLI you can package and deploy your source code using two simple commands:

- sam package
- sam deploy

Alternatively, you can use:

- aws cloudformation package
- aws cloudformation deploy

The SAM CLI is therefore the easiest way to deploy serverless applications on AWS.

CORRECT: "Use the Serverless Application Model" is the correct answer.

INCORRECT: "Use the Serverless Application Repository " is incorrect as this is a managed repository for serverless applications.

INCORRECT: "Use AWS CloudFormation" is incorrect as this would not be the simplest way to package and deploy this infrastructure. Without using SAM, you would need to build out a much more complex AWS CloudFormation template yourself.

INCORRECT: "Use AWS Elastic Beanstalk" is incorrect as Elastic Beanstalk cannot be used to deploy Lambda, API Gateway or DynamoDB.

8. Question

A web application has been deployed on AWS. A developer is concerned about exposure to common exploits that could affect application availability or compromise security. Which AWS service can protect from these threats?

1: AWS Web Application Firewall (WAF)

2: AWS CloudFront

3: Amazon Cognito

4: AWS CloudHSM

Answer: 1

Explanation:

AWS WAF is a web application firewall service that helps protect your web apps from common exploits that could affect app availability, compromise security, or consume excessive resources.

AWS WAF helps protect web applications from attacks by allowing you to configure rules that allow, block, or monitor (count) web requests based on conditions that you define. These conditions include IP addresses, HTTP headers, HTTP body, URI strings, SQL injection and cross-site scripting.

AWS WAF gives you control over which traffic to allow or block to your web applications by defining customizable web security rules.

CORRECT: "AWS Web Application Firewall (WAF)" is the correct answer.

INCORRECT: "AWS CloudFront" is incorrect. CloudFront does provide DDoS attack protection (through AWS Shield), however it is primarily a content delivery network (CDN) so you wouldn't put it in-front of a web application unless you wanted it to cache your content. i.e. its primary use case would not be protection from Internet threats.

INCORRECT: "Amazon Cognito" is incorrect as this is a service for providing sign-up and sign-in capabilities to mobile applications.

INCORRECT: "AWS CloudHSM" is incorrect as this is a service that is used for storing cryptographic keys using a hardware device.

9. Question

A team of developers are adding an API layer to a multicontainer Docker environment running on AWS Elastic Beanstalk. The client-submitted method requests should be passed directly to the backend, without modification. Which integration type is MOST suitable for this solution?

1: AWS

2: HTTP

3: HTTP_PROXY

4: AWS_PROXY

Answer: 3

Explanation:

You choose an API integration type according to the types of integration endpoint you work with and how you want data to pass to and from the integration endpoint. For a Lambda function, you can have the Lambda proxy integration, or the Lambda custom integration.

For an HTTP endpoint, you can have the HTTP proxy integration or the HTTP custom integration. For an AWS service action, you have the AWS integration of the non-proxy type only. API Gateway also supports the mock integration, where API Gateway serves as an integration endpoint to respond to a method request.

As this is a Docker deployment running on Elastic Beanstalk the HTTP integration types are applicable. There are two options:

HTTP: This type of integration lets an API expose HTTP endpoints in the backend. With the HTTP integration, also known as the HTTP custom integration, you must configure both the integration request and integration response. You must set up necessary data mappings from the method request to the integration request, and from the integration response to the method response.

HTTP_PROXY: The HTTP proxy integration allows a client to access the backend HTTP endpoints with a streamlined integration setup on single API method. You do not set the integration request or the integration response. API Gateway passes the incoming request from the client to the HTTP endpoint and passes the outgoing response from the HTTP endpoint to the client.

As we can see from the above explanation, the most suitable integration type for this deployment is going to be the HTTP_PROXY.

CORRECT: "HTTP_PROXY" is the correct answer.

INCORRECT: "HTTP" is incorrect as this is a custom integration that would be used if you need to customize the data mappings.

INCORRECT: "AWS" is incorrect as this type of integration lets an API expose AWS service actions.

INCORRECT: "AWS_PROXY" is incorrect as this type of integration lets an API method be integrated with the Lambda function invocation action with a flexible, versatile, and streamlined integration setup.

10. Question

A company runs a booking system for a medical practice. The AWS SDK is used to communicate with between several AWS services. Due to compliance requirements, the security department has requested that a record is made of all API calls. How can this requirement be met?

1: Use Amazon CloudWatch logs to keep a history of API calls

2: Use AWS X-Ray to trace the API calls and keep a record

3: Use an AWS Lambda to function to continually monitor API calls and log them to an Amazon S3 bucket

4: Use Amazon CloudTrail to keep a history of API calls

Answer: 4

Explanation:

AWS CloudTrail is a service that enables governance, compliance, operational auditing, and risk auditing of your AWS account. With CloudTrail, you can log, continuously monitor, and retain account activity related to actions across your AWS infrastructure.

CloudTrail provides event history of your AWS account activity, including actions taken through the AWS Management Console, AWS SDKs, command line tools, and other AWS services.

This event history simplifies security analysis, resource change tracking, and troubleshooting. In addition, you can use CloudTrail to detect unusual activity in your AWS accounts. These capabilities help simplify operational analysis and troubleshooting.

As this scenario requests that a history of API calls are retained (auditing), AWS CloudTrail is the correct solution to use.

CORRECT: "Use Amazon CloudTrail to keep a history of API calls" is the correct answer.

INCORRECT: "Use Amazon CloudWatch logs to keep a history of API calls" is incorrect as this does not keep a record of API activity. CloudWatch records metrics related to performance.

INCORRECT: "Use AWS X-Ray to trace the API calls and keep a record" is incorrect as X-Ray does not trace API calls for auditing.

INCORRECT: "Use an AWS Lambda to function to continually monitor API calls and log them to an Amazon S3 bucket" is incorrect as this is totally unnecessary when CloudTrail can do this for you.

11. Question

A company is in the process of migrating an application from a monolithic architecture to a microservices-based architecture. The developers need to refactor the application so that the many microservices can asynchronously communicate with each other in a decoupled manner. Which AWS services can be used for asynchronous message passing? (Select TWO)

1: Amazon SQS

2: Amazon Kinesis

3: Amazon ECS

4: AWS Lambda

5: Amazon SNS

Answer: 1,5

Explanation:

Amazon Simple Queue Service (SQS) is a fully managed message queuing service that enables you to decouple and scale microservices, distributed systems, and serverless applications.

Amazon Simple Notification Service (SNS) is a highly available, durable, secure, fully managed pub/sub messaging service that enables you to decouple microservices, distributed systems, and serverless applications.

These services both enable asynchronous message passing in the form of a message bus (SQS) and notifications (SNS).

CORRECT: "Amazon SQS" is the correct answer.

CORRECT: "Amazon SNS" is also a correct answer.

INCORRECT: "Amazon Kinesis" is incorrect. Kinesis is used for streaming data, it is used for real-time analytics, mobile data capture and IoT and similar use cases.

INCORRECT: "Amazon ECS" is incorrect. ECS is a service providing Docker containers on Amazon EC2.

INCORRECT: "AWS Lambda" is incorrect. AWS Lambda is a compute service that runs functions in response to triggers.

12. Question

A developer needs to implement a caching layer in front of an Amazon RDS database. If the caching layer fails, it is time consuming to repopulate cached data so the solution should be designed for maximum uptime. Which solution is best for this scenario?

1: Implement Amazon ElastiCache Memcached

2: Migrate the database to Amazon RedShift

3: Implement Amazon DynamoDB DAX

4: Implement Amazon ElastiCache Redis

Answer: 4

Explanation:

Amazon ElastiCache provides fully managed implementations of two popular in-memory data stores – Redis and Memcached. ElastiCache is a web service that makes it easy to deploy and run Memcached or Redis protocol-compliant server nodes in the cloud.

The in-memory caching provided by ElastiCache can be used to significantly improve latency and throughput for many read-heavy application workloads or compute-intensive workloads. It is common to use ElastiCache as a cache in front of databases such as Amazon RDS.

The two implementations, Memcached, and Redis, each offer different capabilities and limitations. Only Redis supports read replicas and auto-failover.

The Redis implementation must be used if high availability is required, as is necessary for this scenario. Therefore the correct answer is to use Amazon ElastiCache Redis.

CORRECT: "Implement Amazon ElastiCache Redis" is the correct answer.

INCORRECT: "Implement Amazon ElastiCache Memcached" is incorrect as Memcached does not offer read replicas or auto-failover and therefore cannot provide high availability.

INCORRECT: "Migrate the database to Amazon RedShift" is incorrect as RedShift is a data warehouse for use in online analytics processing (OLAP) use cases. It is not suitable to be used as a caching layer.

INCORRECT: "Implement Amazon DynamoDB DAX" is incorrect as DAX is used in front of DynamoDB, not Amazon RDS.

13. Question

An application running on a fleet of EC2 instances use the AWS SDK for Java to copy files into several AWS buckets using access keys stored in environment variables. A Developer has modified the instances to use an assumed IAM role with a more restrictive policy that allows access to only one bucket. However, after applying the change the Developer logs into one of the instances and is still able to write to all buckets. What is the MOST likely explanation for this situation?

1: An IAM inline policy is being used on the IAM role

2: An IAM managed policy is being used on the IAM role

3: The AWS CLI is corrupt and needs to be reinstalled

4: The AWS credential provider looks for instance profile credentials last

Answer: 4

Explanation:

When you initialize a new service client without supplying any arguments, the AWS SDK for Java attempts to find AWS credentials by using the *default credential provider chain* implemented by the DefaultAWSCredentialsProviderChain class. The default credential provider chain looks for credentials in this order:

- **Environment variables**–AWS_ACCESS_KEY_ID and AWS_SECRET_ACCESS_KEY. The AWS SDK for Java uses the EnvironmentVariableCredentialsProvider class to load these credentials.

- **Java system properties**–aws.accessKeyId and aws.secretKey. The AWS SDK for Java uses the SystemPropertiesCredentialsProvider to load these credentials.

- **The default credential profiles file**– typically located at ~/.aws/credentials (location can vary per platform) and shared by many of the AWS SDKs and by the AWS CLI. The AWS SDK for Java uses the ProfileCredentialsProvider to load these credentials.

- **Amazon ECS container credentials**– loaded from the Amazon ECS if the environment variable AWS_CONTAINER_CREDENTIALS_RELATIVE_URI is set. The AWS SDK for Java uses the ContainerCredentialsProvider to load these credentials. You can specify the IP address for this value.

- **Instance profile credentials**– used on EC2 instances and delivered through the Amazon EC2 metadata service. The AWS SDK for Java uses the InstanceProfileCredentialsProvider to load these credentials. You can specify the IP address for this value.

Therefore, the AWS SDK for Java will find the credentials stored in environment variables before it checks for instance provide credentials and will allow access to the extra S3 buckets.

NOTE: The Default Credential Provider Chain is very similar for other SDKs and the CLI as well.

CORRECT: "The AWS credential provider looks for instance profile credentials last" is the correct answer.

INCORRECT: "An IAM inline policy is being used on the IAM role" is incorrect. If an inline policy was also applied to the role with a less restrictive policy it wouldn't matter, as the most restrictive policy would be applied.

INCORRECT: "An IAM managed policy is being used on the IAM role" is incorrect. Though the managed policies are less restrictive by default (read-only or full access), this is not the most likely cause of the situation as we were told the policy is more restrictive and we know the environments variables have access keys in them which will be used before the policy is checked.

INCORRECT: "The AWS CLI is corrupt and needs to be reinstalled" is incorrect. There is a plausible explanation for this situation so no reason to suspect a software bug is to blame.

14. Question

A static website is hosted on Amazon S3 using the bucket name of dctlabs.com. Some HTML pages on the site use JavaScript to download images that are located in the bucket https://dctlabsimages.s3.amazonaws.com/. Users have reported that the images are not being displayed. What is the MOST likely cause?

1: Cross Origin Resource Sharing is not enabled on the dctlabsimages bucket

2: The dctlabsimages bucket is not in the same region as the dctlabs.com bucket

3: Amazon S3 Transfer Acceleration should be enabled on the dctlabs.com bucket

4: Cross Origin Resource Sharing is not enabled on the dctlabs.com bucket

Answer: 1

Explanation:

Cross-origin resource sharing (CORS) defines a way for client web applications that are loaded in one domain to interact with resources in a different domain. With CORS support, you can build rich client-side web applications with Amazon S3 and selectively allow cross-origin access to your Amazon S3 resources.

To configure your bucket to allow cross-origin requests, you create a CORS configuration, which is an XML document with rules that identify the origins that you will allow to access your bucket, the operations (HTTP methods) that will support for each origin, and other operation-specific information.

In this case, you would apply the CORS configuration to the dctlabsimages bucket so that it will allow GET requests from the dctlabs.com origin.

CORRECT: "Cross Origin Resource Sharing is not enabled on the dctlabsimages bucket" is the correct answer.

INCORRECT: "Cross Origin Resource Sharing is not enabled on the dctlabs.com bucket" is incorrect as in this case the images that are being blocked are located in the dctlabsimages bucket. You need to apply the CORS configuration to the dctlabsimages bucket so it allows requests from the dctlabs.com origin.

INCORRECT: "The dctlabsimages bucket is not in the same region as the dctlabs.com bucket" is incorrect as it doesn't matter what regions the buckets are in.

INCORRECT: "Amazon S3 Transfer Acceleration should be enabled on the dctlabs.com bucket" is incorrect as this feature of Amazon S3 is used to speed uploads to S3.

15. Question

A Developer received the following error when attempting to launch an Amazon EC2 instance using the AWS CLI.

An error occurred (UnauthorizedOperation) when calling the RunInstances operation: You are not authorized to perform this operation. Encoded authorization failure message: VNVaHFdCohROkbyT_rlXoRyNTp7vXFJCqnGiwPuyKnsSVf-WSSGK_06H3vKnrkUa3qx5D40hqj9HEG8kznr04Acmi6lvc8m51tfqtsomFSDylK15x96ZrxMW7MjDJLrMkM0BasP vy8ixo1wi6X2b0C-J1ThyWU9lcrGd7WbaRDOiGbBhJtKs1z01WSn2rVa5_7sr5PwEK-ARrC9y5Pl54pmeF6wh7QhSv2pFO0y39WVBajL2GmByFmQ4p8s-6Lcgxy23b4NJdJwWOF4QGxK9HcKof1VTVZ2oIpsI-dH6_0t2DI0BTwaIgmaT7ldontI1p7OGz-3wPgXm67x2NVNgaK63zPxjYNbpl32QuXLKUKNlB9DdkSdoLvsuFlvf-lQOXLPHnZKCWMqrkl87eqKHYpYKyV5c11TlZTAJ3MntTGO_TJ4U9ySYvTzU2LgswYOtKF_O76-13fryGG5dhgOW5NxwCWBj6WT2NSJvqOeLykAFjR_ET4lM6Dl1XYfQlTWCqlzlvlQdLmHJ1jqjp4gW56VcQCdqozLv 2UAg8ldrZlXd0OJ047RQcvvN1lyZN0EIL7dR6RzAAQrftoKMRhZQng6THZs8PZM6wep6-ylnzwfg8J5_FW6G_PwYqO-4VunVtJSTzM_F_8kojGlRmzqy7eCk5or__blisUoslw

What action should the Developer perform to make this error more human-readable?

1: Make a call to AWS KMS to decode the message

2: Use the AWS STS decode-authorization-message API to decode the message

3: Use an open source decoding library to decode the message

4: Use the AWS IAM decode-authorization-message API to decode this message

Answer: 2

Explanation:

The AWS STS decode-authorization-message API decodes additional information about the authorization status of a request from an encoded message returned in response to an AWS request. The output is then decoded into a more human-readable output that can be viewed in a JSON editor.

The following example is the decoded output from the error shown in the question:

{

"DecodedMessage":
"{\"allowed\":false,\"explicitDeny\":false,\"matchedStatements\":{\"items\":[]},\"failures\":{\"items\":[]},\"context\":{\"principal\":{\"id\":\"AIDAXP4J2EKU7YXXG3EJ4\",\"name\":\"Paul\",\"arn\":\"arn:aws:iam::515148227241:user/Paul\"},\"action\":\"ec2:RunInstances\",\"resource\":\"arn:aws:ec2:ap-southeast-2:515148227241:instance/*\",\"conditions\":{\"items\":[{\"key\":\"ec2:InstanceMarketType\",\"values\":{\"items\":[{\"value\":\"on-demand\"}]}},{\"key\":\"aws:Resource\",\"values\":{\"items\":[{\"value\":\"instance/*\"}]}},{\"key\":\"aws:Account\",\"values\":{\"items\":[{\"value\":\"515148227241\"}]}},{\"key\":\"ec2:AvailabilityZone\",\"values\":{\"items\":[{\"value\":\"ap-southeast-2a\"}]}},{\"key\":\"ec2:ebsOptimized\",\"values\":{\"items\":[{\"value\":\"false\"}]}},{\"key\":\"ec2:IsLaunchTemplateResource\",\"values\":{\"items\":[{\"value\":\"false\"}]}},{\"key\":\"ec2:InstanceType\",\"values\":{\"items\":[{\"value\":\"t2.micro\"}]}},{\"key\":\"ec2:RootDeviceType\",\"values\":{\"items\":[{\"value\":\"ebs\"}]}},{\"key\":\"aws:Region\",\"values\":{\"items\":[{\"value\":\"ap-southeast-2\"}]}},{\"key\":\"aws:Service\",\"values\":{\"items\":[{\"value\":\"ec2\"}]}},{\"key\":\"ec2:InstanceID\",\"values\":{\"items\":[{\"value\":\"*\"}]}},{\"key\":\"aws:Type\",\"values\":{\"items\":[{\"value\":\"instance\"}]}},{\"key\":\"ec2:Tenancy\",\"values\":{\"items\":[{\"value\":\"default\"}]}},{\"key\":\"ec2:Region\",\"values\":{\"items\":[{\"value\":\"ap-southeast-2\"}]}},{\"key\":\"aws:ARN\",\"values\":{\"items\":[{\"value\":\"arn:aws:ec2:ap-southeast-2:515148227241:instance/*\"}]}}]}}}}"

}

Therefore, the best answer is to use the AWS STS decode-authorization-message API to decode the message.

CORRECT: "Use the AWS STS decode-authorization-message API to decode the message" is the correct answer.

INCORRECT: "Make a call to AWS KMS to decode the message" is incorrect as the message is not encrypted, it is base64 encoded.

INCORRECT: "Use an open source decoding library to decode the message" is incorrect as you can use the AWS STS decode-authorization-message API.

INCORRECT: "Use the AWS IAM decode-authorization-message API to decode this message" is incorrect as the decode-authorization-message API is associated with STS, not IAM.

16. Question

A company is developing a game for the Android and iOS platforms. The mobile game will securely store user game history and other data locally on the device. The company would like users to be able to use multiple mobile devices and synchronize data between devices. Which service can be used to synchronize the data across mobile devices without the need to create a backend application?

1: AWS Lambda

2: Amazon API Gateway

3: Amazon DynamoDB

4: Amazon Cognito

Answer: 4

Explanation:

Amazon Cognito lets you save end user data in datasets containing key-value pairs. This data is associated with an Amazon Cognito identity, so that it can be accessed across logins and devices. To sync this data between the Amazon Cognito service and an end user's devices, invoke the synchronize method. Each dataset can have a maximum size of 1 MB. You can associate up to 20 datasets with an identity.

The Amazon Cognito Sync client creates a local cache for the identity data. Your app talks to this local cache when it reads and writes keys. This guarantees that all of your changes made on the device are immediately available on the device, even when you are offline. When the synchronize method is called, changes from the service are pulled to the device, and any local changes are pushed to the service. At this point the changes are available to other devices to synchronize.

CORRECT: "Amazon Cognito" is the correct answer.

INCORRECT: "AWS Lambda" is incorrect. AWS Lambda provides serverless functions that run your code, it is not used for mobile client data synchronization.

INCORRECT: "Amazon API Gateway" is incorrect as API Gateway provides APIs for traffic coming into AWS. It is not used for mobile client data synchronization.

INCORRECT: "Amazon DynamoDB" is incorrect as DynamoDB is a NoSQL database. It is not used for mobile client data synchronization.

17. Question

An application is using Amazon DynamoDB as its data store and needs to be able to read 200 items per second as eventually consistent reads. Each item is 12 KB in size.
What value should be set for the table's provisioned throughput for reads?

1: 300 Read Capacity Units

2: 600 Read Capacity Units

3: 1200 Read Capacity Units

4: 150 Read Capacity Units

Answer: 1

Explanation:

With provisioned capacity mode, you specify the number of data reads and writes per second that you require for your application.

Read capacity unit (RCU):

- Each API call to read data from your table is a read request.
- Read requests can be strongly consistent, eventually consistent, or transactional.
- For items up to 4 KB in size, one RCU can perform one *strongly consistent* read request per second.
- Items larger than 4 KB require additional RCUs.
- For items up to 4 KB in size, one RCU can perform two *eventually consistent* read requests per second.
- *Transactional* read requests require two RCUs to perform one read per second for items up to 4 KB.
- For example, a strongly consistent read of an 8 KB item would require two RCUs, an eventually consistent read of an 8 KB item would require one RCU, and a transactional read of an 8 KB item would require four RCUs.

Write capacity unit (WCU):

- Each API call to write data to your table is a write request.
- For items up to 1 KB in size, one WCU can perform one *standard* write request per second.
- Items larger than 1 KB require additional WCUs.
- *Transactional* write requests require two WCUs to perform one write per second for items up to 1 KB.
- For example, a standard write request of a 1 KB item would require one WCU, a standard write request of a 3 KB item would require three WCUs, and a transactional write request of a 3 KB item would require six WCUs.

To determine the number of RCUs required to handle 200 eventually consistent reads per/second with an average item size of 12KB, perform the following steps:

- Determine the average item size by rounding up the next multiple of 4KB (12KB rounds up to 12KB).
- Determine the RCU per item by dividing the item size by 8KB (12KB/8KB = 1.5).
- Multiply the value from step 2 with the number of reads required per second (1.5x200 = 300).

CORRECT: "300 Read Capacity Units" is the correct answer.

INCORRECT: "600 Read Capacity Units" is incorrect. This would be the value for strongly consistent reads.

INCORRECT: "1200 Read Capacity Units" is incorrect. This would be the value for transactional reads.

INCORRECT: "150 Read Capacity Units" is incorrect.

18. Question

An application uses AWS Lambda to process many files. The Lambda function takes approximately 3 minutes to process each file and does not return any important data. A Developer has written a script that will invoke the function using the AWS CLI. What is the FASTEST way to process all the files?

1: Invoke the Lambda function synchronously with the invocation type Event and process the files in parallel

2: Invoke the Lambda function synchronously with the invocation type RequestResponse and process the files sequentially

3: Invoke the Lambda function asynchronously with the invocation type Event and process the files in parallel

4: Invoke the Lambda function asynchronously with the invocation type RequestResponse and process the files sequentially

Answer: 3

Explanation:

You can invoke Lambda functions directly with the Lambda console, the Lambda API, the AWS SDK, the AWS CLI, and AWS toolkits.

You can also configure other AWS services to invoke your function, or you can configure Lambda to read from a stream or queue and invoke your function.

When you invoke a function, you can choose to invoke it synchronously or asynchronously.

- Synchronous invocation:
    - You wait for the function to process the event and return a response.
    - To invoke a function synchronously with the AWS CLI, use the invoke command.
    - The Invocation-type can be used to specify a value of "RequestResponse". This instructs AWS to execute your Lambda function and wait for the function to complete.
- Asynchronous invocation:
    - When you invoke a function asynchronously, you don't wait for a response from the function code.
    - For asynchronous invocation, Lambda handles retries and can send invocation records to a destination.
    - To invoke a function asynchronously, set the invocation type parameter to Event.

The fastest way to process all the files is to use asynchronous invocation and process the files in parallel. To do this you should specify the invocation type of Event

CORRECT: "Invoke the Lambda function asynchronously with the invocation type Event and process the files in parallel" is the correct answer.

INCORRECT: "Invoke the Lambda function synchronously with the invocation type Event and process the files in parallel" is incorrect as the invocation type for a synchronous invocation should be RequestResponse.

INCORRECT: "Invoke the Lambda function synchronously with the invocation type RequestResponse and process the files sequentially" is incorrect as this is not the fastest way of processing the files as Lambda will wait for completion of once file before moving on to the next one.

INCORRECT: "Invoke the Lambda function asynchronously with the invocation type RequestResponse and process the files sequentially" is incorrect as the invocation type RequestResponse is used for synchronous invocations.

19. Question

A development team are creating a mobile application that customers will use to receive notifications and special offers. Users will not be required to log in. What is the MOST efficient method to grant users access to AWS resources?

1: Use an IAM SAML 2.0 identity provider to establish trust

2: Use Amazon Cognito Federated Identities and setup authentication using a Cognito User Pool

3: Use Amazon Cognito to associate unauthenticated users with an IAM role that has limited access to resources

4: Embed access keys in the application that have limited access to resources

Answer: 3

Explanation:

Amazon Cognito Identity Pools can support unauthenticated identities by providing a unique identifier and AWS credentials for users who do not authenticate with an identity provider. If your application allows users who do not log in, you can enable access for unauthenticated identities.

This is the most efficient and secure way to allow unauthenticated access as the process to set it up is simple and the IAM role can be configured with permissions allowing only the access permitted for unauthenticated users.

CORRECT: "Use Amazon Cognito to associate unauthenticated users with an IAM role that has limited access to resources" is the correct answer.

INCORRECT: "Use an IAM SAML 2.0 identity provider to establish trust" is incorrect as we need to allow unauthenticated users access to the AWS resources, not those who have been authenticated elsewhere (i.e. Active Directory).

INCORRECT: "Use Amazon Cognito Federated Identities and setup authentication using a Cognito User Pool" is incorrect as we need to setup unauthenticated access, not authenticated access through a user pool.

INCORRECT: "Embed access keys in the application that have limited access to resources" is incorrect. We should try and avoid embedding access keys in application code, it is better to use the built-in features of Amazon Cognito.

20. Question

A serverless application is used to process customer information and outputs a JSON file to an Amazon S3 bucket. AWS Lambda is used for processing the data. The data is sensitive and should be encrypted. How can a Developer modify the Lambda function to ensure the data is encrypted before it is uploaded to the S3 bucket?

1: Use the GenerateDataKey API, then use the data key to encrypt the file using the Lambda code

2: Enable server-side encryption on the S3 bucket and create a policy to enforce encryption

3: Use the S3 managed key and call the GenerateDataKey API to encrypt the file

4: Use the default KMS key for S3 and encrypt the file using the Lambda code

Answer: 1

Explanation:

The GenerateDataKey API is used with the AWS KMS services and generates a unique symmetric data key. This operation returns a plaintext copy of the data key and a copy that is encrypted under a customer master key (CMK) that you specify. You can use the plaintext key to encrypt your data outside of AWS KMS and store the encrypted data key with the encrypted data.

For this scenario we can use GenerateDataKey to obtain an encryption key from KMS that we can then use within the function code to encrypt the file. This ensures that the file is encrypted BEFORE it is uploaded to Amazon S3.

CORRECT: "Use the GenerateDataKey API, then use the data key to encrypt the file using the Lambda code" is the correct answer.

INCORRECT: "Enable server-side encryption on the S3 bucket and create a policy to enforce encryption" is incorrect. This would not encrypt data before it is uploaded as S3 would only encrypt the data as it is written to storage.

INCORRECT: "Use the S3 managed key and call the GenerateDataKey API to encrypt the file" is incorrect as you do not use an encryption key to call KMS. You call KMS with the GenerateDataKey API to obtain an encryption key. Also, the S3 managed key can only be used within the S3 service.

INCORRECT: "Use the default KMS key for S3 and encrypt the file using the Lambda code" is incorrect. You cannot use the default KMS key for S3 within the Lambda code as it can only be used within the S3 service.

21. Question

A Developer is troubleshooting an issue with a DynamoDB table. The table is used to store order information for a busy online store and uses the order date as the partition key. During busy periods writes to the table are being throttled despite the consumed throughput being well below the provisioned throughput. According to AWS best practices, how can the Developer resolve the issue at the LOWEST cost?

1: Increase the read and write capacity units for the table

2: Add a random number suffix to the partition key values

3: Add a global secondary index to the table

4: Use an Amazon SQS queue to buffer the incoming writes

Answer: 2

Explanation:

DynamoDB stores data as groups of attributes, known as *items*. Items are similar to rows or records in other database systems. DynamoDB stores and retrieves each item based on the primary key value, which must be unique.

Items are distributed across 10-GB storage units, called partitions (physical storage internal to DynamoDB). Each table has one or more partitions, as shown in the following illustration.

DynamoDB uses the partition key's value as an input to an internal hash function. The output from the hash function determines the partition in which the item is stored. Each item's location is determined by the hash value of its partition key.

All items with the same partition key are stored together, and for composite partition keys, are ordered by the sort key value. DynamoDB splits partitions by sort key if the collection size grows bigger than 10 GB.

DynamoDB evenly distributes provisioned throughput—read capacity units (RCUs) and write capacity units (WCUs)—among partitions and automatically supports your access patterns using the throughput you have provisioned. However, if your access pattern exceeds 3000 RCU or 1000 WCU for a single partition key value, your requests might be throttled with a ProvisionedThroughputExceededException error.

To avoid request throttling, design your DynamoDB table with the right partition key to meet your access requirements and provide even distribution of data. Recommendations for doing this include the following:

- Use high cardinality attributes (e.g. email_id, employee_no, customer_id etc.)
- Use composite attributes
- Cache popular items
- Add random numbers or digits from a pre-determined range for write-heavy use cases

In this case there is a hot partition due to the order date being used as the partition key and this is causing writes to be throttled. Therefore, the best solution to ensure the writes are more evenly distributed in this scenario is to add a random number suffix to the partition key values.

CORRECT: "Add a random number suffix to the partition key values" is the correct answer.

INCORRECT: "Increase the read and write capacity units for the table" is incorrect as this will not solve the hot partition issue and we know that the consumed throughput is lower than provisioned throughput.

INCORRECT: "Add a global secondary index to the table" is incorrect as a GSI is used for querying data more efficiently, it will not solve the problem of write performance due to a hot partition.

INCORRECT: "Use an Amazon SQS queue to buffer the incoming writes" is incorrect as this is not the lowest cost option. You would need to have producers and consumers of the queue as well as paying for the queue itself.

22. Question

A company is migrating a stateful web service into the AWS cloud. The objective is to refactor the application to realize the benefits of cloud computing. How can the Developer leading the project refactor the application to enable more elasticity? (Select TWO)

1: Use Amazon CloudFormation and the Serverless Application Model

2: Use Amazon CloudFront with a Web Application Firewall

3: Store the session state in an Amazon RDS database

4: Use an Elastic Load Balancer and Auto Scaling Group

5: Store the session state in an Amazon DynamoDB table

Answer: 4,5

Explanation:

As this is a stateful application the session data needs to be stored somewhere. Amazon DynamoDB is designed to be used for storing session data and it highly scalable. To add elasticity to the architecture an Amazon Elastic Load Balancer (ELB) and Amazon EC2 Auto Scaling group (ASG) can be used.

With this architecture the web service can scale elastically using the ASG and the ELB will distribute traffic to all new instances that the ASG launches. This is a good example of utilizing some of the key benefits of refactoring applications into the AWS cloud.

CORRECT: "Use an Elastic Load Balancer and Auto Scaling Group" is a correct answer.

CORRECT: "Store the session state in an Amazon DynamoDB table" is also a correct answer.

INCORRECT: "Use Amazon CloudFormation and the Serverless Application Model" is incorrect. AWS SAM is used in CloudFormation templates for expressing serverless applications using a simplified syntax. This application is not a serverless application.

INCORRECT: "Use Amazon CloudFront with a Web Application Firewall" is incorrect neither protection from web exploits nor improved performance for content delivery are requirements in this scenario.

INCORRECT: "Store the session state in an Amazon RDS database" is incorrect as RDS is not suitable for storing session state data. DynamoDB is a better fit for this use case.

23. Question

A company uses continuous integration and continuous delivery (CI/CD) systems. A Developer needs to automate the deployment of a software package to Amazon EC2 instances as on-premises virtual servers. Which AWS service can be used for the software deployment?

1: AWS CodePipeline

2: AWS CloudBuild

3: AWS Elastic Beanstalk

4: AWS CodeDeploy

Answer: 4

Explanation:

CodeDeploy is a deployment service that automates application deployments to Amazon EC2 instances, on-premises instances, serverless Lambda functions, or Amazon ECS services.

CodeDeploy can deploy application content that runs on a server and is stored in Amazon S3 buckets, GitHub repositories, or Bitbucket repositories. CodeDeploy can also deploy a serverless Lambda function. You do not need to make changes to your existing code before you can use CodeDeploy.

The image below shows the flow of a typical CodeDeploy in-place deployment.

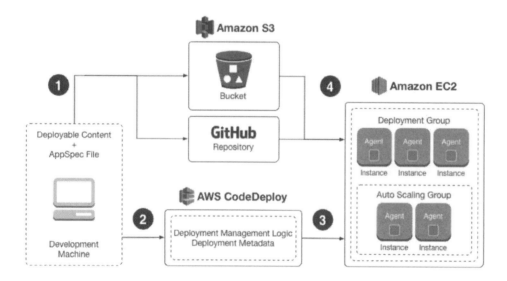

The above deployment could also be directed at on-premises servers. Therefore, the best answer is to use AWS CodeDeploy to deploy the software package to both EC2 instances and on-premises virtual servers.

CORRECT: "AWS CodeDeploy" is the correct answer.

INCORRECT: "AWS CodePipeline" is incorrect. AWS CodePipeline is a fully managed continuous delivery service that helps you automate your release pipelines for fast and reliable application and infrastructure updates. You can use CodeDeploy in a CodePipeline pipeline however it is actually CodeDeploy that deploys the software packages.

INCORRECT: "AWS CloudBuild" is incorrect as this is a build tool, not a deployment tool.

INCORRECT: "AWS Elastic Beanstalk" is incorrect as you cannot deploy software packages to on-premise virtual servers using Elastic Beanstalk

24. Question

A company uses Amazon SQS to decouple an online application that generates memes. The SQS consumers poll the queue regularly to keep throughput high and this is proving to be costly and resource intensive. A Developer has been asked to review the system and propose changes that can reduce costs and the number of empty responses. What would be the BEST approach to MINIMIZING cost?

1: Set the imaging queue visibility Timeout attribute to 20 seconds

2: Set the Imaging queue ReceiveMessageWaitTimeSeconds attribute to 20 seconds

3: Set the imaging queue MessageRetentionPeriod attribute to 20 seconds

4: Set the DelaySeconds parameter of a message to 20 seconds

Answer: 2

Explanation:

The process of consuming messages from a queue depends on whether you use short or long polling. By default, Amazon SQS uses *short polling*, querying only a subset of its servers (based on a weighted random distribution) to determine whether any messages are available for a response. You can use *long polling* to reduce your costs while allowing your consumers to receive messages as soon as they arrive in the queue.

When the wait time for the ReceiveMessage API action is greater than 0, *long polling* is in effect. The maximum long polling wait time is 20 seconds. Long polling helps reduce the cost of using Amazon SQS by eliminating the number of empty responses (when there are no messages available for a ReceiveMessage request) and false empty responses (when messages are available but aren't included in a response).

Therefore, the best way to optimize resource usage and reduce the number of empty responses (and cost) is to configure long polling by setting the Imaging queue ReceiveMessageWaitTimeSeconds attribute to 20 seconds.

CORRECT: "Set the Imaging queue ReceiveMessageWaitTimeSeconds attribute to 20 seconds" is the correct answer.

INCORRECT: "Set the imaging queue visibility Timeout attribute to 20 seconds" is incorrect. This attribute configures message visibility which will not reduce empty responses.

INCORRECT: "Set the imaging queue MessageRetentionPeriod attribute to 20 seconds" is incorrect. This attribute sets the length of time, in seconds, for which Amazon SQS retains a message.

INCORRECT: "Set the DelaySeconds parameter of a message to 20 seconds" is incorrect. This attribute sets the length of time, in seconds, for which the delivery of all messages in the queue is delayed.

25. Question

A Developer has updated an AWS Lambda function and published a new version. To ensure the code is working as expected the Developer needs to initially direct a percentage of traffic to the new version and gradually increase this over time. It is important to be able to rollback if there are any issues reported. What is the BEST way the Developer can implement the migration to the new version SAFELY?

1: Create an Alias, assign the current and new versions and use traffic shifting to assign a percentage of traffic to the new version

2: Create an Amazon Route 53 weighted routing policy pointing to the current and new versions, assign a lower weight to the new version

3: Use an immutable update with a new ASG to deploy the new version in parallel, following testing cutover to the new version

4: Use an Amazon Elastic Load Balancer to direct a percentage of traffic to each target group containing the Lambda function versions

Answer: 1

Explanation:

You can create one or more aliases for your AWS Lambda function. A Lambda alias is like a pointer to a specific Lambda function version. Users can access the function version using the alias ARN.

Each alias has a unique ARN. An alias can only point to a function version, not to another alias. You can update an alias to point to a new version of the function. You can also use traffic shifting to direct a percentage of traffic to a specific version.

This is the recommended way to direct traffic to multiple function versions and shift traffic when testing code updated. Therefore, the best answer is to create an Alias, assign the current and new versions and use traffic shifting to assign a percentage of traffic to the new version.

CORRECT: "Create an Alias, assign the current and new versions and use traffic shifting to assign a percentage of traffic to the new version" is the correct answer.

INCORRECT: "Create an Amazon Route 53 weighted routing policy pointing to the current and new versions, assign a lower weight to the new version" is incorrect. AWS Lambda endpoints are not DNS names that you can route to with Route 53. The best way to route traffic to multiple versions is using an alias.

INCORRECT: "Use an immutable update with a new ASG to deploy the new version in parallel, following testing cutover to the new version" is incorrect as immutable updates are associated with Amazon Elastic Beanstalk and this service does not deploy updates to AWS Lambda.

INCORRECT: "Use an Amazon Elastic Load Balancer to direct a percentage of traffic to each target group containing the Lambda function versions" is incorrect as this introduces an unnecessary layer (complexity and cost) to the architecture. The best choice is to use an alias instead.

26. Question

A Development team is creating a microservices application running on Amazon ECS. The release process workflow of the application requires a manual approval step before the code is deployed into the production environment. What is the BEST way to achieve this using AWS CodePipeline?

1: Use an Amazon SNS notification from the deployment stage

2: Use an approval action in a stage before deployment

3: Disable the stage transition to allow manual approval

4: Disable a stage just prior the deployment stage

Answer: 2

Explanation:

In AWS CodePipeline, you can add an approval action to a stage in a pipeline at the point where you want the pipeline execution to stop so that someone with the required AWS Identity and Access Management permissions can approve or reject the action.

If the action is approved, the pipeline execution resumes. If the action is rejected—or if no one approves or rejects the action within seven days of the pipeline reaching the action and stopping—the result is the same as an action failing, and the pipeline execution does not continue.

In this scenario, the manual approval stage would be placed in the pipeline before the deployment stage that deploys the application update into production.

Therefore, the best answer is to use an approval action in a stage before deployment to production

CORRECT: "Use an approval action in a stage before deployment" is the correct answer.

INCORRECT: "Use an Amazon SNS notification from the deployment stage" is incorrect as this would send a notification when the actual deployment is already occurring.

INCORRECT: "Disable the stage transition to allow manual approval" is incorrect as this requires manual intervention as could be easily missed and allow the deployment to continue.

INCORRECT: "Disable a stage just prior the deployment stage" is incorrect as disabling the stage prior would prevent that stage from running, which may be necessary (could be the build / test stage). It is better to use an approval action in a stage in the pipeline before the deployment occurs

27. Question

A web application is using Amazon Kinesis Data Streams for ingesting IoT data that is then stored before processing for up to 24 hours. How can the Developer implement encryption at rest for data stored in Amazon Kinesis Data Streams?

1: Add a certificate and enable SSL/TLS connections to Kinesis Data Streams

2: Use the Amazon Kinesis Consumer Library (KCL) to encrypt the data

3: Encrypt the data once it is at rest with an AWS Lambda function

4: Enable server-side encryption on Kinesis Data Streams with an AWS KMS CMK

Answer: 4

Explanation:

Amazon Kinesis Data Streams (KDS) is a massively scalable and durable real-time data streaming service. KDS can continuously capture gigabytes of data per second from hundreds of thousands of sources such as website clickstreams, database event streams, financial transactions, social media feeds, IT logs, and location-tracking events.

Server-side encryption is a feature in Amazon Kinesis Data Streams that automatically encrypts data before it's at rest by using an AWS KMS customer master key (CMK) you specify. Data is encrypted before it's written to the Kinesis stream storage layer and decrypted after it's retrieved from storage. As a result, your data is encrypted at rest within the Kinesis Data Streams service. This allows you to meet strict regulatory requirements and enhance the security of your data.

With server-side encryption, your Kinesis stream producers and consumers don't need to manage master keys or cryptographic operations. Your data is automatically encrypted as it enters and leaves the Kinesis Data Streams service, so your data at rest is encrypted. AWS KMS provides all the master keys that are used by the server-side encryption feature. AWS KMS makes it easy to use a CMK for Kinesis that is managed by AWS, a user-specified AWS KMS CMK, or a master key imported into the AWS KMS service.

Therefore, in this scenario the Developer can enable server-side encryption on Kinesis Data Streams with an AWS KMS CMK

CORRECT: "Enable server-side encryption on Kinesis Data Streams with an AWS KMS CMK" is the correct answer.

INCORRECT: "Add a certificate and enable SSL/TLS connections to Kinesis Data Streams" is incorrect as SSL/TLS is already used with Kinesis (you don't need to add a certificate) and this only provides encryption in-transit, not encryption at rest.

INCORRECT: "Use the Amazon Kinesis Consumer Library (KCL) to encrypt the data" is incorrect. The KCL provides design patterns and code for Amazon Kinesis Data Streams consumer applications. The KCL is not used for adding encryption to the data in a stream.

INCORRECT: "Encrypt the data once it is at rest with an AWS Lambda function" is incorrect as this is unnecessary when Kinesis natively supports server-side encryption.

28. Question

A Developer has completed some code updates and needs to deploy the updates to an Amazon Elastic Beanstalk environment. Due to the criticality of the application, the ability to quickly roll back must be prioritized of any other considerations. Which deployment policy should the Developer choose?

1: All at once

2: Rolling

3: Rolling with additional batch

4: Immutable

Answer: 4

Explanation:

AWS Elastic Beanstalk provides several options for how deployments are processed, including deployment policies and options that let you configure batch size and health check behavior during deployments.

Each deployment policy has advantages and disadvantages and it's important to select the best policy to use for each situation. The "immutable" policy will create a new ASG with a whole new set of instances and deploy the updates there.

Immutable:

- Launches new instances in a new ASG and deploys the version update to these instances before swapping traffic to these instances once healthy.

- Zero downtime.

- New code is deployed to new instances using an ASG.

- High cost as double the number of instances running during updates.

- Longest deployment.

- Quick rollback in case of failures.

- Great for production environments.

For this scenario a quick rollback must be prioritized over all other considerations. Therefore, the best choice is "immutable". This deployment policy is the most expensive and longest (duration) option. However, you can roll back quickly and safely as the original instances are all available and unmodified.

CORRECT: "Immutable" is the correct answer.

INCORRECT: "Rolling" is incorrect as this policy requires manual redeployment if there are any issues caused by the update.

INCORRECT: "Rolling with additional batch" is incorrect as this policy requires manual redeployment if there are any issues caused by the update.

INCORRECT: "All at once" is incorrect as this takes the entire environment down at once and requires manual redeployment if there are any issues caused by the update.

29. Question

A Developer needs to configure an Elastic Load Balancer that is deployed through AWS Elastic Beanstalk. Where should the Developer place the load-balancer.config file in the application source bundle?

1: In the root of the source code

2: In the bin folder

3: In the load-balancer.config.root

4: In the .ebextensions folder

Answer: 4

Explanation:

You can add AWS Elastic Beanstalk configuration files (.ebextensions) to your web application's source code to configure your environment and customize the AWS resources that it contains.

Configuration files are YAML- or JSON-formatted documents with a .config file extension that you place in a folder named .ebextensions and deploy in your application source bundle.

For example, you could include a configuration file for setting the load balancer type into:

.ebextensions/load-balancer.config

This example makes a simple configuration change. It modifies a configuration option to set the type of your environment's load balancer to Network Load Balancer:

```
option_settings:
  aws:elasticbeanstalk:environment:
    LoadBalancerType: network
```

Requirements

- **Location** – Place all of your configuration files in a single folder, named .ebextensions, in the root of your source bundle. Folders starting with a dot can be hidden by file browsers, so make sure that the folder is added when you create your source bundle.

- **Naming** – Configuration files must have the .config file extension.

- **Formatting** – Configuration files must conform to YAML or JSON specifications.

- **Uniqueness** – Use each key only once in each configuration file.

Therefore, the Developer should place the file in the .ebextensions folder in the application source bundle.

CORRECT: "In the .ebextensions folder" is the correct answer.

INCORRECT: "In the root of the source code" is incorrect. You need to place .config files in the .ebextensions folder.

INCORRECT: "In the bin folder" is incorrect. You need to place .config files in the .ebextensions folder.

INCORRECT: "In the load-balancer.config.root" is incorrect. You need to place .config files in the .ebextensions folder.

30. Question

A Developer has created the code for a Lambda function saved the code in a file named lambda_function.py. He has also created a template that named template.yaml. The following code is included in the template file:

AWSTemplateFormatVersion: '2010-09-09'

Transform: 'AWS::Serverless-2016-10-31'

Resources:

  microservicehttpendpointpython3:

   Type: 'AWS::Serverless::Function'

   Properties:

    Handler: lambda_function.lambda_handler

CodeUri: .

What commands can the Developer use to prepare and then deploy this template? (Select TWO)

1: Run aws cloudformation package and then aws cloudformation deploy

2: Run sam package and then sam deploy

3: Run aws cloudformation compile and then aws cloudformation deploy

4: Run sam build and then sam package

5: Run aws serverless package and then aws serverless deploy

Answer: 1,2

Explanation:

The template shown is an AWS SAM template for deploying a serverless application. This can be identified by the template header: *Transform: 'AWS::Serverless-2016-10-31'*

The Developer will need to package and then deploy the template. To do this the source code must be available in the same directory or referenced using the "codeuri" parameter. Then, the Developer can use the "aws cloudformation package" or "sam package" commands to prepare the local artifacts (local paths) that your AWS CloudFormation template references.

The command uploads local artifacts, such as source code for an AWS Lambda function or a Swagger file for an AWS API Gateway REST API, to an S3 bucket. The command returns a copy of your template, replacing references to local artifacts with the S3 location where the command uploaded the artifacts.

Once that is complete the template can be deployed using the "aws cloudformation deploy" or "sam deploy" commands. Therefore, the developer has two options to prepare and then deploy this package:

- Run aws cloudformation package and then aws cloudformation deploy
- Run sam package and then sam deploy

CORRECT: "Run aws cloudformation package and then aws cloudformation deploy" is a correct answer.

INCORRECT: "Run sam package and then sam deploy" is also a correct answer.

INCORRECT: "Run aws cloudformation compile and then aws cloudformation deploy" is incorrect as the "compile" command should be replaced with the "package" command.

INCORRECT: "Run sam build and then sam package" is incorrect as the Developer needs to run the "package" command first and then the "deploy" command to actually deploy the function.

INCORRECT: "Run aws serverless package and then aws serverless deploy" is incorrect as there is no AWS CLI command named "serverless".

31. Question

A Developer manages a monitoring service for a fleet of IoT sensors in a major city. The monitoring application uses an Amazon Kinesis Data Stream with a group of EC2 instances processing the data. Amazon CloudWatch custom metrics show that the instances a reaching maximum processing capacity and there are insufficient shards in the Data Stream to handle the rate of data flow. What course of action should the Developer take to resolve the performance issues?

1: Increase the number of EC2 instances to match the number of shards

2: Increase the EC2 instance size and add shards to the stream

3: Increase the EC2 instance size

4: Increase the number of open shards

Answer: 2

Explanation:

By increasing the instance size and number of shards in the Kinesis stream, the developer can allow the instances to handle more record processors, which are running in parallel within the instance. It also allows the stream to properly accommodate the rate of data being sent in. The data capacity of your stream is a function of the number of shards that you specify for the stream. The total capacity of the stream is the sum of the capacities of its shards.

Therefore, the best answer is to increase both the EC2 instance size and add shards to the stream.

CORRECT: "Increase the EC2 instance size and add shards to the stream" is the correct answer.

INCORRECT: "Increase the number of EC2 instances to match the number of shards" is incorrect as you can have an individual instance running multiple KCL workers.

INCORRECT: "Increase the EC2 instance size" is incorrect as the Developer would also need to add shards to the stream to increase the capacity of the stream.

INCORRECT: "Increase the number of open shards" is incorrect as this does not include increasing the instance size or quantity which is required as they are running at capacity.

---

32. Question

A company uses an Amazon Simple Storage Service (SQS) Standard queue for an application. An issue has been identified where applications are picking up messages from the queue that are still being processed causing duplication. What can a Developer do to resolve this issue?

1: Increase the DelaySeconds API action on the queue

2: Increase the VisibilityTimeout API action on the queue

3: Increase the ReceiveMessageWaitTimeSeconds API action on the queue

4: Create a RedrivePolicy for the queue

Answer: 2

Explanation:

When a consumer receives and processes a message from a queue, the message remains in the queue. Amazon SQS doesn't automatically delete the message. Because Amazon SQS is a distributed system, there's no guarantee that the consumer actually receives the message (for example, due to a connectivity issue, or due to an issue in the consumer application). Thus, the consumer must delete the message from the queue after receiving and processing it.

Immediately after a message is received, it remains in the queue. To prevent other consumers from processing the message again, Amazon SQS sets a *visibility timeout*, a period of time during which Amazon SQS prevents other consumers from receiving and processing the message. The default visibility timeout for a message is 30 seconds. The minimum is 0 seconds. The maximum is 12 hours.

Therefore, the best thing the Developer can do in this situation is to increase the VisibilityTimeout API action on the queue

CORRECT: "Increase the VisibilityTimeout API action on the queue" is the correct answer.

INCORRECT: "Increase the DelaySeconds API action on the queue" is incorrect as this controls the length of time, in seconds, for which the delivery of all messages in the queue is delayed.

INCORRECT: "Increase the ReceiveMessageWaitTimeSeconds API action on the queue" is incorrect as this is the length of time, in seconds, for which a ReceiveMessage action waits for a message to arrive. This is used to configure long polling.

INCORRECT: "Create a RedrivePolicy for the queue" is incorrect as this is a string that includes the parameters for the dead-letter queue functionality of the source queue as a JSON object.

33. Question

A Developer is using AWS SAM to create a template for deploying a serverless application. The Developer plans deploy a Lambda function using the template. Which resource type should the Developer specify?

1: AWS::Serverless::Application

2: AWS::Serverless:Function

3: AWS::Serverless:LayerVersion

4: AWS::Serverless:API

Answer: 2

Explanation:

A **serverless application** is a combination of Lambda functions, event sources, and other resources that work together to perform tasks. Note that a serverless application is more than just a Lambda function—it can include additional resources such as APIs, databases, and event source mappings.

AWS SAM templates are an extension of AWS CloudFormation templates, with some additional components that make them easier to work with. To create a Lambda function using an AWS SAM template the Developer can use the AWS::Serverless::Function resource type.

The AWS::Serverless::Function resource type can be used to Create a Lambda function, IAM execution role, and event source mappings that trigger the function.

CORRECT: "AWS::Serverless:Function" is the correct answer.

INCORRECT: "AWS::Serverless::Application" is incorrect as this embeds a serverless application from the AWS Serverless Application Repository or from an Amazon S3 bucket as a nested application.

INCORRECT: "AWS::Serverless:LayerVersion" is incorrect as this creates a Lambda LayerVersion that contains library or runtime code needed by a Lambda Function.

INCORRECT: "AWS::Serverless:API" is incorrect as this creates a collection of Amazon API Gateway resources and methods that can be invoked through HTTPS endpoints.

34. Question

A team of Developers have been assigned to a new project. The team will be collaborating on the development and delivery of a new application and need a centralized private repository for managing source code. The repository should support updates from multiple sources. Which AWS service should the development team use?

1: AWS CodeCommit

2: AWS CodeBuild

3: AWS CodeDeploy

4: AWS CodePipeline

Answer: 1

Explanation:

CodeCommit is a secure, highly scalable, managed source control service that hosts private Git repositories. CodeCommit eliminates the need for you to manage your own source control system or worry about scaling its infrastructure.

You can use CodeCommit to store anything from code to binaries. It supports the standard functionality of Git, so it works seamlessly with your existing Git-based tools.

With CodeCommit, you can:

- **Benefit from a fully managed service hosted by AWS**. CodeCommit provides high service availability and durability and eliminates the administrative overhead of managing your own hardware and software. There is no hardware to provision and scale and no server software to install, configure, and update.

- **Store your code securely**. CodeCommit repositories are encrypted at rest as well as in transit.

- **Work collaboratively on code.** CodeCommit repositories support pull requests, where users can review and comment on each other's code changes before merging them to branches; notifications that automatically send emails to users about pull requests and comments; and more.

- **Easily scale your version control projects**. CodeCommit repositories can scale up to meet your development needs. The service can handle repositories with large numbers of files or branches, large file sizes, and lengthy revision histories.

- **Store anything, anytime**. CodeCommit has no limit on the size of your repositories or on the file types you can store.

- **Integrate with other AWS and third-party services**. CodeCommit keeps your repositories close to your other production resources in the AWS Cloud, which helps increase the speed and frequency of your development lifecycle. It is integrated with IAM and can be used with other AWS services and in parallel with other repositories. **Easily migrate files from other remote repositories**. You can migrate to CodeCommit from any Git-based repository.

- **Use the Git tools you already know**. CodeCommit supports Git commands as well as its own AWS CLI commands and APIs.

Therefore, the development team should select AWS CodeCommit as the repository they use for storing code related to the new project.

CORRECT: "AWS CodeCommit" is the correct answer.

INCORRECT: "AWS CodeBuild" is incorrect. AWS CodeBuild is a fully managed continuous integration (CI) service that compiles source code, runs tests, and produces software packages that are ready to deploy.

INCORRECT: "AWS CodeDeploy" is incorrect. CodeDeploy is a deployment service that automates application deployments to Amazon EC2 instances, on-premises instances, serverless Lambda functions, or Amazon ECS services.

INCORRECT: "AWS CodePipeline" is incorrect. AWS CodePipeline is a fully managed continuous delivery service that helps you automate your release pipelines for fast and reliable application and infrastructure updates.

35. Question

A development team have deployed a new application and users have reported some performance issues. The developers need to enable monitoring for specific metrics with a data granularity of one second. How can this be achieved?

1: Do nothing, CloudWatch uses standard resolution metrics by default

2: Create custom metrics and configure them as standard resolution

3: Create custom metrics and enable detailed monitoring

4: Create custom metrics and configure them as high resolution

Answer: 4

Explanation:

You can publish your own metrics to CloudWatch using the AWS CLI or an API. You can view statistical graphs of your published metrics with the AWS Management Console.

CloudWatch stores data about a metric as a series of data points. Each data point has an associated time stamp. You can even publish an aggregated set of data points called a *statistic set*.

Each metric is one of the following:

- Standard resolution, with data having a one-minute granularity

- High resolution, with data at a granularity of one second

Metrics produced by AWS services are standard resolution by default. When you publish a custom metric, you can define it as either standard resolution or high resolution. When you publish a high-resolution metric, CloudWatch stores it with a resolution of 1 second, and you can read and retrieve it with a period of 1 second, 5 seconds, 10 seconds, 30 seconds, or any multiple of 60 seconds.

High-resolution metrics can give you more immediate insight into your application's sub-minute activity. Keep in mind that every PutMetricData call for a custom metric is charged, so calling PutMetricData more often on a high-resolution metric can lead to higher charges.

Therefore, the best action to take is to Create custom metrics and configure them as high resolution. This will ensure that granularity can be down to 1 second.

CORRECT: "Create custom metrics and configure them as high resolution" is the correct answer.

INCORRECT: "Do nothing, CloudWatch uses standard resolution metrics by default" is incorrect as standard resolution has a granularity of one-minute.

INCORRECT: "Create custom metrics and configure them as standard resolution" is incorrect as standard resolution has a granularity of one-minute.

INCORRECT: "Create custom metrics and enable detailed monitoring" is incorrect as detailed monitoring has a granularity of one-minute.

36. Question

A Developer is deploying an application using Docker containers on Amazon ECS. One of the containers runs a database and should be placed on instances in the "databases" task group. What should the Developer use to control the placement of the database task?

1: Cluster Query Language

2: Task Placement Constraint

3: IAM Group

4: ECS Container Agent

Answer: 2

Explanation:

A *task placement constraint* is a rule that is considered during task placement. Task placement constraints can be specified when either running a task or creating a new service. The task placement constraints can be updated for existing services as well.

Amazon ECS supports the following types of task placement constraints:

distinctInstance

Place each task on a different container instance. This task placement constraint can be specified when either running a task or creating a new service.

memberOf

Place tasks on container instances that satisfy an expression. For more information about the expression syntax for constraints, see Cluster Query Language.

The memberOf task placement constraint can be specified with the following actions:

- Running a task

- Creating a new service

- Creating a new task definition

- Creating a new revision of an existing task definition

The example task placement constraint below uses the memberOf constraint to place tasks on instances in the databases task group. It can be specified with the following actions: CreateService, UpdateService, RegisterTaskDefinition, and RunTask.

```
"placementConstraints": [

  {

    "expression": "task:group == databases",

    "type": "memberOf"

  }

]
```

The Developer should therefore use task placement constraints as in the above example to control the placement of the database task.

CORRECT: "Task Placement Constraint" is the correct answer.

INCORRECT: "Cluster Query Language" is incorrect. Cluster queries are expressions that enable you to group objects. For example, you can group container instances by attributes such as Availability Zone, instance type, or custom metadata.

INCORRECT: "IAM Group" is incorrect as you cannot control task placement on ECS with IAM Groups. IAM groups are used for organizing IAM users and applying policies to them.

INCORRECT: "ECS Container Agent" is incorrect. The Amazon ECS container agent allows container instances to connect to your cluster.

37. Question

An organization has a new AWS account and is setting up IAM users and policies. According to AWS best practices, which of the following strategies should be followed? (Select TWO.)

1: Use groups to assign permissions to users

2: Create standalone policies instead of using inline policies

3: Use user accounts to delegate permissions

4: Create user accounts that can be shared for efficiency

5: Always use customer managed policies instead of AWS managed policies

Answer: 1,2

Explanation:

AWS provide a number of best practices for AWS IAM that help you to secure your resources. The key best practices referenced in this scenario are as follows:

- Use groups to assign permissions to users – this is correct as you should create permissions policies and assign them to groups. Users can be added to the groups to get the permissions they need to perform their jobs.
- Create standalone policies instead of using inline policies (Use Customer Managed Policies Instead of Inline Policies in the AWS best practices) – this refers to creating your own policies that are standalone policies which can be reused multiple times (assigned to multiple entities such as groups, and users). This is better than using inline policies which are directly attached to a single entity.

CORRECT: "Use groups to assign permissions to users" is the correct answer.

CORRECT: "Create standalone policies instead of using inline policies" is the correct answer.

INCORRECT: "Use user accounts to delegate permissions" is incorrect as you should use roles to delegate permissions.

INCORRECT: "Create user accounts that can be shared for efficiency" is incorrect as you should not share user accounts. Always create individual user accounts.

INCORRECT: "Always use customer managed policies instead of AWS managed policies" is incorrect as this is not a best practice. AWS recommend getting started by using AWS managed policies (Get Started Using Permissions with AWS Managed Policies).

38. Question

A Developer is deploying an update to a serverless application that includes AWS Lambda using the AWS Serverless Application Model (SAM). The traffic needs to move from the old Lambda version to the new Lambda version gradually, within the shortest period of time. Which deployment configuration is MOST suitable for these requirements?

1: CodeDeployDefault.LambdaCanary10Percent5Minutes

2: CodeDeployDefault.HalfAtATime

3: CodeDeployDefault.LambdaLinear10PercentEvery1Minute

4: CodeDeployDefault.LambdaLinear10PercentEvery2Minutes

Answer: 1

Explanation:

If you use AWS SAM to create your serverless application, it comes built-in with CodeDeploy to provide gradual Lambda deployments. With just a few lines of configuration, AWS SAM does the following for you:

- Deploys new versions of your Lambda function, and automatically creates aliases that point to the new version.

- Gradually shifts customer traffic to the new version until you're satisfied that it's working as expected, or you roll back the update.

- Defines pre-traffic and post-traffic test functions to verify that the newly deployed code is configured correctly and your application operates as expected.

- Rolls back the deployment if CloudWatch alarms are triggered.

There are several options for how CodeDeploy shifts traffic to the new Lambda version. You can choose from the following:

- **Canary:** Traffic is shifted in two increments. You can choose from predefined canary options. The options specify the percentage of traffic that's shifted to your updated Lambda function version in the first increment, and the interval, in minutes, before the remaining traffic is shifted in the second increment.

- **Linear**: Traffic is shifted in equal increments with an equal number of minutes between each increment. You can choose from predefined linear options that specify the percentage of traffic that's shifted in each increment and the number of minutes between each increment.

- **All-at-once**: All traffic is shifted from the original Lambda function to the updated Lambda function version at once.

Therefore CodeDeployDefault.LambdaCanary10Percent5Minutes is the best answer as this will shift 10 percent of the traffic and then after 5 minutes shift the remainder of the traffic. The entire deployment will take 5 minutes to cut over.

CORRECT: "CodeDeployDefault.LambdaCanary10Percent5Minutes" is the correct answer.

INCORRECT: "CodeDeployDefault.HalfAtATime" is incorrect as this is a CodeDeploy traffic shifting strategy that is not applicable to AWS Lambda. You can use Half at a Time with EC2 and on-premises instances.

INCORRECT: "CodeDeployDefault.LambdaLinear10PercentEvery1Minute" is incorrect as this option will take longer. CodeDeploy will shift 10 percent every 1 minute and therefore the deployment time will be 10 minutes.

INCORRECT: "CodeDeployDefault.LambdaLinear10PercentEvery2Minutes" is incorrect as this option will take longer. CodeDeploy will shift 10 percent every 2 minutes and therefore the deployment time will be 20 minutes.

39. Question

A Developer recently created an Amazon DynamoDB table. The table has the following configuration:

Table details

Table name	table1
Primary partition key	userid (String)
Primary sort key	-

The Developer attempted to add two items for userid "user0001" with unique timestamps and received an error for the second item stating: "The conditional request failed". What MUST the Developer do to resolve the issue?

1: Use the SDK to add the items

2: Update the table with a primary sort key for the timestamp attribute

3: Recreate the table with a composite key consisting of userid and timestamp

4: Add a local secondary index (LSI) for the timestamp attribute

Answer: 3

Explanation:

DynamoDB stores and retrieves data based on a Primary key. There are two types of Primary key:

Partition key – unique attribute (e.g. user ID).

- Value of the Partition key is input to an internal hash function which determines the partition or physical location on which the data is stored.

- If you are using the Partition key as your Primary key, then no two items can have the same partition key.

Composite key – Partition key + Sort key in combination.

- Example is user posting to a forum. Partition key would be the user ID, Sort key would be the timestamp of the post.

- 2 items may have the same Partition key, but they must have a different Sort key.

- All items with the same Partition key are stored together, then sorted according to the Sort key value.

- Allows you to store multiple items with the same partition key.

As stated above, if using a partition key alone as per the configuration provided with the question, then you cannot have two items with the same partition key. The only resolution is to recreate the table with a composite key consisting of the userid and timestamp attributes. In that case the Developer will be able to add multiple items with the same userid as long as the timestamp is unique.

CORRECT: "Recreate the table with a composite key consisting of userid and timestamp" is the correct answer.

INCORRECT: "Update the table with a primary sort key for the timestamp attribute" is incorrect as you cannot update the table in this case, it must be recreated.

INCORRECT: "Add a local secondary index (LSI) for the timestamp attribute" is incorrect as the Developer will still not be able to add multiple entries to the main table for the same userid.

INCORRECT: "Use the SDK to add the items" is incorrect as it doesn't matter whether you use the console, CLI or SDK, the conditional update will still fail with this configuration.

40. Question

A Developer has deployed an AWS Lambda function and an Amazon DynamoDB table. The function code returns data from the DynamoDB table when it receives a request. The Developer needs to implement a front end that can receive HTTP GET requests and proxy the request information to the Lambda function. What is the SIMPLEST and most COST-EFFECTIVE solution?

1: Implement an API Gateway API with Lambda proxy integration

2: Implement an API Gateway API with a POST method

3: Implement an Elastic Load Balancer with a Lambda function target

4: Implement an Amazon Cognito User Pool with a Lambda proxy integration

Answer: 1

Explanation:

Amazon API Gateway Lambda proxy integration is a simple, powerful, and nimble mechanism to build an API with a setup of a single API method. The Lambda proxy integration allows the client to call a single Lambda function in the backend. The function accesses many resources or features of other AWS services, including calling other Lambda functions.

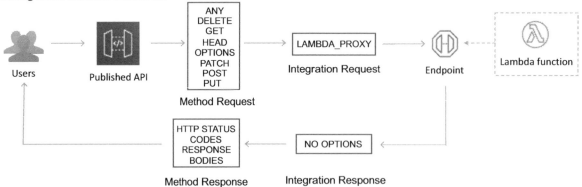

In Lambda proxy integration, when a client submits an API request, API Gateway passes to the integrated Lambda function the raw request as-is, except that the order of the request parameters is not preserved. This request data includes the request headers, query string parameters, URL path variables, payload, and API configuration data.

This solution provides a front end that can listen for HTTP GET requests and then proxy them to the Lambda function and is the simplest option to implement and also the most cost-effective.

CORRECT: "Implement an API Gateway API with Lambda proxy integration" is the correct answer.

INCORRECT: "Implement an API Gateway API with a POST method" is incorrect as a GET method should be implemented. A GET method is a request for data whereas a POST method is a request to upload data.

INCORRECT: "Implement an Elastic Load Balancer with a Lambda function target" is incorrect as though you can do this it is not the simplest or most cost-effective solution.

INCORRECT: "Implement an Amazon Cognito User Pool with a Lambda proxy integration" is incorrect as you cannot create Lambda proxy integrations with Cognito.

41. Question

A Developer needs to write some code to invoke an AWS Lambda function using the AWS Command Line Interface (CLI). Which option must be specified to cause the function to be invoked asynchronously?

1: Set the –invocation-type option to Event

2: Set the –invocation-type option to Invoke

3: Set the –payload option to Asynchronous

4: Set the –qualifier option to Asynchronous

Answer: 1

Explanation:

Several AWS services, such as Amazon Simple Storage Service (Amazon S3) and Amazon Simple Notification Service (Amazon SNS), invoke functions asynchronously to process events.

When you invoke a function asynchronously, you don't wait for a response from the function code. You hand off the event to Lambda and Lambda handles the rest. You can configure how Lambda handles errors and can send invocation records to a downstream resource to chain together components of your application.

The Developer will therefore need to set the –invocation-type option to Event.

CORRECT: "Set the –invocation-type option to Event " is the correct answer.

INCORRECT: "Set the –invocation-type option to Invoke" is incorrect as this is not valid value for this option.

INCORRECT: "Set the –payload option to Asynchronous" is incorrect as this option is used to provide the JSON blob that you want to provide to your Lambda function as input. You cannot supply "asynchronous" as a value.

INCORRECT: "Set the –qualifier option to Asynchronous" is incorrect as this is used to specify a version or alias to invoke a published version of the function. You cannot supply "asynchronous" as a value.

42. Question

A serverless application uses Amazon API Gateway an AWS Lambda function and a Lambda authorizer function. There is a failure with the application and a developer needs to trace and analyze user requests that pass through API Gateway through to the back end services. Which AWS service is MOST suitable for this purpose?

1: Amazon CloudWatch

2: Amazon Inspector

3: VPC Flow Logs

4: AWS X-Ray

Answer: 4

Explanation:

You can use <u>AWS X-Ray</u> to trace and analyze user requests as they travel through your Amazon API Gateway APIs to the underlying services. API Gateway supports X-Ray tracing for all API Gateway endpoint types: Regional, edge-optimized, and private. You can use X-Ray with Amazon API Gateway in all AWS Regions where X-Ray is available.

Because X-Ray gives you an end-to-end view of an entire request, you can analyze latencies in your APIs and their backend services. You can use an X-Ray service map to view the latency of an entire request and that of the downstream services that are integrated with X-Ray. You can also configure sampling rules to tell X-Ray which requests to record and at what sampling rates, according to criteria that you specify.

CORRECT: "AWS X-Ray" is the correct answer.

INCORRECT: "Amazon CloudWatch" is incorrect as it is used to collect metrics and logs. You can use these for troubleshooting however it will be more effective to use AWS X-Ray for analyzing and tracing a distributed application such as this one.

INCORRECT: "Amazon Inspector" is incorrect as this is an automated security assessment service. It is not used for analyzing and tracing serverless applications.

INCORRECT: "VPC Flow Logs" is incorrect as this is a feature that captures information about TCP/IP traffic related to network interfaces in a VPC.

43. Question

A website is being delivered using Amazon CloudFront and a Developer recently modified some images that are displayed on website pages. Upon testing the changes, the Developer noticed that the new versions of the images are not displaying. What should the Developer do to force the new images to be displayed?

1: Delete the images from the origin and then save the new version on the origin

2: Invalidate the old versions of the images on the edge caches

3: Invalidate the old versions of the images on the origin

4: Force an update of the cache

Answer: 2

Explanation:

If you need to remove a file from CloudFront edge caches before it expires, you can do one of the following:

- Invalidate the file from edge caches. The next time a viewer requests the file, CloudFront returns to the origin to fetch the latest version of the file.

- Use file versioning to serve a different version of the file that has a different name. For more information, see <u>Updating Existing Files Using Versioned File Names</u>.

To invalidate files, you can specify either the path for individual files or a path that ends with the * wildcard, which might apply to one file or to many, as shown in the following examples:

- /images/image1.jpg

- /images/image*

- /images/*

Therefore, the Developer should invalidate the old versions of the images on the edge cache as this will remove the cached images and the new versions of the images will then be cached when the next request is received.

CORRECT: "Invalidate the old versions of the images on the edge caches" is the correct answer.

INCORRECT: "Delete the images from the origin and then save the new version on the origin" is incorrect as this will not cause the cache entries to expire. The Developer needs to remove the cached entries to cause a cache miss to occur which will then result in the updated images being cached.

INCORRECT: "Invalidate the old versions of the images on the origin" is incorrect as the Developer needs to invalidate the cache entries on the edge caches, not the images on the origin.

INCORRECT: "Force an update of the cache" is incorrect as there is no way to directly update the cache. The Developer should invalidate the relevant cache entries and then the cache will be updated next time a request is received for the images.

44. Question

A company is using Amazon CloudFront to provide low-latency access to a web application to its global users. The organization must encrypt all traffic between users and CloudFront, and all traffic between CloudFront and the web application. How can these requirements be met? (Select TWO)

1: Use AWS KMS to encrypt traffic between CloudFront and the web application

2: Set the Origin Protocol Policy to "HTTPS Only"

3: Set the Origin's HTTP Port to 443

4: Set the Viewer Protocol Policy to "HTTPS Only" or "Redirect HTTP to HTTPS"

5: Enable the CloudFront option Restrict Viewer Access

Answer: 2,4

Explanation:

This scenario requires encryption of in-flight data which can be done by implementing HTTPS. To do this the organization must configure the Origin Protocol Policy and the Viewer Protocol Policy on the CloudFront Distribution.

Origin Protocol Policy   ○ HTTP Only
                                       ● HTTPS Only
                                       ○ Match Viewer

The Origin Protocol Policy can be used to select whether you want CloudFront to connect to your origin using only HTTP, only HTTPS, or to connect by matching the protocol used by the viewer. For example, if you select Match Viewer for the Origin Protocol Policy, and if the viewer connects to CloudFront using HTTPS, CloudFront will connect to your origin using HTTPS.

Viewer Protocol Policy   ○ HTTP and HTTPS
                                       ● Redirect HTTP to HTTPS
                                       ○ HTTPS Only

If you want CloudFront to allow viewers to access your web content using either HTTP or HTTPS, specify HTTP and HTTPS. If you want CloudFront to redirect all HTTP requests to HTTPS, specify Redirect HTTP to HTTPS. If you want CloudFront to require HTTPS, specify HTTPS Only.

CORRECT: "Set the Origin Protocol Policy to "HTTPS Only"" is a correct answer.

CORRECT: "Set the Viewer Protocol Policy to "HTTPS Only" or "Redirect HTTP to HTTPS"" is also a correct answer.

INCORRECT: "Use AWS KMS to encrypt traffic between CloudFront and the web application" is incorrect as KMS is used for encrypting data at rest.

INCORRECT: "Set the Origin's HTTP Port to 443" is incorrect as you must configure the origin protocol policy to HTTPS. The HTTPS port should be set to 443.

INCORRECT: "Enable the CloudFront option Restrict Viewer Access" is incorrect as this is used to configure whether you want CloudFront to require users to access your content using a signed URL or a signed cookie.

45. Question

A Developer is working on an AWS Lambda function that accesses Amazon DynamoDB. The Lambda function must retrieve an item and update some of its attributes or create the item if it does not exist. The Lambda function has access to the primary key. Which IAM permission should the Developer request for the Lambda function to achieve this functionality?

1: "dynamodb:DeleteItem", "dynamodb:GetItem", and "dynamodb:PutItem"

2: "dynamodb:UpdateItem", "dynamodb:GetItem", and "dynamodb:DescribeTable"

3: "dynamodb:GetRecords", "dynamodb:PutItem", and "dynamodb:UpdateTable"

4: "dynamodb:UpdateItem", "dynamodb:GetItem", and "dynamodb:PutItem"

Answer: 4

Explanation:

The Developer needs the permissions to retrieve items, update/modify items, and create items. Therefore permissions for the following API actions are required:

- GetItem - The GetItem operation returns a set of attributes for the item with the given primary key.
- UpdateItem - Edits an existing item's attributes, or adds a new item to the table if it does not already exist. You can put, delete, or add attribute values.
- PutItem - Creates a new item, or replaces an old item with a new item. If an item that has the same primary key as the new item already exists in the specified table, the new item completely replaces the existing item.

CORRECT: ""dynamodb:UpdateItem", "dynamodb:GetItem", and "dynamodb:PutItem"" is the correct answer.

INCORRECT: ""dynamodb:DeleteItem", "dynamodb:GetItem", and "dynamodb:PutItem"" is incorrect as the Developer does not need the permission to delete items.

INCORRECT: ""dynamodb:UpdateItem", "dynamodb:GetItem", and "dynamodb:DescribeTable"" is incorrect as the Developer does not need to return information about the table (DescribeTable) such as the current status of the table, when it was created, the primary key schema, and any indexes on the table.

INCORRECT: ""dynamodb:GetRecords", "dynamodb:PutItem", and "dynamodb:UpdateTable"" is incorrect as GetRecords is not a valid API action/permission for DynamoDB.

46. Question

A Developer is trying to make API calls using AWS SDK. The IAM user credentials used by the application require multi-factor authentication for all API calls. Which method should the Developer use to access the multi-factor authentication protected API?

1: GetFederationToken

2: GetCallerIdentity

3: GetSessionToken

4: DecodeAuthorizationMessage

Answer: 3

Explanation:

The GetSessionToken API call returns a set of temporary credentials for an AWS account or IAM user. The credentials consist of an access key ID, a secret access key, and a security token. Typically, you use GetSessionToken if you want to use MFA to protect programmatic calls to specific AWS API operations

Therefore, the Developer can use GetSessionToken with an MFA device to make secure API calls using the AWS SDK.

CORRECT: "GetSessionToken" is the correct answer.

INCORRECT: "GetFederationToken" is incorrect as this is used with federated users to return a set of temporary security credentials (consisting of an access key ID, a secret access key, and a security token).

INCORRECT: "GetCallerIdentity" is incorrect as this API action returns details about the IAM user or role whose credentials are used to call the operation.

INCORRECT: "DecodeAuthorizationMessage" is incorrect as this API action decodes additional information about the authorization status of a request from an encoded message returned in response to an AWS request.

47. Question

A company is creating a REST service using an Amazon API Gateway with AWS Lambda integration. The service must run different versions for testing purposes. What would be the BEST way to accomplish this?

1: Use an X-Version header to denote which version is being called and pass that header to the Lambda function(s)

2: Create an API Gateway Lambda authorizer to route API clients to the correct API version

3: Create an API Gateway resource policy to isolate versions and provide context to the Lambda function(s)

4: Deploy the API version as unique stages with unique endpoints and use stage variables to provide further context

Answer: 4

Explanation:

A stage is a named reference to a deployment, which is a snapshot of the API. You use a Stage to manage and optimize a particular deployment. For example, you can configure stage settings to enable caching, customize request throttling, configure logging, define stage variables, or attach a canary release for testing.

Stage variables are name-value pairs that you can define as configuration attributes associated with a deployment stage of a REST API. They act like environment variables and can be used in your API setup and mapping templates.

With stages and stage variables, you can configure different settings for different versions of the application and point to different versions of your Lambda function.

CORRECT: "Deploy the API version as unique stages with unique endpoints and use stage variables to provide further context" is the correct answer.

INCORRECT: "Use an X-Version header to denote which version is being called and pass that header to the Lambda function(s)" is incorrect as you cannot pass a value in a header to a Lambda function and have that determine which version is executed. Versions have unique ARNs and must be connected to separately.

INCORRECT: "Create an API Gateway Lambda authorizer to route API clients to the correct API version" is incorrect as a Lambda authorizer is used for authentication, and different versions of an API are created using stages.

INCORRECT: "Create an API Gateway resource policy to isolate versions and provide context to the Lambda function(s)" is incorrect as resource policies are not used to isolate versions or provide context. In this scenario, stages and stage variables should be used.

48. Question

A set of APIs are exposed to customers using Amazon API Gateway. These APIs have caching enabled on the API Gateway. Customers have asked for an option to invalidate this cache for each of the APIs. What action can be taken to allow API customers to invalidate the API Cache?

1: Ask customers to use AWS credentials to call the InvalidateCache API

2: Ask customers to invoke an AWS API endpoint which invalidates the cache

3: Ask customers to pass an HTTP header called Cache-Control:max-age=0

4: Ask customers to add a query string parameter called INVALIDATE_CACHE" when making an API call

Answer: 3

Explanation:

A client of your API can invalidate an existing cache entry and reload it from the integration endpoint for individual requests. The client must send a request that contains the Cache-Control: max-age=0 header.

The client receives the response directly from the integration endpoint instead of the cache, provided that the client is authorized to do so. This replaces the existing cache entry with the new response, which is fetched from the integration endpoint.

Therefore, the company should ask customers to pass an HTTP header called Cache-Control:max-age=0.

CORRECT: "Ask customers to pass an HTTP header called Cache-Control:max-age=0" is the correct answer.

INCORRECT: "Ask customers to use AWS credentials to call the InvalidateCache API" is incorrect as this API action is used to invalidate the cache but is not the method the clients use to invalidate the cache.

INCORRECT: "Ask customers to invoke an AWS API endpoint which invalidates the cache" is incorrect as you don't invalidate the cache by invoking an endpoint, the HTTP header mentioned in the explanation is required.

INCORRECT: "Ask customers to add a query string parameter called INVALIDATE_CACHE" when making an API call" is incorrect as this is not a valid method of invalidating an API Gateway cache.

49. Question

A Developer is writing a web application that allows users to view images from an Amazon S3 bucket. The users will log in with their Amazon login, as well as Facebook and/or Google accounts. How can the Developer provide this authentication capability?

1: Use Amazon Cognito with web identity federation

2: Use Amazon Cognito with SAML-based identity federation

3: Use AWS IAM Access/Secret keys in the application code to allow Get* on the S3 bucket

4: Use AWS STS AssumeRole in the application code and assume a role with Get* permissions on the S3 bucket

Answer: 1

Explanation:

Amazon Cognito identity pools (federated identities) enable you to create unique identities for your users and federate them with identity providers. With an identity pool, you can obtain temporary, limited-privilege AWS credentials to access other AWS services. Amazon Cognito identity pools support the following identity providers:

- Public providers: Login with Amazon (Identity Pools), Facebook (Identity Pools), Google (Identity Pools) Sign in with Apple (Identity Pools).

- Amazon Cognito User Pools

- Open ID Connect Providers (Identity Pools)

- SAML Identity Providers (Identity Pools)

- Developer Authenticated Identities (Identity Pools)

With the temporary, limited-privilege AWS credentials users will be able to access the images in the S3 bucket. Therefore, the Developer should use Amazon Cognito with web identity federation

CORRECT: "Use Amazon Cognito with web identity federation" is the correct answer.

INCORRECT: "Use Amazon Cognito with SAML-based identity federation" is incorrect as SAML is used with directory sources such as Microsoft Active Directory, not Facebook or Google.

INCORRECT: "Use AWS IAM Access/Secret keys in the application code to allow Get* on the S3 bucket" is incorrect as this insecure and against best practice. Always try to avoid embedding access keys in application code.

INCORRECT: "Use AWS STS AssumeRole in the application code and assume a role with Get* permissions on the S3 bucket" is incorrect as you cannot do this directly through a Facebook or Google login. For this scenario, a Cognito Identity Pool is required to authenticate the user from the social IdP and provide access to the AWS services.

50. Question

A mobile application has hundreds of users. Each user may use multiple devices to access the application. The Developer wants to assign unique identifiers to these users regardless of the device they use. Which of the following methods should be used to obtain unique identifiers?

1: Create a user table in Amazon DynamoDB as key-value pairs of users and their devices. Use these keys as unique identifiers

2: Use IAM-generated access key IDs for the users as the unique identifier, but do not store secret keys

3: Implement developer-authenticated identities by using Amazon Cognito, and get credentials for these identities

4: Assign IAM users and roles to the users. Use the unique IAM resource ID as the unique identifier

Answer: 3

Explanation:

Amazon Cognito supports developer authenticated identities, in addition to web identity federation through Facebook (Identity Pools), Google (Identity Pools), Login with Amazon (Identity Pools), and Sign in with Apple (identity Pools).

With developer authenticated identities, you can register and authenticate users via your own existing authentication process, while still using Amazon Cognito to synchronize user data and access AWS resources.

Using developer authenticated identities involves interaction between the end user device, your backend for authentication, and Amazon Cognito.

Therefore, the Developer can implement developer-authenticated identities by using Amazon Cognito, and get credentials for these identities.

CORRECT: "Implement developer-authenticated identities by using Amazon Cognito, and get credentials for these identities" is the correct answer.

INCORRECT: "Create a user table in Amazon DynamoDB as key-value pairs of users and their devices. Use these keys as unique identifiers" is incorrect as this solution would require additional application logic and would be more complex.

INCORRECT: "Use IAM-generated access key IDs for the users as the unique identifier, but do not store secret keys" is incorrect as it is not a good practice to provide end users of mobile applications with IAM user accounts and access keys. Cognito is a better solution for this use case.

INCORRECT: "Assign IAM users and roles to the users. Use the unique IAM resource ID as the unique identifier" is incorrect. AWS Cognito is better suited to mobile users and with developer authenticated identities the users can be assigned unique identities.

51. Question

A gaming application stores scores for players in an Amazon DynamoDB table that has four attributes: user_id, user_name, user_score, and user_rank. The users are allowed to update their names only. A user is authenticated by web identity federation. Which set of conditions should be added in the policy attached to the role for the dynamodb:PutItem API call?

1.

```
"Condition": {
  "ForAllValues:StringEquals": {
    "dynamodb:LeadingKeys": [
      "${www.amazon.com:user_id}"
    ],
    "dynamodb:Attributes": [
      "user_name"
    ]
  }
}
```

2.

```
"Condition": {
  "ForAllValues:StringEquals": {
    "dynamodb:LeadingKeys": [
      "${www.amazon.com:user_name}"
    ],
    "dynamodb:Attributes": [
      "user_id"
    ]
  }
}
```

3.

```
"Condition": {
  "ForAllValues:StringEquals": {
    "dynamodb:LeadingKeys": [
      "${www.amazon.com:user_id}"
    ],
    "dynamodb:Attributes": [
      "user_name", "user_id"
    ]
```

```
    }
  }
```

4.

```
"Condition": {
  "ForAllValues:StringEquals": {
    "dynamodb:LeadingKeys": [
      "${www.amazon.com:user_name}"
    ],
    "dynamodb:Attributes": [
      "user_name", "user_id"
    ]
  }
}
```

Answer: 1

Explanation:

The users are authenticated by web identity federation. The user_id value should be used to identify the user in the policy and the policy needs to then allow the user to change the user_name value when using the dynamodb:PutItem API call.

The key parts of the code to look for are the dynamodb:LeadingKeys which represents the partition key of the table and the dynamodb:Attributes which represents the items that can be changed.

CORRECT: The answer that includes dynamodb:LeadingKeys identifying user_id and dynamodb:Attributes identifying user_name is the correct answer.

INCORRECT: The other answers provide a few incorrect code samples where either the dynamodb:LeadingKeys identifies user_name (which is incorrect as it is the item to be changed) or dynamodb:Attributes identifying the wrong attributes for modification (should be user_name).

52. Question

A company is running an order processing system on AWS. Amazon SQS is used to queue orders and an AWS Lambda function processes them. The company recently started noticing a lot of orders are failing to process. How can a Developer MOST effectively manage these failures to debug the failed orders later and reprocess them, as necessary?

1: Implement dead-letter queues for failed orders from the order queue

2: Publish failed orders from the order queue to an Amazon SNS topic

3: Log the failed orders from the order queue using Amazon CloudWatch Logs

4: Send failed orders from the order queue to AWS CloudTrail logs

Answer: 1

Explanation:

Amazon SQS supports *dead-letter queues*, which other queues (*source queues*) can target for messages that can't be processed (consumed) successfully. Dead-letter queues are useful for debugging your application or messaging system because they let you isolate problematic messages to determine why their processing doesn't succeed.

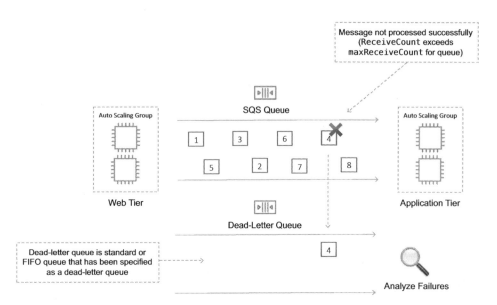

Message not processed successfully
(ReceiveCount exceeds
maxReceiveCount for queue)

SQS Queue

Auto Scaling Group

Web Tier

| 1 | 3 | 6 | 4 |

| 5 | 2 | 7 | 8 |

Auto Scaling Group

Application Tier

Dead-Letter Queue

Dead-letter queue is standard or
FIFO queue that has been specified
as a dead-letter queue

4

Analyze Failures

The Developer should therefore implement dead-letter queues for failed orders from the order queue. This will allow full debugging as the entire message is available for analysis.

CORRECT: "Implement dead-letter queues for failed orders from the order queue" is the correct answer.

INCORRECT: "Publish failed orders from the order queue to an Amazon SNS topic" is incorrect as there is no way to isolate messages that have failed to process when subscribing an SQS queue to an SNS topic.

INCORRECT: "Log the failed orders from the order queue using Amazon CloudWatch Logs" is incorrect as SQS does not publish message success/failure to CloudWatch Logs.

INCORRECT: "Send failed orders from the order queue to AWS CloudTrail logs" is incorrect as CloudTrail records API activity not performance metrics or logs.

53. Question

A Developer must deploy a new AWS Lambda function using an AWS CloudFormation template. Which procedures will deploy a Lambda function? (Select TWO.)

1: Upload the code to an AWS CodeCommit repository, then add a reference to it in an AWS::Lambda::Function resource in the template

2: Create an AWS::Lambda::Function resource in the template, then write the code directly inside the CloudFormation template

3: Upload a ZIP file containing the function code to Amazon S3, then add a reference to it in an AWS::Lambda::Function resource in the template

4: Upload a ZIP file to AWS CloudFormation containing the function code, then add a reference to it in an AWS::Lambda::Function resource in the template

5: Upload the function code to a private Git repository, then add a reference to it in an AWS::Lambda::Function resource in the template

Answer: 2,3

Explanation:

Of the options presented there are two workable procedures for deploying the Lambda function.

Firstly, you can create an AWS::Lambda::Function resource in the template, then write the code directly inside the CloudFormation template. This is possible for simple functions using Node.js or Python which allow you to declare the code inline in the CloudFormation template. For example:

```
Resources:
  MyFunction:
    Type: AWS::Lambda::Function
    Properties:
      Code:
        ZipFile: |
          import json
          def handler(event, context):
              print("Event: %s" % json.dumps(event))
```

The other option is to upload a ZIP file containing the function code to Amazon S3, then add a reference to it in an AWS::Lambda::Function resource in the template. To declare this in your AWS CloudFormation template, you can use the following syntax (within AWS::Lambda::Function Code):

```
{
  "S3Bucket" : String,
  "S3Key" : String,
  "S3ObjectVersion" : String,
  "ZipFile" : String
}
```

CORRECT: "Create an AWS::Lambda::Function resource in the template, then write the code directly inside the CloudFormation template" is a correct answer.

CORRECT: "Upload a ZIP file containing the function code to Amazon S3, then add a reference to it in an AWS::Lambda::Function resource in the template" is also a correct answer.

INCORRECT: "Upload the code to an AWS CodeCommit repository, then add a reference to it in an AWS::Lambda::Function resource in the template" is incorrect as you cannot add a reference to code in a CodeCommit repository.

INCORRECT: "Upload a ZIP file to AWS CloudFormation containing the function code, then add a reference to it in an AWS::Lambda::Function resource in the template" is incorrect as you cannot reference a zip file in CloudFormation.

INCORRECT: "Upload the function code to a private Git repository, then add a reference to it in an AWS::Lambda::Function resource in the template" is incorrect as you cannot reference the function code in a private Git repository.

54. Question

A company is running an application built on AWS Lambda functions. One Lambda function has performance issues when it has to download a 50 MB file from the internet every execution. This function is called multiple times a second. What solution would give the BEST performance increase?

1: Cache the file in the /tmp directory

2: Increase the Lambda maximum execution time

3: Put an Elastic Load Balancer in front of the Lambda function

4: Cache the file in Amazon S3

Answer: 1

Explanation:

The /tmp directory provides 512 MB of storage space that can be used by a function. When a file is cached by a function in the /tmp directory it is available to be used by subsequent executions of the function which will reduce latency.

CORRECT: "Cache the file in the /tmp directory" is the correct answer.

INCORRECT: "Increase the Lambda maximum execution time" is incorrect as the function is not timing out.

INCORRECT: "Put an Elastic Load Balancer in front of the Lambda function" is incorrect as this would not reduce latency or improve performance.

INCORRECT: "Cache the file in Amazon S3" is incorrect as this would not provide better performance as it would still need to be retrieved from S3 for each execution if it is not cached in the /tmp directory.

55. Question

A company is migrating several applications to the AWS cloud. The security team has strict security requirements and mandate that a log of all API calls to AWS resources must be maintained. Which AWS service should be used to record this information for the security team?

1: Amazon CloudWatch

2: AWS CloudTrail

3: Amazon CloudWatch Logs

4: AWS X-Ray

Answer: 2

Explanation:

AWS CloudTrail is a web service that records activity made on your account. A CloudTrail trail can be created which delivers log files to an Amazon S3 bucket. CloudTrail is about logging and saves a history of API calls for your AWS account. It enables governance, compliance, and operational and risk auditing of your AWS account.

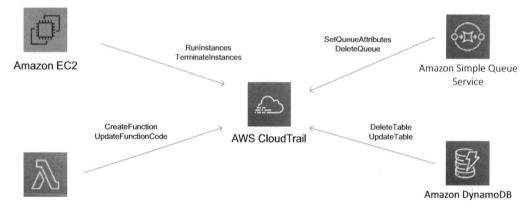

Therefore, AWS CloudTrail is the best solution for maintaining a log of API calls for the security team.

CORRECT: "AWS CloudTrail" is the correct answer.

INCORRECT: "Amazon CloudWatch" is incorrect as this service records metrics related to performance.

INCORRECT: "Amazon CloudWatch Logs" is incorrect as this records log files from services and applications, it does not record a history of API activity.

INCORRECT: "AWS X-Ray" is incorrect as this is used for tracing applications to view performance-related statistics.

56. Question

A Developer has written some code that will connect and pull information from several hundred websites. The code needs to run on a daily schedule and execution time will be less than 60 seconds. Which AWS service will be most suitable and cost-effective?

1: Amazon ECS Fargate

2: Amazon EC2

3: AWS Lambda

4: Amazon API Gateway

Answer: 3

Explanation:

AWS Lambda is a serverless service with a maximum execution time of 900 seconds. This will be the most suitable and cost-effective option for this use case. You can also schedule Lambda functions to run using Amazon CloudWatch Events.

CORRECT: "AWS Lambda" is the correct answer.

INCORRECT: "Amazon ECS Fargate" is incorrect as this is used for running Docker containers and is a better fit for microservices applications rather than running code for a short period of time.

INCORRECT: "Amazon EC2" is incorrect as this would require running EC2 instances which would not be cost-effective.

INCORRECT: "Amazon API Gateway" is incorrect as this service is used for creating APIs, not running code.

57. Question

A team of Developers require access to an AWS account that is a member account in AWS Organizations. The administrator of the master account needs to restrict the AWS services, resources, and API actions that can be accessed by the users in the account. What should the administrator create?

1: A Service Control Policy (SCP)

2: A Tag Policy

3: An Organizational Unit

4: A Consolidated Billing account

Answer: 1

Explanation:

As an administrator of the master account of an organization, you can use service control policies (SCPs) to specify the maximum permissions for member accounts in the organization.

In SCPs, you can restrict which AWS services, resources, and individual API actions the users and roles in each member account can access. You can also define conditions for when to restrict access to AWS services, resources, and API actions.

The following example shows how an SCP can be created to restrict the EC2 instance types that any user can run in the account:

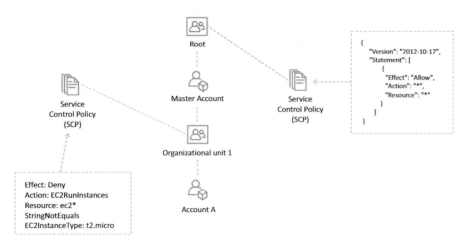

These restrictions even override the administrators of member accounts in the organization. When AWS Organizations blocks access to a service, resource, or API action for a member account, a user or role in that account can't access it. This block remains in effect even if an administrator of a member account explicitly grants such permissions in an IAM policy.

CORRECT: "A Service Control Policy (SCP)" is the correct answer.

INCORRECT: "A Tag Policy" is incorrect as these are used to maintain consistent tags, including the preferred case treatment of tag keys and tag values.

INCORRECT: "An Organizational Unit" is incorrect as this is used to group accounts for administration.

INCORRECT: "A Consolidated Billing account" is incorrect as consolidated billing is not related to controlling access to resources within an account.

58. Question

A three tier web application has been deployed on Amazon EC2 instances using Amazon EC2 Auto Scaling. The EC2 instances in the web tier sometimes receive bursts of traffic and the application tier cannot scale fast enough to keep up with messages sometimes resulting in message loss. How can a Developer decouple the application to prevent loss of messages?

1: Add an Amazon SQS queue between the application tier and the database tier

2: Configure the web tier to publish messages to an SNS topic and subscribe the application tier to the SNS topic

3: Add an Amazon SQS queue between the web tier and the application tier

4: Migrate the database tier to Amazon DynamoDB and enable scalable session handling

Answer: 3

Explanation:

Amazon SQS queues messages received from one application component ready for consumption by another component. A queue is a temporary repository for messages that are awaiting processing. The queue acts as a buffer between the component producing and saving data, and the component receiving the data for processing.

With this scenario the best choice for the Developer is to implement an Amazon SQS queue between the web tier and the application tier. This will mean when the web tier receives bursts of traffic the messages will not overburden the application tier. Instead, they will be placed in the queue and can be processed by the app tier.

CORRECT: "Add an Amazon SQS queue between the web tier and the application tier" is the correct answer.

INCORRECT: "Add an Amazon SQS queue between the application tier and the database tier" is incorrect as the burst of messages are being received by the web tier and it is the application tier that is having difficulty keeping up with demand.

INCORRECT: "Configure the web tier to publish messages to an SNS topic and subscribe the application tier to the SNS topic" is incorrect as SNS is used for notifications and those notifications are not queued, they are sent to all subscribers. The messages being passed in this scenario are better suited to being placed in a queue.

INCORRECT: "Migrate the database tier to Amazon DynamoDB and enable scalable session handling" is incorrect as this is of no relevance to the situation. We don't know what type of database is being used and there is not stated issue with the database layer.

59. Question

A security officer has requested that a Developer enable logging for API actions for all AWS regions to a single Amazon S3 bucket. What is the EASIEST way for the Developer to achieve this requirement?

1: Create an AWS CloudTrail trail and apply it to all regions, configure logging to a single S3 bucket

2: Create an AWS CloudTrail trail in each region, configure logging to a single S3 bucket

3: Create an AWS CloudTrail trail in each region, configure logging to a local bucket, and then use cross-region replication to replicate all logs to a single S3 bucket

4: Create an AWS CloudTrail trail and apply it to all regions, configure logging to a local bucket, and then use cross-region replication to replicate all logs to a single S3 bucket

Answer: 1

Explanation:

The easiest way to achieve the desired outcome is to create an AWS CloudTrail trail and apply it to all regions and configure logging to a single S3 bucket. This is a supported configuration and will achieve the requirement.

CORRECT: "Create an AWS CloudTrail trail and apply it to all regions, configure logging to a single S3 bucket" is the correct answer.

INCORRECT: "Create an AWS CloudTrail trail in each region, configure logging to a single S3 bucket" is incorrect. The Developer should apply a trail to all regions. This will be easier.

INCORRECT: "Create an AWS CloudTrail trail in each region, configure logging to a local bucket, and then use cross-region replication to replicate all logs to a single S3 bucket" is incorrect. This is unnecessary, the Developer can simply create a trail that is applied to all regions and log to a single bucket.

INCORRECT: "Create an AWS CloudTrail trail and apply it to all regions, configure logging to a local bucket, and then use cross-region replication to replicate all logs to a single S3 bucket" is incorrect. This is unnecessary, the Developer can simply create a trail that is applied to all regions and log to a single bucket.

60. Question

A small team of Developers require access to an Amazon S3 bucket. An admin has created a resource-based policy. Which element of the policy should be used to specify the ARNs of the user accounts that will be granted access?

1: Sid

2: Condition

3: Principal

4: Id

Answer: 3

Explanation:

Use the Principal element in a policy to specify the principal that is allowed or denied access to a resource. You cannot use the Principal element in an IAM identity-based policy. You can use it in the trust policies for IAM roles and in resource-based policies. Resource-based policies are policies that you embed directly in an IAM resource.

CORRECT: "Principal" is the correct answer.

INCORRECT: "Condition" is incorrect. The Condition element (or Condition *block*) lets you specify conditions for when a policy is in effect.

INCORRECT: "Sid" is incorrect. The Sid (statement ID) is an optional identifier that you provide for the policy statement.

INCORRECT: "Id" is incorrect. The Id element specifies an optional identifier for the policy.

61. Question

An Amazon DynamoDB table will store authentication credentials for a mobile app. The table must be secured so only a small group of Developers are able to access it. How can table access be secured according to this requirement and following AWS best practice?

1: Attach a permissions policy to an IAM group containing the Developer's IAM user accounts that grants access to the table

2: Attach a resource-based policy to the table and add an IAM group containing the Developer's IAM user accounts as a Principal in the policy

3: Create an AWS KMS resource-based policy to a CMK and grant the developer's user accounts the permissions to decrypt data in the table using the CMK

4: Create a shared user account and attach a permissions policy granting access to the table. Instruct the Developer's to login with the user account

Answer: 1

Explanation:

Amazon DynamoDB supports identity-based policies only. The best practice method to assign permissions to the table is to create a permissions policy that grants access to the table and assigning that policy to an IAM group that contains the Developer's user accounts.

This will provide all users with accounts in the IAM group with the access required to access the DynamoDB table.

CORRECT: "Attach a permissions policy to an IAM group containing the Developer's IAM user accounts that grants access to the table" is the correct answer.

INCORRECT: "Attach a resource-based policy to the table and add an IAM group containing the Developer's IAM user accounts as a Principal in the policy" is incorrect as you cannot assign resource-based policies to DynamoDB tables.

INCORRECT: "Create an AWS KMS resource-based policy to a CMK and grant the developer's user accounts the permissions to decrypt data in the table using the CMK" is incorrect as the questions requires that the Developers can access the table, not to be able to decrypt data.

INCORRECT: "Create a shared user account and attach a permissions policy granting access to the table. Instruct the Developer's to login with the user account" is incorrect as this is against AWS best practice. You should never share user accounts.

62. Question

Based on the following AWS CLI command the resulting output, what has happened here?

```
$ aws lambda invoke --function-name MyFunction  --invocation-type Event --payload
ewogICJrZXkxIjogInZhbHVlMSIsCiAgImtleTIiOiAidmFsdWUyIiwKICAia2V5MyI6ICJ2YWx1ZTMiCn0=
response.json

{
   "StatusCode": 202
}
```

1: An AWS Lambda function has been invoked synchronously and has completed successfully

2: An AWS Lambda function has been invoked synchronously and has not completed successfully

3: An AWS Lambda function has been invoked asynchronously and has completed successfully

4: An AWS Lambda function has been invoked asynchronously and has not completed successfully

Answer: 3

Explanation:

Several AWS services, such as Amazon Simple Storage Service (Amazon S3) and Amazon Simple Notification Service (Amazon SNS), invoke functions asynchronously to process events.

When you invoke a function asynchronously, you don't wait for a response from the function code. You hand off the event to Lambda and Lambda handles the rest. You can configure how Lambda handles errors, and can send invocation records to a downstream resource to chain together components of your application.

The following diagram shows clients invoking a Lambda function asynchronously. Lambda queues the events before sending them to the function.

Asynchronous Invocation

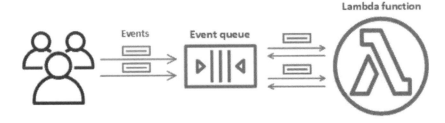

For asynchronous invocation, Lambda places the event in a queue and returns a success response without additional information. A separate process reads events from the queue and sends them to your function. To invoke a function asynchronously, set the invocation type parameter to Event.

In this scenario the Event parameter has been used so we know the function has been invoked asynchronously. For asynchronous invocation the status code 202 indicates a successful execution.

CORRECT: "An AWS Lambda function has been invoked asynchronously and has completed successfully" is the correct answer.

INCORRECT: "An AWS Lambda function has been invoked synchronously and has completed successfully" is incorrect as the Event parameter indicates an asynchronous invocation.

INCORRECT: "An AWS Lambda function has been invoked synchronously and has not completed successfully" is incorrect as the Event parameter indicates an asynchronous invocation (a status code 200 would be a successful execution for a synchronous invocation).

INCORRECT: "An AWS Lambda function has been invoked asynchronously and has not completed successfully" is incorrect as the status code 202 indicates a successful execution.

63. Question

A Developer is creating a service on Amazon ECS and needs to ensure that each task is placed on a different container instance. How can this be achieved?

1: Use a task placement strategy

2: Use a task placement constraint

3: Create a service on Fargate

4: Create a cluster with multiple container instances

Answer: 2

Explanation:

A *task placement constraint* is a rule that is considered during task placement. Task placement constraints can be specified when either running a task or creating a new service.

Amazon ECS supports the following types of task placement constraints:

distinctInstance

Place each task on a different container instance. This task placement constraint can be specified when either running a task or creating a new service.

memberOf

Place tasks on container instances that satisfy an expression. For more information about the expression syntax for constraints, see Cluster Query Language.

The memberOf task placement constraint can be specified with the following actions:

- Running a task

- Creating a new service

- Creating a new task definition

- Creating a new revision of an existing task definition

The following code can be used in a task definition to specify a task placement constraint that ensures that each task will run on a distinct instance:

```
"placementConstraints": [
  {
    "type": "distinctInstance"
  }
]
```

CORRECT: "Use a task placement constraint" is the correct answer.

INCORRECT: "Use a task placement strategy" is incorrect as this is used to select instances for task placement using the binpack, random and spread algorithms.

INCORRECT: "Create a service on Fargate" is incorrect as Fargate spreads tasks across AZs but not instances.

INCORRECT: "Create a cluster with multiple container instances" is incorrect as this will not guarantee that each task runs on a different container instance.

64. Question

An application exports files which must be saved for future use but are not frequently accessed. Compliance requirements necessitate redundant retention of data across AWS regions. Which solution is the MOST cost-effective for these requirements?

1: Amazon S3 with Same-Region Replication (CRR)

2: Amazon DynamoDB with Global Tables

3: AWS Storage Gateway with a replicated file gateway

4: Amazon S3 with Cross-Region Replication (CRR)

Answer: 4

Explanation:

Replication enables automatic, asynchronous copying of objects across Amazon S3 buckets. Buckets that are configured for object replication can be owned by the same AWS account or by different accounts. You can copy objects between different AWS Regions or within the same Region.

To enable object replication, you add a replication configuration to your source bucket. The minimum configuration must provide the following:

- The destination bucket where you want Amazon S3 to replicate objects

- An AWS Identity and Access Management (IAM) role that Amazon S3 can assume to replicate objects on your behalf

You can replicate objects between different AWS Regions or within the same AWS Region.

- **Cross-Region replication** (CRR) is used to copy objects across Amazon S3 buckets in different AWS Regions.

- **Same-Region replication** (SRR) is used to copy objects across Amazon S3 buckets in the same AWS Region.

For this scenario, CRR would be a better fit as the data must be replicated across regions.

CORRECT: "Amazon S3 with Cross-Region Replication (CRR)" is the correct answer.

INCORRECT: "Amazon S3 with Same-Region Replication (CRR)" is incorrect as the requirement is to replicated data across AWS regions.

INCORRECT: "Amazon DynamoDB with Global Tables" is incorrect as this is unlikely to be the most cost-effective solution when data is infrequently accessed. It also may not be possible to store the files in the database, they may need to be referenced from an external location such as S3.

INCORRECT: "AWS Storage Gateway with a replicated file gateway" is incorrect. AWS Storage Gateway connects an on-premises software appliance with cloud-based storage to provide seamless integration. This is not used for replicating data within the AWS cloud across regions.

65. Question

An AWS Lambda function requires several environment variables with secret values. The secret values should be obscured in the Lambda console and API output even for users who have permission to use the key. What is the best way to achieve this outcome and MINIMIZE complexity and latency?

1: Encrypt the secret values client-side using encryption helpers

2: Encrypt the secret values with a customer-managed CMK

3: Store the encrypted values in an encrypted Amazon S3 bucket and reference them from within the code

4: Use an external encryption infrastructure to encrypt the values and add them as environment variables

Answer: 1

Explanation:

You can use environment variables to store secrets securely for use with Lambda functions. Lambda always encrypts environment variables at rest.

Additionally, you can use the following features to customize how environment variables are encrypted.

- **Key configuration** – On a per-function basis, you can configure Lambda to use an encryption key that you create and manage in AWS Key Management Service. These are referred to as *customer managed* customer master keys (CMKs) or customer managed keys. If you don't configure a customer managed key, Lambda uses an AWS managed CMK named aws/lambda, which Lambda creates in your account.

- **Encryption helpers** – The Lambda console lets you encrypt environment variable values client side, before sending them to Lambda. This enhances security further by preventing secrets from being displayed unencrypted in the Lambda console, or in function configuration that's returned by the Lambda API. The console also provides sample code that you can adapt to decrypt the values in your function handler.

The configuration for using encryption helps to encrypt data client-side looks like this:

▼ **Encryption configuration**

Encryption in transit Info

☑ Enable helpers for encryption in transit

AWS KMS key to encrypt at rest
Choose an AWS KMS key to encrypt the environment variables at rest, or simply let Lambda manage the encryption.

○ (default) aws/lambda

◉ Use a customer master key

Customer master key

🔍 arn:aws:kms:ap-southeast-2:515148227241:key/56d9c8ac-c4d0-40d9-9246-; ✕   ⟳

This is the best way to achieve this outcome and minimizes complexity as the encryption infrastructure will still use AWS KMS and be able to decrypt the values during function execution.

CORRECT: "Encrypt the secret values client-side using encryption helpers" is the correct answer.

INCORRECT: "Encrypt the secret values with a customer-managed CMK" is incorrect as this alone will not achieve the desired outcome as the environment variables should be encrypted client-side with the encryption helper to ensure users cannot see the secret values.

INCORRECT: "Store the encrypted values in an encrypted Amazon S3 bucket and reference them from within the code" is incorrect as this would introduce complexity and latency.

INCORRECT: "Use an external encryption infrastructure to encrypt the values and add them as environment variables" is incorrect as this would introduce complexity and latency.

SET 5: PRACTICE QUESTIONS ONLY

For training purposes, go directly to Set 5: Practice Questions, Answers & Explanations

1. Question

An application uses Amazon EC2, and Application Load Balancer and Amazon CloudFront to serve content. The security team have reported malicious activity from a specific range of IP addresses. How can a Developer prevent the application from being targeted by these addresses again?

1: Create a security group rule denying the address range and apply it to the EC2 instances

2: Add a certificate using AWS Certificate Manager (ACM) and encrypt all communications

3: Add a rule to a Web ACL using AWS WAF that denies the IP address ranges

4: Disable the Amazon CloudFront distribution and then reenable it

2. Question

A developer is making some updates to an AWS Lambda function that is part of a serverless application and will be saving a new version. The application is used by hundreds of users and the developer needs to be able to test the updates and be able to rollback if there any issues with user experience. What is the SAFEST way to do this with minimal changes to the application code?

1: Create an alias and point it to the new version. Update the application code to point to the new alias

2: Update the application code to point to the new version

3: Create A records in Route 53 for each function version's ARN. Use a weighted routing policy to direct 20% of traffic to the new version. Add the DNS records to the application code

4: Create an alias and point it to the new and previous versions. Assign a weight of 20% to the new version to direct less traffic. Update the application code to point to the new alias

3. Question

A developer is creating a new application that will store data in a DynamoDB table. Which APIs can be used to read, write and modify individual items in the table?

1: GetItem, PutItem, UpdateItem

2: GetItem, TransactWriteItems, UpdateTable

3: GetItem, PutItem, DeleteItem

4: BatchGetItem, BatchWriteItem, UpdateItem

4. Question

An application running on Amazon EC2 is experiencing intermittent technical difficulties. The developer needs to find a solution for tracking the errors that occur in the application logs and setting up a notification when the error rate exceeds a certain threshold. How can this be achieved with the LEAST complexity?

1: Use CloudTrail to monitor the application log files and send an SNS notification

2: Configure the application to send logs to Amazon S3. Use Amazon Kinesis Analytics to analyze the log files and send an SES notification

3: Configure Amazon CloudWatch Events to monitor the EC2 instances and configure an SNS topic as a target

4: Use CloudWatch Logs to track the number of errors that occur in the application logs and send an SNS notification

5. Question

A website consisting of HTML, images, and client-side JavaScript is being hosted on Amazon S3. The website will be used globally, what's the best way to MINIMIZE latency for global users?

1: Create a CloudFront distribution and configure the S3 website as an origin

2: Host the website from multiple buckets around the world and use Route 53 geolocation-based routing

3: Enable S3 transfer acceleration

4: Create an ElastiCache cluster and configure the S3 website as an origin

6. Question

A team of developers need to be able to collaborate and synchronize multiple distributed code repositories and leverage a pre-configured continuous delivery toolchain for deploying their projects on AWS. The team also require a centralized project dashboard to monitor application activity. Which AWS service should they use?

1: AWS CodePipeline

2: AWS Cloud9

3: AWS CodeStar

4: AWS CodeCommit

7. Question

A developer has created a YAML template file that includes the following header: 'AWS::Serverless-2016-10-31'. Which commands should the developer use to deploy the application?

1: sam package and sam deploy

2: sam package and sam build

3: aws cloudformation create-stack-set

4: aws cloudformation package and aws cloudformation create-stack

8. Question

An application uses multiple Lambda functions to write data to an Amazon RDS database. The Lambda functions must share the same connection string. What is the BEST solution to ensure security and operational efficiency?

1: Use KMS encrypted environment variables within each Lambda function

2: Create a secure string parameter using AWS systems manager parameter store

3: Use a CloudHSM encrypted environment variable that is shared between the functions

4: Embed the connection string within the Lambda function code

9. Question

A company has several AWS accounts used by different departments. Developers use the same CloudFormation template to deploy an application across accounts. What can the developers use to deploy and manage the application with the LEAST operational effort?

1: Create a CloudFormation Stack in an administrator account and use StackSets to update the stacks across multiple accounts

2: Create a CloudFormation Stack in an administrator account and use CloudFormation Change Sets to modify stacks across multiple accounts

3: Migrate the application into an Elastic Beanstalk environment that is shared between multiple accounts

4: Synchronize the applications in multiple accounts using AWS AppSync

10. Question

A company uses an Amazon EC2 web application with Amazon CloudFront to distribute content to its customers globally. The company requires that all traffic is encrypted between the customers and CloudFront, and CloudFront and the web application. What steps need to be taken to enforce this encryption? (Select TWO)

1: Enable Field Level Encryption

2: Set the Origin Protocol Policy to "HTTPS Only"

3: Change the HTTP port to 443 in the Origin Settings

4: Set the Viewer Protocol Policy to "HTTPS Only" or "Redirect HTTP to HTTPS"

5: Use AWS KMS to enforce encryption

11. Question

A developer has a user account in the Development AWS account. He has been asked to modify resources in a Production AWS account. What is the MOST secure way to provide temporary access to the developer?

1: Generate an access key on the second account using the root account and share the access keys with the developer for API access

2: Add the user to a group in the second account that has a role attached granting the necessary permissions

3: Create a cross-account access role, and use sts:AssumeRole API to get short-lived credentials

4: Use AWS KMS to generate cross-account customer master keys and use those get short-lived credentials

12. Question

An application scans an Amazon DynamoDB table once per day to produce a report. The scan is performed in non-peak hours when production usage uses around 50% of the provisioned throughput. How can you MINIMIZE the time it takes to produce the report without affecting production workloads? (Select TWO)

1: Use a Parallel Scan API operation

2: Use a Sequential Scan API operation

3: Increase read capacity units during the scan operation

4: Use the Limit parameter

5: Use pagination to divide results into 1 MB pages

13. Question

A Developer is creating a banking application that will be used to view financial transactions and statistics. The application requires multi-factor authentication to be added to the login protocol. Which service should be used to meet this requirement?

1: AWS IAM with MFA

2: Amazon Cognito User Pool with MFA

3: AWS Directory Service

4: Amazon Cognito Identity Pool with MFA

14. Question

An application is running on a fleet of EC2 instances running behind an Elastic Load Balancer (ELB). The EC2 instances session data in a shared Amazon S3 bucket. Security policy mandates that data must be encrypted in transit. How can the Developer ensure that all data that is sent to the S3 bucket is encrypted in transit?

1: Create an S3 bucket policy that denies any S3 Put request that does not include the x-amz-server-side-encryption

2: Create an S3 bucket policy that denies traffic where SecureTransport is false

3: Configure HTTP to HTTPS redirection on the Elastic Load Balancer

4: Create an S3 bucket policy that denies traffic where SecureTransport is true

15. Question

A gaming application displays the results of games in a leaderboard. The leaderboard is updated by 4 KB messages that are retrieved from an Amazon SQS queue. The updates are received infrequently but the Developer needs to minimize the time between the messages arriving in the queue and the leaderboard being updated. Which technique provides the shortest delay in updating the leaderboard?

1: Reduce the size of the messages with compression before sending them

2: Retrieve the messages from the queue using long polling every 15 seconds

3: Store the message payload in Amazon S3 and use the SQS Extended Client Library for Java

4: Retrieve the messages from the queue using short polling every 10 seconds

16. Question

A developer is creating a serverless application that will use a DynamoDB table. The average item size is 9KB. The application will make 4 strongly consistent reads/sec, and 2 standard write/sec. How many RCUs/WCUs are required?

1: 24 RCU and 18 WCU

2: 12 RCU and 36 WCU

3: 6 RCU and 18 WCU

4: 12 RCU and 18 WCU

17. Question

A monitoring application that keeps track of a large eCommerce website uses Amazon Kinesis for data ingestion. During periods of peak data rates, the Kinesis stream cannot keep up with the incoming data. What step will allow Kinesis data streams to accommodate the traffic during peak hours?

1: Install the Kinesis Producer Library (KPL) for ingesting data into the stream

2: Create an SQS queue and decouple the producers from the Kinesis data stream

3: Increase the shard count of the stream using UpdateShardCount

4: Ingest multiple records into the stream in a single call using PutRecords

18. Question

A Developer has created a serverless function that processes log files. The function should be invoked once every 15 minutes. How can the Developer automatically invoke the function using serverless services?

1: Launch an EC2 Linux instance and add a command to periodically invoke the function to its /etc/crontab file

2: Configure the Lambda scheduler to run based on recurring time value

3: Create an Amazon SNS rule to send a notification to Lambda to instruct it to run

4: Create an Amazon CloudWatch Events rule that is scheduled to run and invoke the function

19. Question

A Developer wants to find a list of items in a global secondary index from an Amazon DynamoDB table. Which DynamoDB API call can the Developer use in order to consume the LEAST number of read capacity units?

1: Scan operation using eventually-consistent reads

2: Query operation using strongly-consistent reads

3: Query operation using eventually-consistent reads

4: Scan operation using strongly-consistent reads

20. Question

A company provides a large number of services on AWS to customers. The customers connect to one or more services directly and the architecture is becoming complex. How can the architecture be refactored to provide a single interface for the services?

1: Amazon API Gateway

2: AWS X-Ray

3: AWS Cognito

4: AWS Single Sign On (SSO)

21. Question

An application writes items to an Amazon DynamoDB table. As the application scales to thousands of instances, calls to the DynamoDB API generate occasional ThrottlingException errors. The application is coded in a language that is incompatible with the AWS SDK. What can be done to prevent the errors from occurring?

1: Add exponential backoff to the application logic

2: Use Amazon SQS as an API message bus

3: Pass API calls through Amazon API Gateway

4: Send the items to DynamoDB through Amazon Kinesis Data Firehose

22. Question

A Developer has created an AWS Lambda function in a new AWS account. The function is expected to be invoked 40 times per second and the execution duration will be around 100 seconds. What MUST the Developer do to ensure there are no errors?

1: Contact AWS Support to increase the concurrent execution limits

2: Implement error handling within the function code

3: Implement a Dead Letter Queue to capture invocation errors

4: Implement tracing with X-Ray

23. Question

You run an ad-supported photo sharing website using Amazon S3 to serve photos to visitors of your site. At some point you find out that other sites have been linking to the photos on your site, causing loss to your business. What is an effective method to mitigate this?

1: Store photos on an EBS volume of the web server

2: Remove public read access and use signed URLs with expiry dates

3: Use CloudFront distributions for static content

4: Block the IPs of the offending websites in Security Groups

24. Question

A company manages an application that stores data in an Amazon DynamoDB table. The company need to keep a record of all new changes made to the DynamoDB table in another table within the same AWS region. What is the MOST suitable way to deliver this requirement?

1: Use Amazon DynamoDB streams

2: Use CloudWatch events

3: Use Amazon CloudTrail

4: Use Amazon DynamoDB snapshots

25. Question

An IT automation architecture uses many AWS Lambda functions invoking one another as a large state machine. The coordination of this state machine is legacy custom code that breaks easily.
Which AWS Service can help refactor and manage the state machine?

1: AWS CodePipeline

2: AWS CodeBuild

3: AWS CloudFormation

4: AWS Step Functions

26. Question

A Developer is deploying an Amazon ECS update using AWS CodeDeploy. In the appspec.yml file, which of the following is a valid structure for the order of hooks that should be specified?

1: BeforeInstall > AfterInstall > AfterAllowTestTraffic > BeforeAllowTraffic > AfterAllowTraffic

2: BeforeInstall > AfterInstall > ApplicationStart > ValidateService

3: BeforeAllowTraffic > AfterAllowTraffic

4: BeforeBlockTraffic > AfterBlockTraffic > BeforeAllowTraffic > AfterAllowTraffic

27. Question

A Developer has setup an Amazon Kinesis Data Stream with 6 shards to ingest a maximum of 2000 records per second. An AWS Lambda function has been configured to process these records. In which order will these records be processed?

1: Lambda will receive each record in the reverse order it was placed into the stream

2: Lambda will receive each record in the exact order it was placed into the stream

3: Lambda will receive each record in the exact order it was placed into the shard. There is no guarantee of order across shards

4: The Developer can select exact order or reverse order using the GetRecords API

28. Question

A Developer created an AWS Lambda function for a serverless application. The Lambda function has been executing for several minutes and the Developer cannot find any log data in CloudWatch Logs. What is the MOST likely explanation for this issue?

1: The Lambda function does not have any explicit log statements for the log data to send it to CloudWatch Logs

2: The Lambda function is missing CloudWatch Logs as a source trigger to send log data

3: The execution role for the Lambda function is missing permissions to write log data to the CloudWatch Logs

4: The Lambda function is missing a target CloudWatch Logs group

29. Question

A Developer is looking for a way to use shorthand syntax to express functions, APIs, databases, and event source mappings. The Developer will test using AWS SAM to create a simple Lambda function using Nodejs.12x. What is the SIMPLEST way for the Developer to get started with a Hello World Lambda function?

1: Install the AWS SAM CLI, run sam init and use one of the AWS Quick Start Templates

2: Install the AWS CLI, run aws sam init and use one of the AWS Quick Start Templates

3: Use the AWS Management Console to access AWS SAM and deploy a Hello World function

4: Use AWS CloudFormation to deploy a Hello World stack using AWS SAM

30. Question

An Amazon Kinesis Data Stream has recently been configured to receive data from sensors in a manufacturing facility. A consumer EC2 instance is configured to process the data every 48 hours and save processing results to an Amazon RedShift data warehouse. Testing has identified a large amount of data is missing. A review of monitoring logs has identified that the sensors are sending data correctly and the EC2 instance is healthy. What is the MOST likely explanation for this issue?

1: Records are retained for 24 hours in the Kinesis Data Stream by default

2: Amazon RedShift is not suitable for storing streaming data

3: The EC2 instance is failing intermittently

4: Amazon Kinesis has too many shards provisioned

31. Question

A Developer is managing an application that includes an Amazon SQS queue. The consumers that process the data from the queue are connecting in short cycles and the queue often does not return messages. The cost for API calls is increasing. How can the Developer optimize the retrieval of messages and reduce cost?

1: Call the ReceiveMessage API with the VisibilityTimeout parameter set to 30

2: Call the ReceiveMessage API with the WaitTimeSeconds parameter set to 20

3: Call the SetQueueAttributes API with the DelaySeconds parameter set to 900

4: Call the SetQueueAttributes API with the maxReceiveCount set to 20

32. Question

A company currently runs a number of legacy automated batch processes for system update management and operational activities. The company are looking to refactor these processes and require a service that can coordinate multiple AWS services into serverless workflows. What is the MOST suitable service for this requirement?

1: Amazon SWF

2: AWS Batch

3: AWS Step Functions

33. Question

A Development team have moved their continuous integration and delivery (CI/CD) pipeline into the AWS Cloud. The team is leveraging AWS CodeCommit for management of source code. The team need to compile their source code, run tests, and produce software packages that are ready for deployment. Which AWS service can deliver these outcomes?

1: AWS CodePipeline

2: AWS CodeCommit

3: AWS CodeBuild

4: AWS Cloud9

34. Question

Every time an Amazon EC2 instance is launched, certain metadata about the instance should be recorded in an Amazon DynamoDB table. The data is gathered and written to the table by an AWS Lambda function. What is the MOST efficient method of invoking the Lambda function?

1: Create a CloudWatch Event with an event pattern looking for EC2 state changes and a target set to use the Lambda function

2: Create a CloudWatch alarm that triggers the Lambda function based on log streams indicating an EC2 state change in CloudWatch logs

3: Create a CloudTrail trail alarm that triggers the Lambda function based on the RunInstances API action

4: Configure detailed monitoring on Amazon EC2 and create an alarm that triggers the Lambda function in initialization

35. Question

A Developer is migrating Docker containers to Amazon ECS. A large number of containers will be deployed across some newly deployed ECS containers instances using the same instance type. High availability is provided within the microservices architecture. Which task placement strategy requires the LEAST configuration for this scenario?

1: binpack

2: random

3: spread

4: Fargate

36. Question

A Developer has noticed some suspicious activity in her AWS account and is concerned that the access keys associated with her IAM user account may have been compromised. What is the first thing the Developer do in should do in this situation?

1: Delete her IAM user account

2: Delete the compromised access keys

3: Report the incident to AWS Support

4: Change her IAM User account password

37. Question

A Developer needs to setup a new serverless application that includes AWS Lambda and Amazon API Gateway as part of a single stack. The Developer needs to be able to locally build and test the serverless applications before deployment on AWS. Which service should the Developer use?

1: AWS CloudFormation

2: AWS Elastic Beanstalk

3: AWS CodeBuild

4: AWS Serverless Application Model (SAM)

38. Question

An application needs to read up to 100 items at a time from an Amazon DynamoDB. Each item is up to 100MB in size and all attributes must be retrieved. What is the BEST way to minimize latency?

1: Use GetItem and use a projection expression

2: Use BatchGetItem

3: Use a Scan operation with pagination

4: Use a Query operation with a FilterExpression

39. Question

A Developer manages a website running behind an Elastic Load Balancer in the us-east-1 region. The Developer has recently deployed an identical copy of the website in us-west-1 and needs to send 20% of the traffic to the new site. How can the Developer achieve this requirement?

1: Use an Amazon Route 53 Geolocation Routing Policy

2: Use a blue/green deployment with Amazon Elastic Beanstalk

3: Use a blue/green deployment with Amazon CodeDeploy

4: Use an Amazon Route 53 Weighted Routing Policy

40. Question

A Development team are deploying an AWS Lambda function that will be used by a production application. The function code will be updated regularly, and new versions will be published. The development team do not want to modify application code to point to each new version. How can the Development team setup a static ARN that will point to the latest published version?

1: Publish a mutable version and point it to the $LATEST version

2: Use an unqualified ARN

3: Setup an Alias that will point to the latest version

4: Setup a Route 53 Alias record that points to the published version

41. Question

An application is being instrumented to send trace data using AWS X-Ray. A Developer needs to upload segment documents using JSON-formatted strings to X-Ray using the API. Which API action should the developer use?

1: The PutTraceSegments API action

2: The PutTelemetryRecords API action

3: The UpdateGroup API action

42. Question

A three-tier application is being migrated from an on-premises data center. The application includes an Apache Tomcat web tier, an application tier running on Linux, and a MySQL back end. A Developer must refactor the application to run on the AWS cloud. The cloud-based application must be fault tolerant and elastic. How can the Developer refactor the web tier and application tier? (Select TWO)

1: Create an Amazon CloudFront distribution for the web tier

2: Create an Auto Scaling group of EC2 instances for both the web tier and application tier

3: Use a multi-AZ Amazon RDS database for the back end using the MySQL engine

4: Implement an Elastic Load Balancer for the application tier

5: Implement an Elastic Load Balancer for both the web tier and the application tier

43. Question

A Developer has joined a team and needs to connect to the AWS CodeCommit repository using SSH. What should the Developer do to configure access using Git?

1: On the Developer's IAM account, under security credentials, choose to create HTTPS Git credentials for AWS CodeCommit

2: On the Developer's IAM account, under security credentials, choose to create an access key and secret ID

3: Create an account on Github and user those login credentials to login to AWS CodeCommit

4: Generate an SSH public and private key. Upload the public key to the Developer's IAM account

44. Question

A large quantity of sensitive data must be encrypted. A Developer will use a custom CMK to generate the encryption key. The key policy currently looks like this:

```
{
  "Sid": "Allow Key Usage",
  "Effect": "Allow",
  "Principal": {"AWS": [
    "arn:aws:iam::111122223333:user/CMKUser"
  ]},
  "Action": [
    "kms:Encrypt",
    "kms:Decrypt",
    "kms:ReEncrypt*",
    "kms:DescribeKey"
  ],
  "Resource": "*"
}
```

What API action must be added to the key policy?

1: kms:EnableKey

2: kms:GenerateDataKey*

3: kms:CreateKey

4: kms:GetKeyPolicy

45. Question

A Developer needs to access AWS CodeCommit over SSH. The SSH keys configured to access AWS CodeCommit are tied to a user with the following permissions:

```
{
    "version": "2012-10-17"
    "Statement": [
      {
        "Effect": "Allow",
        "Action": [
          "codecommit:BatchGetRepositories",
          "codecommit:Get*"
          "codecommit:List*",
          "codecommit:GitPull"
        ],
      "Resource": "*"
      }
    ]
}
```

The Developer needs to create/delete branches. Which specific IAM permissions need to be added based on the principle of least privilege?

1: "codecommit:CreateBranch" and "codecommit:DeleteBranch"

2: "codecommit:Put*:"

3: "codecommit:Update*"

4: "codecommit:*"

46. Question

An application uses Amazon Kinesis Data Streams to ingest and process large streams of data records in real time. Amazon EC2 instances consume and process the data using the Amazon Kinesis Client Library (KCL). The application handles the failure scenarios and does not require standby workers. The application reports that a specific shard is receiving more data than expected. To adapt to the changes in the rate of data flow, the "hot" shard is resharded.

Assuming that the initial number of shards in the Kinesis data stream is 6, and after resharding the number of shards increased to 8, what is the maximum number of EC2 instances that can be deployed to process data from all the shards?

1: 12

2: 8

3: 6

4: 1

47. Question

What does an Amazon SQS delay queue accomplish?

1: Messages are hidden for a configurable amount of time when they are first added to the queue

2: Messages are hidden for a configurable amount of time after they are consumed from the queue

3: The consumer can poll the queue for a configurable amount of time before retrieving a message

4: Message cannot be deleted for a configurable amount of time after they are consumed from the queue

48. Question

An organization needs to add encryption in-transit to an existing website running behind an Elastic Load Balancer. The website's Amazon EC2 instances are CPU-constrained and therefore load on their CPUs should not be increased. What should be done to secure the website? (Select TWO)

1: Configure an Elastic Load Balancer with SSL pass-through

2: Configure SSL certificates on an Elastic Load Balancer

3: Configure an Elastic Load Balancer with a KMS CMK

4: Install SSL certificates on the EC2 instances

5: Configure an Elastic Load Balancer with SSL termination

49. Question

A company is running a Docker application on Amazon ECS. The application must scale based on user load in the last 15 seconds. How should the Developer instrument the code so that the requirement can be met?

1: Create a high-resolution custom Amazon CloudWatch metric for user activity data, then publish data every 30 seconds

2: Create a high-resolution custom Amazon CloudWatch metric for user activity data, then publish data every 5 seconds

3: Create a standard-resolution custom Amazon CloudWatch metric for user activity data, then publish data every 30 seconds

4: Create a standard-resolution custom Amazon CloudWatch metric for user activity data, then publish data every 5 seconds

50. Question

A company needs a fully-managed source control service that will work in AWS. The service must ensure that revision control synchronizes multiple distributed repositories by exchanging sets of changes peer-to-peer. All users need to work productively even when not connected to a network. Which source control service should be used?

1: Subversion

2: AWS CodeBuild

3: AWS CodeCommit

4: AWS CodeStar

51. Question

A Developer needs to return a list of items in a global secondary index from an Amazon DynamoDB table. Which DynamoDB API call can the Developer use in order to consume the LEAST number of read capacity units?

1: Scan operation using eventually-consistent reads

2: Query operation using strongly-consistent reads

3: Query operation using eventually-consistent reads

4: Scan operation using strongly-consistent reads

52. Question

A Developer is writing an AWS Lambda function that processes records from an Amazon Kinesis Data Stream. The Developer must write the function so that it sends a notice to Administrators that includes the processed data. How should the Developer write the function?

1: Separate the Lambda handler from the core logic

2: Use Amazon CloudWatch Events to send the processed data

3: Publish the processed data to an Amazon SNS topic

4: Push the processed data to Amazon SQS

53. Question

An application is running on a cluster of Amazon EC2 instances. The application has received an error when trying to read objects stored within an Amazon S3 bucket. The bucket is encrypted with server-side encryption and AWS KMS managed keys (SSE-KMS). The error is as follows:

Service: AWSKMS; Status Code: 400, Error Code: ThrottlingException

Which combination of steps should be taken to prevent this failure? (Select TWO)

1: Contact AWS support to request an AWS KMS rate limit increase

2: Perform error retries with exponential backoff in the application code

3: Contact AWS support to request an S3 rate limit increase

4: Import a customer master key (CMK) with a larger key size

5: Use more than once customer master key (CMK) to encrypt S3 data

54. Question

A Developer is creating an AWS Lambda function that generates a new file each time it runs. Each new file must be checked into an AWS CodeCommit repository hosted in the same AWS account. How should the Developer accomplish this?

1: When the Lambda function starts, use the Git CLI to clone the repository. Check the new file into the cloned repository and push the change

2: After the new file is created in Lambda, use cURL to invoke the CodeCommit API. Send the file to the repository

3: Use an AWS SDK to instantiate a CodeCommit client. Invoke the put_file method to add the file to the repository

4: Upload the new file to an Amazon S3 bucket. Create an AWS Step Function to accept S3 events. In the Step Function, add the new file to the repository

55. Question

A Developer needs to run some code using Lambda in response to an event and forward the execution result to another application using a pub/sub notification. How can the Developer accomplish this?

1: Configure a CloudWatch Events alarm the triggers based on Lambda execution success and route the execution results to Amazon SNS

2: Configure a Lambda "on success" destination and route the execution results to Amazon SNS

3: Configure a Lambda "on success" destination and route the execution results to Amazon SQS

4: Configure a CloudWatch Events alarm the triggers based on Lambda execution success and route the execution results to Amazon SQS

56. Question

An application runs on Amazon EC2 and generates log files. A Developer needs to centralize the log files so they can be queried and retained. What is the EASIEST way for the Developer to centralize the log files?

1: Install the Amazon CloudWatch Logs agent and collect the logs from the instances

2: Create a script that copies the log files to Amazon S3 and use a cron job to run the script on a recurring schedule

3: Create a script that uses the AWS SDK to collect and send the log files to Amazon CloudWatch Logs

4: Setup a CloudWatch Events rule to trigger an SNS topic when an application log file is generated

57. Question

A company needs to encrypt a large quantity of data. The data encryption keys must be generated from a dedicated, tamper-resistant hardware device. To deliver these requirements, which AWS service should the company use?

1: AWS KMS

2: AWS CloudHSM

3: AWS Certificate Manager

4: AWS IAM

58. Question

A Developer needs to restrict all users and roles from using a list of API actions within a member account in AWS Organizations. The Developer needs to deny access to a few specific API actions. What is the MOST efficient way to do this?

1: Create a deny list and specify the API actions to deny

2: Create an allow list and specify the API actions to deny

3: Create an IAM policy that denies the API actions for all users and roles

4: Create an IAM policy that allows only the unrestricted API actions

59. Question

A development team require a fully-managed source control service that is compatible with Git. Which service should they use?

1: AWS CodeDeploy

2: AWS Cloud9

3: AWS CodePipeline

4: AWS CodeCommit

60. Question

How can a Developer view a summary of proposed changes to an AWS CloudFormation stack without implementing the changes in production?

1: Create a StackSet

2: Create a Change Set

3: Use drift detection

4: Use a direct update

61. Question

Based on the following AWS CLI command the resulting output, what has happened here?

$ aws lambda invoke --function-name MyFunction --payload
ewogICJrZXkxIjogInZhbHVlMSIsCiAgImtleTIiOiAidmFsdWUyIiwKICAia2V5MyI6ICJ2YWx1ZTMiCn0=
response.json

```
{

  "StatusCode": 200

}
```

1: An AWS Lambda function has been invoked synchronously and has completed successfully

2: An AWS Lambda function has been invoked synchronously and has not completed successfully

3: An AWS Lambda function has been invoked asynchronously and has completed successfully

4: An AWS Lambda function has been invoked asynchronously and has not completed successfully

62. Question

A Developer must run a shell script on Amazon EC2 Linux instances each time they are launched by an Amazon EC2 Auto Scaling group. What is the SIMPLEST way to run the script?

1: Add the script to the user data when creating the launch configuration

2: Configure Amazon CloudWatch Events to trigger the AWS CLI when an instance is launched and run the script

3: Package the script in a zip file with some AWS Lambda source code. Upload to Lambda and run the function when instances are launched

4: Run the script using the AWS Systems Manager Run Command

63. Question

A Developer has created a task definition that includes the following JSON code:

```
"placementConstraints": [

  {

    "expression": "task:group == databases",

    "type": "memberOf"

  }

]
```

What will be the effect for tasks using this task definition?

1: They will become members of a task group called "databases"

2: They will not be placed on container instances in the "databases" task group

3: They will be placed on container instances in the "databases" task group

4: They will not be allowed to run unless they have the "databases" tag assigned

64. Question

Data must be loaded into an application each week for analysis. The data is uploaded to an Amazon S3 bucket from several offices around the world. Latency is slowing the uploads and delaying the analytics job. What is the SIMPLEST way to improve upload times?

1: Upload to a local Amazon S3 bucket within each region and enable Cross-Region Replication (CRR)

2: Upload via a managed AWS VPN connection

3: Upload to Amazon CloudFront and then download from the local cache to the S3 bucket

4: Upload using Amazon S3 Transfer Acceleration

65. Question

An AWS Lambda function must be connected to an Amazon VPC private subnet that does not have Internet access. The function also connects to an Amazon DynamoDB table. What MUST a Developer do to enable access to the DynamoDB table?

1: Attach an Internet Gateway

2: Configure a VPC endpoint

3: Create a route table

4: Attach an ENI to the DynamoDB table

SET 5: PRACTICE QUESTIONS, ANSWERS & EXPLANATIONS

1. Question

An application uses Amazon EC2, and Application Load Balancer and Amazon CloudFront to serve content. The security team have reported malicious activity from a specific range of IP addresses. How can a Developer prevent the application from being targeted by these addresses again?

1: Create a security group rule denying the address range and apply it to the EC2 instances

2: Add a certificate using AWS Certificate Manager (ACM) and encrypt all communications

3: Add a rule to a Web ACL using AWS WAF that denies the IP address ranges

4: Disable the Amazon CloudFront distribution and then reenable it

Answer: 3

Explanation:

You use AWS WAF to control how an Amazon CloudFront distribution, an Amazon API Gateway API, or an Application Load Balancer responds to web requests.

- **Web ACLs** – You use a web access control list (ACL) to protect a set of AWS resources. You create a web ACL and define its protection strategy by adding rules. Rules define criteria for inspecting web requests and specify how to handle requests that match the criteria. You set a default action for the web ACL that indicates whether to block or allow through those requests that pass the rules inspections.

- **Rules** – Each rule contains a statement that defines the inspection criteria, and an action to take if a web request meets the criteria. When a web request meets the criteria, that's a match. You can use rules to block matching requests or to allow matching requests through. You can also use rules just to count matching requests.

- **Rules groups** – You can use rules individually or in reusable rule groups. AWS Managed Rules and AWS Marketplace sellers provide managed rule groups for your use. You can also define your own rule groups.

After you create your web ACL, you can associate it with one or more AWS resources. The resource types that you can protect using AWS WAF web ACLs are Amazon CloudFront distributions, Amazon API Gateway APIs, and Application Load Balancers.

CORRECT: "Add a rule to a Web ACL using AWS WAF that denies the IP address ranges" is the correct answer.

INCORRECT: "Create a security group rule denying the address range and apply it to the EC2 instances" is incorrect as you cannot add deny rules to security groups.

INCORRECT: "Add a certificate using AWS Certificate Manager (ACM) and encrypt all communications" is incorrect as this will not prevent attacks from coming in from the specific IP ranges. This will simply enabled SSL/TLS for communications from clients.

INCORRECT: "Disable the Amazon CloudFront distribution and then reenable it" is incorrect as this will do nothing to stop future attacks from occurring.

2. Question

A developer is making some updates to an AWS Lambda function that is part of a serverless application and will be saving a new version. The application is used by hundreds of users and the developer needs to be able to test the updates and be able to rollback if there any issues with user experience. What is the SAFEST way to do this with minimal changes to the application code?

1: Create an alias and point it to the new version. Update the application code to point to the new alias

2: Update the application code to point to the new version

3: Create A records in Route 53 for each function version's ARN. Use a weighted routing policy to direct 20% of traffic to the new version. Add the DNS records to the application code

4: Create an alias and point it to the new and previous versions. Assign a weight of 20% to the new version to direct less traffic. Update the application code to point to the new alias

Answer: 4

Explanation:

You can create one or more aliases for your AWS Lambda function. A Lambda alias is like a pointer to a specific Lambda function version. Users can access the function version using the alias ARN.

You can point an alias a multiple versions of your function code and then assign a weighting to direct certain amounts of traffic to each version. This enables a blue/green style of deployment and means it's easy to roll back to the older version by simply updating the weighting if issues occur with user experience.

CORRECT: "Create an alias and point it to the new and previous versions. Assign a weight of 20% to the new version to direct less traffic. Update the application code to point to the new alias" is the correct answer.

INCORRECT: "Create an alias and point it to the new version. Update the application code to point to the new alias" is incorrect as it is better to point the alias at both the new and previous versions of the function code so that it is easier to roll back with fewer application code changes.

INCORRECT: "Update the application code to point to the new version" is incorrect as if you do this you will have to change the application code again to roll back in the event of issues. You will also need to update the application code every time you publish a new version, so this is not a best practice strategy.

INCORRECT: "Create A records in Route 53 for each function version's ARN. Use a weighted routing policy to direct 20% of traffic to the new version. Add the DNS records to the application code" is incorrect as you cannot create Route 53 DNS records that point to an ARN.

3. Question

A developer is creating a new application that will store data in a DynamoDB table. Which APIs can be used to read, write and modify individual items in the table?

1: GetItem, PutItem, UpdateItem

2: GetItem, TransactWriteItems, UpdateTable

3: GetItem, PutItem, DeleteItem

4: BatchGetItem, BatchWriteItem, UpdateItem

Answer: 1

Explanation:

The GetItem operation returns a set of attributes for the item with the given primary key. If there is no matching item, GetItem does not return any data and there will be no Item element in the response.

PutItem creates a new item or replaces an old item with a new item. If an item that has the same primary key as the new item already exists in the specified table, the new item completely replaces the existing item.

UpdateItem edits an existing item's attributes or adds a new item to the table if it does not already exist. You can put, delete, or add attribute values. You can also perform a conditional update on an existing item (insert a new attribute name-value pair if it doesn't exist or replace an existing name-value pair if it has certain expected attribute values).

CORRECT: "GetItem, PutItem, UpdateItem" is the correct answer.

INCORRECT: "GetItem, TransactWriteItems, UpdateTable" is incorrect as TransactWriteItems is a synchronous write operation that groups up to 25 action requests. In this scenario we are updating individual items.

INCORRECT: "GetItem, PutItem, DeleteItem" is incorrect as DeleteItem will delete single items in a table by primary key. We do not want to delete, we want to modify so UpdateItem should be used instead.

INCORRECT: "BatchGetItem, BatchWriteItem, UpdateItem" is incorrect as BatchGetItem and BatchGetItem are used when you have multiple items to read/write. In this scenario we are updating individual items.

4. Question

An application running on Amazon EC2 is experiencing intermittent technical difficulties. The developer needs to find a solution for tracking the errors that occur in the application logs and setting up a notification when the error rate exceeds a certain threshold. How can this be achieved with the LEAST complexity?

1: Use CloudTrail to monitor the application log files and send an SNS notification

2: Configure the application to send logs to Amazon S3. Use Amazon Kinesis Analytics to analyze the log files and send an SES notification

3: Configure Amazon CloudWatch Events to monitor the EC2 instances and configure an SNS topic as a target

4: Use CloudWatch Logs to track the number of errors that occur in the application logs and send an SNS notification

Answer: 4

Explanation:

You can use CloudWatch Logs to monitor applications and systems using log data. For example, CloudWatch Logs can track the number of errors that occur in your application logs and send you a notification whenever the rate of errors exceeds a threshold you specify.

CloudWatch Logs uses your log data for monitoring; so, no code changes are required. For example, you can monitor application logs for specific literal terms (such as "NullReferenceException") or count the number of occurrences of a literal term at a particular position in log data (such as "404" status codes in an Apache access log).

When the term you are searching for is found, CloudWatch Logs reports the data to a CloudWatch metric that you specify. Log data is encrypted while in transit and while it is at rest.

CORRECT: "Use CloudWatch Logs to track the number of errors that occur in the application logs and send an SNS notification" is the correct answer.

INCORRECT: "Use CloudTrail to monitor the application log files and send an SNS notification" is incorrect as CloudTrail logs API activity in your account, it does not monitor application logs.

INCORRECT: "Configure the application to send logs to Amazon S3. Use Amazon Kinesis Analytics to analyze the log files and send an SES notification" is incorrect. This is a much more complex solution and is not a full solution as it does not include a method of loading the data into Kinesis. Amazon SES is also not suitable for notifications, SNS should be used which can also send emails if required.

INCORRECT: "Configure Amazon CloudWatch Events to monitor the EC2 instances and configure an SNS topic as a target" is incorrect as it monitors AWS services for changes in state. You can monitor EC2, but not the application within the EC2 instance.

5. Question

A website consisting of HTML, images, and client-side JavaScript is being hosted on Amazon S3. The website will be used globally, what's the best way to MINIMIZE latency for global users?

1: Create a CloudFront distribution and configure the S3 website as an origin

2: Host the website from multiple buckets around the world and use Route 53 geolocation-based routing

3: Enable S3 transfer acceleration

4: Create an ElastiCache cluster and configure the S3 website as an origin

Answer: 1

Explanation:

To serve a static website hosted on Amazon S3, you can deploy a CloudFront distribution using one of these configurations:

- Using a REST API endpoint as the origin with access restricted by an <u>origin access identity (OAI)</u>
- Using a website endpoint as the origin with anonymous (public) access allowed
- Using a website endpoint as the origin with access restricted by a Referer header

All assets of this website are static (HTML, images, client-side JavaScript), therefore this website is compatible with both S3 static websites and Amazon CloudFront. The simplest way to minimize latency is to create a CloudFront distribution and configure the static website as an origin.

CORRECT: "Create a CloudFront distribution and configure the S3 website as an origin" is the correct answer.

INCORRECT: "Host the website from multiple buckets around the world and use Route 53 geolocation-based routing" is incorrect as this not a good way to solve this problem. With this configuration you would need to keep multiple copies of the website files in sync (and pay for more storage space) which is less than ideal.

INCORRECT: "Enable S3 transfer acceleration" is incorrect as transfer acceleration is used for improving the speed of uploads to an S3 bucket, not downloads.

INCORRECT: "Create an ElastiCache cluster and configure the S3 website as an origin" is incorrect as you cannot use an ElastiCache cluster as the front-end to an S3 static website (nor does it solve the problem of reducing latency around the world).

6. Question

A team of developers need to be able to collaborate and synchronize multiple distributed code repositories and leverage a pre-configured continuous delivery toolchain for deploying their projects on AWS. The team also require a centralized project dashboard to monitor application activity. Which AWS service should they use?

1: AWS CodePipeline

2: AWS Cloud9

3: AWS CodeStar

4: AWS CodeCommit

Answer: 3

Explanation:

AWS CodeStar enables you to quickly develop, build, and deploy applications on AWS. AWS CodeStar provides a unified user interface, enabling you to easily manage your software development activities in one place. With AWS CodeStar, you can set up your entire continuous delivery toolchain in minutes, allowing you to start releasing code faster. AWS CodeStar makes it easy for your whole team to work together securely, allowing you to easily manage access and add owners, contributors, and viewers to your projects.

Each AWS CodeStar project comes with a project management dashboard, including an integrated issue tracking capability powered by Atlassian JIRA Software. With the AWS CodeStar project dashboard, you can easily track progress across your entire software development process, from your backlog of work items to teams' recent code deployments.

CORRECT: "AWS CodeStar" is the correct answer.

INCORRECT: "AWS CodePipeline" is incorrect as it does not offer the collaboration and project management dashboard features of CodeStar.

INCORRECT: "AWS Cloud9" is incorrect as it is a cloud-based integrated development environment (IDE) that lets you write, run, and debug your code with just a browser.

INCORRECT: "AWS CodeCommit" is incorrect. CodeCommit is a fully managed source control service that hosts Git-based repositories. However, it does not offer the collaboration and project management dashboard features of CodeStar or the pre-configured continuous delivery toolchain.

7. Question

A developer has created a YAML template file that includes the following header: 'AWS::Serverless-2016-10-31'. Which commands should the developer use to deploy the application?

1: sam package and sam deploy

2: sam package and sam build

3: aws cloudformation create-stack-set

4: aws cloudformation package and aws cloudformation create-stack

Answer: 1

Explanation:

The AWS Serverless Application Model (SAM) is an open-source framework for building serverless applications. It provides shorthand syntax to express functions, APIs, databases, and event source mappings. With just a few lines per resource, you can define the application you want and model it using YAML.

The "Transform" header indicates that the developer is creating a SAM template as it has the value: Transform: 'AWS::Serverless-2016-10-31'

Therefore, there are two sets of commands that can be used to package and deploy using SAM:

Use either:

- sam package
- sam deploy

Or use:

- aws cloudformation package
- aws cloudformation deploy

CORRECT: "sam package and sam deploy" is the correct answer.

INCORRECT: "sam package and sam build" is incorrect as "sam build" is used to build your Lambda function code, not to package and deploy it.

INCORRECT: "aws cloudformation create-stack-set" is incorrect as this creates a stack set and is not used when deploying using AWS SAM.

INCORRECT: "aws cloudformation package and aws cloudformation create-stack" is incorrect as when using AWS SAM you should use "aws cloudformation deploy" instead for the second command.

8. Question

An application uses multiple Lambda functions to write data to an Amazon RDS database. The Lambda functions must share the same connection string. What is the BEST solution to ensure security and operational efficiency?

1: Use KMS encrypted environment variables within each Lambda function

2: Create a secure string parameter using AWS systems manager parameter store

3: Use a CloudHSM encrypted environment variable that is shared between the functions

4: Embed the connection string within the Lambda function code

Answer: 2

Explanation:

AWS Systems Manager Parameter Store provides secure, hierarchical storage for configuration data management and secrets management. You can store data such as passwords, database strings, and license codes as parameter values.

You can store values as plaintext (unencrypted data) or ciphertext (encrypted data). You can then reference values by using the unique name that you specified when you created the parameter.

A secure string parameter is any sensitive data that needs to be stored and referenced in a secure manner. If you have data that you don't want users to alter or reference in plaintext, such as passwords or license keys, create those parameters using the SecureString datatype.

If you choose the SecureString datatype when you create a parameter, then Parameter Store uses an AWS Key Management Service (KMS) customer master key (CMK) to encrypt the parameter value.

This is the most secure and operationally efficient way to meet this requirement. The connection string will be encrypted and only needs to be managed in one place where it can be shared by the multiple Lambda functions.

CORRECT: "Create a secure string parameter using AWS systems manage parameter store" is the correct answer.

INCORRECT: "Use KMS encrypted environment variables within each Lambda function" is incorrect as this would require more operational overhead when managing any changes to the connection string.

INCORRECT: "Use a CloudHSM encrypted environment variable that is shared between the functions" is incorrect as you cannot encrypt Lambda environment variables with CloudHSM (use KMS instead).

INCORRECT: "Embed the connection string within the Lambda function code" is incorrect as this is not secure or operationally efficient.

9. Question

A company has several AWS accounts used by different departments. Developers use the same CloudFormation template to deploy an application across accounts. What can the developers use to deploy and manage the application with the LEAST operational effort?

1: Create a CloudFormation Stack in an administrator account and use StackSets to update the stacks across multiple accounts

2: Create a CloudFormation Stack in an administrator account and use CloudFormation Change Sets to modify stacks across multiple accounts

3: Migrate the application into an Elastic Beanstalk environment that is shared between multiple accounts

4: Synchronize the applications in multiple accounts using AWS AppSync

Answer: 1

Explanation:

AWS CloudFormation StackSets extends the functionality of stacks by enabling you to create, update, or delete stacks across multiple accounts and regions with a single operation.

Using an administrator account, you define and manage an AWS CloudFormation template, and use the template as the basis for provisioning stacks into selected target accounts across specified regions.

Using StackSets for this scenario will work well and result in the least operational overhead in creating, updating and deleting CloudFormation stacks across multiple accounts.

CORRECT: "Create a CloudFormation Stack in an administrator account and use StackSets to update the stacks across multiple accounts" is the correct answer.

INCORRECT: "Create a CloudFormation Stack in an administrator account and use CloudFormation Change Sets to modify stacks across multiple accounts" is incorrect. Change sets allow you to preview how proposed changes to a stack might impact your running resources.

INCORRECT: "Migrate the application into an Elastic Beanstalk environment that is shared between multiple accounts" is incorrect because we don't even know if the application is compatible with Elastic Beanstalk and you cannot "share" environments between multiple accounts.

INCORRECT: "Synchronize the applications in multiple accounts using AWS AppSync" is incorrect. AWS AppSync can perform synchronization and real-time updates between applications but it requires development and is not suitable for solving this challenge.

10. Question

A company uses an Amazon EC2 web application with Amazon CloudFront to distribute content to its customers globally. The company requires that all traffic is encrypted between the customers and CloudFront, and CloudFront and the web application. What steps need to be taken to enforce this encryption? (Select TWO)

1: Enable Field Level Encryption

2: Set the Origin Protocol Policy to "HTTPS Only"

3: Change the HTTP port to 443 in the Origin Settings

4: Set the Viewer Protocol Policy to "HTTPS Only" or "Redirect HTTP to HTTPS"

5: Use AWS KMS to enforce encryption

Answer: 2,4

Explanation:

To ensure encryption between the origin (Amazon EC2) and CloudFront you need to set the Origin Protocol Policy to "HTTPS Only" This is configured in the origin settings and can be seen in the image below:

To ensure encryption between CloudFront and the end users you need to change the Viewer Protocol Policy to "HTTPS Only" or "Redirect HTTP to HTTPS". This is configured in the cache behavior and can be seen in the image below:

CORRECT: "Set the Origin Protocol Policy to "HTTPS Only"" is the correct answer.

CORRECT: "Set the Viewer Protocol Policy to "HTTPS Only" or "Redirect HTTP to HTTPS"" is also a correct answer.

INCORRECT: "Enable Field Level Encryption" is incorrect. This is used to add another layer of security to sensitive data such as credit card numbers.

INCORRECT: "Change the HTTP port to 443 in the Origin Settings" is incorrect. You should not change the HTTP port to 443, instead change Origin Protocol Policy to HTTPS.

INCORRECT: "Use AWS KMS to enforce encryption" is incorrect. AWS KMS is not used for enforcing encryption on CloudFront. AWS KMS is used for creating and managing encryption keys.

11. Question

A developer has a user account in the Development AWS account. He has been asked to modify resources in a Production AWS account. What is the MOST secure way to provide temporary access to the developer?

1: Generate an access key on the second account using the root account and share the access keys with the developer for API access

2: Add the user to a group in the second account that has a role attached granting the necessary permissions

3: Create a cross-account access role, and use sts:AssumeRole API to get short-lived credentials

4: Use AWS KMS to generate cross-account customer master keys and use those get short-lived credentials

Answer: 3

Explanation:

This should be implemented using a role in the Production account and a group in the Development account. The developer in the Development account would then be added to the group. The role in the Production account would provide the necessary access and would allow the group in the Development account to assume the role.

Therefore, the most secure way to achieve the required access is to use a role in the Production account that the user is able to assume and then the user can request short-lived credentials from the Security Token Service (STS).

CORRECT: "Create a cross-account access role, and use sts:AssumeRole API to get short-lived credentials" is the correct answer.

INCORRECT: "Generate an access key on the second account using the root account and share the access keys with the developer for API access" is incorrect as this is highly insecure. You should never share access keys across user accounts, and you should especially not use access keys associated with the root account.

INCORRECT: "Add the user to a group in the second account that has a role attached granting the necessary permissions" is incorrect as you cannot add a user to a group in a different AWS account.

INCORRECT: "Use AWS KMS to generate cross-account customer master keys and use those get short-lived credentials" is incorrect as you do not use AWS KMS CMKs for obtaining short-lived credentials from the STS service. CMKs are used for encrypting data.

12. Question

An application scans an Amazon DynamoDB table once per day to produce a report. The scan is performed in non-peak hours when production usage uses around 50% of the provisioned throughput. How can you MINIMIZE the time it takes to produce the report without affecting production workloads? (Select TWO)

1: Use a Parallel Scan API operation

2: Use a Sequential Scan API operation

3: Increase read capacity units during the scan operation

4: Use the Limit parameter

Answer: 1,4

Explanation:

By default, the Scan operation processes data sequentially. Amazon DynamoDB returns data to the application in 1 MB increments, and an application performs additional Scan operations to retrieve the next 1 MB of data.

The larger the table or index being scanned, the more time the Scan takes to complete. In addition, a sequential Scan might not always be able to fully use the provisioned read throughput capacity: Even though DynamoDB distributes a large table's data across multiple physical partitions, a Scan operation can only read one partition at a time. For this reason, the throughput of a Scan is constrained by the maximum throughput of a single partition.

To address these issues, the Scan operation can logically divide a table or secondary index into multiple *segments*, with multiple application workers scanning the segments in parallel. Each worker can be a thread (in programming languages that support multithreading) or an operating system process. To perform a parallel scan, each worker issues its own Scan request with the following parameters:

- Segment — A segment to be scanned by a particular worker. Each worker should use a different value for Segment.

- TotalSegments — The total number of segments for the parallel scan. This value must be the same as the number of workers that your application will use.

To make the most of your table's provisioned throughput, you'll want to use the Parallel Scan API operation so that your scan is distributed across your table's partitions. However, you also need to ensure the scan doesn't consume your table's provisioned throughput and cause the critical parts of your application to be throttled.

To control the amount of data returned per request, use the Limit parameter. This can help prevent situations where one worker consumes all of the provisioned throughput, at the expense of all other workers.

Therefore, the best solution to this problem is to use a parallel scan API operation with the Limit parameter.

CORRECT: "Use a Parallel Scan API operation " is the correct answer.

CORRECT: "Use the Limit parameter" is also a correct answer.

INCORRECT: "Use a Sequential Scan API operation" is incorrect as this would take more time and the question requests that we minimize the time it takes to complete the scan.

INCORRECT: "Increase read capacity units during the scan operation" is incorrect as this would increase cost and we still need a solution to ensure we maximize usage of available throughput without affecting production workloads.

INCORRECT: "Use pagination to divide results into 1 MB pages" is incorrect as this does only divides the results into pages, it does not segment and limit the amount of throughput used.

13. Question

A Developer is creating a banking application that will be used to view financial transactions and statistics. The application requires multi-factor authentication to be added to the login protocol. Which service should be used to meet this requirement?

1: AWS IAM with MFA

2: Amazon Cognito User Pool with MFA

3: AWS Directory Service

4: Amazon Cognito Identity Pool with MFA

Answer: 2

Explanation:

A user pool is a user directory in Amazon Cognito. With a user pool, your users can sign in to your web or mobile app through Amazon Cognito. Your users can also sign in through social identity providers like Google, Facebook, Amazon, or Apple, and through SAML identity providers.

User pools provide:

- Sign-up and sign-in services.

- A built-in, customizable web UI to sign in users.

- Social sign-in with Facebook, Google, Login with Amazon, and Sign in with Apple, as well as sign-in with SAML identity providers from your user pool.

- User directory management and user profiles.

- Security features such as multi-factor authentication (MFA), checks for compromised credentials, account takeover protection, and phone and email verification.

- Customized workflows and user migration through AWS Lambda triggers.

Multi-factor authentication (MFA) increases security for your app by adding another authentication method, and not relying solely on username and password. You can choose to use SMS text messages, or time-based one-time (TOTP) passwords as second factors in signing in your users.

For this scenario you would want to set the MFA setting to "Required" as the data is highly secure.

CORRECT: "Amazon Cognito User Pool with MFA" is the correct answer.

INCORRECT: "Amazon Cognito Identity Pool with MFA" is incorrect

INCORRECT: "AWS IAM with MFA" is incorrect. With IAM your user accounts are maintained in your AWS account rather than in a Cognito User Pool. For logging into a web or mobile app it is better to create and manage your users in a Cognito User Pool and add MFA to the User Pool for extra security.

INCORRECT: "AWS Directory Service" is incorrect as this is a managed Active Directory service. For a web or mobile application using AWS Cognito User Pools is a better solution for storing your user accounts and authenticating to the application.

14. Question

An application is running on a fleet of EC2 instances running behind an Elastic Load Balancer (ELB). The EC2 instances session data in a shared Amazon S3 bucket. Security policy mandates that data must be encrypted in transit. How can the Developer ensure that all data that is sent to the S3 bucket is encrypted in transit?

1: Create an S3 bucket policy that denies any S3 Put request that does not include the x-amz-server-side-encryption

2: Create an S3 bucket policy that denies traffic where SecureTransport is false

3: Configure HTTP to HTTPS redirection on the Elastic Load Balancer

4: Create an S3 bucket policy that denies traffic where SecureTransport is true

Answer: 2

Explanation:

At the Amazon S3 bucket level, you can configure permissions through a bucket policy. For example, you can limit access to the objects in a bucket by IP address range or specific IP addresses. Alternatively, you can make the objects accessible only through HTTPS.

The following bucket policy allows access to Amazon S3 objects only through HTTPS (the policy was generated with the AWS Policy Generator).

```
{
    "Version": "2012-10-17",
    "Id": "Policy1504640911349",
    "Statement": [
        {
            "Sid": "Stmt1504640908907",
            "Effect": "Deny",
            "Principal": "*",
            "Action": "s3:GetObject",
            "Resource": "arn:aws:s3:::/*",
            "Condition": {
                "Bool": {
                    "aws:SecureTransport": "false"
                }
            }
        }
    ]
}
```

Here the bucket policy explicitly denies ("Effect": "Deny") all read access ("Action": "s3:GetObject") from anybody who browses ("Principal": "*") to Amazon S3 objects within an Amazon S3 bucket if they are not accessed through HTTPS ("aws:SecureTransport": "false").

CORRECT: "Create an S3 bucket policy that denies traffic where SecureTransport is false" is the correct answer.

INCORRECT: "Create an S3 bucket policy that denies traffic where SecureTransport is true" is incorrect. This will not work as it is denying traffic that IS encrypted in transit.

INCORRECT: "Create an S3 bucket policy that denies any S3 Put request that does not include the x-amz-server-side-encryption" is incorrect. This will ensure that the data is encrypted at rest, but not in-transit.

INCORRECT: "Configure HTTP to HTTPS redirection on the Elastic Load Balancer" is incorrect. This will ensure the client traffic reaching the ELB is encrypted however we need to ensure the traffic from the EC2 instances to S3 is encrypted and the ELB is not involved in this communication.

15. Question

A gaming application displays the results of games in a leaderboard. The leaderboard is updated by 4 KB messages that are retrieved from an Amazon SQS queue. The updates are received infrequently but the Developer needs to minimize the time between the messages arriving in the queue and the leaderboard being updated. Which technique provides the shortest delay in updating the leaderboard?

1: Reduce the size of the messages with compression before sending them

2: Retrieve the messages from the queue using long polling every 15 seconds

3: Store the message payload in Amazon S3 and use the SQS Extended Client Library for Java

4: Retrieve the messages from the queue using short polling every 10 seconds

Answer: 2

Explanation:

The process of consuming messages from a queue depends on whether you use short or long polling. By default, Amazon SQS uses *short polling*, querying only a subset of its servers (based on a weighted random distribution) to determine whether any messages are available for a response.

You can use *long polling* to reduce your costs while allowing your consumers to receive messages as soon as they arrive in the queue. When the wait time for the ReceiveMessage API action is greater than 0, *long polling* is in effect. The maximum long polling wait time is 20 seconds.

Long polling helps reduce the cost of using Amazon SQS by eliminating the number of empty responses (when there are no messages available for a <u>ReceiveMessage</u> request) and false empty responses (when messages are available but aren't included in a response). It also returns messages as soon as they become available.

CORRECT: "Retrieve the messages from the queue using long polling every 15 seconds" is the correct answer.

INCORRECT: "Retrieve the messages from the queue using short polling every 10 seconds" is incorrect as short polling is configured when the WaitTimeSeconds parameter of a <u>ReceiveMessage</u> request is set to 0. Any number above zero indicates long polling is in effect.

INCORRECT: "Reduce the size of the messages with compression before sending them" is incorrect as this will not mean messages are picked up earlier and there is no reason to compress messages that are 4 KB in size.

INCORRECT: "Store the message payload in Amazon S3 and use the SQS Extended Client Library for Java" is incorrect as this is unnecessary for messages of this size and will also not result in the shortest delay when updating the leaderboard.

16. Question

A developer is creating a serverless application that will use a DynamoDB table. The average item size is 9KB. The application will make 4 strongly consistent reads/sec, and 2 standard write/sec. How many RCUs/WCUs are required?

1: 24 RCU and 18 WCU

2: 12 RCU and 36 WCU

3: 6 RCU and 18 WCU

4: 12 RCU and 18 WCU

Answer: 4

Explanation:

With provisioned capacity mode, you specify the number of data reads and writes per second that you require for your application.

Read capacity unit (RCU):

- Each API call to read data from your table is a read request.
- Read requests can be strongly consistent, eventually consistent, or transactional.
- For items up to 4 KB in size, one RCU can perform one *strongly consistent* read request per second.
- Items larger than 4 KB require additional RCUs.
- For items up to 4 KB in size, one RCU can perform two *eventually consistent* read requests per second.
- *Transactional* read requests require two RCUs to perform one read per second for items up to 4 KB.
- For example, a strongly consistent read of an 8 KB item would require two RCUs, an eventually consistent read of an 8 KB item would require one RCU, and a transactional read of an 8 KB item would require four RCUs.

Write capacity unit (WCU):

- Each API call to write data to your table is a write request.
- For items up to 1 KB in size, one WCU can perform one *standard* write request per second.

- Items larger than 1 KB require additional WCUs.
- *Transactional* write requests require two WCUs to perform one write per second for items up to 1 KB.
- For example, a standard write request of a 1 KB item would require one WCU, a standard write request of a 3 KB item would require three WCUs, and a transactional write request of a 3 KB item would require six WCUs.

To determine the number of RCUs required to handle 4 strongly consistent reads per/second with an average item size of 9KB, perform the following steps:

1. Determine the average item size by rounding up the next multiple of 4KB (9KB rounds up to 12KB).
2. Determine the RCU per item by dividing the item size by 4KB (12KB/4KB = 3).
3. Multiply the value from step 2 with the number of reads required per second (3x4 = 12).

To determine the number of WCUs required to handle 2 standard writes per/second with an average item size of 9KB, simply multiply the average item size by the number of writes required (9x2=18).

CORRECT: "12 RCU and 18 WCU" is the correct answer.

INCORRECT: "24 RCU and 18 WCU" is incorrect. This would be the correct answer for transactional reads and standard writes.

INCORRECT: "12 RCU and 36 WCU" is incorrect. This would be the correct answer for strongly consistent reads and transactional writes.

INCORRECT: "6 RCU and 18 WCU" is incorrect. This would be the correct answer for eventually consistent reads and standard writes

17. Question

A monitoring application that keeps track of a large eCommerce website uses Amazon Kinesis for data ingestion. During periods of peak data rates, the Kinesis stream cannot keep up with the incoming data. What step will allow Kinesis data streams to accommodate the traffic during peak hours?

1: Install the Kinesis Producer Library (KPL) for ingesting data into the stream

2: Create an SQS queue and decouple the producers from the Kinesis data stream

3: Increase the shard count of the stream using UpdateShardCount

4: Ingest multiple records into the stream in a single call using PutRecords

Answer: 3

Explanation:

The UpdateShardCount API action updates the shard count of the specified stream to the specified number of shards.

Updating the shard count is an asynchronous operation. Upon receiving the request, Kinesis Data Streams returns immediately and sets the status of the stream to UPDATING. After the update is complete, Kinesis Data Streams sets the status of the stream back to ACTIVE.

Depending on the size of the stream, the scaling action could take a few minutes to complete. You can continue to read and write data to your stream while its status is UPDATING.

To update the shard count, Kinesis Data Streams performs splits or merges on individual shards. This can cause short-lived shards to be created, in addition to the final shards. These short-lived shards count towards your total shard limit for your account in the Region.

When using this operation, we recommend that you specify a target shard count that is a multiple of 25% (25%, 50%, 75%, 100%). You can specify any target value within your shard limit. However, if you specify a target that isn't a multiple of 25%, the scaling action might take longer to complete.

This operation has the following default limits. By default, you cannot do the following:

- Scale more than ten times per rolling 24-hour period per stream

- Scale up to more than double your current shard count for a stream

- Scale down below half your current shard count for a stream

- Scale up to more than 500 shards in a stream

- Scale a stream with more than 500 shards down unless the result is less than 500 shards

- Scale up to more than the shard limit for your account

Note that the question specifically states that the Kinesis data stream cannot keep up with incoming data. This indicates that the producers are attempting to add records to the stream but there are not enough shards to keep up with demand. Therefore, we need to add additional shards and can do this using the UpdateShardCount API action.

CORRECT: "Increase the shard count of the stream using UpdateShardCount" is the correct answer.

INCORRECT: "Install the Kinesis Producer Library (KPL) for ingesting data into the stream" is incorrect as that will help the producers to be more efficient and increase write throughput to a Kinesis data stream. However, this will not help as the Kinesis data stream already cannot keep up with the incoming demand.

INCORRECT: "Create an SQS queue and decouple the producers from the Kinesis data stream " is incorrect. You cannot decouple a Kinesis producer from a Kinesis data stream using SQS. Kinesis is more than capable of keeping up with demand, it just needs more shards in this case.

INCORRECT: "Ingest multiple records into the stream in a single call using PutRecords" is incorrect as the stream is already overloaded, we need more shards, not more data to be written.

18. Question

A Developer has created a serverless function that processes log files. The function should be invoked once every 15 minutes. How can the Developer automatically invoke the function using serverless services?

1: Launch an EC2 Linux instance and add a command to periodically invoke the function to its /etc/crontab file

2: Configure the Lambda scheduler to run based on recurring time value

3: Create an Amazon SNS rule to send a notification to Lambda to instruct it to run

4: Create an Amazon CloudWatch Events rule that is scheduled to run and invoke the function

Answer: 4

Explanation:

Amazon CloudWatch Events delivers a near real-time stream of system events that describe changes in Amazon Web Services (AWS) resources. Using simple rules that you can quickly set up, you can match events and route them to one or more target functions or streams.

You can use Amazon CloudWatch Events to invoke the Lambda function on a recurring schedule of 15 minutes. This solution is entirely automated and serverless.

CORRECT: "Create an Amazon CloudWatch Events rule that is scheduled to run and invoke the function" is the correct answer.

INCORRECT: "Launch an EC2 Linux instance and add a command to periodically invoke the function to its /etc/crontab file " is incorrect as this is automatic but it is not serverless.

INCORRECT: "Configure the Lambda scheduler to run based on recurring time value" is incorrect as there is no Lambda scheduler that can be used.

INCORRECT: "Create an Amazon SNS rule to send a notification to Lambda to instruct it to run" is incorrect as you cannot invoke a function by sending a notification to it from Amazon SNS.

19. Question

A Developer wants to find a list of items in a global secondary index from an Amazon DynamoDB table. Which DynamoDB API call can the Developer use in order to consume the LEAST number of read capacity units?

1: Scan operation using eventually-consistent reads

2: Query operation using strongly-consistent reads

3: Query operation using eventually-consistent reads

4: Scan operation using strongly-consistent reads

Answer: 3

Explanation:

Amazon DynamoDB provides fast access to items in a table by specifying primary key values. However, many applications might benefit from having one or more secondary (or alternate) keys available, to allow efficient access to data with attributes other than the primary key. To address this, you can create one or more secondary indexes on a table and issue Query or Scan requests against these indexes.

A *secondary index* is a data structure that contains a subset of attributes from a table, along with an alternate key to support Query operations. You can retrieve data from the index using a Query, in much the same way as you use Query with a table. A table can have multiple secondary indexes, which give your applications access to many different query patterns.

You can also issue scan operations on a global secondary index however it is less efficient as it will return all items in the index.

CORRECT: "Query operation using eventually-consistent reads" is the correct answer.

INCORRECT: "Query operation using strongly-consistent reads" is incorrect. Strongly consistent reads require more RCUs and also are not supported on a global secondary index (they are supported on local secondary indexes).

INCORRECT: "Scan operation using eventually-consistent reads" is incorrect as a scan is less efficient than a query and will therefore use more RCUs.

INCORRECT: "Scan operation using strongly-consistent reads" is incorrect as a scan is less efficient than a query and will therefore use more RCUs.

20. Question

A company provides a large number of services on AWS to customers. The customers connect to one or more services directly and the architecture is becoming complex. How can the architecture be refactored to provide a single interface for the services?

1: Amazon API Gateway

2: AWS X-Ray

3: AWS Cognito

4: AWS Single Sign On (SSO)

Answer: 1

Explanation:

Amazon API Gateway is a fully managed service that makes it easy for developers to create, publish, maintain, monitor, and secure APIs at any scale. APIs act as the "front door" for applications to access data, business logic, or functionality from your backend services.

Using API Gateway, you can create RESTful APIs and WebSocket APIs that enable real-time two-way communication applications. API Gateway supports containerized and serverless workloads, as well as web applications.

API Gateway can be used as the single interface for consumers of the services provided by the organization in this scenario. This solution will simplify the architecture.

CORRECT: "Amazon API Gateway" is the correct answer.

INCORRECT: "AWS X-Ray" is incorrect. AWS X-Ray is used for analyzing and debugging applications.

INCORRECT: "AWS Cognito" is incorrect. AWS Cognito is used for adding sign-up, sign-in and access control to web and mobile apps.

INCORRECT: "AWS Single Sign On (SSO)" is incorrect. AWS SSO is used to provide central management of multiple AWS accounts and business applications and to provide single sign-on to accounts.

21. Question

An application writes items to an Amazon DynamoDB table. As the application scales to thousands of instances, calls to the DynamoDB API generate occasional ThrottlingException errors. The application is coded in a language that is incompatible with the AWS SDK. What can be done to prevent the errors from occurring?

1: Add exponential backoff to the application logic

2: Use Amazon SQS as an API message bus

3: Pass API calls through Amazon API Gateway

4: Send the items to DynamoDB through Amazon Kinesis Data Firehose

Answer: 1

Explanation:

Implementing error retries and exponential backoff is a good way to resolve this issue. Exponential backoff can improve an application's reliability by using progressively longer waits between retries. If you're using an AWS SDK, this logic is built-in. If you're not using an AWS SDK, consider manually implementing exponential backoff.

Additional options for preventing throttling from occurring include:

- Distribute read and write operations as evenly as possible across your table. A hot partition can degrade the overall performance of your table. For more information, see Designing Partition Keys to Distribute Your Workload Evenly.

- Implement a caching solution. If your workload is mostly read access to static data, then query results can be delivered much faster if the data is in a well-designed cache rather than in a database. DynamoDB Accelerator (DAX) is a caching service that offers fast in-memory performance for your application. You can also use Amazon ElastiCache.

CORRECT: "Add exponential backoff to the application logic" is the correct answer.

INCORRECT: "Use Amazon SQS as an API message bus" is incorrect. SQS is used for decoupling (messages, nut not APIs), however for this scenario it would add extra cost and complexity.

INCORRECT: "Pass API calls through Amazon API Gateway" is incorrect. For this scenario we don't want to add an additional layer in when we can simply configure the application to back off and retry.

INCORRECT: "Send the items to DynamoDB through Amazon Kinesis Data Firehose" is incorrect as DynamoDB is not a supported destination for Kinesis Data Firehose.

22. Question

A Developer has created an AWS Lambda function in a new AWS account. The function is expected to be invoked 40 times per second and the execution duration will be around 100 seconds. What MUST the Developer do to ensure there are no errors?

1: Contact AWS Support to increase the concurrent execution limits

2: Implement error handling within the function code

3: Implement a Dead Letter Queue to capture invocation errors

4: Implement tracing with X-Ray

Answer: 1

Explanation:

Concurrency is the number of requests that your function is serving at any given time. When your function is invoked, Lambda allocates an instance of it to process the event. When the function code finishes running, it can handle another request. If the function is invoked again while a request is still being processed, another instance is allocated, which increases the function's concurrency.

In this scenario the Lambda function will be invoked 40 times per second and run for 100 seconds. Therefore, there can be up to 4,000 executions running concurrently which is above the default per-region limit of 1,000 concurrent executions.

This can be easily rectified by contacting AWS support and requesting the concurrent execution limit to be increased.

CORRECT: "Contact AWS Support to increase the concurrent execution limits" is the correct answer.

INCORRECT: "Implement error handling within the function code" is incorrect. Though this could be useful it is not something that must be done based on what we know about this scenario.

INCORRECT: "Implement a Dead Letter Queue to capture invocation errors" is incorrect as this would be implemented for message handling requirements.

INCORRECT: "Implement tracing with X-Ray" is incorrect. X-Ray can be used to analyze and debug distributed applications. We don't know of any specific issues with this function yet so this is not something that must be done.

23. Question

You run an ad-supported photo sharing website using Amazon S3 to serve photos to visitors of your site. At some point you find out that other sites have been linking to the photos on your site, causing loss to your business. What is an effective method to mitigate this?

1: Store photos on an EBS volume of the web server

2: Remove public read access and use signed URLs with expiry dates

3: Use CloudFront distributions for static content

4: Block the IPs of the offending websites in Security Groups

Answer: 2

Explanation:

When Amazon S3 objects are private, only the object owner has permission to access these objects. However, the object owner can optionally share objects with others by creating a presigned URL, using their own security credentials, to grant time-limited permission to download the objects.

When you create a presigned URL for your object, you must provide your security credentials, specify a bucket name, an object key, specify the HTTP method (GET to download the object) and expiration date and time. The presigned URLs are valid only for the specified duration.

Anyone who receives the presigned URL can then access the object. In this scenario, the photos can be shared with the owner's website but not with any other 3rd parties. This will stop other sites from linking to the photos as they will not display anywhere else.

CORRECT: "Remove public read access and use signed URLs with expiry dates" is the correct answer.

INCORRECT: "Store photos on an EBS volume of the web server" is incorrect as this does not add any more control over content visibility in the website.

INCORRECT: "Use CloudFront distributions for static content" is incorrect as this alone will not protect the content. You can also use pre-signed URLs with CloudFront, but this isn't mentioned.

INCORRECT: "Block the IPs of the offending websites in Security Groups" is incorrect as you can only configure allow rules in security groups so this would be hard to manage.

24. Question

A company manages an application that stores data in an Amazon DynamoDB table. The company need to keep a record of all new changes made to the DynamoDB table in another table within the same AWS region. What is the MOST suitable way to deliver this requirement?

1: Use Amazon DynamoDB streams

2: Use CloudWatch events

3: Use Amazon CloudTrail

4: Use Amazon DynamoDB snapshots

Answer: 1

Explanation:

A *DynamoDB stream* is an ordered flow of information about changes to items in a DynamoDB table. When you enable a stream on a table, DynamoDB captures information about every modification to data items in the table.

Whenever an application creates, updates, or deletes items in the table, DynamoDB Streams writes a stream record with the primary key attributes of the items that were modified. A *stream record* contains information about a data modification to a single item in a DynamoDB table. You can configure the stream so that the stream records capture additional information, such as the "before" and "after" images of modified items.

This is the best way to capture a record of new changes made to the DynamoDB table. Another table can then be populated with this data so the data is stored persistently.

CORRECT: "Use Amazon DynamoDB streams" is the correct answer.

INCORRECT: "Use CloudWatch events" is incorrect. CloudWatch Events delivers a near real-time stream of system events that describe changes in Amazon Web Services (AWS) resources. However, it does not capture the information that changes in a DynamoDB table so is unsuitable for this purpose.

INCORRECT: "Use Amazon CloudTrail" is incorrect as CloudTrail records a history of API calls on your account. It is used for creating an audit trail of events.

INCORRECT: "Use Amazon DynamoDB snapshots" is incorrect as snapshots only capture a point in time, they are not used for recording item-level changes.

An IT automation architecture uses many AWS Lambda functions invoking one another as a large state machine. The coordination of this state machine is legacy custom code that breaks easily. Which AWS Service can help refactor and manage the state machine?

1: AWS CodePipeline

2: AWS CodeBuild

3: AWS CloudFormation

4: AWS Step Functions

Answer: 4

Explanation:

AWS Step Functions lets you coordinate multiple AWS services into serverless workflows so you can build and update apps quickly. Using Step Functions, you can design and run workflows that stitch together services, such as AWS Lambda, AWS Fargate, and Amazon SageMaker, into feature-rich applications.

Workflows are made up of a series of steps, with the output of one step acting as input into the next. Application development is simpler and more intuitive using Step Functions, because it translates your workflow into a state machine diagram that is easy to understand, easy to explain to others, and easy to change.

Step Functions automatically triggers and tracks each step, and retries when there are errors, so your application executes in order and as expected. With Step Functions, you can craft long-running workflows such as machine learning model training, report generation, and IT automation.

Therefore, AWS Step Functions is the best AWS service to use when refactoring the application away from the legacy code.

CORRECT: "AWS Step Functions" is the correct answer.

INCORRECT: "AWS CloudFormation" is incorrect as CloudFormation is used for deploying resources no AWS but not for ongoing automation.

INCORRECT: "AWS CodePipeline" is incorrect as this is used as part of a continuous integration and delivery (CI/CD) pipeline to deploy software updates to applications.

INCORRECT: "AWS CodeBuild" is incorrect as this an AWS build/test service.

26. Question

A Developer is deploying an Amazon ECS update using AWS CodeDeploy. In the appspec.yml file, which of the following is a valid structure for the order of hooks that should be specified?

1: BeforeInstall > AfterInstall > AfterAllowTestTraffic > BeforeAllowTraffic > AfterAllowTraffic

2: BeforeInstall > AfterInstall > ApplicationStart > ValidateService

3: BeforeAllowTraffic > AfterAllowTraffic

4: BeforeBlockTraffic > AfterBlockTraffic > BeforeAllowTraffic > AfterAllowTraffic

Answer: 1

Explanation:

The content in the 'hooks' section of the AppSpec file varies, depending on the compute platform for your deployment. The 'hooks' section for an EC2/On-Premises deployment contains mappings that link deployment lifecycle event hooks to one or more scripts.

The 'hooks' section for a Lambda or an Amazon ECS deployment specifies Lambda validation functions to run during a deployment lifecycle event. If an event hook is not present, no operation is executed for that event. This section is required only if you are running scripts or Lambda validation functions as part of the deployment.

The following code snippet shows a valid example of the structure of hooks for an Amazon ECS deployment:

```
Hooks:
   - BeforeInstall: "LambdaFunctionToValidateBeforeInstall"
   - AfterInstall: "LambdaFunctionToValidateAfterTraffic"
   - AfterAllowTestTraffic: "LambdaFunctionToValidateAfterTestTrafficStarts"
   - BeforeAllowTraffic: "LambdaFunctionToValidateBeforeAllowingProductionTraffic"
   - AfterAllowTraffic: "LambdaFunctionToValidateAfterAllowingProductionTraffic"
```

Therefore, in this scenario a valid structure for the order of hooks that should be specified in the appspec.yml file is: BeforeInstall > AfterInstall > AfterAllowTestTraffic > BeforeAllowTraffic > AfterAllowTraffic

CORRECT: "BeforeInstall > AfterInstall > AfterAllowTestTraffic > BeforeAllowTraffic > AfterAllowTraffic" is the correct answer.

INCORRECT: "BeforeInstall > AfterInstall > ApplicationStart > ValidateService" is incorrect as this would be valid for Amazon EC2.

INCORRECT: "BeforeAllowTraffic > AfterAllowTraffic" is incorrect as this would be valid for AWS Lambda.

INCORRECT: "BeforeBlockTraffic > AfterBlockTraffic > BeforeAllowTraffic > AfterAllowTraffic" is incorrect as this is a partial listing of hooks for Amazon EC2 but is incomplete.

27. Question

A Developer has setup an Amazon Kinesis Data Stream with 6 shards to ingest a maximum of 2000 records per second. An AWS Lambda function has been configured to process these records. In which order will these records be processed?

1: Lambda will receive each record in the reverse order it was placed into the stream

2: Lambda will receive each record in the exact order it was placed into the stream

3: Lambda will receive each record in the exact order it was placed into the shard. There is no guarantee of order across shards

4: The Developer can select exact order or reverse order using the GetRecords API

Answer: 3

Explanation:

Amazon Kinesis Data Streams (KDS) is a massively scalable and durable real-time data streaming service. KDS can continuously capture gigabytes of data per second from hundreds of thousands of sources such as website clickstreams, database event streams, financial transactions, social media feeds, IT logs, and location-tracking events.

KDS receives data from producers, and the data is stored in shards. Consumers then take the data and process it. In this case the AWS Lambda function is consuming the records from the shards.

In this scenario an application will be producing records and placing them in the stream (step 1). The AWS Lambda function will then consume the records (step 2) and will then execute the function by assuming the execution role specified (step 3).

A shard is an append-only log and a unit of streaming capability. A shard contains an ordered sequence of records ordered by arrival time. The order is guaranteed within a shard but not across shards.

Therefore, the best answer to this question is that AWS Lambda will receive each record in the exact order it was placed into the shard but there is no guarantee of order across shards

CORRECT: "Lambda will receive each record in the exact order it was placed into the shard. There is no guarantee of order across shards" is the correct answer.

INCORRECT: "Lambda will receive each record in the exact order it was placed into the stream " is incorrect as there are multiple shards in the stream and the order of records is not guaranteed across shards.

INCORRECT: "Lambda will receive each record in the reverse order it was placed into the stream" is incorrect as the order is guaranteed within a shard.

INCORRECT: "The Developer can select exact order or reverse order using the GetRecords API" is incorrect as you cannot choose the order you receive records with the GetRecords API.

28. Question

A Developer created an AWS Lambda function for a serverless application. The Lambda function has been executing for several minutes and the Developer cannot find any log data in CloudWatch Logs. What is the MOST likely explanation for this issue?

1: The Lambda function does not have any explicit log statements for the log data to send it to CloudWatch Logs

2: The Lambda function is missing CloudWatch Logs as a source trigger to send log data

3: The execution role for the Lambda function is missing permissions to write log data to the CloudWatch Logs

4: The Lambda function is missing a target CloudWatch Logs group

Answer: 3

Explanation:

AWS Lambda automatically monitors Lambda functions on your behalf, reporting metrics through Amazon CloudWatch. To help you troubleshoot failures in a function, Lambda logs all requests handled by your function and also automatically stores logs generated by your code through Amazon CloudWatch Logs.

Lambda automatically integrates with CloudWatch Logs and pushes all logs from your code to a CloudWatch Logs group associated with a Lambda function, which is named /aws/lambda/<function name>.

An AWS Lambda function's execution role grants it permission to access AWS services and resources. You provide this role when you create a function, and Lambda assumes the role when your function is invoked. You can create an execution role for development that has permission to send logs to Amazon CloudWatch and upload trace data to AWS X-Ray.

For the lambda function to create log stream and publish logs to cloudwatch, the lambda execution role needs to have the following permissions:

```
{
    "Statement": [
        {
            "Action": [
                "logs:CreateLogGroup",
                "logs:CreateLogStream",
                "logs:PutLogEvents"
            ],
            "Effect": "Allow",
            "Resource": "arn:aws:logs:*:*:*"
        }
    ]
}
```

The most likely cause of this issue is that the execution role assigned to the Lambda function does not have the permissions (shown above) to write to CloudWatch Logs.

CORRECT: "The execution role for the Lambda function is missing permissions to write log data to the CloudWatch Logs" is the correct answer.

INCORRECT: "The Lambda function does not have any explicit log statements for the log data to send it to CloudWatch Logs" is incorrect as this is not required, Lambda automatically logs data to CloudWatch logs and just needs the permissions to do so.

INCORRECT: "The Lambda function is missing a target CloudWatch Logs group" is incorrect as the CloudWatch Logs group will be created automatically if the function has sufficient permissions.

INCORRECT: "The Lambda function is missing CloudWatch Logs as a source trigger to send log data" is incorrect as CloudWatch Logs is a destination, not a source in this case. However, you do not need to configure CloudWatch Logs as a destination, it is automatic.

29. Question

A Developer is looking for a way to use shorthand syntax to express functions, APIs, databases, and event source mappings. The Developer will test using AWS SAM to create a simple Lambda function using Nodejs.12x. What is the SIMPLEST way for the Developer to get started with a Hello World Lambda function?

1: Install the AWS SAM CLI, run sam init and use one of the AWS Quick Start Templates

2: Install the AWS CLI, run aws sam init and use one of the AWS Quick Start Templates

3: Use the AWS Management Console to access AWS SAM and deploy a Hello World function

4: Use AWS CloudFormation to deploy a Hello World stack using AWS SAM

Answer: 1

Explanation:

The sam init command initializes a serverless application with an AWS SAM template. The template provides a folder structure for your Lambda functions and is connected to an event source such as APIs, S3 buckets, or DynamoDB tables. This application includes everything you need to get started and to eventually extend it into a production-scale application.

This is the simplest way for the Developer to quickly get started with testing AWS SAM. Before the Developer can use the "sam" commands it is necessary to install the AWS SAM CLI. This is separate to the AWS CLI.

CORRECT: "Install the AWS SAM CLI, run sam init and use one of the AWS Quick Start Templates" is the correct answer.

INCORRECT: "Install the AWS CLI, run aws sam init and use one of the AWS Quick Start Templates" is incorrect as "sam init" is not an AWS CLI command, therefore you cannot put "aws" in front of "sam".

INCORRECT: "Use the AWS Management Console to access AWS SAM and deploy a Hello World function" is incorrect as you cannot access AWS SAM through the console. You can, however, access the Serverless Application Repository through the console and deploy SAM templates.

INCORRECT: "Use AWS CloudFormation to deploy a Hello World stack using AWS SAM" is incorrect as though AWS SAM does use CloudFormation you cannot deploy SAM templates through the AWS CloudFormation console. You must use the SAM CLI or deploy using the Serverless Application Repository.

30. Question

An Amazon Kinesis Data Stream has recently been configured to receive data from sensors in a manufacturing facility. A consumer EC2 instance is configured to process the data every 48 hours and save processing results to an Amazon RedShift data warehouse. Testing has identified a large amount of data is missing. A review of monitoring logs has identified that the sensors are sending data correctly and the EC2 instance is healthy. What is the MOST likely explanation for this issue?

1: Records are retained for 24 hours in the Kinesis Data Stream by default

2: Amazon RedShift is not suitable for storing streaming data

3: The EC2 instance is failing intermittently

4: Amazon Kinesis has too many shards provisioned

Answer: 1

Explanation:

Amazon Kinesis Data Streams supports changes to the data record retention period of your stream. A Kinesis data stream is an ordered sequence of data records meant to be written to and read from in real time. Data records are therefore stored in shards in your stream temporarily. The time period from when a record is added to when it is no longer accessible is called the *retention period*. A Kinesis data stream stores records from 24 hours by default, up to 168 hours.

You can increase the retention period up to 168 hours using the IncreaseStreamRetentionPeriod operation. You can decrease the retention period down to a minimum of 24 hours using the DecreaseStreamRetentionPeriod operation. The request syntax for both operations includes the stream name and the retention period in hours. Finally, you can check the current retention period of a stream by calling the DescribeStream operation.

Both operations are easy to use. The following is an example of changing the retention period using the AWS CLI:

```
aws kinesis increase-stream-retention-period --stream-name retentionPeriodDemo --retention-period-hours 72
```

Therefore, the most likely explanation is that the message retention period is set at the 24-hour default.

CORRECT: "Records are retained for 24 hours in the Kinesis Data Stream by default" is the correct answer.

INCORRECT: "Amazon RedShift is not suitable for storing streaming data" is incorrect. In this architecture Amazon Kinesis is responsible for receiving streaming data and storing it in a stream. The EC2 instances can then process and store the data in a number of different destinations including Amazon RedShift.

INCORRECT: "The EC2 instance is failing intermittently" is incorrect as the question states that a review of monitoring logs indicates that the EC2 instance is healthy. If it was failing intermittently this should be recorded in the logs.

INCORRECT: "Amazon Kinesis has too many shards provisioned" is incorrect as this would just mean that the Kinesis Stream has more capacity, not less.

31. Question

A Developer is managing an application that includes an Amazon SQS queue. The consumers that process the data from the queue are connecting in short cycles and the queue often does not return messages. The cost for API calls is increasing. How can the Developer optimize the retrieval of messages and reduce cost?

1: Call the ReceiveMessage API with the VisibilityTimeout parameter set to 30

2: Call the ReceiveMessage API with the WaitTimeSeconds parameter set to 20

3: Call the SetQueueAttributes API with the DelaySeconds parameter set to 900

4: Call the SetQueueAttributes API with the maxReceiveCount set to 20

Answer: 2

Explanation:

The process of consuming messages from a queue depends on whether you use short or long polling. By default, Amazon SQS uses *short polling*, querying only a subset of its servers (based on a weighted random distribution) to determine whether any messages are available for a response. You can use *long polling* to reduce your costs while allowing your consumers to receive messages as soon as they arrive in the queue.

When you consume messages from a queue using short polling, Amazon SQS samples a subset of its servers (based on a weighted random distribution) and returns messages from only those servers. Thus, a particular ReceiveMessage request might not return all of your messages. However, if you have fewer than 1,000 messages in your queue, a subsequent request will return your messages. If you keep consuming from your queues, Amazon SQS samples all of its servers, and you receive all of your messages.

When the wait time for the ReceiveMessage API action is greater than 0, *long polling* is in effect. The maximum long polling wait time is 20 seconds. Long polling helps reduce the cost of using Amazon SQS by eliminating the number of empty responses (when there are no messages available for a ReceiveMessage request) and false empty responses (when messages are available but aren't included in a response)

Therefore, the Developer should call the ReceiveMessage API with the WaitTimeSeconds parameter set to 20 to enable long polling.

CORRECT: "Call the ReceiveMessage API with the WaitTimeSeconds parameter set to 20 " is the correct answer.

INCORRECT: "Call the ReceiveMessage API with the VisibilityTimeout parameter set to 30" is incorrect

INCORRECT: "Call the SetQueueAttributes API with the DelaySeconds parameter set to 900" is incorrect

INCORRECT: "Call the SetQueueAttributes API with the maxReceiveCount set to 20" is incorrect

32. Question

A company currently runs a number of legacy automated batch processes for system update management and operational activities. The company are looking to refactor these processes and require a service that can coordinate multiple AWS services into serverless workflows. What is the MOST suitable service for this requirement?

1: Amazon SWF

2: AWS Batch

3: AWS Step Functions

4: AWS Lambda

Answer: 3

Explanation:

AWS Step Functions is a web service that enables you to coordinate the components of distributed applications and microservices using visual workflows. You build applications from individual components that each perform a discrete function, or *task*, allowing you to scale and change applications quickly.

Step Functions provides a reliable way to coordinate components and step through the functions of your application. Step Functions offers a graphical console to visualize the components of your application as a series of steps. It automatically triggers and tracks each step, and retries when there are errors, so your application executes in order and as expected, every time. Step Functions logs the state of each step, so when things go wrong, you can diagnose and debug problems quickly.

CORRECT: "AWS Step Functions" is the correct answer.

INCORRECT: "Amazon SWF" is incorrect. You can think of Amazon SWF as a fully-managed state tracker and task coordinator in the Cloud. It does not coordinate serverless workflows.

INCORRECT: "AWS Batch" is incorrect as this is used to run batch computing jobs on Amazon EC2 and is therefore not serverless.

INCORRECT: "AWS Lambda" is incorrect as though it is serverless, it does not provide a native capability to coordinate multiple AWS services.

33. Question

A Development team have moved their continuous integration and delivery (CI/CD) pipeline into the AWS Cloud. The team is leveraging AWS CodeCommit for management of source code. The team need to compile their source code, run tests, and produce software packages that are ready for deployment. Which AWS service can deliver these outcomes?

1: AWS CodePipeline

2: AWS CodeCommit

3: AWS CodeBuild

4: AWS Cloud9

Answer: 3

Explanation:

AWS CodeBuild is a fully managed build service in the cloud. CodeBuild compiles your source code, runs unit tests, and produces artifacts that are ready to deploy. CodeBuild eliminates the need to provision, manage, and scale your own build servers. It provides prepackaged build environments for popular programming languages and build tools such as Apache Maven, Gradle, and more.

You can also customize build environments in CodeBuild to use your own build tools. CodeBuild scales automatically to meet peak build requests.

CodeBuild provides these benefits:

- **Fully managed** – CodeBuild eliminates the need to set up, patch, update, and manage your own build servers.

- **On demand** – CodeBuild scales on demand to meet your build needs. You pay only for the number of build minutes you consume.

- **Out of the box** – CodeBuild provides preconfigured build environments for the most popular programming languages. All you need to do is point to your build script to start your first build.

Therefore, AWS CodeBuild is the best service to use to compile the Development team's source code, run tests, and produce software packages that are ready for deployment.

CORRECT: "AWS CodeBuild" is the correct answer.

INCORRECT: "AWS CodeCommit" is incorrect. The team are already using CodeCommit for its correct purpose, which is to manage source code. CodeCommit cannot perform compiling of source code, testing, or package creation.

INCORRECT: "AWS CodePipeline" is incorrect. AWS CodePipeline is a fully managed continuous delivery service that helps you automate your release pipelines for fast and reliable application and infrastructure updates.

INCORRECT: "AWS Cloud9" is incorrect. AWS Cloud9 is a cloud-based integrated development environment (IDE) that lets you write, run, and debug your code with just a browser.

34. Question

Every time an Amazon EC2 instance is launched, certain metadata about the instance should be recorded in an Amazon DynamoDB table. The data is gathered and written to the table by an AWS Lambda function. What is the MOST efficient method of invoking the Lambda function?

1: Create a CloudWatch Event with an event pattern looking for EC2 state changes and a target set to use the Lambda function

2: Create a CloudWatch alarm that triggers the Lambda function based on log streams indicating an EC2 state change in CloudWatch logs

3: Create a CloudTrail trail alarm that triggers the Lambda function based on the RunInstances API action

4: Configure detailed monitoring on Amazon EC2 and create an alarm that triggers the Lambda function in initialization

Answer: 1

Explanation:

Amazon CloudWatch Events delivers a near real-time stream of system events that describe changes in Amazon Web Services (AWS) resources. Using simple rules that you can quickly set up, you can match events and route them to one or more target functions or streams. CloudWatch Events becomes aware of operational changes as they occur. CloudWatch Events responds to these operational changes and takes corrective action as necessary, by sending messages to respond to the environment, activating functions, making changes, and capturing state information.

In this scenario the only workable solution is to create a CloudWatch Event with an event pattern looking for EC2 state changes and a target set to use the Lambda function.

CORRECT: "Create a CloudWatch Event with an event pattern looking for EC2 state changes and a target set to use the Lambda function" is the correct answer.

INCORRECT: "Create a CloudWatch alarm that triggers the Lambda function based on log streams indicating an EC2 state change in CloudWatch logs" is incorrect as Amazon EC2 does not create a log group or log stream by default.

INCORRECT: "Create a CloudTrail trail alarm that triggers the Lambda function based on the RunInstances API action" is incorrect as you would need to create a CloudWatch alarm for CloudTrail events (CloudTrail does not have its own alarm feature).

INCORRECT: "Configure detailed monitoring on Amazon EC2 and create an alarm that triggers the Lambda function in initialization" is incorrect as you cannot trigger a Lambda function on EC2 instances initialization using detailed monitoring (or the EC2 console).

35. Question

A Developer is migrating Docker containers to Amazon ECS. A large number of containers will be deployed across some newly deployed ECS containers instances using the same instance type. High availability is provided within the microservices architecture. Which task placement strategy requires the LEAST configuration for this scenario?

1: binpack

2: random

3: spread

4: Fargate

Answer: 2

Explanation:

When a task that uses the EC2 launch type is launched, Amazon ECS must determine where to place the task based on the requirements specified in the task definition, such as CPU and memory. Similarly, when you scale down the task count, Amazon ECS must determine which tasks to terminate. You can apply task placement strategies and constraints to customize how Amazon ECS places and terminates tasks. Task placement strategies and constraints are not supported for tasks using the Fargate launch type. By default, Fargate tasks are spread across Availability Zones.

A *task placement strategy* is an algorithm for selecting instances for task placement or tasks for termination. For example, Amazon ECS can select instances at random, or it can select instances such that tasks are distributed evenly across a group of instances.

Amazon ECS supports the following task placement strategies:

- binpack

Place tasks based on the least available amount of CPU or memory. This minimizes the number of instances in use.

- random

Place tasks randomly.

- spread

Place tasks evenly based on the specified value. Accepted values are instanceId (or host, which has the same effect), or any platform or custom attribute that is applied to a container instance, such as attribute:ecs.availability-zone. Service tasks are spread based on the tasks from that service. Standalone tasks are spread based on the tasks from the same task group.

Therefore, for this scenario the random task placement strategy is most suitable as it requires the least configuration.

CORRECT: "random" is the correct answer.

INCORRECT: "spread" is incorrect. As high availability is taken care of within the containers there is no need to use a spread strategy to ensure HA.

INCORRECT: "binpack" is incorrect as there is no need to pack the containers onto the fewest instances based on CPU or memory.

INCORRECT: "Fargate" is incorrect as this is not a task placement strategy, it is a serverless service for running containers.

36. Question

A Developer has noticed some suspicious activity in her AWS account and is concerned that the access keys associated with her IAM user account may have been compromised. What is the first thing the Developer do in should do in this situation?

1: Delete her IAM user account

2: Delete the compromised access keys

3: Report the incident to AWS Support

4: Change her IAM User account password

Answer: 2

Explanation:

In this case the Developer's access keys may have been compromised so the first step would be to invalidate the access keys by deleting them.

The next step would then be to determine if any temporary security credentials have been issued an invalidating those too to prevent any further misuse.

The user account and user account password have not been compromised so they do not need to be deleted / changed as a first step. However, changing the account password would typically be recommended as a best practice in this situation.

CORRECT: "Delete the compromised access keys" is the correct answer.

INCORRECT: "Delete her IAM user account" is incorrect. This user account has not been compromised based on the available information, just the access keys. Deleting the access keys will prevent further misuse of the AWS account.

INCORRECT: "Report the incident to AWS Support" is incorrect is a good practice but not the first step. The Developer should first attempt to mitigate any further misuse of the account by deleting the access keys.

INCORRECT: "Change her IAM User account password" is incorrect as she does not have any evidence that the account has been compromised, just the access keys. However, it would be a good practice to change the password, just not the first thing to do.

37. Question

A Developer needs to setup a new serverless application that includes AWS Lambda and Amazon API Gateway as part of a single stack. The Developer needs to be able to locally build and test the serverless applications before deployment on AWS. Which service should the Developer use?

1: AWS CloudFormation

2: AWS Elastic Beanstalk

3: AWS CodeBuild

4: AWS Serverless Application Model (SAM)

Answer: 4

Explanation:

The AWS Serverless Application Model (AWS SAM) is an open-source framework that you can use to build serverless applications on AWS. A **serverless application** is a combination of Lambda functions, event sources, and other resources that work together to perform tasks.

AWS SAM provides you with a simple and clean syntax to describe the functions, APIs, permissions, configurations, and events that make up a serverless application.

The example AWS SAM template file below creates an AWS Lambda function and a simple Amazon API Gateway API with a Get method and a /greeting resource:

```
AWSTemplateFormatVersion: '2010-09-09'
Transform: 'AWS::Serverless-2016-10-31'
Description: 'Creates simple function and API resource'
Resources:
    LambdaFunctionWithAPI:
        Type: AWS::Serverless::Function
        Properties:
          Handler: index.handler
          Runtime: nodejs12.x
          Policies:
          Events:
            HttpPost:
              Type: Api
              Properties:
                Path: '/greeting'
                Method: get
```

The AWS SAM CLI lets you locally build, test, and debug serverless applications that are defined by AWS SAM templates. The CLI provides a Lambda-like execution environment locally. It helps you catch issues upfront by providing parity with the actual Lambda execution environment.

CORRECT: "AWS Serverless Application Model (SAM)" is the correct answer.

INCORRECT: "AWS CloudFormation" is incorrect as you cannot perform local build and test with AWS CloudFormation.

INCORRECT: "AWS Elastic Beanstalk" is incorrect as you cannot deploy serverless applications or perform local build and test with Elastic Beanstalk.

INCORRECT: "AWS CodeBuild" is incorrect as you cannot perform local build and test with AWS CodeBuild.

38. Question

An application needs to read up to 100 items at a time from an Amazon DynamoDB. Each item is up to 100MB in size and all attributes must be retrieved. What is the BEST way to minimize latency?

1: Use GetItem and use a projection expression

2: Use BatchGetItem

3: Use a Scan operation with pagination

4: Use a Query operation with a FilterExpression

Answer: 2

Explanation:

The BatchGetItem operation returns the attributes of one or more items from one or more tables. You identify requested items by primary key.

A single operation can retrieve up to 16 MB of data, which can contain as many as 100 items. In order to minimize response latency, BatchGetItem retrieves items in parallel.

By default, BatchGetItem performs eventually consistent reads on every table in the request. If you want strongly consistent reads instead, you can set ConsistentRead to true for any or all tables.

CORRECT: "Use BatchGetItem" is the correct answer.

INCORRECT: "Use GetItem and use a projection expression" is incorrect as this will limit the attributes returned and will retrieve the items sequentially which results in more latency.

INCORRECT: "Use a Scan operation with pagination" is incorrect as a Scan operation is the least efficient way to retrieve the data as all items in the table are returned and then filtered. Pagination just breaks the results into pages.

INCORRECT: "Use a Query operation with a FilterExpression" is incorrect as this would limit the results that are returned.

39. Question

A Developer manages a website running behind an Elastic Load Balancer in the us-east-1 region. The Developer has recently deployed an identical copy of the website in us-west-1 and needs to send 20% of the traffic to the new site. How can the Developer achieve this requirement?

1: Use an Amazon Route 53 Geolocation Routing Policy

2: Use a blue/green deployment with Amazon Elastic Beanstalk

3: Use a blue/green deployment with Amazon CodeDeploy

4: Use an Amazon Route 53 Weighted Routing Policy

Answer: 4

Explanation:

Weighted routing lets you associate multiple resources with a single domain name (example.com) or subdomain name (acme.example.com) and choose how much traffic is routed to each resource. This can be useful for a variety of purposes, including load balancing and testing new versions of software.

In this case the Developer can use a weighted routing policy to direct 20% of the incoming traffic to the new site as required.

CORRECT: "Use an Amazon Route 53 Weighted Routing Policy" is the correct answer.

INCORRECT: "Use an Amazon Route 53 Geolocation Routing Policy" is incorrect as the Developer should use a weighted routing policy for this requirement as a specified percentage of traffic needs to be directed to the new website.

INCORRECT: "Use a blue/green deployment with Amazon Elastic Beanstalk" is incorrect as the question does not state that Elastic Beanstalk is being used and the new website has already been deployed.

INCORRECT: "Use a blue/green deployment with Amazon CodeDeploy" is incorrect as the question does not state that Amazon CodeDeploy is being used and the website has already been deployed.

40. Question

A Development team are deploying an AWS Lambda function that will be used by a production application. The function code will be updated regularly, and new versions will be published. The development team do not want to modify application code to point to each new version. How can the Development team setup a static ARN that will point to the latest published version?

1: Publish a mutable version and point it to the $LATEST version

2: Use an unqualified ARN

3: Setup an Alias that will point to the latest version

4: Setup a Route 53 Alias record that points to the published version

Answer: 3

Explanation:

You can create one or more aliases for your AWS Lambda function. A Lambda alias is like a pointer to a specific Lambda function version. Users can access the function version using the alias ARN.

This is the best way to setup the Lambda function so you don't need to modify the application code when a new version is published. Instead, the developer will simply need to update the Alias to point to the new version:

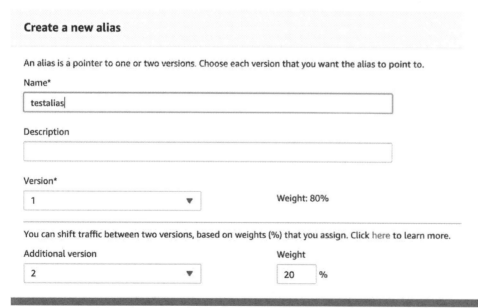

As you can see above you can also point to multiple versions and send a percentage of traffic to each. This is great for testing new code.

CORRECT: "Setup an Alias that will point to the latest version" is the correct answer.

INCORRECT: "Publish a mutable version and point it to the $LATEST version" is incorrect as all published versions are immutable (cannot be modified) and you cannot modify a published version to point to the $LATEST version.

INCORRECT: "Use an unqualified ARN" is incorrect as this is an ARN that does not have a version number which means it points to the $LATEST version, not to a published version (as published versions always have version numbers).

INCORRECT: "Setup a Route 53 Alias record that points to the published version" is incorrect as you cannot point a Route 53 Alias record to an AWS Lambda function.

41. Question

An application is being instrumented to send trace data using AWS X-Ray. A Developer needs to upload segment documents using JSON-formatted strings to X-Ray using the API. Which API action should the developer use?

1: The PutTraceSegments API action

2: The PutTelemetryRecords API action

3: The UpdateGroup API action

4: The GetTraceSummaries API action

Answer: 1

Explanation:

You can send trace data to X-Ray in the form of segment documents. A segment document is a JSON formatted string that contains information about the work that your application does in service of a request. Your application can record data about the work that it does itself in segments, or work that uses downstream services and resources in subsegments.

Segments record information about the work that your application does. A segment, at a minimum, records the time spent on a task, a name, and two IDs. The trace ID tracks the request as it travels between services. The segment ID tracks the work done for the request by a single service.

Example Minimal complete segment:

```
{
    "name" : "Scorekeep",
    "id" : "70de5b6f19ff9a0a",
    "start_time" : 1.478293361271E9,
    "trace_id" : "1-581cf771-a006649127e371903a2de979",
    "end_time" : 1.478293361449E9
}
```

You can upload segment documents with the PutTraceSegments API. The API has a single parameter, TraceSegmentDocuments, that takes a list of JSON segment documents.

Therefore, the Developer should use the PutTraceSegments API action.

CORRECT: "The PutTraceSegments API action" is the correct answer.

INCORRECT: "The PutTelemetryRecords API action" is incorrect as this is used by the AWS X-Ray daemon to upload telemetry.

INCORRECT: "The UpdateGroup API action" is incorrect as this updates a group resource.

INCORRECT: "The GetTraceSummaries API action" is incorrect as this retrieves IDs and annotations for traces available for a specified time frame using an optional filter.

42. Question

A three-tier application is being migrated from an on-premises data center. The application includes an Apache Tomcat web tier, an application tier running on Linux, and a MySQL back end. A Developer must refactor the application to run on the AWS cloud. The cloud-based application must be fault tolerant and elastic. How can the Developer refactor the web tier and application tier? (Select TWO)

1: Create an Amazon CloudFront distribution for the web tier

2: Create an Auto Scaling group of EC2 instances for both the web tier and application tier

3: Use a multi-AZ Amazon RDS database for the back end using the MySQL engine

4: Implement an Elastic Load Balancer for the application tier

5: Implement an Elastic Load Balancer for both the web tier and the application tier

Answer: 2,5

Explanation:

The key requirements in this scenario are to add fault tolerances and elasticity to the web tier and application tier. Note that no specific requirements for the back end have been included.

To add elasticity to the web and application tiers the Developer should create Auto Scaling groups of EC2 instances. We know that the application tier runs on Linux and the web tier runs on Apache Tomcat (which could be on Linux or Windows). Therefore, these workloads are suitable for an ASG and this will ensure the number of instances dynamically scales out and in based on actual usage.

To add fault tolerance to the web and application tiers the Developer should add an Elastic Load Balancer. This will ensure that if the number of EC2 instances are changed by the ASG, the load balancer is able to distribute traffic to them. This also assists with elasticity.

CORRECT: "Create an Auto Scaling group of EC2 instances for both the web tier and application tier" is a correct answer.

CORRECT: "Implement an Elastic Load Balancer for both the web tier and the application tier" is also a correct answer.

INCORRECT: "Create an Amazon CloudFront distribution for the web tier" is incorrect as CloudFront is used for performance reasons, not elasticity or fault tolerance. You would use CloudFront to get content closer to end users around the world.

INCORRECT: "Use a multi-AZ Amazon RDS database for the back end using the MySQL engine" is incorrect as the question does not ask for fault tolerance of the back end, only the web tier and the application tier.

INCORRECT: "Implement an Elastic Load Balancer for the application tier" is incorrect. An Elastic Load Balancer should be implemented for both the web tier and the application tier as that is how we ensure fault tolerance and elasticity for both of those tiers.

43. Question

A Developer has joined a team and needs to connect to the AWS CodeCommit repository using SSH. What should the Developer do to configure access using Git?

1: On the Developer's IAM account, under security credentials, choose to create HTTPS Git credentials for AWS CodeCommit

2: On the Developer's IAM account, under security credentials, choose to create an access key and secret ID

3: Create an account on Github and user those login credentials to login to AWS CodeCommit

4: Generate an SSH public and private key. Upload the public key to the Developer's IAM account

Answer: 4

Explanation:

You need to configure your Git client to communicate with CodeCommit repositories. As part of this configuration, you provide IAM credentials that CodeCommit can use to authenticate you. IAM supports CodeCommit with three types of credentials:

- Git credentials, an IAM -generated user name and password pair you can use to communicate with CodeCommit repositories over HTTPS.

- SSH keys, a locally generated public-private key pair that you can associate with your IAM user to communicate with CodeCommit repositories over SSH.

- AWS access keys, which you can use with the credential helper included with the AWS CLI to communicate with CodeCommit repositories over HTTPS.

As the Developer is going to use SSH, he first needs to generate an SSH private and public key. These can then be used for authentication. The method of creating these depends on the operating system the Developer is using. Then, the Developer can upload the public key (by copying the contents of the file) into his IAM account under security credentials.

CORRECT: "Generate an SSH public and private key. Upload the public key to the Developer's IAM account" is the correct answer.

INCORRECT: "On the Developer's IAM account, under security credentials, choose to create HTTPS Git credentials for AWS CodeCommit" is incorrect as this method is used for creating credentials when you want to connect to CodeCommit using HTTPS.

INCORRECT: "Create an account on Github and user those login credentials to login to AWS CodeCommit" is incorrect as you cannot login to AWS CodeCommit using credentials from Github.

INCORRECT: "On the Developer's IAM account, under security credentials, choose to create an access key and secret ID" is incorrect as though you can use access keys to authenticated to CodeCommit, this requires the credential helper, and enables access over HTTPS.

44. Question

A large quantity of sensitive data must be encrypted. A Developer will use a custom CMK to generate the encryption key. The key policy currently looks like this:

```
{
  "Sid": "Allow Key Usage",
  "Effect": "Allow",
  "Principal": {"AWS": [
    "arn:aws:iam::111122223333:user/CMKUser"
  ]},
  "Action": [
    "kms:Encrypt",
    "kms:Decrypt",
```

```
  "kms:ReEncrypt*",
  "kms:DescribeKey"
],
"Resource": "*"
}
```

What API action must be added to the key policy?

1: kms:EnableKey

2: kms:GenerateDataKey*

3: kms:CreateKey

4: kms:GetKeyPolicy

Answer: 2

Explanation:

A key policy is a document that uses JSON (JavaScript Object Notation) to specify permissions. You can work with these JSON documents directly, or you can use the AWS Management Console to work with them using a graphical interface called the *default view*.

The key policy supplied with this question is missing the GenerateDataKey API action which is a permission that is required to generate a data encryption key. A data encryption key is required to encrypt large amounts of data as a CMK can only encrypt up to 4 KB.

The GenerateDataKey API Generates a unique symmetric data key. This operation returns a plaintext copy of the data key and a copy that is encrypted under a customer master key (CMK) that you specify. You can use the plaintext key to encrypt your data outside of AWS KMS and store the encrypted data key with the encrypted data.

CORRECT: "kms:GenerateDataKey" is the correct answer.

INCORRECT: "kms:EnableKey" is incorrect as this sets the key state of a customer master key (CMK) to enabled. It allows you to use the CMK for cryptographic operations.

INCORRECT: "kms:CreateKey" is incorrect as this creates a unique customer managed customer master key (CMK) in your AWS account and Region. In this case the CMK already exists, the Developer needs to create a data encryption key.

INCORRECT: "kms:GetKeyPolicy" is incorrect as this simply gets a key policy attached to the specified customer master key (CMK).

45. Question

A Developer needs to access AWS CodeCommit over SSH. The SSH keys configured to access AWS CodeCommit are tied to a user with the following permissions:

```
{
  "version": "2012-10-17"
  "Statement": [
    {
      "Effect": "Allow",
      "Action": [
        "codecommit:BatchGetRepositories",
```

```
    "codecommit:Get*"

    "codecommit:List*",

    "codecommit:GitPull"

  ],

  "Resource": "*"

  }

 ]

}
```

The Developer needs to create/delete branches. Which specific IAM permissions need to be added based on the principle of least privilege?

1: "codecommit:CreateBranch" and "codecommit:DeleteBranch"

2: "codecommit:Put*:"

3: "codecommit:Update*"

4: "codecommit:*"

Answer: 1

Explanation:

The permissions assigned to the user account are missing the privileges to create and delete branches in AWS CodeCommit. The Developer needs to be assigned these permissions but according to the principal of least privilege it's important to ensure no additional permissions are assigned.

The following API actions can be used to work with branches:

- CreateBranch , which creates a branch in a specified repository.

- DeleteBranch , which deletes the specified branch in a repository unless it is the default branch.

- GetBranch , which returns information about a specified branch.

- ListBranches , which lists all branches for a specified repository.

- UpdateDefaultBranch , which changes the default branch for a repository.

Therefore, the best answer is to add the "codecommit:CreateBranch" and "codecommit:DeleteBranch" permissions to the permissions policy.

CORRECT: "codecommit:CreateBranch" and "codecommit:DeleteBranch" is the correct answer.

INCORRECT: "codecommit:Put*:" is incorrect. The wildcard (*) will allow any API action starting with "Put", however the only options are put-file and put-repository-triggers, neither of which is related to branches.

INCORRECT: "codecommit:Update*" is incorrect. The wildcard (*) will allow any API action starting with "Update", however none of the options available are suitable for working with branches.

INCORRECT: "codecommit:*" is incorrect as this would allow any API action which does not follow the principal of least privilege.

46. Question

An application uses Amazon Kinesis Data Streams to ingest and process large streams of data records in real time. Amazon EC2 instances consume and process the data using the Amazon Kinesis Client Library (KCL). The application handles the failure scenarios and does not require standby workers. The application reports that a specific shard is receiving more data than expected. To adapt to the changes in the rate of data flow, the "hot" shard is resharded.

Assuming that the initial number of shards in the Kinesis data stream is 6, and after resharding the number of shards increased to 8, what is the maximum number of EC2 instances that can be deployed to process data from all the shards?

1: 12

2: 8

3: 6

4: 1

Answer: 2

Explanation:

Typically, when you use the KCL, you should ensure that the number of instances does not exceed the number of shards (except for failure standby purposes). Each shard is processed by exactly one KCL worker and has exactly one corresponding record processor, so you never need multiple instances to process one shard. However, one worker can process any number of shards, so it's fine if the number of shards exceeds the number of instances.

In this scenario, the number of shards has been increased to 8. Therefore, the maximum number of instances that can be deployed is 8 as the number of instances cannot exceed the number of shards.

CORRECT: "8" is the correct answer.

INCORRECT: "6" is incorrect as this is not the maximum number of instances that can be deployed to process 8 shards. The maximum number of instances should be the same as the number of shards.

INCORRECT: "12" is incorrect as the number of instances exceeds the number of shards. You should ensure that the number of instances does not exceed the number of shards

INCORRECT: "1" is incorrect as this is not the maximum number of instances that can be deployed to process 8 shards. The maximum number of instances should be the same as the number of shards.

47. Question

What does an Amazon SQS delay queue accomplish?

1: Messages are hidden for a configurable amount of time when they are first added to the queue

2: Messages are hidden for a configurable amount of time after they are consumed from the queue

3: The consumer can poll the queue for a configurable amount of time before retrieving a message

4: Message cannot be deleted for a configurable amount of time after they are consumed from the queue

Answer: 1

Explanation:

Delay queues let you postpone the delivery of new messages to a queue for a number of seconds, for example, when your consumer application needs additional time to process messages.

If you create a delay queue, any messages that you send to the queue remain invisible to consumers for the duration of the delay period. The default (minimum) delay for a queue is 0 seconds. The maximum is 15 minutes.

Therefore, the correct explanation is that with an Amazon SQS Delay Queue messages are hidden for a configurable amount of time when they are first added to the queue

CORRECT: "Messages are hidden for a configurable amount of time when they are first added to the queue" is the correct answer.

INCORRECT: "Messages are hidden for a configurable amount of time after they are consumed from the queue" is incorrect. They are hidden when they are added to the queue.

INCORRECT: "The consumer can poll the queue for a configurable amount of time before retrieving a message" is incorrect. A delay queue simply delays visibility of the message, it does not affect polling behavior.

INCORRECT: "Message cannot be deleted for a configurable amount of time after they are consumed from the queue" is incorrect. That is what a visibility timeout achieves.

48. Question

An organization needs to add encryption in-transit to an existing website running behind an Elastic Load Balancer. The website's Amazon EC2 instances are CPU-constrained and therefore load on their CPUs should not be increased. What should be done to secure the website? (Select TWO)

1: Configure an Elastic Load Balancer with SSL pass-through

2: Configure SSL certificates on an Elastic Load Balancer

3: Configure an Elastic Load Balancer with a KMS CMK

4: Install SSL certificates on the EC2 instances

5: Configure an Elastic Load Balancer with SSL termination

Answer: 2,5

Explanation:

The company need to add security to their website by encrypting traffic in-transit using HTTPS. This requires adding SSL/TLS certificates to enable the encryption. The process of encrypting and decrypting data is CPU intensive and therefore the company need to avoid adding certificates to the EC2 instances as that will place further load on their CPUs.

Therefore, the solution is to configure SSL certificates on the Elastic Load Balancer and then configure SSL termination. This can be done by adding a certificate to a HTTPS listener on the load balancer.

CORRECT: "Configure SSL certificates on an Elastic Load Balancer" is a correct answer.

CORRECT: "Configure an Elastic Load Balancer with SSL termination" is a correct answer.

INCORRECT: "Configure an Elastic Load Balancer with SSL pass-through" is incorrect as with pass-through the SSL session must be terminated on the EC2 instances which should be avoided as they are CPU-constrained.

INCORRECT: "Configure an Elastic Load Balancer with a KMS CMK" is incorrect as a KMS CMK is used to encrypt data at rest, it is not used for in-transit encryption.

INCORRECT: "Install SSL certificates on the EC2 instances" is incorrect as this would increase the load on the CPUs

49. Question

A company is running a Docker application on Amazon ECS. The application must scale based on user load in the last 15 seconds. How should the Developer instrument the code so that the requirement can be met?

1: Create a high-resolution custom Amazon CloudWatch metric for user activity data, then publish data every 30 seconds

2: Create a high-resolution custom Amazon CloudWatch metric for user activity data, then publish data every 5 seconds

3: Create a standard-resolution custom Amazon CloudWatch metric for user activity data, then publish data every 30 seconds

4: Create a standard-resolution custom Amazon CloudWatch metric for user activity data, then publish data every 5 seconds

Answer: 2

Explanation:

Metrics produced by AWS services are standard resolution by default. When you publish a custom metric, you can define it as either standard resolution or high resolution. When you publish a high-resolution metric, CloudWatch stores it with a resolution of 1 second, and you can read and retrieve it with a period of 1 second, 5 seconds, 10 seconds, 30 seconds, or any multiple of 60 seconds.

User activity is not a standard CloudWatch metric and as stated above for the resolution we need in this scenario a custom CloudWatch metric is required anyway. Therefore, for this scenario the Developer should create a high-resolution custom Amazon CloudWatch metric for user activity data and publish the data every 5 seconds.

CORRECT: "Create a high-resolution custom Amazon CloudWatch metric for user activity data, then publish data every 5 seconds" is the correct answer.

INCORRECT: "Create a high-resolution custom Amazon CloudWatch metric for user activity data, then publish data every 30 seconds" is incorrect as the resolution is lower than required which will not provide the granularity required.

INCORRECT: "Create a standard-resolution custom Amazon CloudWatch metric for user activity data, then publish data every 30 seconds" is incorrect as standard resolution metrics have a granularity of one minute.

INCORRECT: "Create a standard-resolution custom Amazon CloudWatch metric for user activity data, then publish data every 5 seconds" is incorrect as standard resolution metrics have a granularity of one minute.

50. Question

A company needs a fully-managed source control service that will work in AWS. The service must ensure that revision control synchronizes multiple distributed repositories by exchanging sets of changes peer-to-peer. All users need to work productively even when not connected to a network. Which source control service should be used?

1: Subversion

2: AWS CodeBuild

3: AWS CodeCommit

4: AWS CodeStar

Answer: 3

Explanation:

AWS CodeCommit is a version control service hosted by Amazon Web Services that you can use to privately store and manage assets (such as documents, source code, and binary files) in the cloud.

A repository is the fundamental version control object in CodeCommit. It's where you securely store code and files for your project. It also stores your project history, from the first commit through the latest changes. You can share your repository with other users so you can work together on a project. If you add AWS tags to repositories, you can set up notifications so that repository users receive email about events (for example, another user commenting on code).

You can also change the default settings for your repository, browse its contents, and more. You can create triggers for your repository so that code pushes or other events trigger actions, such as emails or code functions. You can even configure a repository on your local computer (a local repo) to push your changes to more than one repository.

CORRECT: "AWS CodeCommit" is the correct answer.

INCORRECT: "Subversion" is incorrect as this is not a fully managed source control system

INCORRECT: "AWS CodeBuild" is incorrect as this is a service used for building and testing code.

INCORRECT: "AWS CodeStar" is incorrect as this is not a source control system; it integrates with source control systems such as CodeCommit.

51. Question

A Developer needs to return a list of items in a global secondary index from an Amazon DynamoDB table. Which DynamoDB API call can the Developer use in order to consume the LEAST number of read capacity units?

1: Scan operation using eventually-consistent reads

2: Query operation using strongly-consistent reads

3: Query operation using eventually-consistent reads

4: Scan operation using strongly-consistent reads

Answer: 3

Explanation:

The Query operation finds items based on primary key values. You can query any table or secondary index that has a composite primary key (a partition key and a sort key).

For items up to 4 KB in size, one RCU equals one strongly consistent read request per second or two eventually consistent read requests per second. Therefore, using eventually consistent reads uses fewer RCUs.

CORRECT: "Query operation using eventually-consistent reads" is the correct answer.

INCORRECT: "Query operation using strongly-consistent reads" is incorrect as strongly-consistent reads use more RCUs than eventually consistent reads.

INCORRECT: "Scan operation using eventually-consistent reads" is incorrect. The Scan operation returns one or more items and item attributes by accessing every item in a table or a secondary index and therefore uses more RCUs than a query operation.

INCORRECT: "Scan operation using strongly-consistent reads" is incorrect. The Scan operation returns one or more items and item attributes by accessing every item in a table or a secondary index and therefore uses more RCUs than a query operation.

52. Question

A Developer is writing an AWS Lambda function that processes records from an Amazon Kinesis Data Stream. The Developer must write the function so that it sends a notice to Administrators that includes the processed data. How should the Developer write the function?

1: Separate the Lambda handler from the core logic

2: Use Amazon CloudWatch Events to send the processed data

3: Publish the processed data to an Amazon SNS topic

4: Push the processed data to Amazon SQS

Answer: 3

Explanation:

With Destinations, you can route asynchronous function results as an execution record to a destination resource without writing additional code. An execution record contains details about the request and response in JSON format including version, timestamp, request context, request payload, response context, and response payload.

For each execution status such as *Success* or *Failure* you can choose one of four destinations: another Lambda function, SNS, SQS, or EventBridge. Lambda can also be configured to route different execution results to different destinations.

In this scenario the Developer can publish the processed data to an Amazon SNS topic by using an Amazon SNS destination.

CORRECT: "Publish the processed data to an Amazon SNS topic" is the correct answer.

INCORRECT: "Separate the Lambda handler from the core logic" is incorrect as this will not assist with sending a notification to administrators.

INCORRECT: "Use Amazon CloudWatch Events to send the processed data" is incorrect as CloudWatch Events is used for tracking state changes, not forwarding execution results

INCORRECT: "Push the processed data to Amazon SQS" is incorrect as SQS will not notify the administrators, SNS should be used.

53. Question

An application is running on a cluster of Amazon EC2 instances. The application has received an error when trying to read objects stored within an Amazon S3 bucket. The bucket is encrypted with server-side encryption and AWS KMS managed keys (SSE-KMS). The error is as follows:

Service: AWSKMS; Status Code: 400, Error Code: ThrottlingException

Which combination of steps should be taken to prevent this failure? (Select TWO)

1: Contact AWS support to request an AWS KMS rate limit increase

2: Perform error retries with exponential backoff in the application code

3: Contact AWS support to request an S3 rate limit increase

4: Import a customer master key (CMK) with a larger key size

5: Use more than once customer master key (CMK) to encrypt S3 data

Answer: 1,2

Explanation:

AWS KMS establishes quotas for the number of API operations requested in each second. When you exceed an API request quota, AWS KMS *throttles* the request, that is, it rejects an otherwise valid request and returns a ThrottlingException error like the following one.

```
You have exceeded the rate at which you may call KMS. Reduce the frequency of your calls.
(Service: AWSKMS; Status Code: 400; Error Code: ThrottlingException; Request ID: <ID>
```

As the error indicates, one of the recommendations is to reduce the frequency of calls which can be implemented by using exponential backoff logic in the application code. It is also possible to contact AWS and request an increase in the quota.

CORRECT: "Contact AWS support to request an AWS KMS rate limit increase" is a correct answer.

CORRECT: "Perform error retries with exponential backoff in the application code" is a correct answer.

INCORRECT: "Contact AWS support to request an S3 rate limit increase" is incorrect as the error indicates throttling in AWS KMS.

INCORRECT: "Import a customer master key (CMK) with a larger key size" is incorrect as the key size does not affect the quota for requests to AWS KMS.

INCORRECT: "Use more than once customer master key (CMK) to encrypt S3 data" is incorrect as the issue is not the CMK it is the request quota on AWS KMS.

54. Question

A Developer is creating an AWS Lambda function that generates a new file each time it runs. Each new file must be checked into an AWS CodeCommit repository hosted in the same AWS account. How should the Developer accomplish this?

1: When the Lambda function starts, use the Git CLI to clone the repository. Check the new file into the cloned repository and push the change

2: After the new file is created in Lambda, use cURL to invoke the CodeCommit API. Send the file to the repository

3: Use an AWS SDK to instantiate a CodeCommit client. Invoke the put_file method to add the file to the repository

4: Upload the new file to an Amazon S3 bucket. Create an AWS Step Function to accept S3 events. In the Step Function, add the new file to the repository

Answer: 3

Explanation:

The Developer can use the AWS SDK to instantiate a CodeCommit client. For instance, the code might include the following:

```
import boto3


client = boto3.client('codecommit')
```

The client can then be used with put_file which adds or updates a file in a branch in an AWS CodeCommit repository, and generates a commit for the addition in the specified branch.

The request syntax is as follows:

```
response = client.put_file(
    repositoryName='string',
    branchName='string',
    fileContent=b'bytes',
    filePath='string',
    fileMode='EXECUTABLE'|'NORMAL'|'SYMLINK',
    parentCommitId='string',
    commitMessage='string',
    name='string',
    email='string'
)
```

CORRECT: "Use an AWS SDK to instantiate a CodeCommit client. Invoke the put_file method to add the file to the repository" is the correct answer.

INCORRECT: "When the Lambda function starts, use the Git CLI to clone the repository. Check the new file into the cloned repository and push the change" is incorrect as there is no need to clone a repository, a file just needs to be added to an existing repository.

INCORRECT: "After the new file is created in Lambda, use cURL to invoke the CodeCommit API. Send the file to the repository" is incorrect as a URL cannot be used to invoke a CodeCommit client and upload and check in the file.

INCORRECT: "Upload the new file to an Amazon S3 bucket. Create an AWS Step Function to accept S3 events. In the Step Function, add the new file to the repository" is incorrect as Step Functions is not triggered by S3 events.

55. Question

A Developer needs to run some code using Lambda in response to an event and forward the execution result to another application using a pub/sub notification. How can the Developer accomplish this?

1: Configure a CloudWatch Events alarm the triggers based on Lambda execution success and route the execution results to Amazon SNS

2: Configure a Lambda "on success" destination and route the execution results to Amazon SNS

3: Configure a Lambda "on success" destination and route the execution results to Amazon SQS

4: Configure a CloudWatch Events alarm the triggers based on Lambda execution success and route the execution results to Amazon SQS

Answer: 2

Explanation:

With Destinations, you can send asynchronous function execution results to a destination resource without writing code. A function execution result includes version, timestamp, request context, request payload, response context, and response payload. For each execution status (i.e. Success and Failure), you can choose one destination from four options: another Lambda function, an SNS topic, an SQS standard queue, or EventBridge.

For this scenario, the code will be run by Lambda and the execution result will then be sent to the SNS topic. The application that is subscribed to the SNS topics will then receive the notification.

CORRECT: "Configure a Lambda "on success" destination and route the execution results to Amazon SNS" is the correct answer.

INCORRECT: "Configure a CloudWatch Events alarm the triggers based on Lambda execution success and route the execution results to Amazon SNS" is incorrect as CloudWatch Events is used to track changes in the state of AWS resources. To forward execution results from Lambda a destination should be used.

INCORRECT: "Configure a Lambda "on success" destination and route the execution results to Amazon SQS" is incorrect as SQS is a message queue not a pub/sub notification service.

INCORRECT: "Configure a CloudWatch Events alarm the triggers based on Lambda execution success and route the execution results to Amazon SQS" is incorrect as CloudWatch Events is used to track changes in the state of AWS resources. To forward execution results from Lambda a destination should be used (with an SNS topic).

56. Question

An application runs on Amazon EC2 and generates log files. A Developer needs to centralize the log files so they can be queried and retained. What is the EASIEST way for the Developer to centralize the log files?

1: Install the Amazon CloudWatch Logs agent and collect the logs from the instances

2: Create a script that copies the log files to Amazon S3 and use a cron job to run the script on a recurring schedule

3: Create a script that uses the AWS SDK to collect and send the log files to Amazon CloudWatch Logs

4: Setup a CloudWatch Events rule to trigger an SNS topic when an application log file is generated

Answer: 1

Explanation:

You can use Amazon CloudWatch Logs to monitor, store, and access your log files from Amazon Elastic Compute Cloud (Amazon EC2) instances, AWS CloudTrail, Route 53, and other sources.

CloudWatch Logs enables you to centralize the logs from all of your systems, applications, and AWS services that you use, in a single, highly scalable service. You can then easily view them, search them for specific error codes or patterns, filter them based on specific fields, or archive them securely for future analysis.

To collect logs from Amazon EC2 and on-premises instances it is necessary to install an agent. There are two options: the unified CloudWatch Agent which collects logs and advanced metrics (such as memory usage), or the older CloudWatch Logs agent which only collects logs from Linux servers.

CORRECT: "Install the Amazon CloudWatch Logs agent and collect the logs from the instances" is the correct answer.

INCORRECT: "Create a script that copies the log files to Amazon S3 and use a cron job to run the script on a recurring schedule" is incorrect as the best place to move the log files to for querying and long term retention would be CloudWatch Logs. It is also easier to use the agent than to create and maintain a script.

INCORRECT: "Create a script that uses the AWS SDK to collect and send the log files to Amazon CloudWatch Logs" is incorrect as this is not the easiest way to achieve this outcome. It will be easier to use the CloudWatch Logs agent.

INCORRECT: "Setup a CloudWatch Events rule to trigger an SNS topic when an application log file is generated" is incorrect as CloudWatch Events does not collect log files, it monitors state changes in resources.

57. Question

A company needs to encrypt a large quantity of data. The data encryption keys must be generated from a dedicated, tamper-resistant hardware device. To deliver these requirements, which AWS service should the company use?

1: AWS KMS

2: AWS CloudHSM

3: AWS Certificate Manager

4: AWS IAM

Answer: 2

Explanation:

The AWS CloudHSM service helps you meet corporate, contractual, and regulatory compliance requirements for data security by using dedicated Hardware Security Module (HSM) instances within the AWS cloud.

A Hardware Security Module (HSM) provides secure key storage and cryptographic operations within a tamper-resistant hardware device. CloudHSM allows you to securely generate, store, and manage cryptographic keys used for data encryption in a way that keys are accessible only by you.

CORRECT: "AWS CloudHSM" is the correct answer.

INCORRECT: "AWS KMS" is incorrect as it uses shared infrastructure (multi-tenant) and is therefore not a dedicated HSM.

INCORRECT: "AWS Certificate Manager" is incorrect as this is used to generate and manage SSL/TLS certificates, it does not generate data encryption keys.

INCORRECT: "AWS IAM" is incorrect as this service is not involved with generating encryption keys.

58. Question

A Developer needs to restrict all users and roles from using a list of API actions within a member account in AWS Organizations. The Developer needs to deny access to a few specific API actions. What is the MOST efficient way to do this?

1: Create a deny list and specify the API actions to deny

2: Create an allow list and specify the API actions to deny

3: Create an IAM policy that denies the API actions for all users and roles

4: Create an IAM policy that allows only the unrestricted API actions

Answer: 1

Explanation:

Service control policies (SCPs) are one type of policy that you can use to manage your organization. SCPs offer central control over the maximum available permissions for all accounts in your organization, allowing you to ensure your accounts stay within your organization's access control guidelines.

You can configure the SCPs in your organization to work as either of the following:

- A deny list – actions are allowed by default, and you specify what services and actions are prohibited

- An allow list – actions are prohibited by default, and you specify what services and actions are allowed

As there are only a few API actions to restrict the most efficient strategy for this scenario is to create a deny list and specify the specific actions that are prohibited.

CORRECT: "Create a deny list and specify the API actions to deny" is the correct answer.

INCORRECT: "Create an allow list and specify the API actions to deny" is incorrect as with an allow list you specify the API actions to allow.

INCORRECT: "Create an IAM policy that denies the API actions for all users and roles" is incorrect as you cannot create deny policies in IAM. IAM policies implicitly deny access unless you explicitly allow permissions.

INCORRECT: "Create an IAM policy that allows only the unrestricted API actions" is incorrect. This will not work for administrative users such as the root account (as they have extra permissions) so an SCP must be used.

59. Question

A development team require a fully-managed source control service that is compatible with Git. Which service should they use?

1: AWS CodeDeploy

2: AWS Cloud9

3: AWS CodePipeline

4: AWS CodeCommit

Answer: 4

Explanation:

AWS CodeCommit is a version control service hosted by Amazon Web Services that you can use to privately store and manage assets (such as documents, source code, and binary files) in the cloud. CodeCommit is a fully-managed service that hosts secure Git-based repositories.

CORRECT: "AWS CodeCommit" is the correct answer.

INCORRECT: "AWS CodeDeploy" is incorrect. CodeDeploy is a deployment service that automates application deployments to Amazon EC2 instances, on-premises instances, serverless Lambda functions, or Amazon ECS services.

INCORRECT: "AWS CodePipeline" is incorrect. AWS CodePipeline is a fully managed continuous delivery service that helps you automate your release pipelines for fast and reliable application and infrastructure updates.

INCORRECT: "AWS Cloud9" is incorrect. AWS Cloud9 is a cloud-based integrated development environment (IDE) that lets you write, run, and debug your code with just a browser.

60. Question

How can a Developer view a summary of proposed changes to an AWS CloudFormation stack without implementing the changes in production?

1: Create a StackSet

2: Create a Change Set

3: Use drift detection

4: Use a direct update

Answer: 2

Explanation:

When you need to update a stack, understanding how your changes will affect running resources before you implement them can help you update stacks with confidence. Change sets allow you to preview how proposed changes to a stack might impact your running resources.

AWS CloudFormation makes the changes to your stack only when you decide to execute the change set, allowing you to decide whether to proceed with your proposed changes or explore other changes by creating another change set. You can create and manage change sets using the AWS CloudFormation console, AWS CLI, or AWS CloudFormation API.

CORRECT: "Create a Change Set" is the correct answer.

INCORRECT: "Create a StackSet" is incorrect as StackSets are used to create, update, or delete stacks across multiple accounts and regions with a single operation.

INCORRECT: "Use drift detection" is incorrect as this is used to detect when a configuration deviates from the template configuration.

INCORRECT: "Use a direct update" is incorrect as this will directly update the production resources.

61. Question

Based on the following AWS CLI command the resulting output, what has happened here?

$ aws lambda invoke --function-name MyFunction --payload
ewogICJrZXkxIjogInZhbHVlMSIsCiAgImtleTIiOiAidmFsdWUyIiwKICAia2V5MyI6ICJ2YWx1ZTMiCn0=
response.json

{

   "StatusCode": 200

}

1: An AWS Lambda function has been invoked synchronously and has completed successfully

2: An AWS Lambda function has been invoked synchronously and has not completed successfully

3: An AWS Lambda function has been invoked asynchronously and has completed successfully

4: An AWS Lambda function has been invoked asynchronously and has not completed successfully

Answer: 1

Explanation:

When you invoke a function synchronously, Lambda runs the function and waits for a response. When the function execution ends, Lambda returns the response from the function's code with additional data, such as the version of the function that was executed. To invoke a function synchronously with the AWS CLI, use the invoke command.

The following diagram shows clients invoking a Lambda function synchronously. Lambda sends the events directly to the function and sends the function's response back to the invoker.

Synchronous Invocation

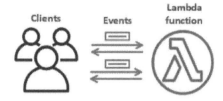

We know the function has been run synchronously as the --invocation-type Event parameter has not been included. Also, the status code 200 indicates a successful execution of a synchronous execution.

CORRECT: "An AWS Lambda function has been invoked synchronously and has completed successfully" is the correct answer.

INCORRECT: "An AWS Lambda function has been invoked synchronously and has not completed successfully" is incorrect as the status code 200 indicates a successful execution.

INCORRECT: "An AWS Lambda function has been invoked asynchronously and has completed successfully" is incorrect as the --invocation-type Event has parameter is not included so this is not an asynchronous invocation.

INCORRECT: "An AWS Lambda function has been invoked asynchronously and has not completed successfully" is incorrect as the --invocation-type Event has parameter is not included so this is not an asynchronous invocation.

62. Question

A Developer must run a shell script on Amazon EC2 Linux instances each time they are launched by an Amazon EC2 Auto Scaling group. What is the SIMPLEST way to run the script?

1: Add the script to the user data when creating the launch configuration

2: Configure Amazon CloudWatch Events to trigger the AWS CLI when an instance is launched and run the script

3: Package the script in a zip file with some AWS Lambda source code. Upload to Lambda and run the function when instances are launched

4: Run the script using the AWS Systems Manager Run Command

Answer: 1

Explanation:

The simplest option is to add the script to the user data when creating the launch configuration. User data is information that is parsed when the EC2 instances are launched. When you add a script to the user data in a launch configuration all instances that are launched by that Auto Scaling group will run the script.

CORRECT: "Add the script to the user data when creating the launch configuration" is the correct answer.

INCORRECT: "Configure Amazon CloudWatch Events to trigger the AWS CLI when an instance is launched and run the script" is incorrect as you cannot trigger the AWS CLI using CloudWatch Events and the script may not involve AWS CLI commands.

INCORRECT: "Package the script in a zip file with some AWS Lambda source code. Upload to Lambda and run the function when instances are launched" is incorrect as Lambda does not run shell scripts. You could program the requirements into the function code however you still need a trigger which is not mentioned in this option.

INCORRECT: "Run the script using the AWS Systems Manager Run Command" is incorrect as this is not the simplest method. For most Linux AMIs (except Amazon Linux) the developer's would need to install the agent on the operating system. They would also then need to create a mechanism of triggering the run command.

63. Question

A Developer has created a task definition that includes the following JSON code:

"placementConstraints": [

  {

    "expression": "task:group == databases",

    "type": "memberOf"

  }

]

What will be the effect for tasks using this task definition?

1: They will become members of a task group called "databases"

2: They will not be placed on container instances in the "databases" task group

3: They will be placed on container instances in the "databases" task group

4: They will not be allowed to run unless they have the "databases" tag assigned

Answer: 3

Explanation:

A *task placement constraint* is a rule that is considered during task placement. Task placement constraints can be specified when either running a task or creating a new service.

The memberOf task placement constraint places tasks on container instances that satisfy an expression.

The memberOf task placement constraint can be specified with the following actions:

- Running a task
- Creating a new service
- Creating a new task definition
- Creating a new revision of an existing task definition

The example JSON code uses the memberOf constraint to place tasks on instances in the databases task group. It can be specified with the following actions: CreateService, UpdateService, RegisterTaskDefinition, and RunTask.

CORRECT: "They will be placed on container instances in the "databases" task group" is the correct answer.

INCORRECT: "They will become members of a task group called "databases"" is incorrect. They will be placed on container instances in the "databases" task group.

INCORRECT: "They will not be placed on container instances in the "databases" task group" is incorrect. This statement ensures the tasks ARE placed on the container instances in the "databases" task group.

INCORRECT: "They will not be allowed to run unless they have the "databases" tag assigned" is incorrect. This JSON code is not related to tagging of the tasks.

64. Question

Data must be loaded into an application each week for analysis. The data is uploaded to an Amazon S3 bucket from several offices around the world. Latency is slowing the uploads and delaying the analytics job. What is the SIMPLEST way to improve upload times?

1: Upload to a local Amazon S3 bucket within each region and enable Cross-Region Replication (CRR)

2: Upload via a managed AWS VPN connection

3: Upload to Amazon CloudFront and then download from the local cache to the S3 bucket

4: Upload using Amazon S3 Transfer Acceleration

Answer: 4

Explanation:

Amazon S3 Transfer Acceleration enables fast, easy, and secure transfers of files over long distances between your client and an S3 bucket. Transfer Acceleration takes advantage of Amazon CloudFront's globally distributed edge locations. As the data arrives at an edge location, data is routed to Amazon S3 over an optimized network path.

You might want to use Transfer Acceleration on a bucket for various reasons, including the following:

- You have customers that upload to a centralized bucket from all over the world.

- You transfer gigabytes to terabytes of data on a regular basis across continents.

- You are unable to utilize all of your available bandwidth over the Internet when uploading to Amazon S3.

CORRECT: "Upload using Amazon S3 Transfer Acceleration" is the correct answer.

INCORRECT: "Upload to a local Amazon S3 bucket within each region and enable Cross-Region Replication (CRR)" is incorrect as this would not speed up the upload as the process introduces more latency.

INCORRECT: "Upload via a managed AWS VPN connection" is incorrect as this still uses the public Internet and there's no real latency advantages here.

INCORRECT: "Upload to Amazon CloudFront and then download from the local cache to the S3 bucket" is incorrect. This is going to require some time to propagate to the cache and requires some manual work in retrieving the data. The simplest solution is to use S3 Transfer Acceleration which basically does this for you.

65. Question

An AWS Lambda function must be connected to an Amazon VPC private subnet that does not have Internet access. The function also connects to an Amazon DynamoDB table. What MUST a Developer do to enable access to the DynamoDB table?

1: Attach an Internet Gateway

2: Configure a VPC endpoint

3: Create a route table

4: Attach an ENI to the DynamoDB table

Answer: 2

Explanation:

To connect to AWS services from a private subnet with no internet access, use VPC endpoints. A *VPC endpoint* for DynamoDB enables resources in a VPC to use their private IP addresses to access DynamoDB with no exposure to the public internet.

When you create a VPC endpoint for DynamoDB, any requests to a DynamoDB endpoint within the Region (for example, *dynamodb.us-west-2.amazonaws.com*) are routed to a private DynamoDB endpoint within the Amazon network.

CORRECT: "Configure a VPC endpoint" is the correct answer.

INCORRECT: "Attach an Internet Gateway" is incorrect as you do not attach these to a private subnet.

INCORRECT: "Create a route table" is incorrect as a route table will exist for all subnets and it does not help to route out from a private subnet via the Internet unless an entry for a NAT Gateway or Instance is added.

INCORRECT: "Attach an ENI to the DynamoDB table" is incorrect as you do not attach Elastic Network Interfaces to DynamoDB tables.

SET 6: PRACTICE QUESTIONS ONLY

For training purposes, go directly to Set 6: Practice Questions, Answers & Explanations

1. Question

A developer has created a Docker image and uploaded it to an Amazon Elastic Container Registry (ECR) repository. How can the developer pull the image to his workstation using the docker client?

1: Run aws ec2 get-login-password use the output to login in then issue a docker pull command specifying the image name using registry/repository[:tag]

2: Run the docker pull command specifying the image name using registry/repository[:tag]

3: Run aws ecr describe-images --repository-name repositoryname

4: Run docker login with an IAM key pair then issue a docker pull command specifying the image name using registry/repository[@digest]

2. Question

A company is designing a new application that will store thousands of terabytes of data. They need a fully managed NoSQL data store that provides low-latency and can store key-value pairs. Which type of database should they use?

1: Amazon RDS

2: Amazon ElastiCache

3: Amazon S3

4: Amazon DynamoDB

3. Question

The manager of a development team is setting up a shared S3 bucket for team members. The manager would like to use a single policy to allow each user to have access to their objects in the S3 bucket. Which feature can be used to generalize the policy?

1: Principal

2: Condition

3: Variable

4: Resource

4. Question

An independent software vendor (ISV) uses Amazon S3 and Amazon CloudFront to distribute software updates. They would like to provide their premium customers with access to updates faster. What is the MOST efficient way to distribute these updates only to the premium customers? (Select TWO)

1: Create a signed cookie and associate it with the Amazon S3 distribution

2: Create a signed URL with access to the content and distribute it to the premium customers

3: Use an access control list (ACL) on the Amazon S3 bucket to restrict access based on IP address

4: Create an origin access identity (OAI) and associate it with the distribution and configure permissions

5: Use an IAM policy to restrict access to the content using a condition attribute and specify the IP addresses of the premium customers

5. Question

An Amazon RDS database is experiencing a high volume of read requests that are slowing down the database. Which fully managed, in-memory AWS database service can assist with offloading reads from the RDS database?

1: Amazon RDS Read Replica

2: Amazon Aurora Serverless

3: Amazon ElastiCache Redis

4: Memcached on Amazon EC2

6. Question

A developer is creating a multi-tier web application. The front-end will place messages in an Amazon SQS queue for the back-end to process. Each job includes a file that is 1GB in size. What MUST the developer do to ensure this works as expected?

1: Increase the maximum message size of the queue from 256KB to 1GB

2: Store the large files in DynamoDB and use the SQS Extended Client Library for Java to manage SQS messages

3: Create a FIFO queue that supports large files

4: Store the large files in Amazon S3 and use the SQS Extended Client Library for Java to manage SQS messages

7. Question

A serverless application composed of multiple Lambda functions has been deployed. A developer is setting up AWS CodeDeploy to manage the deployment of code updates. The developer would like a 10% of the traffic to be shifted to the new version in equal increments, 10 minutes apart. Which setting should be chosen for configuring how traffic is shifted?

1: Canary

2: Linear

3: All-at-once

4: Blue/green

8. Question

A company has a global presence and managers must submit large quantities of reporting data to an Amazon S3 bucket located in the us-east-1 region on weekly basis. Uploads have been slow recently, how can you improve data throughput and upload times?

1: Enable S3 Transfer Acceleration on the S3 bucket

2: Use S3 Multi-part upload

3: Create an AWS Direct Connect connection from each remote office

4: Use an AWS Managed VPN

9. Question

A developer is building a Docker application on Amazon ECS that will use an Application Load Balancer (ALB). The developer needs to configure the port mapping between the host port and container port. Where is this setting configured?

1: Host definition

2: Task definition

3: Service scheduler

4: Container instance

10. Question

A developer is designing a web application that will be used by thousands of users. The users will sign up using their email addresses and the application will store attributes for each user. Which service should the developer use to enable users to sign-up for the web application?

1: Amazon Cognito Sync

2: Amazon Cognito user pool

3: AWS Inspector

4: AWS AppSync

11. Question

An application resizes images that are uploaded to an Amazon S3 bucket. Amazon S3 event notifications are used to trigger an AWS Lambda function that resizes the images. The processing time for each image is less than one second. A large amount of images are expected to be received in a short burst of traffic. How will AWS Lambda accommodate the workload?

1: Lambda will scale out and execute the requests concurrently

2: Lambda will process the images sequentially in the order they are received

3: Lambda will collect and then batch process the images in a single execution

4: Lambda will scale the memory allocated to the function to increase the amount of CPU available to process many images

12. Question

A Developer is creating multiple AWS Lambda functions that will be using an external library that is not included in the standard Lambda libraries. What is the BEST way to make these libraries available to the functions?

1: Include the external library with the function code

2: Create a deployment package that includes the external library

3: Store the files in Amazon S3 and reference them from your function code

4: Create a layer in Lambda that includes the external library

13. Question

A Developer is creating a social networking app for games that uses a single Amazon DynamoDB table. All users' saved game data is stored in the single table, but users should not be able to view each other's data. How can the Developer restrict user access so they can only view their own data?

1: Restrict access to specific items based on certain primary key values

2: Use separate access keys for each user to call the API and restrict access to specific items based on access key ID

3: Use an identity-based policy that restricts read access to the table to specific principals

4: Read records from DynamoDB and discard irrelevant data client-side

14. Question

A Development team are developing a micro-services application that will use Docker containers on Amazon ECS. There will be 6 distinct services included in the architecture. Each service requires specific permissions to various AWS services. What is the MOST secure way to grant the services the necessary permissions?

1: Create a new Identity and Access Management (IAM) instance profile containing the required permissions for the various ECS services, then associate that instance role with the underlying EC2 instances

2: Create six separate IAM roles, each containing the required permissions for the associated ECS service, then configure each ECS task definition to reference the associated IAM role

3: Create six separate IAM roles, each containing the required permissions for the associated ECS service, then create an IAM group and configure the ECS cluster to reference that group

4: Create a single IAM policy and use principal statements referencing the ECS tasks and assigning the required permissions, then apply the policy to the ECS service

15. Question

A company is reviewing their security practices. According to AWS best practice, how should access keys be managed to improve security? (Select TWO)

1: Delete all access keys for the root account IAM user

2: Embed access keys directly into code

3: Rotate access keys daily

4: Use different access keys for different applications

5: Use the same access key in all applications for consistency

16. Question

A Developer is creating an application that will utilize an Amazon DynamoDB table for storing session data. The data being stored is expected to be around 4.5KB in size and the application will make 20 eventually consistent reads/sec, and 12 standard writes/sec. How many RCUs/WCUs are required?

1: 40 RCU and 60 WCU

2: 20 RCU and 60 WCU

3: 40 RCU and 120 WCU

4: 10 RCU and 24 WCU

17. Question

A monitoring application that keeps track of a large eCommerce website uses Amazon Kinesis for data ingestion. During periods of peak data rates, the producers are not making best use of the available shards. What step will allow the producers to better utilize the available shards and increase write throughput to the Kinesis data stream?

1: Install the Kinesis Producer Library (KPL) for ingesting data into the stream

2: Create an SQS queue and decouple the producers from the Kinesis data stream

3: Increase the shard count of the stream using UpdateShardCount

4: Ingest multiple records into the stream in a single call using BatchWriteItem

18. Question

A Developer is creating an AWS Lambda function that will process medical images. The function is dependent on several libraries that are not available in the Lambda runtime environment. Which strategy should be used to create the Lambda deployment package?

1: Create a ZIP file with the source code and all dependent libraries

2: Create a ZIP file with the source code and a script that installs the dependent libraries at runtime

3: Create a ZIP file with the source code. Stage the dependent libraries on an Amazon S3 bucket indicated by the Lambda environment variable LIBRARY_PATH

4: Create a ZIP file with the source code and a buildspec.yaml file that installs the dependent libraries on AWS Lambda

19. Question

A company use Amazon CloudFront to deliver application content to users around the world. A Developer has made an update to some files in the origin however users have reported that they are still getting the old files. How can the Developer ensure that the old files are replaced in the cache with the LEAST disruption?

1: Invalidate the files from the edge caches

2: Create a new origin with the new files and remove the old origin

3: Disable the CloudFront distribution and enable it again to update all the edge locations

4: Add code to Lambda@Edge that updates the files in the cache

20. Question

A Developer is creating a serverless website with content that includes HTML files, images, videos, and JavaScript (client-side scripts). Which combination of services should the Developer use to create the website?

1: Amazon S3 and Amazon CloudFront

2: Amazon EC2 and Amazon ElastiCache

3: Amazon ECS and Redis

4: AWS Lambda and Amazon API Gateway

21. Question

A Developer needs to update an Amazon ECS application that was deployed using AWS CodeDeploy. What file does the Developer need to update to push the change through CodeDeploy?

1: dockerrun.aws.json

2: buildspec.yml

3: appspec.yml

4: ebextensions.config

22. Question

A Development team wants to instrument their code to provide more detailed information to AWS X-Ray than simple outgoing and incoming requests. This will generate large amounts of data, so the Development team wants to implement indexing so they can filter the data. What should the Development team do to achieve this?

1: Add metadata to the segment document

2: Configure the necessary X-Ray environment variables

3: Install required plugins for the appropriate AWS SDK

4: Add annotations to the segment document

23. Question

An organization has an Amazon S3 bucket containing premier content that they intend to make available to only paid subscribers of their website. The objects in the S3 bucket are private to prevent inadvertent exposure of the premier content to non-paying website visitors. How can the organization provide only paid subscribers the ability to download the premier content in the S3 bucket?

1: Apply a bucket policy that grants anonymous users to download the content from the S3 bucket

2: Generate a pre-signed object URL for the premier content file when a paid subscriber requests a download

3: Add a bucket policy that requires Multi-Factor Authentication for requests to access the S3 bucket objects

4: Enable server-side encryption on the S3 bucket for data protection against the non-paying website visitors

24. Question

A serverless application uses Amazon API Gateway, AWS Lambda and DynamoDB. The application writes statistical data that is constantly received from sensors. The data is analyzed soon after it is written to the database and is then not required. What is the EASIEST method to remove stale data and optimize database size?

1: Enable the TTL attribute and add expiry timestamps to items

2: Use atomic counters to decrement the data when it becomes stale

3: Scan the table for stale data and delete it once every hour

4: Delete the table and recreate it every hour

25. Question

A Development team are creating a financial trading application. The application requires sub-millisecond latency for processing trading requests. Amazon DynamoDB is used to store the trading data. During load testing the Development team found that in periods of high utilization the latency is too high and read capacity must be significantly over-provisioned to avoid throttling. How can the Developers meet the latency requirements of the application?

1: Use Amazon DynamoDB Accelerator (DAX) to cache the data

2: Create a Global Secondary Index (GSI) for the trading data

3: Use exponential backoff in the application code for DynamoDB queries

4: Store the trading data in Amazon S3 and use Transfer Acceleration

26. Question

A Developer is deploying an Amazon EC2 update using AWS CodeDeploy. In the appspec.yml file, which of the following is a valid structure for the order of hooks that should be specified?

1: BeforeInstall > AfterInstall > AfterAllowTestTraffic > BeforeAllowTraffic > AfterAllowTraffic

2: BeforeInstall > AfterInstall > ApplicationStart > ValidateService

3: BeforeAllowTraffic > AfterAllowTraffic

4: BeforeBlockTraffic > AfterBlockTraffic > BeforeAllowTraffic > AfterAllowTraffic

27. Question

An application will ingest data at a very high throughput from several sources and stored in an Amazon S3 bucket for subsequent analysis. Which AWS service should a Developer choose for this requirement?

1: Amazon Kinesis Data Firehose

2: Amazon S3 Transfer Acceleration

3: Amazon Kinesis Data Analytics

4: Amazon Simple Queue Service (SQS)

28. Question

A mobile application has thousands of users. Each user may use multiple devices to access the application. The Developer wants to assign unique identifiers to these users regardless of the device they use. Which of the below is the BEST method to obtain unique identifiers?

1: Create a user table in Amazon DynamoDB with key-value pairs of users and their devices. Use these keys as unique identifiers

2: Use IAM-generated access key IDs for the users as the unique identifier, but do not store secret keys

3: Implement developer-authenticated identities by using Amazon Cognito and get credentials for these identities

4: Assign IAM users and roles to the users. Use the unique IAM resource ID as the unique identifier

29. Question

A manufacturing company is creating a new RESTful API that their customers can use to query the status of orders. The endpoint for customer queries will be http://www.manufacturerdomain.com/status/customerID

Which of the following application designs will meet the requirements? (Select TWO)

1: Amazon SQS; Amazon SNS

2: Elastic Load Balancing; Amazon EC2

3: Amazon ElastiCache; Amazon Elacticsearch Service

4: Amazon API Gateway; AWS Lambda

5: Amazon S3; Amazon CloudFront

30. Question

A solution requires a serverless service for receiving streaming data and loading it directly into an Amazon Elasticsearch datastore. Which AWS service would be suitable for this requirement?

1: Amazon Kinesis Data Streams

2: Amazon Kinesis Data Analytics

3: Amazon Kinesis Data Firehose

4: Amazon Simple Queue Service (SQS)

31. Question

A serverless application uses an AWS Lambda function, Amazon API Gateway API and an Amazon DynamoDB table. The Lambda function executes 10 times per second and takes 3 seconds to complete each execution. How many concurrent executions will the Lambda function require?

1: 3

2: 12

3: 10

4: 30

32. Question

An application that is being migrated to AWS and refactored requires a storage service. The storage service should support provide a standards-based REST web service interface and store objects based on keys. Which AWS service would be MOST suitable?

1: Amazon S3

2: Amazon DynamoDB

3: Amazon EBS

4: Amazon EFS

33. Question

A company will be hiring a large number of Developers for a series of projects. The Develops will bring their own devices to work and the company want to ensure consistency in tooling. The Developers must be able to write, run, and debug applications with just a browser, without needing to install or maintain a local Integrated Development Environment (IDE). Which AWS service should the Developers use?

1: AWS CodeCommit

2: AWS Cloud9

3: AWS X-Ray

4: AWS CodeDeploy

34. Question

A Development team manage a hybrid cloud environment. They would like to collect system-level metrics from on-premises servers and Amazon EC2 instances. How can the Development team collect this information MOST efficiently?

1: Use CloudWatch for monitoring EC2 instances and custom AWS CLI scripts using the put-metric-data API

2: Install the CloudWatch agent on the on-premises servers and EC2 instances

3: Install the CloudWatch agent on the EC2 instances and use a cron job on the on-premises servers

4: Use CloudWatch detailed monitoring for both EC2 instances and on-premises servers

35. Question

A Developer is migrating Docker containers to Amazon ECS. A large number of containers will be deployed onto an existing ECS cluster that uses container instances of different instance types. Which task placement strategy can be used to minimize the number of container instances used based on available memory?

1: binpack

2: random

3: spread

4: distinctInstance

36. Question

An organization has encrypted a large quantity of data. To protect their data encryption keys they are planning to use envelope encryption. Which of the following processes is a correct implementation of envelope encryption?

1: Encrypt plaintext data with a data key and then encrypt the data key with a top-level plaintext master key.

2: Encrypt plaintext data with a master key and then encrypt the master key with a top-level plaintext data key

3: Encrypt plaintext data with a data key and then encrypt the data key with a top-level encrypted master key

4: Encrypt plaintext data with a master key and then encrypt the master key with a top-level encrypted data key

37. Question

A mobile application runs as a serverless application on AWS. A Developer needs to create a push notification feature that sends periodic message to subscribers. How can the Developer send the notification from the application?

1: Publish a message to an Amazon SQS Queue

2: Publish a notification to Amazon CloudWatch Events

3: Publish a notification to an Amazon SNS Topic

4: Publish a message to an Amazon SWF Workflow

38. Question

An Amazon ElastiCache cluster has been placed in front of a large Amazon RDS database. To reduce cost the ElastiCache cluster should only cache items that are actually requested. How should ElastiCache be optimized?

1: Only cache database writes

2: Enable a TTL on cached data

3: Use a write-through caching strategy

4: Use a lazy loading caching strategy

39. Question

A retail organization stores stock information in an Amazon RDS database. An application reads and writes data to the database. A Developer has been asked to provide read access to the database from a reporting application in another region. Which configuration would provide BEST performance for the reporting application without impacting the performance of the main database?

1: Implement a cross-region multi-AZ deployment in the region where the reporting application will run

2: Create a snapshot of the database and create a new database from the snapshot in the region where the reporting application will run

3: Implement a cross-region read replica in the region where the reporting application will run

4: Implement a read replica in another AZ and configure the reporting application to connect to the read replica using a VPN connection

40. Question

An Auto Scaling Group (ASG) of Amazon EC2 instances is being created for processing messages from an Amazon SQS queue. To ensure the EC2 instances are cost-effective a Developer would like to configure the ASG to maintain aggregate CPU utilization at 70%. Which type of scaling policy should the Developer choose?

1: Step Scaling Policy

2: Simple Scaling Policy

3: Scheduled Scaling Policy

4: Target Tracking Scaling Policy

41. Question

An application collects data from sensors in a manufacturing facility. The data is stored in an Amazon SQS Standard queue by an AWS Lambda function and an Amazon EC2 instance processes the data and stores it in an Amazon RedShift data warehouse. A fault in the sensors' software is causing occasional duplicate messages to be sent. Timestamps on the duplicate messages show they are generated within a few seconds of the primary message. How a can a Developer prevent duplicate data being stored in the data warehouse?

1: Use a FIFO queue and configure the Lambda function to add a message deduplication token to the message body

2: Use a FIFO queue and configure the Lambda function to add a message group ID to the messages generated by each individual sensor

3: Send a ChangeMessageVisibility call with VisibilityTimeout set to 30 seconds after the receipt of every message from the queue

4: Configure a redrive policy, specify a destination Dead-Letter queue, and set the maxReceiveCount to 1

42. Question

A Developer is publishing custom metrics for Amazon EC2 using the Amazon CloudWatch CLI. The Developer needs to add further context to the metrics being published by organizing them by EC2 instance and Auto Scaling Group. What should the Developer add to the CLI command when publishing the metrics using put-metric-data

1: The --dimensions parameter

2: The --namespace parameter

3: The --statistic-values parameter

4: The --metric-name parameter

43. Question

A legacy application is being refactored into a microservices architecture running on AWS. The microservice will include several AWS Lambda functions. A Developer will use AWS Step Functions to coordinate function execution. How should the Developer proceed?

1: Create an AWS CloudFormation stack using a YAML-formatted template

2: Create a state machine using the Amazon States Language

3: Create a workflow using the StartExecution API action

4: Create a layer in AWS Lambda and add the functions to the layer

44. Question

A company has sensitive data that must be encrypted. The data is made up of 1 GB objects and there is a total of 150 GB of data. What is the BEST approach for a Developer to encrypt the data using AWS KMS?

1: Make an Encrypt API call to encrypt the plaintext data as ciphertext using a customer master key (CMK)

2: Make an Encrypt API call to encrypt the plaintext data as ciphertext using a customer master key (CMK) with imported key material

3: Make a GenerateDataKey API call that returns a plaintext key and an encrypted copy of a data key. Use the plaintext key to encrypt the data

4: Make a GenerateDataKeyWithoutPlaintext API call that returns an encrypted copy of a data key. Use the encrypted key to encrypt the data

45. Question

A nightly batch job loads 1 million new records in to a DynamoDB table. The records are only needed for one hour, and the table needs to be empty by the next night's batch job. Which is the MOST efficient and cost-effective method to provide an empty table?

1: Use DeleteItem using a ConditionExpression

2: Use BatchWriteItem to empty all of the rows

3: Write a recursive function that scans and calls out DeleteItem

4: Create and then delete the table after the task has completed

46. Question

A Developer is creating an AWS Lambda function to process a stream of data from an Amazon Kinesis Data Stream. When the Lambda function parses the data and encounters a missing field, it exits the function with an error. The function is generating duplicate records from the Kinesis stream. When the Developer looks at the stream output without the Lambda function, there are no duplicate records. What is the reason for the duplicates?

1: The Lambda function did not advance the Kinesis stream point to the next record after the error

2: The Lambda event source used asynchronous invocation, resulting in duplicate records

3: The Lambda function did not handle the error, and the Lambda service attempted to reprocess the data

4: The Lambda function is not keeping up with the amount of data coming from the stream

47. Question

A Developer has code running on Amazon EC2 instances that needs read-only access to an Amazon DynamoDB table. What is the MOST secure approach the Developer should take to accomplish this task?

1: Create a user access key for each EC2 instance with read-only access to DynamoDB. Place the keys in the code. Redeploy the code as keys rotate

2: Use an IAM role with an AmazonDynamoDBReadOnlyAccess policy applied to the EC2 instances

3: Run all code with only AWS account root user access keys to ensure maximum access to services

4: Use an IAM role with Administrator access applied to the EC2 instance

48. Question

A company is migrating an on-premises web application to AWS. The web application runs on a single server and stores session data in memory. On AWS the company plan to implement multiple Amazon EC2 instances behind an Elastic Load Balancer (ELB). The company want to refactor the application so that data is resilient if an instance fails and user downtime is minimized. Where should the company move session data to MOST effectively reduce downtime and make users' session data more fault tolerant?

1: An Amazon ElastiCache for Redis cluster

2: A second Amazon EBS volume

3: The web server's primary disk

4: An Amazon EC2 instance dedicated to session data

49. Question

A Developer is creating a script to automate the deployment process for a serverless application. The Developer wants to use an existing AWS Serverless Application Model (SAM) template for the application. What should the Developer use for the project? (Select TWO)

1: Call aws cloudformation package to create the deployment package. Call aws cloudformation deploy to deploy the package afterward

2: Call sam package to create the deployment package. Call sam deploy to deploy the package afterward

3: Call aws s3 cp to upload the AWS SAM template to Amazon S3. Call aws lambda update-function-code to create the application

4: Create a ZIP package locally and call aws serverlessrepo create-application to create the application

5: Create a ZIP package and upload it to Amazon S3. Call aws cloudformation create-stack to create the application

50. Question

A website delivers images stored in an Amazon S3 bucket. The site uses Amazon Cognito-enabled and guest users without logins need to be able to view the images from the S3 bucket. How can a Developer enable access for guest users to the AWS resources?

1: Create a blank user ID in a user pool, add to the user group, and grant access to AWS resources

2: Create a new identity pool, enable access to unauthenticated identities, and grant access to AWS resources

3: Create a new user pool, enable access to unauthenticated identities, and grant access to AWS resources

4: Create a new user pool, disable authentication access, and grant access to AWS resources

51. Question

A company has a website that is developed in PHP and WordPress and is launched using AWS Elastic Beanstalk. There is a new version of the website that needs to be deployed in the Elastic Beanstalk environment. The company cannot tolerate having the website offline if an update fails. Deployments must have minimal impact and rollback as soon as possible. What deployment method should be used?

1: All at once

2: Rolling

3: Snapshots

4: Immutable

52. Question

A company is building an application to track athlete performance using an Amazon DynamoDB table. Each item in the table is identified by a partition key (user_id) and a sort key (sport_name). The table design is shown below:

- **Partition key: user_id**
- **Sort Key: sport_name**
- **Attributes: score, score_datetime**

A Developer is asked to write a leaderboard application to display the top performers (user_id) based on the score for each sport_name.

What process will allow the Developer to extract results MOST efficiently from the DynamoDB table?

1: Use a DynamoDB query operation with the key attributes of user_id and sport_name and order the results based on the score attribute

2: Create a global secondary index with a partition key of sport_name and a sort key of score, and get the results

3: Use a DynamoDB scan operation to retrieve scores and user_id based on sport_name, and order the results based on the score attribute

4: Create a local secondary index with a primary key of sport_name and a sort key of score and get the results based on the score attribute

53. Question

A Developer wants the ability to roll back to a previous version of an AWS Lambda function in the event of errors caused by a new deployment. How can the Developer achieve this with MINIMAL impact on users?

1: Change the application to use an alias that points to the current version. Deploy the new version of the code. Update the alias to use the newly deployed version. If too many errors are encountered, point the alias back to the previous version

2: Change the application to use an alias that points to the current version. Deploy the new version of the code. Update the alias to direct 10% of users to the newly deployed version. If too many errors are encountered, send 100% of traffic to the previous version

3: Change the application to use a version ARN that points to the latest published version. Deploy the new version of the code. Update the application to point to the ARN of the new version of the code. If too many errors are encountered, point the application back to the ARN of the previous version

4: Change the application to use the $LATEST version. Update and save code. If too many errors are encountered, modify and save the code

54. Question

A company is migrating an application with a website and MySQL database to the AWS Cloud. The company require the application to be refactored so it offers high availability and fault tolerance. How should a Developer refactor the application? (Select TWO)

1: Migrate the website to an Auto Scaling group of EC2 instances across a single AZ and use an Elastic Load Balancer

2: Migrate the website to an Auto Scaling group of EC2 instances across multiple AZs and use an Elastic Load Balancer

3: Migrate the MySQL database to an Amazon RDS instance with a Read Replica in another AZ

4: Migrate the MySQL database to an Amazon RDS Multi-AZ deployment

5: Migrate the MySQL database to an Amazon DynamoDB with Global Tables

55. Question

A company runs many microservices applications that use Docker containers. The company are planning to migrate the containers to Amazon ECS. The workloads are highly variable and therefore the company prefers to be charged per running task. Which solution is the BEST fit for the company's requirements?

1: Amazon ECS with the EC2 launch type

2: Amazon ECS with the Fargate launch type

3: An Amazon ECS Service with Auto Scaling

4: An Amazon ECS Cluster with Auto Scaling

56. Question

A company has hired a team of remote Developers. The Developers need to work programmatically with AWS resources from their laptop computers. Which security components MUST the Developers use to authenticate? (Select TWO)

1: Access key ID

2: Secret access key

3: Console password

4: IAM user ID

5: MFA device

57. Question

A Developer created an AWS Lambda function and then attempted to add an on failure destination but received the following error:

The function's execution role does not have permissions to call SendMessage on arn:aws:sqs:us-east-1:515148212435:FailureDestination

How can the Developer resolve this issue MOST securely?

1: Add the AWSLambdaSQSQueueExecutionRole AWS managed policy to the function's execution role

2: Create a customer managed policy with all read/write permissions to SQS and attach the policy to the function's execution role

3: Add a permissions policy to the SQS queue allowing the SendMessage action and specify the AWS account number

4: Add the Lambda function to a group with administrative privileges

58. Question

A Developer is creating an application that uses Amazon EC2 instances and must be highly available and fault tolerant. How should the Developer configure the VPC?

1: Create multiple subnets within a single availability zone in the region

2: Create a subnet in each availability zone in the region

3: Create an Internet Gateway for every availability zone

4: Create a cluster placement group for the EC2 instances

59. Question

A company has released a new application on AWS. The company are concerned about security and require a tool that can automatically assess applications for exposure, vulnerabilities, and deviations from best practices. Which AWS service should they use?

1: Amazon Inspector

2: AWS Shield

3: AWS WAF

4: AWS Secrets Manager

60. Question

A Developer has lost their access key ID and secret access key for programmatic access. What should the Developer do?

1: Contact AWS support and request a password reset

2: Generate a new key pair from the EC2 management console

3: Reset the AWS account access keys

4: Disable and delete the users' access key and generate a new set

61. Question

An application includes multiple Auto Scaling groups of Amazon EC2 instances. Each group corresponds to a different subdomain of example.com, including forum.example.com and myaccount.example.com. An Elastic Load Balancer will be used to distribute load from a single HTTPS listener. Which type of Elastic Load Balancer MUST a Developer use in this scenario?

1: Application Load Balancer

2: Network Load Balancer

3: Classic Load Balancer

4: Task Load Balancer

62. Question

A Developer has created a task definition that includes the following JSON code:

"placementConstraints": [

  {

    "expression": "attribute:ecs.instance-type =~ t2.*",

    "type": "memberOf"

  }

]

What will be the effect for tasks using this task definition?

1: They will be placed only on container instances using the T2 instance type

2: They will be placed only on container instances of T2 or T3 instance types

3: They will be added to distinct instances using the T2 instance type

4: They will be spread across all instances except for T2 instances

63. Question

A Java based application generates email notifications to customers using Amazon SNS. The emails must contain links to access data in a secured Amazon S3 bucket. What is the SIMPLEST way to maintain security of the bucket whilst allowing the customers to access specific objects?

1: Use the AWS SDK for Java with GeneratePresignedUrlRequest to create a presigned URL

2: Use the AWS SDK for Java to update the bucket Access Control List to allow the customers to access the bucket

3: Use the AWS SDK for Java with the AWS STS service to gain temporary security credentials

4: Use the AWS SDK for Java to assume a role with AssumeRole to gain temporary security credentials

64. Question

An application will generate thumbnails from objects uploaded to an Amazon S3 bucket. The Developer has created the bucket configuration and the AWS Lambda function and has formulated the following AWS CLI command:

aws lambda add-permission --function-name CreateThumbnail --principal s3.amazonaws.com --statement-id s3invoke --action "lambda:InvokeFunction" --source-arn arn:aws:s3:::digitalcloudbucket-source --source-account 523107438921

What will be achieved by running the AWS CLI command?

1: The Amazon S3 service principal (s3.amazonaws.com) will be granted permissions to perform the lambda:InvokeFunction action

2: The Lambda function CreateThumbnail will be granted permissions to access the objects in the digitalcloudbucket-source bucket

3: The Amazon S3 service principal (s3.amazonaws.com) will be granted permissions to perform the create an event-source mapping with the digitalcloudbucket-source bucket

4: A Lambda function will be created called CreateThumbnail with an Amazon SNS event source mapping that executes the function when objects are uploaded

65. Question

An application uses Amazon EC2 instances, AWS Lambda functions and an Amazon SQS queue. The Developer must ensure all communications are within an Amazon VPC using private IP addresses. How can this be achieved? (Select TWO)

1: Create the Amazon SQS queue within a VPC

2: Create a VPC endpoint for AWS Lambda

3: Add the AWS Lambda function to the VPC

4: Create a VPC endpoint for Amazon SQS

5: Create a VPN and connect the services to the VPG

SET 6: PRACTICE QUESTIONS, ANSWERS & EXPLANATIONS

1. Question

A developer has created a Docker image and uploaded it to an Amazon Elastic Container Registry (ECR) repository. How can the developer pull the image to his workstation using the docker client?

1: Run aws ec2 get-login-password use the output to login in then issue a docker pull command specifying the image name using registry/repository[:tag]

2: Run the docker pull command specifying the image name using registry/repository[:tag]

3: Run aws ecr describe-images --repository-name repositoryname

4: Run docker login with an IAM key pair then issue a docker pull command specifying the image name using registry/repository[@digest]

Answer: 1

Explanation:

If you would like to run a Docker image that is available in Amazon ECR, you can pull it to your local environment with the docker pull command. You can do this from either your default registry or from a registry associated with another AWS account.

Docker CLI does not support standard AWS authentication methods, so client authentication must be handled so that ECR knows who is requesting to push or pull an image. To do this you can issue the aws ec2 get-login or aws ec2 get-login-password (AWS CLI v2) and then use the output to login using docker login and then issue a docker pull command specifying the image name using registry/repository[:tag]

CORRECT: "Run aws ec2 get-login-password use the output to login in then issue a docker pull command specifying the image name using registry/repository[:tag]" is the correct answer.

INCORRECT: "Run the docker pull command specifying the image name using registry/repository[:tag]" is incorrect as you first need to authenticate to get an access token so you can pull the image down.

INCORRECT: "Run aws ecr describe-images --repository-name repositoryname" is incorrect as this would just list the images available in the repository.

INCORRECT: "Run docker login with an IAM key pair then issue a docker pull command specifying the image name using registry/repository[@digest]" is incorrect as you cannot run docker login with an IAM key pair.

2. Question

A company is designing a new application that will store thousands of terabytes of data. They need a fully managed NoSQL data store that provides low-latency and can store key-value pairs. Which type of database should they use?

1: Amazon RDS

2: Amazon ElastiCache

3: Amazon S3

4: Amazon DynamoDB

Answer: 4

Explanation:

Amazon DynamoDB is a fully managed NoSQL database. With DynamoDB, you can create database tables that can store and retrieve any amount of data and serve any level of request traffic. You can scale up or scale down your tables' throughput capacity without downtime or performance degradation.

DynamoDB is a key-value database. A key-value database is a type of nonrelational database that uses a simple key-value method to store data. A key-value database stores data as a collection of key-value pairs in which a key serves as a unique identifier. Both keys and values can be anything, ranging from simple objects to complex compound objects.

CORRECT: "Amazon DynamoDB" is the correct answer.

INCORRECT: "Amazon RDS" is incorrect as RDS is a SQL (not a NoSQL) type of database.

INCORRECT: "Amazon ElastiCache" is incorrect as ElastiCache is a SQL (not a NoSQL) type of database. ElastiCache is an in-memory database typically used for caching data.

INCORRECT: "Amazon S3" is incorrect as S3 is not a NoSQL database. S3 is an object storage system.

3. Question

The manager of a development team is setting up a shared S3 bucket for team members. The manager would like to use a single policy to allow each user to have access to their objects in the S3 bucket. Which feature can be used to generalize the policy?

1: Principal

2: Condition

3: Variable

4: Resource

Answer: 3

Explanation:

In some cases, you might not know the exact name of the resource when you write the policy. You might want to generalize the policy so it works for many users without having to make a unique copy of the policy for each user. For example, consider writing a policy to allow each user to have access to his or her own objects in an Amazon S3 bucket.

Instead of that explicitly specifies the user's name as part of the resource, create a single group policy that works for any user in that group. You can do this by using *policy variables*, a feature that lets you specify placeholders in a policy. When the policy is evaluated, the policy variables are replaced with values that come from the context of the request itself.

The following example shows a policy for an Amazon S3 bucket that uses a policy variable.

```
{
  "Version": "2012-10-17",
  "Statement": [
    {
      "Action": ["s3:ListBucket"],
      "Effect": "Allow",
      "Resource": ["arn:aws:s3:::mybucket"],
      "Condition": {"StringLike": {"s3:prefix": ["${aws:username}/*"]}}
    },
    {
      "Action": [
        "s3:GetObject",
        "s3:PutObject"
      ],
      "Effect": "Allow",
      "Resource": ["arn:aws:s3:::mybucket/${aws:username}/*"]
    }
  ]
}
```

When this policy is evaluated, IAM replaces the variable ${aws:username}with the friendly name of the actual current user. This means that a single policy applied to a group of users can control access to a bucket by using the username as part of the resource's name.

CORRECT: "Variable" is the correct answer.

INCORRECT: "Condition" is incorrect. The Condition element (or Condition *block*) lets you specify conditions for when a policy is in effect.

INCORRECT: "Principal" is incorrect. You can use the Principal element in a policy to specify the principal that is allowed or denied access to a resource. However, in this scenario a variable is needed to create a generic policy that can provide the necessary permissions to different principals using variables.

INCORRECT: "Resource" is incorrect. The Resource element specifies the object or objects that the statement covers.

4. Question

An independent software vendor (ISV) uses Amazon S3 and Amazon CloudFront to distribute software updates. They would like to provide their premium customers with access to updates faster. What is the MOST efficient way to distribute these updates only to the premium customers? (Select TWO)

1: Create a signed cookie and associate it with the Amazon S3 distribution

2: Create a signed URL with access to the content and distribute it to the premium customers

3: Use an access control list (ACL) on the Amazon S3 bucket to restrict access based on IP address

4: Create an origin access identity (OAI) and associate it with the distribution and configure permissions

5: Use an IAM policy to restrict access to the content using a condition attribute and specify the IP addresses of the premium customers

Answer: 2,4

Explanation:

To restrict access to content that you serve from Amazon S3 buckets, you create CloudFront signed URLs or signed cookies to limit access to files in your Amazon S3 bucket, and then you create a special CloudFront user called an origin access identity (OAI) and associate it with your distribution. Then you configure permissions so that CloudFront can use the OAI to access and serve files to your users, but users can't use a direct URL to the S3 bucket to access a file there. Taking these steps help you maintain secure access to the files that you serve through CloudFront.

CORRECT: "Create a signed URL with access to the content and distribute it to the premium customers" is the correct answer.

CORRECT: "Create an origin access identity (OAI) and associate it with the distribution and configure permissions" is the correct answer.

INCORRECT: "Create a signed cookie and associate it with the Amazon S3 distribution" is incorrect as you cannot associated signed cookies with Amazon S3 and a distribution is a CloudFront concept, not an S3 concept.

INCORRECT: "Use an access control list (ACL) on the Amazon S3 bucket to restrict access based on IP address" is incorrect as you cannot restrict access to buckets by IP address when using an ACL.

INCORRECT: "Use an IAM policy to restrict access to the content using a condition attribute and specify the IP addresses of the premium customers " is incorrect. You can restrict access to buckets using policy statements with conditions based on source IP address. However, this is cumbersome to manage as IP addresses change (and you need to know all your customer's IPs in the first place). Also, because the content is being cached on CloudFront, this would not stop others accessing it anyway.

5. Question

An Amazon RDS database is experiencing a high volume of read requests that are slowing down the database. Which fully managed, in-memory AWS database service can assist with offloading reads from the RDS database?

1: Amazon RDS Read Replica

2: Amazon Aurora Serverless

3: Amazon ElastiCache Redis

4: Memcached on Amazon EC2

Answer: 3

Explanation:

ElastiCache is a web service that makes it easy to deploy and run Memcached or Redis protocol-compliant server nodes in the cloud. The in-memory caching provided by ElastiCache can be used to significantly improve latency and throughput for many read-heavy application workloads or compute-intensive workloads.

This is a fully managed AWS service and is ideal for offloading reads from the main database to reduce the performance impact.

CORRECT: "Amazon ElastiCache Redis" is the correct answer.

INCORRECT: "Amazon RDS Read Replica" is incorrect as it is not an in-memory database. RDS Read Replicas can be used for offloading reads from the main database, however.

INCORRECT: "Amazon Aurora Serverless" is incorrect. Aurora Serverless is not an in-memory solution, nor is it suitable for functioning as a method of offloading reads from RDS databases.

INCORRECT: "Memcached on Amazon EC2" is incorrect as this is an implementation of Memcached running on EC2 and therefore is not a fully managed AWS service.

6. Question

A developer is creating a multi-tier web application. The front-end will place messages in an Amazon SQS queue for the back-end to process. Each job includes a file that is 1GB in size. What MUST the developer do to ensure this works as expected?

1: Increase the maximum message size of the queue from 256KB to 1GB

2: Store the large files in DynamoDB and use the SQS Extended Client Library for Java to manage SQS messages

3: Create a FIFO queue that supports large files

4: Store the large files in Amazon S3 and use the SQS Extended Client Library for Java to manage SQS messages

Answer: 4

Explanation:

You can use Amazon S3 and the Amazon SQS Extended Client Library for Java to manage Amazon SQS messages. This is especially useful for storing and consuming messages up to 2 GB in size. Unless your application requires repeatedly creating queues and leaving them inactive or storing large amounts of data in your queue, consider using Amazon S3 for storing your data.

You can use the Amazon SQS Extended Client Library for Java library to do the following:

- Specify whether messages are always stored in Amazon S3 or only when the size of a message exceeds 256 KB.

- Send a message that references a single message object stored in an Amazon S3 bucket.

- Get the corresponding message object from an Amazon S3 bucket.

- Delete the corresponding message object from an Amazon S3 bucket.

Note: Amazon SQS only supports messages up to 256KB in size. Therefore, the extended client library for Java must be used.

CORRECT: "Store the large files in Amazon S3 and use the SQS Extended Client Library for Java to manage SQS messages" is the correct answer.

INCORRECT: "Increase the maximum message size of the queue from 256KB to 1GB" is incorrect as you cannot increase the maximum message size above 256KB.

INCORRECT: "Store the large files in DynamoDB and use the SQS Extended Client Library for Java to manage SQS messages" is incorrect as you should store the files in Amazon S3.

INCORRECT: "Create a FIFO queue that supports large files " is incorrect as FIFO queues also have a maximum message size of 256KB.

7. Question

A serverless application composed of multiple Lambda functions has been deployed. A developer is setting up AWS CodeDeploy to manage the deployment of code updates. The developer would like a 10% of the traffic to be shifted to the new version in equal increments, 10 minutes apart. Which setting should be chosen for configuring how traffic is shifted?

1: Canary

2: Linear

3: All-at-once

4: Blue/green

Answer: 2

Explanation:

A deployment configuration is a set of rules and success and failure conditions used by CodeDeploy during a deployment. These rules and conditions are different, depending on whether you deploy to an EC2/On-Premises compute platform or an AWS Lambda compute platform.

The following table lists the predefined configurations available for AWS Lambda deployments.

Deployment Configuration	Description
CodeDeployDefault.LambdaCanary10Percent5Minutes	Shifts 10 percent of traffic in the first increment. The remaining 90 percent is deployed five minutes later.
CodeDeployDefault.LambdaCanary10Percent10Minutes	Shifts 10 percent of traffic in the first increment. The remaining 90 percent is deployed 10 minutes later.
CodeDeployDefault.LambdaCanary10Percent15Minutes	Shifts 10 percent of traffic in the first increment. The remaining 90 percent is deployed 15 minutes later.
CodeDeployDefault.LambdaCanary10Percent30Minutes	Shifts 10 percent of traffic in the first increment. The remaining 90 percent is deployed 30 minutes later.
CodeDeployDefault.LambdaLinear10PercentEvery1Minute	Shifts 10 percent of traffic every minute until all traffic is shifted.
CodeDeployDefault.LambdaLinear10PercentEvery2Minutes	Shifts 10 percent of traffic every two minutes until all traffic is shifted.
CodeDeployDefault.LambdaLinear10PercentEvery3Minutes	Shifts 10 percent of traffic every three minutes until all traffic is shifted.
CodeDeployDefault.LambdaLinear10PercentEvery10Minutes	Shifts 10 percent of traffic every 10 minutes until all traffic is shifted.
CodeDeployDefault.LambdaAllAtOnce	Shifts all traffic to the updated Lambda functions at once.

As you can see from the table above, the linear option shifts a specific amount of traffic in equal increments of time. Therefore, the following option should be chosen:

CodeDeployDefault.LambdaLinear10PercentEvery10Minutes

CORRECT: "Linear" is the correct answer.

INCORRECT: "Canary" is incorrect as it does not shift traffic in equal increments.

INCORRECT: "All-at-once" is incorrect as it shifts all traffic at once.

INCORRECT: "Blue/green" is incorrect as it is a type of deployment, not a setting for traffic shifting.

8. Question

A company has a global presence and managers must submit large quantities of reporting data to an Amazon S3 bucket located in the us-east-1 region on weekly basis. Uploads have been slow recently, how can you improve data throughput and upload times?

1: Enable S3 Transfer Acceleration on the S3 bucket

2: Use S3 Multi-part upload

3: Create an AWS Direct Connect connection from each remote office

4: Use an AWS Managed VPN

Answer: 1

Explanation:

Amazon S3 Transfer Acceleration enables fast, easy, and secure transfers of files over long distances between your client and an S3 bucket. Transfer Acceleration takes advantage of Amazon CloudFront's globally distributed edge locations. As the data arrives at an edge location, data is routed to Amazon S3 over an optimized network path.

You might want to use Transfer Acceleration on a bucket for various reasons, including the following:

- You have customers that upload to a centralized bucket from all over the world.

- You transfer gigabytes to terabytes of data on a regular basis across continents.

- You are unable to utilize all of your available bandwidth over the Internet when uploading to Amazon S3.

Therefore, Amazon S3 Transfer Acceleration is an ideal solution for this use case and will result in improved throughput and upload times.

CORRECT: "Enable S3 Transfer Acceleration on the S3 bucket" is the correct answer.

INCORRECT: "Use S3 Multi-part upload" is incorrect. Multi-part upload will perform multiple uploads in parallel which does improve performance however Transfer Acceleration will utilize CloudFront and result in much improved performance over multi-part upload.

INCORRECT: "Create an AWS Direct Connect connection from each remote office" is incorrect as Direct Connect is used to connect from a data center into an AWS region that is local to the data center, not somewhere else in the world (though Direct Connect Gateway can do this). This would also be an extremely expensive solution.

INCORRECT: "Use an AWS Managed VPN" is incorrect as this is used to create an encrypted tunnel into a VPC and will not result in improved upload performance for S3 uploads.

9. Question

A developer is building a Docker application on Amazon ECS that will use an Application Load Balancer (ALB). The developer needs to configure the port mapping between the host port and container port. Where is this setting configured?

1: Host definition

2: Task definition

3: Service scheduler

4: Container instance

Answer: 2

Explanation:

Port mappings allow containers to access ports on the host container instance to send or receive traffic. Port mappings are specified as part of the container definition.

The container definition settings are specified within the task definition. The relevant settings are:

containerPort - the port number on the container that is bound to the user-specified or automatically assigned host port.

hostPort - the port number on the container instance to reserve for your container.

With an ALB you can use Dynamic port mapping which makes it easier to run multiple tasks on the same Amazon ECS service on an Amazon ECS cluster. This is configured by setting the host port to 0, as in the image below:

CORRECT: "Task definition" is the correct answer.

INCORRECT: "Host definition" is incorrect as there's no such thing.

INCORRECT: "Service scheduler" is incorrect as the service scheduler is responsible for scheduling tasks and placing those tasks.

INCORRECT: "Container instance" is incorrect as you don't specify any settings on the container instance to control the host and container port mappings.

10. Question

A developer is designing a web application that will be used by thousands of users. The users will sign up using their email addresses and the application will store attributes for each user. Which service should the developer use to enable users to sign-up for the web application?

1: Amazon Cognito Sync

2: Amazon Cognito user pool

3: AWS Inspector

4: AWS AppSync

Answer: 2

Explanation:

A user pool is a user directory in Amazon Cognito. With a user pool, your users can sign in to your web or mobile app through Amazon Cognito. Your users can also sign in through social identity providers like Google, Facebook, Amazon, or Apple, and through SAML identity providers.

Whether your users sign in directly or through a third party, all members of the user pool have a directory profile that you can access through a Software Development Kit (SDK).

User pools provide:

- Sign-up and sign-in services.

- A built-in, customizable web UI to sign in users.

- Social sign-in with Facebook, Google, Login with Amazon, and Sign in with Apple, as well as sign-in with SAML identity providers from your user pool.

- User directory management and user profiles.

- Security features such as multi-factor authentication (MFA), checks for compromised credentials, account takeover protection, and phone and email verification.

- Customized workflows and user migration through AWS Lambda triggers.

After successfully authenticating a user, Amazon Cognito issues JSON web tokens (JWT) that you can use to secure and authorize access to your own APIs, or exchange for AWS credentials.

Therefore, an Amazon Cognito user pool is the best solution for enabling sign-up to the new web application.

CORRECT: "Amazon Cognito user pool" is the correct answer.

INCORRECT: "Amazon Cognito Sync" is incorrect as it is used to synchronize user profile data across mobile devices and the web without requiring your own backend.

INCORRECT: "AWS Inspector" is incorrect. Amazon Inspector is an automated security assessment service that helps improve the security and compliance of applications deployed on AWS.

INCORRECT: "AWS AppSync" is incorrect. AWS AppSync simplifies application development by letting you create a flexible API to securely access, manipulate, and combine data from one or more data sources.

11. Question

An application resizes images that are uploaded to an Amazon S3 bucket. Amazon S3 event notifications are used to trigger an AWS Lambda function that resizes the images. The processing time for each image is less than one second. A large amount of images are expected to be received in a short burst of traffic. How will AWS Lambda accommodate the workload?

1: Lambda will scale out and execute the requests concurrently

2: Lambda will process the images sequentially in the order they are received

3: Lambda will collect and then batch process the images in a single execution

4: Lambda will scale the memory allocated to the function to increase the amount of CPU available to process many images

Answer: 1

Explanation:

The first time you invoke your function, AWS Lambda creates an instance of the function and runs its handler method to process the event. When the function returns a response, it stays active and waits to process additional events. If you invoke the function again while the first event is being processed, Lambda initializes another instance, and the function processes the two events concurrently.

Your functions' concurrency is the number of instances that serve requests at a given time. For an initial burst of traffic, your functions' cumulative concurrency in a Region can reach an initial level of between 500 and 3000, which varies per Region.

Burst Concurrency Limits:

- 3000 – US West (Oregon), US East (N. Virginia), Europe (Ireland).

- 1000 – Asia Pacific (Tokyo), Europe (Frankfurt).

- 500 – Other Regions.

After the initial burst, your functions' concurrency can scale by an additional 500 instances each minute. This continues until there are enough instances to serve all requests, or until a concurrency limit is reached.

The default account limit is up to 1000 executions per second, per region (can be increased).

CORRECT: "Lambda will scale out and execute the requests concurrently" is the correct answer.

INCORRECT: "Lambda will process the images sequentially in the order they are received" is incorrect as Lambda uses concurrency to process multiple events in parallel.

INCORRECT: "Lambda will collect and then batch process the images in a single execution" is incorrect as Lambda never collects requests and then processes them at a later time. Lambda always uses concurrency to process requests in parallel.

INCORRECT: "Lambda will scale the memory allocated to the function to increase the amount of CPU available to process many images" is incorrect as Lambda does not automatically scale memory/CPU and processes requests in parallel, not sequentially.

12. Question

A Developer is creating multiple AWS Lambda functions that will be using an external library that is not included in the standard Lambda libraries. What is the BEST way to make these libraries available to the functions?

1: Include the external library with the function code

2: Create a deployment package that includes the external library

3: Store the files in Amazon S3 and reference them from your function code

4: Create a layer in Lambda that includes the external library

Answer: 4

Explanation:

You can configure your Lambda function to pull in additional code and content in the form of layers. A layer is a ZIP archive that contains libraries, a custom runtime, or other dependencies. With layers, you can use libraries in your function without needing to include them in your deployment package.

Layers let you keep your deployment package small, which makes development easier. You can avoid errors that can occur when you install and package dependencies with your function code.

When a Lambda function configured with a Lambda layer is executed, AWS downloads any specified layers and extracts them to the /opt directory on the function execution environment. Each runtime then looks for a language-specific folder under the /opt directory.

One of the best practices for AWS Lambda functions is to minimize your deployment package size to its runtime necessities in order to reduce the amount of time that it takes for your deployment package to be downloaded and unpacked ahead of invocation.

Therefore, it is preferable to use layers to store the external libraries to optimize performance of the function. Using layers means that the external library will also be available to all of the Lambda functions that the Developer is creating.

CORRECT: "Create a layer in Lambda that includes the external library" is the correct answer.

INCORRECT: "Include the external library with the function code" is incorrect as you should not include an external library within the function code. Even if possible, this would result in bloated code that could slow down execution time.

INCORRECT: "Create a deployment package that includes the external library" is incorrect as the best practice is to minimize package sizes to runtime necessities. Also, this would require including the library in all function deployment packages whereas with layers we can create a single layer that is used by all functions.

INCORRECT: "Store the files in Amazon S3 and reference them from your function code" is incorrect as this would likely result in increased latency of your function execution. Instead you should either package the library in the deployment package for your function or use layers (preferable in this scenario).

13. Question

A Developer is creating a social networking app for games that uses a single Amazon DynamoDB table. All users' saved game data is stored in the single table, but users should not be able to view each other's data. How can the Developer restrict user access so they can only view their own data?

1: Restrict access to specific items based on certain primary key values

2: Use separate access keys for each user to call the API and restrict access to specific items based on access key ID

3: Use an identity-based policy that restricts read access to the table to specific principals

4: Read records from DynamoDB and discard irrelevant data client-side

Answer: 1

Explanation:

In DynamoDB, you have the option to specify conditions when granting permissions using an IAM policy. For example, you can:

- Grant permissions to allow users read-only access to certain items and attributes in a table or a secondary index.

- Grant permissions to allow users write-only access to certain attributes in a table, based upon the identity of that user.

To implement this kind of fine-grained access control, you write an IAM permissions policy that specifies conditions for accessing security credentials and the associated permissions. You then apply the policy to IAM users, groups, or roles that you create using the IAM console. Your IAM policy can restrict access to individual items in a table, access to the attributes in those items, or both at the same time.

You use the IAM Condition element to implement a fine-grained access control policy. By adding a Condition element to a permissions policy, you can allow or deny access to items and attributes in

DynamoDB tables and indexes, based upon your particular business requirements. You can also grant permissions on a table, but restrict access to specific items in that table based on certain primary key values.

CORRECT: "Restrict access to specific items based on certain primary key values" is the correct answer.

INCORRECT: "Use separate access keys for each user to call the API and restrict access to specific items based on access key ID" is incorrect. You cannot restrict access based on access key ID.

INCORRECT: "Use an identity-based policy that restricts read access to the table to specific principals" is incorrect as this would only restrict read access to the entire table, not to specific items in the table.

INCORRECT: "Read records from DynamoDB and discard irrelevant data client-side" is incorrect as this is inefficient and insecure as it will use more RCUs and has more potential to leak the information.

14. Question

A Development team are developing a micro-services application that will use Docker containers on Amazon ECS. There will be 6 distinct services included in the architecture. Each service requires specific permissions to various AWS services. What is the MOST secure way to grant the services the necessary permissions?

1: Create a new Identity and Access Management (IAM) instance profile containing the required permissions for the various ECS services, then associate that instance role with the underlying EC2 instances

2: Create six separate IAM roles, each containing the required permissions for the associated ECS service, then configure each ECS task definition to reference the associated IAM role

3: Create six separate IAM roles, each containing the required permissions for the associated ECS service, then create an IAM group and configure the ECS cluster to reference that group

4: Create a single IAM policy and use principal statements referencing the ECS tasks and assigning the required permissions, then apply the policy to the ECS service

Answer: 2

Explanation:

With IAM roles for Amazon ECS tasks, you can specify an IAM role that can be used by the containers in a task. Applications must sign their AWS API requests with AWS credentials, and this feature provides a strategy for managing credentials for your applications to use, similar to the way that Amazon EC2 instance profiles provide credentials to EC2 instances.

Instead of creating and distributing your AWS credentials to the containers or using the EC2 instance's role, you can associate an IAM role with an ECS task definition or RunTask API operation. The applications in the task's containers can then use the AWS SDK or CLI to make API requests to authorized AWS services.

Therefore, the most secure solution is to use a separate IAM role with the specific permissions required for an individual service and associate that role to the relevant ECS task definition. This should then be repeated for the remaining 5 services.

CORRECT: "Create six separate IAM roles, each containing the required permissions for the associated ECS service, then configure each ECS task definition to reference the associated IAM role" is the correct answer.

INCORRECT: "Create six separate IAM roles, each containing the required permissions for the associated ECS service, then create an IAM group and configure the ECS cluster to reference that group" is incorrect. The IAM role should be applied to the ECS task definition, not the ECS cluster.

INCORRECT: "Create a new Identity and Access Management (IAM) instance profile containing the required permissions for the various ECS services, then associate that instance role with the underlying EC2 instances" is incorrect. With IAM Roles for Tasks you apply the permissions directly to the task definition. This means multiple services can share the underlying EC2 instance and only have the minimum privileges required.

INCORRECT: "Create a single IAM policy and use principal statements referencing the ECS tasks and assigning the required permissions, then apply the policy to the ECS service" is incorrect. Identity-based policies attached to the ECS service can be used to control permissions for viewing, launching, and managing resources within ECS. However, for this solution we need to control the permissions for an ECS task to access other AWS services. For this we need to use IAM Roles for Tasks.

15. Question

A company is reviewing their security practices. According to AWS best practice, how should access keys be managed to improve security? (Select TWO)

1: Delete all access keys for the root account IAM user

2: Embed access keys directly into code

3: Rotate access keys daily

4: Use different access keys for different applications

5: Use the same access key in all applications for consistency

Answer: 1,4

Explanation:

When you access AWS programmatically, you use an access key to verify your identity and the identity of your applications. An access key consists of an access key ID (something like AKIAIOSFODNN7EXAMPLE) and a secret access key (something like wJalrXUtnFEMI/K7MDENG/bPxRfiCYEXAMPLEKEY).

Anyone who has your access key has the same level of access to your AWS resources that you do. Steps to protect access keys include the following:

- Remove (or Don't Generate) Account Access Key – this is especially important for the root account.
- Use Temporary Security Credentials (IAM Roles) Instead of Long-Term Access Keys.
- Don't embed access keys directly into code.
- Use different access keys for different applications.
- Rotate access keys periodically.
- Remove unused access keys.
- Configure multi-factor authentication for your most sensitive operations.

CORRECT: "Delete all access keys for the root account IAM user" is the correct answer.

CORRECT: "Use different access keys for different applications" is the correct answer.

INCORRECT: "Embed access keys directly into code" is incorrect. This is not a best practice as this is something that should be avoided as much as possible.

INCORRECT: "Rotate access keys daily" is incorrect. Though this would be beneficial from a security perspective it may be hard to manage so this is not an AWS recommended best practice. AWS recommend you rotate access keys "periodically", not "daily".

INCORRECT: "Use the same access key in all applications for consistency" is incorrect. The best practice is to use different access keys for different applications.

16. Question

A Developer is creating an application that will utilize an Amazon DynamoDB table for storing session data. The data being stored is expected to be around 4.5KB in size and the application will make 20 eventually consistent reads/sec, and 12 standard writes/sec. How many RCUs/WCUs are required?

1: 40 RCU and 60 WCU

2: 20 RCU and 60 WCU

3: 40 RCU and 120 WCU

4: 10 RCU and 24 WCU

Answer: 2

Explanation:

With provisioned capacity mode, you specify the number of data reads and writes per second that you require for your application.

Read capacity unit (RCU):

- Each API call to read data from your table is a read request.
- Read requests can be strongly consistent, eventually consistent, or transactional.
- For items up to 4 KB in size, one RCU can perform one *strongly consistent* read request per second.
- Items larger than 4 KB require additional RCUs.
- For items up to 4 KB in size, one RCU can perform two *eventually consistent* read requests per second.
- *Transactional* read requests require two RCUs to perform one read per second for items up to 4 KB.
- For example, a strongly consistent read of an 8 KB item would require two RCUs, an eventually consistent read of an 8 KB item would require one RCU, and a transactional read of an 8 KB item would require four RCUs.

Write capacity unit (WCU):

- Each API call to write data to your table is a write request.
- For items up to 1 KB in size, one WCU can perform one *standard* write request per second.
- Items larger than 1 KB require additional WCUs.
- *Transactional* write requests require two WCUs to perform one write per second for items up to 1 KB.
- For example, a standard write request of a 1 KB item would require one WCU, a standard write request of a 3 KB item would require three WCUs, and a transactional write request of a 3 KB item would require six WCUs.

To determine the number of RCUs required to handle 20 eventually consistent reads per/second with an average item size of 4.5KB, perform the following steps:

- Determine the average item size by rounding up the next multiple of 4KB (4.5KB rounds up to 8KB).
- Determine the RCU per item by dividing the item size by 8KB (8KB/8KB = 1).
- Multiply the value from step 2 with the number of reads required per second (1x20 = 20).

To determine the number of WCUs required to handle 12 standard writes per/second with an average item size of 8KB, simply multiply the average item size by the number of writes required (5x12=60).

CORRECT: "20 RCU and 60 WCU" is the correct answer.

INCORRECT: "40 RCU and 60 WCU" is incorrect. This would be the correct answer for strongly consistent reads and standard writes.

INCORRECT: "40 RCU and 120 WCU" is incorrect. This would be the correct answer for strongly consistent reads and transactional writes.

INCORRECT: "6 RCU and 18 WCU" is incorrect.

17. Question

A monitoring application that keeps track of a large eCommerce website uses Amazon Kinesis for data ingestion. During periods of peak data rates, the producers are not making best use of the available shards. What step will allow the producers to better utilize the available shards and increase write throughput to the Kinesis data stream?

1: Install the Kinesis Producer Library (KPL) for ingesting data into the stream

2: Create an SQS queue and decouple the producers from the Kinesis data stream

3: Increase the shard count of the stream using UpdateShardCount

4: Ingest multiple records into the stream in a single call using BatchWriteItem

Answer: 1

Explanation:

An Amazon Kinesis Data Streams producer is an application that puts user data records into a Kinesis data stream (also called *data ingestion*). The Kinesis Producer Library (KPL) simplifies producer application development, allowing developers to achieve high write throughput to a Kinesis data stream.

The KPL is an easy-to-use, highly configurable library that helps you write to a Kinesis data stream. It acts as an intermediary between your producer application code and the Kinesis Data Streams API actions. The KPL performs the following primary tasks:

- Writes to one or more Kinesis data streams with an automatic and configurable retry mechanism

- Collects records and uses PutRecords to write multiple records to multiple shards per request

- Aggregates user records to increase payload size and improve throughput

- Integrates seamlessly with the Kinesis Client Library (KCL) to de-aggregate batched records on the consumer

- Submits Amazon CloudWatch metrics on your behalf to provide visibility into producer performance

The question states that the producers are not making best use of the available shards. Therefore, we understand that there are adequate shards available but the producers are either not discovering them or are not writing records at sufficient speed to best utilize the shards.

We therefore need to install the Kinesis Producer Library (KPL) for ingesting data into the stream.

CORRECT: "Install the Kinesis Producer Library (KPL) for ingesting data into the stream" is the correct answer.

INCORRECT: "Create an SQS queue and decouple the producers from the Kinesis data stream " is incorrect. In this case we need to ensure our producers are discovering shards and writing records to best utilize those shards.

INCORRECT: "Increase the shard count of the stream using UpdateShardCount" is incorrect. The problem statement is that the producers are not making best use of the available shards. We don't need to add more shards, we need to make sure the producers are discovering and then fully utilizing the shards that are available.

INCORRECT: "Ingest multiple records into the stream in a single call using BatchWriteItem" is incorrect. This API is used with DynamoDB, not Kinesis.

18. Question

A Developer is creating an AWS Lambda function that will process medical images. The function is dependent on several libraries that are not available in the Lambda runtime environment. Which strategy should be used to create the Lambda deployment package?

1: Create a ZIP file with the source code and all dependent libraries

2: Create a ZIP file with the source code and a script that installs the dependent libraries at runtime

3: Create a ZIP file with the source code. Stage the dependent libraries on an Amazon S3 bucket indicated by the Lambda environment variable LIBRARY_PATH

4: Create a ZIP file with the source code and a buildspec.yaml file that installs the dependent libraries on AWS Lambda

Answer: 1

Explanation:

A deployment package is a ZIP archive that contains your function code and dependencies. You need to create a deployment package if you use the Lambda API to manage functions, or if you need to include libraries and dependencies other than the AWS SDK.

You can upload the package directly to Lambda, or you can use an Amazon S3 bucket, and then upload it to Lambda. If the deployment package is larger than 50 MB, you must use Amazon S3.

If your function depends on libraries not included in the Lambda runtime, you can install them to a local directory and include them in your deployment package.

CORRECT: "Create a ZIP file with the source code and all dependent libraries" is the correct answer.

INCORRECT: "Create a ZIP file with the source code and a script that installs the dependent libraries at runtime" is incorrect as though it is possible to call a script within the function code, this would need to run every time and pull in the files which would cause latency.

INCORRECT: "Create a ZIP file with the source code. Stage the dependent libraries on an Amazon S3 bucket indicated by the Lambda environment variable LIBRARY_PATH" is incorrect as you cannot map an external path to a Lambda function using an environment variable.

INCORRECT: "Create a ZIP file with the source code and a buildspec.yaml file that installs the dependent libraries on AWS Lambda" is incorrect as a buildspec.yaml file that is used by AWS CodeBuild to run a build. The libraries need to be included in the package zip file for the Lambda function.

19. Question

A company use Amazon CloudFront to deliver application content to users around the world. A Developer has made an update to some files in the origin however users have reported that they are still getting the old files. How can the Developer ensure that the old files are replaced in the cache with the LEAST disruption?

1: Invalidate the files from the edge caches

2: Create a new origin with the new files and remove the old origin

3: Disable the CloudFront distribution and enable it again to update all the edge locations

4: Add code to Lambda@Edge that updates the files in the cache

Answer: 1

Explanation:

If you need to remove files from CloudFront edge caches before they expire you can invalidate the files from the edge caches. To invalidate files, you can specify either the path for individual files or a path that ends with the * wildcard, which might apply to one file or to many, as shown in the following examples:

- /images/image1.jpg
- /images/image*
- /images/*

You can submit a specified number of invalidation paths each month for free. If you submit more than the allotted number of invalidation paths in a month, you pay a fee for each invalidation path that you submit.

CORRECT: "Invalidate the files from the edge caches" is the correct answer.

INCORRECT: "Create a new origin with the new files and remove the old origin" is incorrect as this would be more disruptive and costly as the entire cache would need to be updated.

INCORRECT: "Disable the CloudFront distribution and enable it again to update all the edge locations" is incorrect as this will cause an outage (disruption) and will not replace files that have not yet expired.

INCORRECT: "Add code to Lambda@Edge that updates the files in the cache" is incorrect as there's no value in running code in Lambda@Edge to update the files. Instead the files in the cache can be invalidated.

20. Question

A Developer is creating a serverless website with content that includes HTML files, images, videos, and JavaScript (client-side scripts). Which combination of services should the Developer use to create the website?

1: Amazon S3 and Amazon CloudFront

2: Amazon EC2 and Amazon ElastiCache

3: Amazon ECS and Redis

4: AWS Lambda and Amazon API Gateway

Answer: 1

Explanation:

You can use Amazon S3 to host a static website. On a *static* website, individual webpages include static content. They might also contain client-side scripts.

To host a static website on Amazon S3, you configure an Amazon S3 bucket for website hosting and then upload your website content to the bucket. When you configure a bucket as a static website, you enable static website hosting, set permissions, and add an index document.

To get content closer to users for better performance you can also use Amazon CloudFront in front of the S3 static website. To serve a static website hosted on Amazon S3, you can deploy a CloudFront distribution using one of these configurations:

- Using a REST API endpoint as the origin with access restricted by an origin access identity (OAI)

- Using a website endpoint as the origin with anonymous (public) access allowed

- Using a website endpoint as the origin with access restricted by a Referer header

Therefore, the combination of services should be Amazon S3 and Amazon CloudFront

CORRECT: "Amazon S3 and Amazon CloudFront" is the correct answer.

INCORRECT: "Amazon EC2 and Amazon ElastiCache" is incorrect. The website is supposed to be serverless and neither of these services are serverless as they both use Amazon EC2 instances.

INCORRECT: "Amazon ECS and Redis" is incorrect. These services are also not serverless. Also Redis is an in-memory cache and is typically placed in front of a database, not a Docker container.

INCORRECT: "AWS Lambda and Amazon API Gateway" is incorrect. These are both serverless services however for serving content such as HTML files, images, videos, and client-side JavaScript, Amazon S3 and CloudFront are more appropriate.

21. Question

A Developer needs to update an Amazon ECS application that was deployed using AWS CodeDeploy. What file does the Developer need to update to push the change through CodeDeploy?

1: dockerrun.aws.json

2: buildspec.yml

3: appspec.yml

4: ebextensions.config

Answer: 3

Explanation:

In CodeDeploy, a revision contains a version of the source files CodeDeploy will deploy to your instances or scripts CodeDeploy will run on your instances. You plan the revision, add an AppSpec file to the revision, and then push the revision to Amazon S3 or GitHub. After you push the revision, you can deploy it.

For a deployment to an Amazon ECS compute platform:

- The AppSpec file specifies the Amazon ECS task definition used for the deployment, a container name and port mapping used to route traffic, and optional Lambda functions run after deployment lifecycle events.
- A revision is the same as an AppSpec file.
- An AppSpec file can be written using JSON or YAML.
- An AppSpec file can be saved as a text file or entered directly into a console when you create a deployment.

Therefore, the appspec.yml file needs to be updated by the Developer.

CORRECT: "appspec.yml" is the correct answer.

INCORRECT: "dockerrun.aws.json" is incorrect. A Dockerrun.aws.json file describes how to deploy a remote Docker image as an Elastic Beanstalk application.

INCORRECT: "buildspec.yml" is incorrect. A *build spec* is a collection of build commands and related settings, in YAML format, that CodeBuild uses to run a build using AWS CodeBuild.

INCORRECT: "ebextensions.config" is incorrect. The .ebextensions folder in the source code for an Elastic Beanstalk application is used for .config files that configure the environment and customize resources.

22. Question

A Development team wants to instrument their code to provide more detailed information to AWS X-Ray than simple outgoing and incoming requests. This will generate large amounts of data, so the Development team wants to implement indexing so they can filter the data. What should the Development team do to achieve this?

1: Add metadata to the segment document

2: Configure the necessary X-Ray environment variables

3: Install required plugins for the appropriate AWS SDK

4: Add annotations to the segment document

Answer: 4

Explanation:

AWS X-Ray makes it easy for developers to analyze the behavior of their production, distributed applications with end-to-end tracing capabilities. You can use X-Ray to identify performance bottlenecks, edge case errors, and other hard to detect issues.

When you instrument your application, the X-Ray SDK records information about incoming and outgoing requests, the AWS resources used, and the application itself. You can add other information to the segment document as annotations and metadata. Annotations and metadata are aggregated at the trace level and can be added to any segment or subsegment.

Annotations are simple key-value pairs that are indexed for use with filter expressions. Use annotations to record data that you want to use to group traces in the console, or when calling the GetTraceSummaries API. X-Ray indexes up to 50 annotations per trace.

Metadata are key-value pairs with values of any type, including objects and lists, but that are not indexed. Use metadata to record data you want to store in the trace but don't need to use for searching traces.

You can view annotations and metadata in the segment or subsegment details in the X-Ray console.

In this scenario, we need to add annotations to the segment document so that the data that needs to be filtered is indexed.

CORRECT: "Add annotations to the segment document" is the correct answer.

INCORRECT: "Add metadata to the segment document" is incorrect as metadata is not indexed for filtering.

INCORRECT: "Configure the necessary X-Ray environment variables" is incorrect as this will not result in indexing of the required data.

INCORRECT: "Install required plugins for the appropriate AWS SDK" is incorrect as there are no plugin requirements for the AWS SDK to support this solution as the annotations feature is available in AWS X-Ray.

23. Question

An organization has an Amazon S3 bucket containing premier content that they intend to make available to only paid subscribers of their website. The objects in the S3 bucket are private to prevent inadvertent exposure of the premier content to non-paying website visitors. How can the organization provide only paid subscribers the ability to download the premier content in the S3 bucket?

1: Apply a bucket policy that grants anonymous users to download the content from the S3 bucket

2: Generate a pre-signed object URL for the premier content file when a paid subscriber requests a download

3: Add a bucket policy that requires Multi-Factor Authentication for requests to access the S3 bucket objects

4: Enable server-side encryption on the S3 bucket for data protection against the non-paying website visitors

Answer: 2

Explanation:

When Amazon S3 objects are private, only the object owner has permission to access these objects. However, the object owner can optionally share objects with others by creating a presigned URL, using their own security credentials, to grant time-limited permission to download the objects.

When you create a presigned URL for your object, you must provide your security credentials, specify a bucket name, an object key, specify the HTTP method (GET to download the object) and expiration date and time. The presigned URLs are valid only for the specified duration.

Anyone who receives the presigned URL can then access the object. In this scenario, a pre-signed URL can be generated only for paying customers and they will be the only website visitors who can view the premier content.

CORRECT: "Generate a pre-signed object URL for the premier content file when a paid subscriber requests a download" is the correct answer.

INCORRECT: "Apply a bucket policy that grants anonymous users to download the content from the S3 bucket" is incorrect as this would provide everyone the ability to download the content.

INCORRECT: "Add a bucket policy that requires Multi-Factor Authentication for requests to access the S3 bucket objects" is incorrect as this would be very difficult to manage. Using pre-signed URLs that are dynamically generated by an application for premier users would be much simpler.

INCORRECT: "Enable server-side encryption on the S3 bucket for data protection against the non-paying website visitors" is incorrect as this is encryption at rest and S3 will simply unencrypt the objects when users attempt to read them. This provides privacy protection for data at rest but does not restrict access.

24. Question

A serverless application uses Amazon API Gateway, AWS Lambda and DynamoDB. The application writes statistical data that is constantly received from sensors. The data is analyzed soon after it is written to the database and is then not required. What is the EASIEST method to remove stale data and optimize database size?

1: Enable the TTL attribute and add expiry timestamps to items

2: Use atomic counters to decrement the data when it becomes stale

3: Scan the table for stale data and delete it once every hour

4: Delete the table and recreate it every hour

Answer: 1

Explanation:

Time to Live (TTL) for Amazon DynamoDB lets you define when items in a table expire so that they can be automatically deleted from the database. With TTL enabled on a table, you can set a timestamp for deletion on a per-item basis, allowing you to limit storage usage to only those records that are relevant.

TTL is useful if you have continuously accumulating data that loses relevance after a specific time period (for example, session data, event logs, usage patterns, and other temporary data). If you have sensitive data that must be retained only for a certain amount of time according to contractual or regulatory obligations, TTL helps you ensure that it is removed promptly and as scheduled.

Therefore, the best answer is to enable the TTL attribute and add expiry timestamps to items.

CORRECT: "Enable the TTL attribute and add expiry timestamps to items" is the correct answer.

INCORRECT: "Use atomic counters to decrement the data when it becomes stale" is incorrect. Atomic counters are useful for incrementing or decrementing the value of an attribute. A good use case is counting website visitors.

INCORRECT: "Scan the table for stale data and delete it once every hour" is incorrect as this is costly in terms of RCUs and WCUs. It also may result in data that has just been written but not analyzed yet.

INCORRECT: "Delete the table and recreate it every hour" is incorrect. The table is constantly being written to and the analysis of data happens soon after the data is written. Therefore, there isn't a good time to delete and recreate the table as data loss is likely to occur at any time.

25. Question

A Development team are creating a financial trading application. The application requires sub-millisecond latency for processing trading requests. Amazon DynamoDB is used to store the trading data. During load testing the Development team found that in periods of high utilization the latency is too high and read capacity must be significantly over-provisioned to avoid throttling. How can the Developers meet the latency requirements of the application?

1: Use Amazon DynamoDB Accelerator (DAX) to cache the data

2: Create a Global Secondary Index (GSI) for the trading data

3: Use exponential backoff in the application code for DynamoDB queries

4: Store the trading data in Amazon S3 and use Transfer Acceleration

Answer: 1

Explanation:

Amazon DynamoDB is designed for scale and performance. In most cases, the DynamoDB response times can be measured in single-digit milliseconds. However, there are certain use cases that require response times in microseconds. For these use cases, DynamoDB Accelerator (DAX) delivers fast response times for accessing eventually consistent data.

DAX is a DynamoDB-compatible caching service that enables you to benefit from fast in-memory performance for demanding applications. DAX addresses three core scenarios:

- As an in-memory cache, DAX reduces the response times of eventually consistent read workloads by an order of magnitude from single-digit milliseconds to microseconds.
- DAX reduces operational and application complexity by providing a managed service that is API-compatible with DynamoDB. Therefore, it requires only minimal functional changes to use with an existing application.
- For read-heavy or bursty workloads, DAX provides increased throughput and potential operational cost savings by reducing the need to overprovision read capacity units. This is especially beneficial for applications that require repeated reads for individual keys.

In this scenario the question is calling for sub-millisecond (e.g. microsecond) latency and this is required for read traffic as evidenced by the need to over-provision reads. Therefore, DynamoDB DAX would be the best solution for reducing the latency and meeting the requirements.

CORRECT: "Use Amazon DynamoDB Accelerator (DAX) to cache the data" is the correct answer.

INCORRECT: "Create a Global Secondary Index (GSI) for the trading data" is incorrect as a GSI is used to speed up queries on non-key attributes. There is no requirement here for a Global Secondary Index.

INCORRECT: "Use exponential backoff in the application code for DynamoDB queries" is incorrect as this may reduce the requirement for over-provisioning reads but it will not solve the problem of reducing latency. With this solution the application performance will be worse, it's a case of reducing cost along with performance.

INCORRECT: "Store the trading data in Amazon S3 and use Transfer Acceleration" is incorrect as this will not reduce the latency of the application. Transfer Acceleration is used for improving performance of uploads of data to Amazon S3.

26. Question

A Developer is deploying an Amazon EC2 update using AWS CodeDeploy. In the appspec.yml file, which of the following is a valid structure for the order of hooks that should be specified?

1: BeforeInstall > AfterInstall > AfterAllowTestTraffic > BeforeAllowTraffic > AfterAllowTraffic

2: BeforeInstall > AfterInstall > ApplicationStart > ValidateService

3: BeforeAllowTraffic > AfterAllowTraffic

4: BeforeBlockTraffic > AfterBlockTraffic > BeforeAllowTraffic > AfterAllowTraffic

Answer: 2

Explanation:

The content in the 'hooks' section of the AppSpec file varies, depending on the compute platform for your deployment. The 'hooks' section for an EC2/On-Premises deployment contains mappings that link deployment lifecycle event hooks to one or more scripts.

The 'hooks' section for a Lambda or an Amazon ECS deployment specifies Lambda validation functions to run during a deployment lifecycle event. If an event hook is not present, no operation is executed for that event. This section is required only if you are running scripts or Lambda validation functions as part of the deployment.

The following code snippet shows a valid example of the structure of hooks for an Amazon EC2 deployment:

```
∨ hooks:
∨   BeforeInstall:
      - location: Scripts/UnzipResourceBundle.sh
      - location: Scripts/UnzipDataBundle.sh
∨   AfterInstall:
∨     - location: Scripts/RunResourceTests.sh
        timeout: 180
∨   ApplicationStart:
∨     - location: Scripts/RunFunctionalTests.sh
        timeout: 3600
∨   ValidateService:
∨     - location: Scripts/MonitorService.sh
        timeout: 3600
        runas: codedeployuser
```

Therefore, in this scenario a valid structure for the order of hooks that should be specified in the appspec.yml file is: BeforeInstall > AfterInstall > ApplicationStart > ValidateService

CORRECT: "BeforeInstall > AfterInstall > ApplicationStart > ValidateService" is the correct answer.

INCORRECT: "BeforeInstall > AfterInstall > AfterAllowTestTraffic > BeforeAllowTraffic > AfterAllowTraffic" is incorrect as this would be valid for Amazon ECS.

INCORRECT: "BeforeAllowTraffic > AfterAllowTraffic" is incorrect as this would be valid for AWS Lambda.

INCORRECT: "BeforeBlockTraffic > AfterBlockTraffic > BeforeAllowTraffic > AfterAllowTraffic" is incorrect as this is a partial listing of hooks for Amazon EC2 but is incomplete.

27. Question

An application will ingest data at a very high throughput from several sources and stored in an Amazon S3 bucket for subsequent analysis. Which AWS service should a Developer choose for this requirement?

1: Amazon Kinesis Data Firehose

2: Amazon S3 Transfer Acceleration

3: Amazon Kinesis Data Analytics

4: Amazon Simple Queue Service (SQS)

Answer: 1

Explanation:

Amazon Kinesis Data Firehose is the easiest way to reliably load streaming data into data lakes, data stores and analytics tools. It can capture, transform, and load streaming data into Amazon S3, Amazon Redshift, Amazon Elasticsearch Service, and Splunk, enabling near real-time analytics with existing business intelligence tools and dashboards.

A destination is the data store where your data will be delivered. Firehose Destinations include:

- Amazon S3.

- Amazon Redshift.

- Amazon Elasticsearch Service.

- Splunk.

For Amazon S3 destinations, streaming data is delivered to your S3 bucket. If data transformation is enabled, you can optionally back up source data to another Amazon S3 bucket.

The best choice of AWS service for this scenario is to use Amazon Kinesis Data Firehose as it can ingest large amounts of data at extremely high throughput and load that data into an Amazon S3 bucket

CORRECT: "Amazon Kinesis Data Firehose" is the correct answer.

INCORRECT: "Amazon S3 Transfer Acceleration" is incorrect as this is a service used for improving the performance of uploads into Amazon S3. It is not suitable for ingesting streaming data.

INCORRECT: "Amazon Kinesis Data Analytics" is incorrect as this service is used for processing and analyzing real-time, streaming data. The easiest way to load streaming data into a data store for analysing at a later time is Kinesis Data Firehose

INCORRECT: "Amazon Simple Queue Service (SQS)" is incorrect as this is not the best solution for this scenario. With SQS you need a producer to place the messages on the queue and then consumers to process the messages and load them into Amazon S3. Kinesis Data Firehose can do this natively without the need for consumers.

28. Question

A mobile application has thousands of users. Each user may use multiple devices to access the application. The Developer wants to assign unique identifiers to these users regardless of the device they use. Which of the below is the BEST method to obtain unique identifiers?

1: Create a user table in Amazon DynamoDB with key-value pairs of users and their devices. Use these keys as unique identifiers

2: Use IAM-generated access key IDs for the users as the unique identifier, but do not store secret keys

3: Implement developer-authenticated identities by using Amazon Cognito and get credentials for these identities

4: Assign IAM users and roles to the users. Use the unique IAM resource ID as the unique identifier

Answer: 3

Explanation:

Amazon Cognito lets you add user sign-up, sign-in, and access control to your web and mobile apps quickly and easily. Amazon Cognito provides authentication, authorization, and user management for your web and mobile apps.

Amazon Cognito identity pools enable you to create unique identities for your users and authenticate them with identity providers. With an identity, you can obtain temporary, limited-privilege AWS credentials to access other AWS services.

Amazon Cognito supports developer authenticated identities, in addition to web identity federation through Facebook (Identity Pools), Google (Identity Pools), and Login with Amazon (Identity Pools).

With developer authenticated identities, you can register and authenticate users via your own existing authentication process, while still using Amazon Cognito to synchronize user data and access AWS resources. Using developer authenticated identities involves interaction between the end user device, your backend for authentication, and Amazon Cognito.

In this scenario, this would be the best method of obtaining unique identifiers for each user. This is natively supported through Amazon Cognito.

CORRECT: "Implement developer-authenticated identities by using Amazon Cognito and get credentials for these identities" is the correct answer.

INCORRECT: "Create a user table in Amazon DynamoDB with key-value pairs of users and their devices. Use these keys as unique identifiers" is incorrect. This is not the best method of implementing this requirement as it requires more custom implementation and management.

INCORRECT: "Use IAM-generated access key IDs for the users as the unique identifier, but do not store secret keys" is incorrect. As this is a mobile application it is a good use case for Amazon Cognito so authentication can be handled without needing to create IAM users.

INCORRECT: "Assign IAM users and roles to the users. Use the unique IAM resource ID as the unique identifier" is incorrect as this mobile application is a good use case for Amazon Cognito. With Cognito the authentication can be handled using identities in Cognito itself or a federated identity provider. Therefore, the users will not have identities in IAM.

29. Question

A manufacturing company is creating a new RESTful API that their customers can use to query the status of orders. The endpoint for customer queries will be
http://www.manufacturerdomain.com/status/customerID

Which of the following application designs will meet the requirements? (Select TWO)

1: Amazon SQS; Amazon SNS

2: Elastic Load Balancing; Amazon EC2

3: Amazon ElastiCache; Amazon Elacticsearch Service

4: Amazon API Gateway; AWS Lambda

5: Amazon S3; Amazon CloudFront

Answer: 2, 4

Explanation:

This scenario includes a web application that will use RESTful API calls to determine the status of orders and dynamically return the results back to the company's customers. Therefore, the two best options are as per below:

- Amazon API Gateway; AWS Lambda – this choice includes API Gateway which is provides managed REST APIs and Lambda which can run the backend code for the application. This is a good solution for this scenario.
- Elastic Load Balancing; Amazon EC2 – with this choice the ELB can load balance to one or more EC2 instances which can run the RESTful APIs and compute functions. This is also a good choice but could be more costly (operationally and financially).

None of the other options provide a workable solution for this scenario.

CORRECT: "Elastic Load Balancing; Amazon EC2" is a correct answer.

CORRECT: "Amazon API Gateway; AWS Lambda" is a correct answer.

INCORRECT: "Amazon SQS; Amazon SNS" is incorrect as these services are used for queuing and sending notifications. They are not suitable for hosting a REST API.

INCORRECT: "Amazon ElastiCache; Amazon Elacticsearch Service" is incorrect as ElastiCache is an in-memory caching service and Elasticsearch is used for searching. These do not provide a suitable solution for this scenario.

INCORRECT: "Amazon S3; Amazon CloudFront" is incorrect as though you can host a static website on Amazon S3 with CloudFront caching the content, this is a static website only and you cannot host an API.

30. Question

A solution requires a serverless service for receiving streaming data and loading it directly into an Amazon Elasticsearch datastore. Which AWS service would be suitable for this requirement?

1: Amazon Kinesis Data Streams

2: Amazon Kinesis Data Analytics

3: Amazon Kinesis Data Firehose

4: Amazon Simple Queue Service (SQS)

Answer: 3

Explanation:

Amazon Kinesis Data Firehose is the easiest way to load streaming data into data stores and analytics tools. It can capture, transform, and load streaming data into Amazon S3, Amazon Redshift, Amazon Elasticsearch Service, and Splunk, enabling near real-time analytics with existing business intelligence tools and dashboards you're already using today.

Firehose is a fully managed service that automatically scales to match the throughput of your data and requires no ongoing administration. It can also batch, compress, and encrypt the data before loading it, minimizing the amount of storage used at the destination and increasing security.

CORRECT: "Amazon Kinesis Data Firehose" is the correct answer.

INCORRECT: "Amazon Kinesis Data Streams" is incorrect as with Kinesis Data Streams you need consumers running on EC2 instances or AWS Lambda for processing the data from the stream. It therefore will not load data directly to a datastore.

INCORRECT: "Amazon Kinesis Data Analytics" is incorrect as this service is used for performing analytics on streaming data using Structured Query Language (SQL queries.

INCORRECT: "Amazon Simple Queue Service (SQS)" is incorrect as this is a message queueing service. You would need servers to place messages on the queue and then other servers to process messages from the queue and store them in Elasticsearch.

31. Question

A serverless application uses an AWS Lambda function, Amazon API Gateway API and an Amazon DynamoDB table. The Lambda function executes 10 times per second and takes 3 seconds to complete each execution. How many concurrent executions will the Lambda function require?

1: 3

2: 12

3: 10

4: 30

Answer: 4

Explanation:

Concurrency is the number of requests that your function is serving at any given time. When your function is invoked, Lambda allocates an instance of it to process the event. When the function code finishes running, it can handle another request. If the function is invoked again while a request is still being processed, another instance is allocated, which increases the function's concurrency.

To calculate the concurrency requirements for the Lambda function simply multiply the number of executions per second (10) by the time it takes to complete the execution (3).

Therefore, for this scenario the calculation is 10 x 3 = 30.

CORRECT: "30" is the correct answer.

INCORRECT: "10" is incorrect. Please use the formula above to calculate concurrency requirements.

INCORRECT: "12" is incorrect. Please use the formula above to calculate concurrency requirements.

INCORRECT: "3" is incorrect. Please use the formula above to calculate concurrency requirements.

32. Question

An application that is being migrated to AWS and refactored requires a storage service. The storage service should support provide a standards-based REST web service interface and store objects based on keys. Which AWS service would be MOST suitable?

1: Amazon S3

2: Amazon DynamoDB

3: Amazon EBS

4: Amazon EFS

Answer: 1

Explanation:

Amazon S3 is object storage built to store and retrieve any amount of data from anywhere on the Internet. Amazon S3 uses standards-based REST and SOAP interfaces designed to work with any internet-development toolkit.

Amazon S3 is a simple key-based object store. The key is the name of the object and the value is the actual data itself. Keys can be any string, and they can be constructed to mimic hierarchical attributes.

CORRECT: "Amazon S3" is the correct answer.

INCORRECT: "Amazon DynamoDB" is incorrect. DynamoDB is a key/value database service that provides tables to store your data. This is not the most suitable solution for this requirement as the cost will be higher and there are more design considerations that need to be addressed.

INCORRECT: "Amazon EBS" is incorrect as this is a block-based storage system with which you attach volumes to Amazon EC2 instances. It is not a key-based object storage system.

INCORRECT: "Amazon EFS" is incorrect as this is a filesystem that you mount to Amazon EC2 instances, it is also not a key-based object storage system.

33. Question

A company will be hiring a large number of Developers for a series of projects. The Develops will bring their own devices to work and the company want to ensure consistency in tooling. The Developers must be able to write, run, and debug applications with just a browser, without needing to install or maintain a local Integrated Development Environment (IDE). Which AWS service should the Developers use?

1: AWS CodeCommit

2: AWS Cloud9

3: AWS X-Ray

4: AWS CodeDeploy

Answer: 2

Explanation:

AWS Cloud9 is an integrated development environment, or *IDE*. The AWS Cloud9 IDE offers a rich code-editing experience with support for several programming languages and runtime debuggers, and a built-in terminal. It contains a collection of tools that you use to code, build, run, test, and debug software, and helps you release software to the cloud.

You access the AWS Cloud9 IDE through a web browser. You can configure the IDE to your preferences. You can switch color themes, bind shortcut keys, enable programming language-specific syntax coloring and code formatting, and more.

CORRECT: "AWS Cloud9" is the correct answer.

INCORRECT: "AWS CodeCommit" is incorrect. AWS CodeCommit is a fully-managed source control service that hosts secure Git-based repositories. It is not an IDE.

INCORRECT: "AWS CodeDeploy" is incorrect. CodeDeploy is a deployment service that automates application deployments to Amazon EC2 instances, on-premises instances, serverless Lambda functions, or Amazon ECS services.

INCORRECT: "AWS X-Ray" is incorrect. AWS X-Ray helps developers analyze and debug production, distributed applications, such as those built using a microservices architecture.

34. Question

A Development team manage a hybrid cloud environment. They would like to collect system-level metrics from on-premises servers and Amazon EC2 instances. How can the Development team collect this information MOST efficiently?

1: Use CloudWatch for monitoring EC2 instances and custom AWS CLI scripts using the put-metric-data API

2: Install the CloudWatch agent on the on-premises servers and EC2 instances

3: Install the CloudWatch agent on the EC2 instances and use a cron job on the on-premises servers

4: Use CloudWatch detailed monitoring for both EC2 instances and on-premises servers

Answer: 2

Explanation:

The unified CloudWatch agent can be installed on both on-premises servers and Amazon EC2 instances using multiple operating system versions. It enables you to do the following:

- Collect more system-level metrics from Amazon EC2 instances across operating systems. The metrics can include in-guest metrics, in addition to the metrics for EC2 instances.

- Collect system-level metrics from on-premises servers. These can include servers in a hybrid environment as well as servers not managed by AWS.

- Retrieve custom metrics from your applications or services using the StatsD and collectd protocols.

- Collect logs from Amazon EC2 instances and on-premises servers, running either Linux or Windows Server.

Therefore, the Development team should install the CloudWatch agent on the on-premises servers and EC2 instances. This will allow them to collect system-level metrics from servers and instances across the hybrid cloud environment.

CORRECT: "Install the CloudWatch agent on the on-premises servers and EC2 instances" is the correct answer.

INCORRECT: "Use CloudWatch for monitoring EC2 instances and custom AWS CLI scripts using the put-metric-data API" is incorrect as this is not the most efficient option as you must write and maintain custom scripts. It is better to use the CloudWatch agent as it provides all the functionality required.

INCORRECT: "Install the CloudWatch agent on the EC2 instances and use a cron job on the on-premises servers" is incorrect as the answer does not even specify what the cron job is going to do / use for gathering and sending the data.

INCORRECT: "Use CloudWatch detailed monitoring for both EC2 instances and on-premises servers" is incorrect as this would not do anything for the on-premises instances.

35. Question

A Developer is migrating Docker containers to Amazon ECS. A large number of containers will be deployed onto an existing ECS cluster that uses container instances of different instance types. Which task placement strategy can be used to minimize the number of container instances used based on available memory?

1: binpack

2: random

3: spread

4: distinctInstance

Answer: 1

Explanation:

When a task that uses the EC2 launch type is launched, Amazon ECS must determine where to place the task based on the requirements specified in the task definition, such as CPU and memory. Similarly, when you scale down the task count, Amazon ECS must determine which tasks to terminate. You can apply task placement strategies and constraints to customize how Amazon ECS places and terminates tasks. Task placement strategies and constraints are not supported for tasks using the Fargate launch type. By default, Fargate tasks are spread across Availability Zones.

A *task placement strategy* is an algorithm for selecting instances for task placement or tasks for termination. For example, Amazon ECS can select instances at random, or it can select instances such that tasks are distributed evenly across a group of instances.

Amazon ECS supports the following task placement strategies:

- binpack

Place tasks based on the least available amount of CPU or memory. This minimizes the number of instances in use.

- random

Place tasks randomly.

- spread

Place tasks evenly based on the specified value. Accepted values are instanceId (or host, which has the same effect), or any platform or custom attribute that is applied to a container instance, such as attribute:ecs.availability-zone. Service tasks are spread based on the tasks from that service. Standalone tasks are spread based on the tasks from the same task group.

The Developer should use the binpack task placement strategy using available memory to determine the placement of tasks. This will minimize the number of container instances required.

CORRECT: "binpack" is the correct answer.

INCORRECT: "random" is incorrect as this would just randomly assign the tasks across the available container instances in the cluster.

INCORRECT: "spread" is incorrect as this would attempt to spread the tasks across the cluster instances for better high availability.

INCORRECT: "distinctInstance" is incorrect as this is a task placement constraint, not a strategy. This constraint would result in the tasks being each placed on a separate instance which would not assist with meeting the requirements.

36. Question

An organization has encrypted a large quantity of data. To protect their data encryption keys they are planning to use envelope encryption. Which of the following processes is a correct implementation of envelope encryption?

1: Encrypt plaintext data with a data key and then encrypt the data key with a top-level plaintext master key.

2: Encrypt plaintext data with a master key and then encrypt the master key with a top-level plaintext data key

3: Encrypt plaintext data with a data key and then encrypt the data key with a top-level encrypted master key

4: Encrypt plaintext data with a master key and then encrypt the master key with a top-level encrypted data key

Answer: 1

Explanation:

When you encrypt your data, your data is protected, but you have to protect your encryption key. One strategy is to encrypt it. *Envelope encryption* is the practice of encrypting plaintext data with a data key, and then encrypting the data key under another key.

You can even encrypt the data encryption key under another encryption key and encrypt that encryption key under another encryption key. But, eventually, one key must remain in plaintext so you can decrypt the keys and your data. This top-level plaintext key encryption key is known as the *master key*.

Envelope encryption offers several benefits:

- **Protecting data keys**

    When you encrypt a data key, you don't have to worry about storing the encrypted data key, because the data key is inherently protected by encryption. You can safely store the encrypted data key alongside the encrypted data.

- **Encrypting the same data under multiple master keys**

    Encryption operations can be time consuming, particularly when the data being encrypted are large objects. Instead of re-encrypting raw data multiple times with different keys, you can re-encrypt only the data keys that protect the raw data.

- **Combining the strengths of multiple algorithms**

    In general, symmetric key algorithms are faster and produce smaller ciphertexts than public key algorithms. But public key algorithms provide inherent separation of roles and easier key management. Envelope encryption lets you combine the strengths of each strategy.

As described above, the process that should be implemented is to encrypt plaintext data with a data key and then encrypt the data key with a top-level plaintext master key.

CORRECT: "Encrypt plaintext data with a data key and then encrypt the data key with a top-level plaintext master key" is the correct answer.

INCORRECT: "Encrypt plaintext data with a master key and then encrypt the master key with a top-level plaintext data key" is incorrect as the master key is the top-level key.

INCORRECT: "Encrypt plaintext data with a data key and then encrypt the data key with a top-level encrypted master key" is incorrect as the top-level master key must be unencrypted so it can be used to decrypt data.

INCORRECT: "Encrypt plaintext data with a master key and then encrypt the master key with a top-level encrypted data key" is incorrect as the master key is the top-level key.

37. Question

A mobile application runs as a serverless application on AWS. A Developer needs to create a push notification feature that sends periodic message to subscribers. How can the Developer send the notification from the application?

1: Publish a message to an Amazon SQS Queue

2: Publish a notification to Amazon CloudWatch Events

3: Publish a notification to an Amazon SNS Topic

4: Publish a message to an Amazon SWF Workflow

Answer: 3

Explanation:

With Amazon SNS, you have the ability to send push notification messages directly to apps on mobile devices. Push notification messages sent to a mobile endpoint can appear in the mobile app as message alerts, badge updates, or even sound alerts.

You send push notification messages to both mobile devices and desktops using one of the following supported push notification services:

- Amazon Device Messaging (ADM)

- Apple Push Notification Service (APNs) for both iOS and Mac OS X

- Baidu Cloud Push (Baidu)

- Firebase Cloud Messaging (FCM)

- Microsoft Push Notification Service for Windows Phone (MPNS)

- Windows Push Notification Services (WNS)

To send a notification to an Amazon SNS subscriber, the application needs to send the notification to an Amazon SNS Topic. Amazon SNS will then send the notification to the relevant subscribers.

CORRECT: "Publish a notification to an Amazon SNS Topic" is the correct answer.

INCORRECT: "Publish a message to an Amazon SQS Queue" is incorrect as SQS is a message queue service, not a notification service.

INCORRECT: "Publish a notification to Amazon CloudWatch Events" is incorrect as CloudWatch Events will not be able to send notifications to mobile app users.

INCORRECT: "Publish a message to an Amazon SWF Workflow" is incorrect as SWF is a workflow orchestration service and it is not used for publishing messages to mobile app users.

38. Question

An Amazon ElastiCache cluster has been placed in front of a large Amazon RDS database. To reduce cost the ElastiCache cluster should only cache items that are actually requested. How should ElastiCache be optimized?

1: Only cache database writes

2: Enable a TTL on cached data

3: Use a write-through caching strategy

4: Use a lazy loading caching strategy

Answer: 4

Explanation:

There are two caching strategies available: Lazy Loading and Write-Through:

Lazy Loading

- Loads the data into the cache only when necessary (if a cache miss occurs).

- Lazy loading avoids filling up the cache with data that won't be requested.

- If requested data is in the cache, ElastiCache returns the data to the application.

- If the data is not in the cache or has expired, ElastiCache returns a null.

- The application then fetches the data from the database and writes the data received into the cache so that it is available for next time.

- Data in the cache can become stale if Lazy Loading is implemented without other strategies (such as TTL).

Write Through

- When using a write through strategy, the cache is updated whenever a new write or update is made to the underlying database.

- Allows cache data to remain up-to-date.

- Can add wait time to write operations in your application.

- Without a TTL you can end up with a lot of cached data that is never read.

CORRECT: "Use a lazy loading caching strategy" is the correct answer.

INCORRECT: "Use a write-through caching strategy" is incorrect as this will load all database items into the cache increasing cost.

INCORRECT: "Only cache database writes" is incorrect as you cannot cache writes, only reads.

INCORRECT: "Enable a TTL on cached data" is incorrect. This would help expire stale items but it is not a cache optimization strategy that will cache only items that are requested.

39. Question

A retail organization stores stock information in an Amazon RDS database. An application reads and writes data to the database. A Developer has been asked to provide read access to the database from a reporting application in another region. Which configuration would provide BEST performance for the reporting application without impacting the performance of the main database?

1: Implement a cross-region multi-AZ deployment in the region where the reporting application will run

2: Create a snapshot of the database and create a new database from the snapshot in the region where the reporting application will run

3: Implement a cross-region read replica in the region where the reporting application will run

4: Implement a read replica in another AZ and configure the reporting application to connect to the read replica using a VPN connection

Answer: 3

Explanation:

With Amazon RDS, you can create a MariaDB, MySQL, Oracle, or PostgreSQL read replica in a different AWS Region than the source DB instance. Creating a cross-Region read replica isn't supported for SQL Server on Amazon RDS.

You create a read replica in a different AWS Region to do the following:

- Improve your disaster recovery capabilities.

- Scale read operations into an AWS Region closer to your users.

- Make it easier to migrate from a data center in one AWS Region to a data center in another AWS Region.

Creating a read replica in a different AWS Region from the source instance is similar to creating a replica in the same AWS Region. You can use the AWS Management Console, run the create-db-instance-read-replica command, or call the CreateDBInstanceReadReplica API operation.

Creating read replica in the region where the reporting application is going to run will provide the best performance as latency will be much lower than connecting across regions. As the database is a replica it will also be continuously updated using asynchronous replication so the reporting application will have the latest data available.

CORRECT: "Implement a cross-region read replica in the region where the reporting application will run" is the correct answer.

INCORRECT: "Implement a cross-region multi-AZ deployment in the region where the reporting application will run" is incorrect as multi-AZ is used across availability zones, not regions.

INCORRECT: "Create a snapshot of the database and create a new database from the snapshot in the region where the reporting application will run" is incorrect as this would be OK from a performance perspective but the database would not receive ongoing updates from the main database so the data would quickly become out of date.

INCORRECT: "Implement a read replica in another AZ and configure the reporting application to connect to the read replica using a VPN connection" is incorrect as this would result in much higher latency than having the database in the local region close to the reporting application and would impact performance.

40. Question

An Auto Scaling Group (ASG) of Amazon EC2 instances is being created for processing messages from an Amazon SQS queue. To ensure the EC2 instances are cost-effective a Developer would like to configure the ASG to maintain aggregate CPU utilization at 70%. Which type of scaling policy should the Developer choose?

1: Step Scaling Policy

2: Simple Scaling Policy

3: Scheduled Scaling Policy

4: Target Tracking Scaling Policy

Answer: 4

Explanation:

With target tracking scaling policies, you select a scaling metric and set a target value. Amazon EC2 Auto Scaling creates and manages the CloudWatch alarms that trigger the scaling policy and calculates the scaling adjustment based on the metric and the target value. The scaling policy adds or removes capacity as required to keep the metric at, or close to, the specified target value. In addition to keeping the metric close to the target value, a target tracking scaling policy also adjusts to the changes in the metric due to a changing load pattern.

For example, you can use target tracking scaling to:

- Configure a target tracking scaling policy to keep the average aggregate CPU utilization of your Auto Scaling group at 40 percent.

- Configure a target tracking scaling policy to keep the request count per target of your Elastic Load Balancing target group at 1000 for your Auto Scaling group.

The target tracking scaling policy is therefore the best choice for this scenario.

CORRECT: "Target Tracking Scaling Policy" is the correct answer.

INCORRECT: "Step Scaling Policy" is incorrect. (explanation below)

INCORRECT: "Simple Scaling Policy" is incorrect. (explanation below)

With step scaling and simple scaling, you choose scaling metrics and threshold values for the CloudWatch alarms that trigger the scaling process. You also define how your Auto Scaling group should be scaled when a threshold is in breach for a specified number of evaluation periods.

INCORRECT: "Scheduled Scaling Policy" is incorrect as this is used to schedule a scaling action at a specific time and date rather than dynamically adjusting according to load.

41. Question

An application collects data from sensors in a manufacturing facility. The data is stored in an Amazon SQS Standard queue by an AWS Lambda function and an Amazon EC2 instance processes the data and stores it in an Amazon RedShift data warehouse. A fault in the sensors' software is causing occasional duplicate messages to be sent. Timestamps on the duplicate messages show they are generated within a few seconds of the primary message. How a can a Developer prevent duplicate data being stored in the data warehouse?

1: Use a FIFO queue and configure the Lambda function to add a message deduplication token to the message body

2: Use a FIFO queue and configure the Lambda function to add a message group ID to the messages generated by each individual sensor

3: Send a ChangeMessageVisibility call with VisibilityTimeout set to 30 seconds after the receipt of every message from the queue

4: Configure a redrive policy, specify a destination Dead-Letter queue, and set the maxReceiveCount to 1

Answer: 1

Explanation:

FIFO (First-In-First-Out) queues are designed to enhance messaging between applications when the order of operations and events is critical, or where duplicates can't be tolerated.

In FIFO queues, messages are ordered based on message group ID. If multiple hosts (or different threads on the same host) send messages with the same message group ID to a FIFO queue, Amazon SQS stores the messages in the order in which they arrive for processing. To ensure that Amazon SQS preserves the order in which messages are sent and received, ensure that each producer uses a unique message group ID to send all its messages.

FIFO queue logic applies only per message group ID. Each message group ID represents a distinct ordered message group within an Amazon SQS queue. For each message group ID, all messages are sent and received in strict order. However, messages with different message group ID values might be sent and received out of order. You must associate a message group ID with a message. If you don't provide a message group ID, the action fails. If you require a single group of ordered messages, provide the same message group ID for messages sent to the FIFO queue.

Therefore, the Developer can use a FIFO queue and configure the Lambda function to add a message deduplication token to the message body. This will ensure that the messages are deduplicated before being picked up for processing by the Amazon EC2 instance.

CORRECT: "Use a FIFO queue and configure the Lambda function to add a message deduplication token to the message body" is the correct answer.

INCORRECT: "Use a FIFO queue and configure the Lambda function to add a message group ID to the messages generated by each individual sensor" is incorrect. The message group ID is the tag that specifies that a message belongs to a specific message group. Messages that belong to the same message group are always processed one by one, in a strict order relative to the message group.

INCORRECT: "Send a ChangeMessageVisibility call with VisibilityTimeout set to 30 seconds after the receipt of every message from the queue" is incorrect as this will just change the visibility timeout for the message which will prevent others from seeing it until it has been processed and deleted from the queue. This doesn't stop a message with duplicate data being processed.

INCORRECT: "Configure a redrive policy, specify a destination Dead-Letter queue, and set the maxReceiveCount to 1" is incorrect as without a FIFO queue and a message deduplication ID duplicate messages will still enter the queue. The redrive policy only applies to individual messages for which processing has failed a number of times as specified in the maxReceiveCount.

42. Question

A Developer is publishing custom metrics for Amazon EC2 using the Amazon CloudWatch CLI. The Developer needs to add further context to the metrics being published by organizing them by EC2 instance and Auto Scaling Group. What should the Developer add to the CLI command when publishing the metrics using put-metric-data

1: The --dimensions parameter

2: The --namespace parameter

3: The --statistic-values parameter

4: The --metric-name parameter

Answer: 1

Explanation:

You can publish your own metrics to CloudWatch using the AWS CLI or an API. You can view statistical graphs of your published metrics with the AWS Management Console.

CloudWatch stores data about a metric as a series of data points. Each data point has an associated time stamp. You can even publish an aggregated set of data points called a *statistic set*.

In custom metrics, the --dimensions parameter is common. A dimension further clarifies what the metric is and what data it stores. You can have up to 10 dimensions in one metric, and each dimension is defined by a name and value pair. There are two dimensions associated with the EC2 namespace. These organize the metrics by Auto Scaling Group and Per-Instance metrics. Therefore, the Developer should the --dimensions parameter.

CORRECT: "The --dimensions parameter" is the correct answer.

INCORRECT: "The --namespace parameter" is incorrect as a *namespace* is a container for CloudWatch metrics. To add further context the Developer should use a *dimension*.

INCORRECT: "The --statistic-values parameter" is incorrect as this is a parameter associated with the publishing of statistic sets.

INCORRECT: "The --metric-name parameter" is incorrect as this simply provides the name for the metric that is being published.

43. Question

A legacy application is being refactored into a microservices architecture running on AWS. The microservice will include several AWS Lambda functions. A Developer will use AWS Step Functions to coordinate function execution. How should the Developer proceed?

1: Create an AWS CloudFormation stack using a YAML-formatted template

2: Create a state machine using the Amazon States Language

3: Create a workflow using the StartExecution API action

4: Create a layer in AWS Lambda and add the functions to the layer

Answer: 2

Explanation:

AWS Step Functions is a web service that enables you to coordinate the components of distributed applications and microservices using visual workflows. You build applications from individual components that each perform a discrete function, or *task*, allowing you to scale and change applications quickly.

The following are key features of AWS Step Functions:

- Step Functions is based on the concepts of tasks and state machines.

- You define state machines using the JSON-based Amazon States Language.

- The Step Functions console displays a graphical view of your state machine's structure. This provides a way to visually check your state machine's logic and monitor executions.

The Developer needs to create a state machine using the Amazon States Language as this is how you can create an executable state machine that includes the Lambda functions that must be coordinated.

CORRECT: "Create a state machine using the Amazon States Language" is the correct answer.

INCORRECT: "Create an AWS CloudFormation stack using a YAML-formatted template" is incorrect as AWS Step Functions does not use CloudFormation. The Developer needs to create a state machine.

INCORRECT: "Create a workflow using the StartExecution API action" is incorrect as workflows are associated with Amazon SWF whereas the StartExecution API action is a Step Functions action for executing a state machine.

INCORRECT: "Create a layer in AWS Lambda and add the functions to the layer" is incorrect as a layer is a ZIP archive that contains libraries, a custom runtime, or other dependencies that you can use to pull additional code into a Lambda function.

44. Question

A company has sensitive data that must be encrypted. The data is made up of 1 GB objects and there is a total of 150 GB of data. What is the BEST approach for a Developer to encrypt the data using AWS KMS?

1: Make an Encrypt API call to encrypt the plaintext data as ciphertext using a customer master key (CMK)

2: Make an Encrypt API call to encrypt the plaintext data as ciphertext using a customer master key (CMK) with imported key material

3: Make a GenerateDataKey API call that returns a plaintext key and an encrypted copy of a data key. Use the plaintext key to encrypt the data

4: Make a GenerateDataKeyWithoutPlaintext API call that returns an encrypted copy of a data key. Use the encrypted key to encrypt the data

Answer: 3

Explanation:

To encrypt large quantities of data with the AWS Key Management Service (KMS), you must use a data encryption key rather than a customer master keys (CMK). This is because a CMK can only encrypt up to 4KB in a single operation and in this scenario the objects are 1 GB in size.

To create a data key, call the GenerateDataKey operation. AWS KMS uses the CMK that you specify to generate a data key. The operation returns a plaintext copy of the data key and a copy of the data key encrypted under the CMK.

AWS KMS cannot use a data key to encrypt data. But you can use the data key outside of KMS, such as by using OpenSSL or a cryptographic library like the AWS Encryption SDK. Data can then be encrypted using the plaintext data key.

Therefore, the Developer should make a GenerateDataKey API call that returns a plaintext key and an encrypted copy of a data key, and then use the plaintext key to encrypt the data.

CORRECT: "Make a GenerateDataKey API call that returns a plaintext key and an encrypted copy of a data key. Use the plaintext key to encrypt the data" is the correct answer.

INCORRECT: "Make an Encrypt API call to encrypt the plaintext data as ciphertext using a customer master key (CMK)" is incorrect as you cannot use a CMK to encrypt objects over 4 KB in size.

INCORRECT: "Make an Encrypt API call to encrypt the plaintext data as ciphertext using a customer master key (CMK) with imported key material" is incorrect as you cannot use a CMK to encrypt objects over 4 KB in size.

INCORRECT: "Make a GenerateDataKeyWithoutPlaintext API call that returns an encrypted copy of a data key. Use the encrypted key to encrypt the data" is incorrect as you need to encrypt data with a plaintext data key.

45. Question

A nightly batch job loads 1 million new records in to a DynamoDB table. The records are only needed for one hour, and the table needs to be empty by the next night's batch job. Which is the MOST efficient and cost-effective method to provide an empty table?

1: Use DeleteItem using a ConditionExpression

2: Use BatchWriteItem to empty all of the rows

3: Write a recursive function that scans and calls out DeleteItem

4: Create and then delete the table after the task has completed

Answer: 4

Explanation:

The key requirements here are to be efficient and cost-effective. Therefore, it's important to choose the option that requires the fewest API calls. As the table is only required for a short period of time, the most efficient and cost-effective option is to simply delete and recreate the table.

The following API actions can be used to perform this operation programmatically:

- CreateTable - The CreateTable operation adds a new table to your account.
- DeleteTable - The DeleteTable operation deletes a table and all of its items.

This solution means fewer API calls and also the table is not consuming RCUs/WCUs whilst not being used. Therefore, the best option is to create and then delete the table after the task has completed.

CORRECT: "Create and then delete the table after the task has completed" is the correct answer.

INCORRECT: "Use DeleteItem using a ConditionExpression" is incorrect as this will use more RCUs and WCUs and is not cost-effective.

INCORRECT: "Use BatchWriteItem to empty all of the rows" is incorrect. The BatchWriteItem operation puts or deletes multiple items (not rows) in one or more tables. This would use more RCUs and WCUs and is not cost-effective.

INCORRECT: "Write a recursive function that scans and calls out DeleteItem" is incorrect as scans are the least efficient and cost-effective option as all items must be retrieved from the table.

46. Question

A Developer is creating an AWS Lambda function to process a stream of data from an Amazon Kinesis Data Stream. When the Lambda function parses the data and encounters a missing field, it exits the function with an error. The function is generating duplicate records from the Kinesis stream. When the Developer looks at the stream output without the Lambda function, there are no duplicate records. What is the reason for the duplicates?

1: The Lambda function did not advance the Kinesis stream point to the next record after the error

2: The Lambda event source used asynchronous invocation, resulting in duplicate records

3: The Lambda function did not handle the error, and the Lambda service attempted to reprocess the data

4: The Lambda function is not keeping up with the amount of data coming from the stream

Answer: 3

Explanation:

When you invoke a function, two types of error can occur. Invocation errors occur when the invocation request is rejected before your function receives it. Function errors occur when your function's code or runtime returns an error.

Depending on the type of error, the type of invocation, and the client or service that invokes the function, the retry behavior and the strategy for managing errors varies. Function errors occur when your function code or the runtime that it uses return an error.

In this case, with an event source mapping from a stream (Kinesis Data Stream), Lambda retries the entire batch of items. Therefore, the best explanation is that the Lambda function did not handle the error, and the Lambda service attempted to reprocess the data.

CORRECT: "The Lambda function did not handle the error, and the Lambda service attempted to reprocess the data" is the correct answer.

INCORRECT: "The Lambda function did not advance the Kinesis stream point to the next record after the error" is incorrect. Lambda does not advance a stream "point" to the next record. It processed records in batches.

INCORRECT: "The Lambda event source used asynchronous invocation, resulting in duplicate records" is incorrect as Lambda processes records from Kinesis Data Streams synchronously.

INCORRECT: "The Lambda function is not keeping up with the amount of data coming from the stream" is incorrect as Lambda can scale seamlessly to handle the load coming from the stream.

47. Question

A Developer has code running on Amazon EC2 instances that needs read-only access to an Amazon DynamoDB table. What is the MOST secure approach the Developer should take to accomplish this task?

1: Create a user access key for each EC2 instance with read-only access to DynamoDB. Place the keys in the code. Redeploy the code as keys rotate

2: Use an IAM role with an AmazonDynamoDBReadOnlyAccess policy applied to the EC2 instances

3: Run all code with only AWS account root user access keys to ensure maximum access to services

4: Use an IAM role with Administrator access applied to the EC2 instance

Answer: 2

Explanation:

According to the principal of least privilege the Developer needs to provide the minimum permissions that application requires. The application needs read-only access and therefore an IAM role with an AmazonDynamoDBReadOnlyAccess policy applied that only provides read-only access to DynamoDB is secure.

This role can be applied to the EC2 instance through the management console or programmatically by creating an instance profile and attaching the role to the instance profile. The EC2 instance can then assume the role and get read-only access to DynamoDB.

CORRECT: "Use an IAM role with an AmazonDynamoDBReadOnlyAccess policy applied to the EC2 instances" is the correct answer.

INCORRECT: "Create a user access key for each EC2 instance with read-only access to DynamoDB. Place the keys in the code. Redeploy the code as keys rotate" is incorrect as access keys are less secure than using roles as the keys are stored in the code.

INCORRECT: "Run all code with only AWS account root user access keys to ensure maximum access to services" is incorrect as this is highly insecure as the access keys are stored in code and these access keys provide full permissions to the AWS account.

INCORRECT: "Use an IAM role with Administrator access applied to the EC2 instance" is incorrect as this does not follow the principal of least privilege and is therefore less secure. The role used should have read-only access to DynamoDB.

48. Question

A company is migrating an on-premises web application to AWS. The web application runs on a single server and stores session data in memory. On AWS the company plan to implement multiple Amazon EC2 instances behind an Elastic Load Balancer (ELB). The company want to refactor the application so that data is resilient if an instance fails and user downtime is minimized. Where should the company move session data to MOST effectively reduce downtime and make users' session data more fault tolerant?

1: An Amazon ElastiCache for Redis cluster

2: A second Amazon EBS volume

3: The web server's primary disk

4: An Amazon EC2 instance dedicated to session data

Answer: 1

Explanation:

ElastiCache is a fully managed, low latency, in-memory data store that supports either Memcached or Redis. The Redis engine supports multi-AZ and high availability.

With ElastiCache the company can move the session data to a high-performance, in-memory data store that is well suited to this use case. This will provide high availability for the session data in the case of EC2 instance failure and will reduce downtime for users.

CORRECT: "An Amazon ElastiCache for Redis cluster" is the correct answer.

INCORRECT: "A second Amazon EBS volume" is incorrect as the session data needs to be highly available so should not be stored on an EC2 instance.

INCORRECT: "The web server's primary disk" is incorrect as the session data needs to be highly available so should not be stored on an EC2 instance.

INCORRECT: "An Amazon EC2 instance dedicated to session data" is incorrect as the session data needs to be highly available so should not be stored on an EC2 instance.

49. Question

A Developer is creating a script to automate the deployment process for a serverless application. The Developer wants to use an existing AWS Serverless Application Model (SAM) template for the application. What should the Developer use for the project? (Select TWO)

1: Call aws cloudformation package to create the deployment package. Call aws cloudformation deploy to deploy the package afterward

2: Call sam package to create the deployment package. Call sam deploy to deploy the package afterward

3: Call aws s3 cp to upload the AWS SAM template to Amazon S3. Call aws lambda update-function-code to create the application

4: Create a ZIP package locally and call aws serverlessrepo create-application to create the application

5: Create a ZIP package and upload it to Amazon S3. Call aws cloudformation create-stack to create the application

Answer: 1,2

Explanation:

The AWS Serverless Application Model (SAM) is an open-source framework for building serverless applications. It provides shorthand syntax to express functions, APIs, databases, and event source mappings. With just a few lines per resource, you can define the application you want and model it using YAML. During deployment, SAM transforms and expands the SAM syntax into AWS CloudFormation syntax, enabling you to build serverless applications faster.

To get started with building SAM-based applications, use the AWS SAM CLI. SAM CLI provides a Lambda-like execution environment that lets you locally build, test, and debug applications defined by SAM templates. You can also use the SAM CLI to deploy your applications to AWS.

With the SAM CLI you can package and deploy your source code using two simple commands:

- sam package
- sam deploy

Alternatively, you can use:

- aws cloudformation package
- aws cloudformation deploy

Therefore, the Developer can use either the sam or aws cloudformation CLI commands to package and deploy the serverless application.

CORRECT: "Call aws cloudformation package to create the deployment package. Call aws cloudformation deploy to deploy the package afterward" is a correct answer.

CORRECT: "Call sam package to create the deployment package. Call sam deploy to deploy the package afterward" is a correct answer.

INCORRECT: "Call aws s3 cp to upload the AWS SAM template to Amazon S3. Call aws lambda update-function-code to create the application" is incorrect as this is not how to use a SAM template. With SAM the commands mentioned above must be run.

INCORRECT: "Create a ZIP package locally and call aws serverlessrepo create-application to create the application" is incorrect as this is not the correct way to use a SAM template.

INCORRECT: "Create a ZIP package and upload it to Amazon S3. Call aws cloudformation create-stack to create the application" is incorrect as this is not required when deploying a SAM template.

50. Question

A website delivers images stored in an Amazon S3 bucket. The site uses Amazon Cognito-enabled and guest users without logins need to be able to view the images from the S3 bucket. How can a Developer enable access for guest users to the AWS resources?

1: Create a blank user ID in a user pool, add to the user group, and grant access to AWS resources

2: Create a new identity pool, enable access to unauthenticated identities, and grant access to AWS resources

3: Create a new user pool, enable access to unauthenticated identities, and grant access to AWS resources

4: Create a new user pool, disable authentication access, and grant access to AWS resources

Answer: 2

Explanation:

Amazon Cognito identity pools provide temporary AWS credentials for users who are guests (unauthenticated) and for users who have been authenticated and received a token. An identity pool is a store of user identity data specific to your account.

Amazon Cognito identity pools support both authenticated and unauthenticated identities. Authenticated identities belong to users who are authenticated by any supported identity provider. Unauthenticated identities typically belong to guest users.

- To configure authenticated identities with a public login provider, see <u>Identity Pools (Federated Identities) External Identity Providers</u>.

- To configure your own backend authentication process, see <u>Developer Authenticated Identities (Identity Pools)</u>.

Therefore, the Developer should create a new identity pool, enable access to unauthenticated identities, and grant access to AWS resources.

CORRECT: "Create a new identity pool, enable access to unauthenticated identities, and grant access to AWS resources" is the correct answer.

INCORRECT: "Create a blank user ID in a user pool, add to the user group, and grant access to AWS resources" is incorrect as you must use identity pools for unauthenticated users.

INCORRECT: "Create a new user pool, enable access to unauthenticated identities, and grant access to AWS resources" is incorrect as you must use identity pools for unauthenticated users.

INCORRECT: "Create a new user pool, disable authentication access, and grant access to AWS resources" is incorrect as you must use identity pools for unauthenticated users.

---

51. Question

A company has a website that is developed in PHP and WordPress and is launched using AWS Elastic Beanstalk. There is a new version of the website that needs to be deployed in the Elastic Beanstalk environment. The company cannot tolerate having the website offline if an update fails. Deployments must have minimal impact and rollback as soon as possible. What deployment method should be used?

1: All at once

2: Rolling

3: Snapshots

4: Immutable

Answer: 4

Explanation:

AWS Elastic Beanstalk provides several options for how deployments are processed, including deployment policies and options that let you configure batch size and health check behavior during deployments.

All at once:

- Deploys the new version to all instances simultaneously.

Rolling:

- Update a few instances at a time (bucket), and then move onto the next bucket once the first bucket is healthy (downtime for 1 bucket at a time).

Rolling with additional batch:

- Like Rolling but launches new instances in a batch ensuring that there is full availability.

Immutable:

- Launches new instances in a new ASG and deploys the version update to these instances before swapping traffic to these instances once healthy.

- Zero downtime.

Blue / Green deployment:

- Zero downtime and release facility.

- Create a new "stage" environment and deploy updates there.

For this scenario, the best choice is Immutable as this is the safest option when you cannot tolerate downtime and also provides a simple way of rolling back should an issue occur.

CORRECT: "Immutable" is the correct answer.

INCORRECT: "All at once" is incorrect as this will take all instances down and cause a total outage.

INCORRECT: "Snapshots" is incorrect as this is not a deployment method you can use with Elastic Beanstalk.

INCORRECT: "Rolling" is incorrect as this will reduce the capacity of the application and it is more difficult to roll back as you must redeploy the old version to the instances.

52. Question

A company is building an application to track athlete performance using an Amazon DynamoDB table. Each item in the table is identified by a partition key (user_id) and a sort key (sport_name). The table design is shown below:

- **Partition key: user_id**
- **Sort Key: sport_name**
- **Attributes: score, score_datetime**

A Developer is asked to write a leaderboard application to display the top performers (user_id) based on the score for each sport_name.

What process will allow the Developer to extract results MOST efficiently from the DynamoDB table?

1: Use a DynamoDB query operation with the key attributes of user_id and sport_name and order the results based on the score attribute

2: Create a global secondary index with a partition key of sport_name and a sort key of score, and get the results

3: Use a DynamoDB scan operation to retrieve scores and user_id based on sport_name, and order the results based on the score attribute

4: Create a local secondary index with a primary key of sport_name and a sort key of score and get the results based on the score attribute

Answer: 2

Explanation:

The Developer needs to be able to sort the scores for each sport and then extract the highest performing athletes. In this case BOTH the partition key and sort key must be different which means a Global Secondary index is required (as a Local Secondary index only has a different sort key). The GSI would be configured as follows:

- Partition key: sport_name
- Sort Key: score

The results will then be listed in order of the highest score for each sport which is exactly what is required.

CORRECT: "Create a global secondary index with a partition key of sport_name and a sort key of score, and get the results" is the correct answer.

INCORRECT: "Create a local secondary index with a primary key of sport_name and a sort key of score and get the results based on the score attribute" is incorrect as an LSI cannot be created after table creation and also only has a different sort key, not a different partition key.

INCORRECT: "Use a DynamoDB query operation with the key attributes of user_id and sport_name and order the results based on the score attribute" is incorrect as this is less efficient compared to using a GSI.

INCORRECT: "Use a DynamoDB scan operation to retrieve scores and user_id based on sport_name, and order the results based on the score attribute" is incorrect as this is the least efficient option as a scan returns every item in the table (more RCUs).

53. Question

A Developer wants the ability to roll back to a previous version of an AWS Lambda function in the event of errors caused by a new deployment. How can the Developer achieve this with MINIMAL impact on users?

1: Change the application to use an alias that points to the current version. Deploy the new version of the code. Update the alias to use the newly deployed version. If too many errors are encountered, point the alias back to the previous version

2: Change the application to use an alias that points to the current version. Deploy the new version of the code. Update the alias to direct 10% of users to the newly deployed version. If too many errors are encountered, send 100% of traffic to the previous version

3: Change the application to use a version ARN that points to the latest published version. Deploy the new version of the code. Update the application to point to the ARN of the new version of the code. If too many errors are encountered, point the application back to the ARN of the previous version

4: Change the application to use the $LATEST version. Update and save code. If too many errors are encountered, modify and save the code

Answer: 2

Explanation:

You can create one or more aliases for your AWS Lambda function. A Lambda alias is like a pointer to a specific Lambda function version. Users can access the function version using the alias ARN.

You can update the versions that an alias points to and you can also add multiple versions and use weightings to direct a percentage of traffic to a new version of the code.

For this example, the best choice is to use an alias and direct 10% of traffic to the new version. If errors are encountered the rollback is easy (change the pointer in the alias) and a minimum of impact has been made to users.

CORRECT: "Change the application to use an alias that points to the current version. Deploy the new version of the code. Update the alias to direct 10% of users to the newly deployed version. If too many errors are encountered, send 100% of traffic to the previous version" is the correct answer.

INCORRECT: "Change the application to use an alias that points to the current version. Deploy the new version of the code. Update the alias to use the newly deployed version. If too many errors are encountered, point the alias back to the previous version" is incorrect. This is not the best answer as 100% of the users will be directed to the new version so if any errors do occur more users will be affected.

INCORRECT: "Change the application to use a version ARN that points to the latest published version. Deploy the new version of the code. Update the application to point to the ARN of the new version of the code. If too many errors are encountered, point the application back to the ARN of the previous version" is incorrect. This answer involves a lot of updates to the application that could be completely avoided by using an alias.

INCORRECT: "Change the application to use the $LATEST version. Update and save code. If too many errors are encountered, modify and save the code" is incorrect as this is against best practice. The $LATEST is the unpublished version of the code where you make changes. You should publish to a version when the code is ready for deployment.

54. Question

A company is migrating an application with a website and MySQL database to the AWS Cloud. The company require the application to be refactored so it offers high availability and fault tolerance. How should a Developer refactor the application? (Select TWO)

1: Migrate the website to an Auto Scaling group of EC2 instances across a single AZ and use an Elastic Load Balancer

2: Migrate the website to an Auto Scaling group of EC2 instances across multiple AZs and use an Elastic Load Balancer

3: Migrate the MySQL database to an Amazon RDS instance with a Read Replica in another AZ

4: Migrate the MySQL database to an Amazon RDS Multi-AZ deployment

5: Migrate the MySQL database to an Amazon DynamoDB with Global Tables

Answer: 2,4

Explanation:

The key requirements are to add high availability and fault tolerance to the application. To do this the Developer should put the website into an Auto Scaling group of EC2 instances across multiple AZs. An Elastic Load Balancer can be deployed in front of the EC2 instances to distribute incoming connections. This solution is highly available and fault tolerant.

For the MySQL database the Developer should use Amazon RDS with the MySQL engine. To provide fault tolerance the Developer should configure Amazon RDS as a Multi-AZ deployment which will create a standby instance in another AZ that can be failed over to.

CORRECT: "Migrate the website to an Auto Scaling group of EC2 instances across multiple AZs and use an Elastic Load Balancer" is a correct answer.

CORRECT: "Migrate the MySQL database to an Amazon RDS Multi-AZ deployment" is also a correct answer.

INCORRECT: "Migrate the website to an Auto Scaling group of EC2 instances across a single AZ and use an Elastic Load Balancer" is incorrect as to be fully fault tolerant the solution should be spread across multiple AZs.

INCORRECT: "Migrate the MySQL database to an Amazon RDS instance with a Read Replica in another AZ" is incorrect as read replicas are used for performance, not fault tolerance

INCORRECT: "Migrate the MySQL database to an Amazon DynamoDB with Global Tables" is incorrect as the MySQL database is a relational database so it is a better fit to be migrated to Amazon RDS rather than DynamoDB.

55. Question

A company runs many microservices applications that use Docker containers. The company are planning to migrate the containers to Amazon ECS. The workloads are highly variable and therefore the company prefers to be charged per running task. Which solution is the BEST fit for the company's requirements?

1: Amazon ECS with the EC2 launch type

2: Amazon ECS with the Fargate launch type

3: An Amazon ECS Service with Auto Scaling

4: An Amazon ECS Cluster with Auto Scaling

Answer: 2

Explanation:

The key requirement is that the company should be charged per running task. Therefore, the best answer is to use Amazon ECS with the Fargate launch type as with this model AWS charge you for running tasks rather than running container instances.

The Fargate launch type allows you to run your containerized applications without the need to provision and manage the backend infrastructure. You just register your task definition and Fargate launches the container for you. The Fargate Launch Type is a serverless infrastructure managed by AWS.

CORRECT: "Amazon ECS with the Fargate launch type" is the correct answer.

INCORRECT: "Amazon ECS with the EC2 launch type" is incorrect as with this launch type you pay for running container instances (EC2 instances).

INCORRECT: "An Amazon ECS Service with Auto Scaling" is incorrect as this does not specify the launch type. You can run an ECS Service on the Fargate or EC2 launch types.

INCORRECT: "An Amazon ECS Cluster with Auto Scaling" is incorrect as this does not specify the launch type. You can run an ECS Cluster on the Fargate or EC2 launch types.

56. Question

A company has hired a team of remote Developers. The Developers need to work programmatically with AWS resources from their laptop computers. Which security components MUST the Developers use to authenticate? (Select TWO)

1: Access key ID

2: Secret access key

3: Console password

4: IAM user ID

5: MFA device

Answer: 1,2

Explanation:

Access keys consist of two parts: an access key ID (for example, AKIAIOSFODNN7EXAMPLE) and a secret access key (for example, wJalrXUtnFEMI/K7MDENG/bPxRfiCYEXAMPLEKEY). You use access keys to sign programmatic requests that you make to AWS if you use AWS CLI commands (using the SDKs) or using AWS API operations.

For this scenario, the Developers will be connecting programmatically to AWS resources and will therefore be required to use an access key ID and secret access key.

CORRECT: "Access key ID" is a correct answer.

CORRECT: "Secret access key" is a correct answer.

INCORRECT: "Console password " is incorrect as this is used for accessing AWS via the console with an IAM user ID and is not used for programmatic access.

INCORRECT: "IAM user ID" is incorrect as the IAM user ID is used with the password (see above) to access the AWS management console.

INCORRECT: "MFA device" is incorrect as this is not required for making programmatic requests but can be added for additional security

57. Question

A Developer created an AWS Lambda function and then attempted to add an on failure destination but received the following error:

The function's execution role does not have permissions to call SendMessage on arn:aws:sqs:us-east-1:515148212435:FailureDestination

How can the Developer resolve this issue MOST securely?

1: Add the AWSLambdaSQSQueueExecutionRole AWS managed policy to the function's execution role

2: Create a customer managed policy with all read/write permissions to SQS and attach the policy to the function's execution role

3: Add a permissions policy to the SQS queue allowing the SendMessage action and specify the AWS account number

4: Add the Lambda function to a group with administrative privileges

Answer: 2

Explanation:

The Lambda function needs the privileges to use the SendMessage API action on the Amazon SQS queue. The permissions should be assigned to the function's execution role. The AWSLambdaSQSQueueExecutionRole AWS managed policy cannot be used as this policy does not provide the SendMessage action.

The Developer should therefore create a customer managed policy with read/write permissions to SQS and attach the policy to the function's execution role.

CORRECT: "Create a customer managed policy with all read/write permissions to SQS and attach the policy to the function's execution role" is the correct answer.

INCORRECT: "Add the AWSLambdaSQSQueueExecutionRole AWS managed policy to the function's execution role" is incorrect as this does not provide the necessary permissions.

INCORRECT: "Add a permissions policy to the SQS queue allowing the SendMessage action and specify the AWS account number" is incorrect as this would allow any resource in the AWS account to write to the queue which is less secure.

INCORRECT: "Add the Lambda function to a group with administrative privileges" is incorrect as you cannot add a Lambda function to an IAM group.

58. Question

A Developer is creating an application that uses Amazon EC2 instances and must be highly available and fault tolerant. How should the Developer configure the VPC?

1: Create multiple subnets within a single availability zone in the region

2: Create a subnet in each availability zone in the region

3: Create an Internet Gateway for every availability zone

4: Create a cluster placement group for the EC2 instances

Answer: 2

Explanation:

To ensure high availability and fault tolerance the Developer should create a subnet within each availability zone. The EC2 instances should then be distributed between these subnets.

The Developer would likely use Amazon EC2 Auto Scaling which will automatically launch instances in each subnet and then Elastic Load Balancing to distributed incoming traffic.

CORRECT: "Create a subnet in each availability zone in the region" is the correct answer.

INCORRECT: "Create multiple subnets within a single availability zone in the region" is incorrect as this will not provide fault tolerance in the event that the AZ becomes unavailable.

INCORRECT: "Create an Internet Gateway for every availability zone" is incorrect as there is a single Internet Gateway per VPC.

INCORRECT: "Create a cluster placement group for the EC2 instances" is incorrect as this is used for ensuring low latency access between EC2 instances in a single availability zone.

59. Question

A company has released a new application on AWS. The company are concerned about security and require a tool that can automatically assess applications for exposure, vulnerabilities, and deviations from best practices. Which AWS service should they use?

1: Amazon Inspector

2: AWS Shield

3: AWS WAF

4: AWS Secrets Manager

Answer: 1

Explanation:

Amazon Inspector is an automated security assessment service that helps improve the security and compliance of applications deployed on AWS. Amazon Inspector automatically assesses applications for exposure, vulnerabilities, and deviations from best practices.

After performing an assessment, Amazon Inspector produces a detailed list of security findings prioritized by level of severity. These findings can be reviewed directly or as part of detailed assessment reports which are available via the Amazon Inspector console or API.

CORRECT: "Amazon Inspector" is the correct answer.

INCORRECT: "AWS Shield" is incorrect as this service is used to protect from distributed denial of service (DDoS) attacks.

INCORRECT: "AWS WAF" is incorrect as this is a web application firewall.

INCORRECT: "AWS Secrets Manager" is incorrect as this service is used to store secure secrets.

60. Question

A Developer has lost their access key ID and secret access key for programmatic access. What should the Developer do?

1: Contact AWS support and request a password reset

2: Generate a new key pair from the EC2 management console

3: Reset the AWS account access keys

4: Disable and delete the users' access key and generate a new set

Answer: 4

Explanation:

Access keys consist of two parts:

- **The access key identifier**. This is not a secret, and can be seen in the IAM console wherever access keys are listed, such as on the user summary page.

- **The secret access key**. This is provided when you initially create the access key pair. Just like a password, it ***cannot be retrieved later***. If you lost your secret access key, then you must create a new access key pair. If you already have the <u>maximum number of access keys</u>, you must delete an existing pair before you can create another.

Therefore, the Developer should disable and delete their access keys and generate a new set.

CORRECT: "Disable and delete the users' access key and generate a new set" is the correct answer.

INCORRECT: "Contact AWS support and request a password reset" is incorrect as a user name and password are used for console access, not programmatic access.

INCORRECT: "Generate a new key pair from the EC2 management console" is incorrect as a key pair is used for accessing EC2 instances, not for programmatic access to work with AWS services.

INCORRECT: "Reset the AWS account access keys" is incorrect as these are the access keys associated with the root account rather than the users' individual IAM account.

61. Question

An application includes multiple Auto Scaling groups of Amazon EC2 instances. Each group corresponds to a different subdomain of example.com, including forum.example.com and myaccount.example.com. An Elastic Load Balancer will be used to distribute load from a single HTTPS listener. Which type of Elastic Load Balancer MUST a Developer use in this scenario?

1: Application Load Balancer

2: Network Load Balancer

3: Classic Load Balancer

4: Task Load Balancer

Answer: 1

Explanation:

With an Application Load Balancer it is possible to route requests based on the domain name specified in the Host header. This means you can route traffic coming in to forum.example.com and myaccount.example.com to different target groups.

The Application Load Balancer is the only Elastic Load Balancer provided by AWS that can perform host-based routing.

CORRECT: "Application Load Balancer" is the correct answer.

INCORRECT: "Network Load Balancer" is incorrect as this type of ELB routes traffic based on information at the connection layer (L4).

INCORRECT: "Classic Load Balancer" is incorrect as it does not support any kind of host or path-based routing or even target groups.

INCORRECT: "Task Load Balancer" is incorrect as this is not a type of ELB.

62. Question

A Developer has created a task definition that includes the following JSON code:

"placementConstraints": [

```
    {

      "expression": "attribute:ecs.instance-type =~ t2.*",

      "type": "memberOf"

    }

]
```

What will be the effect for tasks using this task definition?

1: They will be placed only on container instances using the T2 instance type

2: They will be placed only on container instances of T2 or T3 instance types

3: They will be added to distinct instances using the T2 instance type

4: They will be spread across all instances except for T2 instances

Answer: 1

Explanation:

A *task placement constraint* is a rule that is considered during task placement. Task placement constraints can be specified when either running a task or creating a new service.

The memberOf task placement constraint places tasks on container instances that satisfy an expression.

The memberOf task placement constraint can be specified with the following actions:

- Running a task

- Creating a new service

- Creating a new task definition

- Creating a new revision of an existing task definition

The example JSON code uses the memberOf constraint to place tasks on T2 instances. It can be specified with the following actions: CreateService, UpdateService, RegisterTaskDefinition, and RunTask.

CORRECT: "They will be placed only on container instances using the T2 instance type" is the correct answer.

INCORRECT: "They will be added to distinct instances using the T2 instance type" is incorrect. The memberOf constraint does not choose distinct instances.

INCORRECT: "They will be placed only on container instances of T2 or T3 instance types" is incorrect as only T2 instance types will be used. The wildcard means any T2 instance type such as t2.micro or t2.large.

INCORRECT: "They will be spread across all instances except for T2 instances" is incorrect as this code ensures the instances WILL be placed on T2 instance types.

63. Question

A Java based application generates email notifications to customers using Amazon SNS. The emails must contain links to access data in a secured Amazon S3 bucket. What is the SIMPLEST way to maintain security of the bucket whilst allowing the customers to access specific objects?

1: Use the AWS SDK for Java with GeneratePresignedUrlRequest to create a presigned URL

2: Use the AWS SDK for Java to update the bucket Access Control List to allow the customers to access the bucket

3: Use the AWS SDK for Java with the AWS STS service to gain temporary security credentials

4: Use the AWS SDK for Java to assume a role with AssumeRole to gain temporary security credentials

Answer: 1

Explanation:

A presigned URL gives you access to the object identified in the URL, provided that the creator of the presigned URL has permissions to access that object. That is, if you receive a presigned URL to upload an object, you can upload the object only if the creator of the presigned URL has the necessary permissions to upload that object.

You can use the AWS SDK for Java to generate a presigned URL that you, or anyone you give the URL, can use to upload an object to Amazon S3. When you use the URL to upload an object, Amazon S3 creates the object in the specified bucket.

If an object with the same key that is specified in the presigned URL already exists in the bucket, Amazon S3 replaces the existing object with the uploaded object. To successfully complete an upload, you must do the following:

- Specify the HTTP PUT verb when creating the GeneratePresignedUrlRequest and HttpURLConnection objects.

- Interact with the HttpURLConnection object in some way after finishing the upload. The following example accomplishes this by using the HttpURLConnection object to check the HTTP response code.

CORRECT: "Use the AWS SDK for Java with GeneratePresignedUrlRequest to create a presigned URL" is the correct answer.

INCORRECT: "Use the AWS SDK for Java to update the bucket Access Control List to allow the customers to access the bucket" is incorrect. Bucket ACLs are used to grant access to predefined groups and accounts and are not suitable for this purpose.

INCORRECT: "Use the AWS SDK for Java with the AWS STS service to gain temporary security credentials" is incorrect as this requires the creation of policies and security credentials and is not as simple as creating a presigned URL.

INCORRECT: "Use the AWS SDK for Java to assume a role with AssumeRole to gain temporary security credentials" is incorrect as this requires the creation of policies and security credentials and is not as simple as creating a presigned URL.

64. Question

An application will generate thumbnails from objects uploaded to an Amazon S3 bucket. The Developer has created the bucket configuration and the AWS Lambda function and has formulated the following AWS CLI command:

aws lambda add-permission --function-name CreateThumbnail --principal s3.amazonaws.com --statement-id s3invoke --action "lambda:InvokeFunction" --source-arn arn:aws:s3:::digitalcloudbucket-source --source-account 523107438921

What will be achieved by running the AWS CLI command?

1: The Amazon S3 service principal (s3.amazonaws.com) will be granted permissions to perform the lambda:InvokeFunction action

2: The Lambda function CreateThumbnail will be granted permissions to access the objects in the digitalcloudbucket-source bucket

3: The Amazon S3 service principal (s3.amazonaws.com) will be granted permissions to perform the create an event-source mapping with the digitalcloudbucket-source bucket

4: A Lambda function will be created called CreateThumbnail with an Amazon SNS event source mapping that executes the function when objects are uploaded

Answer: 1

Explanation:

In this scenario the Developer is using an AWS Lambda function to process images that are uploaded to an Amazon S3 bucket. The AWS Lambda function has been created and the notification settings on the bucket have been configured. The last thing to do is to grant permissions for the Amazon S3 service principal to invoke the function.

The Lambda CLI add-permission command grants the Amazon S3 service principal (s3.amazonaws.com) permissions to perform the lambda:InvokeFunction action.

CORRECT: "The Amazon S3 service principal (s3.amazonaws.com) will be granted permissions to perform the lambda:InvokeFunction action" is the correct answer.

INCORRECT: "The Lambda function CreateThumbnail will be granted permissions to access the objects in the digitalcloudbucket-source bucket" is incorrect as the CLI command grants S3 the ability to execute the Lambda function.

INCORRECT: "The Amazon S3 service principal (s3.amazonaws.com) will be granted permissions to perform the create an event-source mapping with the digitalcloudbucket-source bucket" is incorrect as event source mappings are created with services such as Kinesis, DynamoDB, and SQS.

INCORRECT: "A Lambda function will be created called CreateThumbnail with an Amazon SNS event source mapping that executes the function when objects are uploaded" is incorrect. This solution does not use Amazon SNS, the S3 notification invokes the Lambda function directly.

65. Question

An application uses Amazon EC2 instances, AWS Lambda functions and an Amazon SQS queue. The Developer must ensure all communications are within an Amazon VPC using private IP addresses. How can this be achieved? (Select TWO)

1: Create the Amazon SQS queue within a VPC

2: Create a VPC endpoint for AWS Lambda

3: Add the AWS Lambda function to the VPC

4: Create a VPC endpoint for Amazon SQS

5: Create a VPN and connect the services to the VPG

Answer: 3,4

Explanation:

This solution can be achieved by adding the AWS Lambda function to a VPC through the function configuration and by creating a VPC endpoint for Amazon SQS. This will result in the services using purely private IP addresses to communicate without traversing the public Internet.

CORRECT: "Add the AWS Lambda function to the VPC" is a correct answer.

CORRECT: "Create a VPC endpoint for Amazon SQS" is also a correct answer.

INCORRECT: "Create the Amazon SQS queue within a VPC" is incorrect as you cannot create a queue within a VPC as Amazon SQS is a public service.

INCORRECT: "Create a VPC endpoint for AWS Lambda" is incorrect as you cannot create a VPC endpoint for AWS Lambda. You can, however, connect a Lambda function to a VPC.

INCORRECT: "Create a VPN and connect the services to the VPG" is incorrect as you cannot create a VPN between each of these services.

CONCLUSION

Congratulations on completing these exam-difficulty practice tests! We truly hope that these high-quality questions along with the supporting explanations helped to fully prepare you for the AWS Certified Developer Associate exam.

The DVA-C01 exam covers a broad set of technologies and it's vital to ensure you are armed with the knowledge to answer whatever questions come up in your certification exam. So it's best to review these practice questions until you're confident in all areas. We recommend re-taking these practice tests until you consistently score 80% or higher - that's when you're ready to sit the exam and achieve a great score!

Reach out and Connect

We want you to have a 5-star learning experience. If anything is not 100% to your liking, please email us at feedback@digitalcloud.training. We promise to address all questions and concerns. We really want you to get great value from these training resources.

The AWS platform is evolving quickly, and the exam tracks these changes with a typical lag of around 6 months. We are therefore reliant on student feedback to keep track of what is appearing in the exam. If there are any topics in your exam that weren't covered in our training resources, please provide us with feedback using this form https://digitalcloud.training/student-feedback/. We appreciate any feedback that will help us further improve our AWS training resources.

To discuss any exam-specific questions you may have, please join the discussion on Slack. Visit https://digitalcloud.training/contact/ for instructions.

Also, remember to join our private Facebook group to ask questions and share knowledge and exam tips with the AWS community: https://www.facebook.com/groups/awscertificationqa

Limited Time Bonus Offer

As a special bonus, we are now offering **FREE Access to the Exam Simulator** on the Digital Cloud Training website. The exam simulator randomly selects 65 questions from our pool of 390 questions - mimicking the real AWS exam environment. The practice exam has the same format, style, time limit, and passing score as the real AWS exam.

To gain FREE access to all 390 Practice Questions, simply send us a **screenshot of your review on Amazon** to info@digitalcloud.training with "CDASIM" in the subject line. You will then get FREE access to our Online Exam Simulator within 48 hours. Should you encounter ANY problems with your review, please reach out. We're here to support you on your cloud journey.

Your reviews help us improve our courses and help your fellow AWS students make the right choices. We celebrate every honest review and truly appreciate it. You can leave a review at any time by visiting amazon.com/ryp or your local amazon store (e.g. amazon.co.uk/ryp).

Download your FREE PDF version of this book

Based on the feedback we've received from our Amazon clients, we understand that studying complex diagrams in black and white or accessing reference links from a kindle may NOT offer the best learning experience.

That's why we've decided to provide you with this PDF at no additional charge. This extended version includes additional diagrams, images and reference links that will enable you to access additional information. To download your free version, simply scan the QR code below or visit:

https://digitalcloud.training/aws-certified-developer-associate-cheat-sheets-amazon-customers-only/

Best wishes for your AWS certification journey!

OTHER BOOKS & COURSES BY NEAL DAVIS

AWS Certified Developer Associate Instructor-led Video Course

AVAILABLE ON DIGITALCLOUD.TRAINING

This brand-new **AWS Certified Developer Associate Exam Training** for the **AWS Certified Developer Associate certification exam** (DVA-C01) is packed with over 28 hours of comprehensive video lessons, hands-on labs, quizzes and exam-crams. With our mixture of in-depth theory, architectural diagrams and hands-on training, you'll learn how to architect and build applications on **Amazon Web Services**, fully preparing you for the **AWS Developer Certification** exam. With this complete **AWS Developer training** course, you have everything you need to comfortably pass the **AWS Developer Certification** exam at the first attempt.

How is this Course Different?

We are big believers in using practical exercises to improve memory retention and contextualize knowledge. We have included many hours of hands-on guided exercises, so you get to build a practical skillset. The course also includes many visual slides to help you understand the concepts. All practical exercises are backed by architectural diagrams so you can visualize what you're developing on Amazon Web Services. By the end of this course, you will have acquired a strong experience-based skillset on AWS along with the confidence to ace your **AWS Certified Developer Associate exam** first time!

With this **AWS Developer training**, you'll learn AWS Serverless using AWS Lambda, API Gateway, DynamoDB & Cognito, get hands-on with AWS Databases including DynamoDB, build Microservices architectures with Docker containers on Amazon ECS and create Continuous Integration and Delivery (CI/CD) pipelines with AWS CodeCommit, CodeDeploy, and CodePipeline. All of this and so MUCH more!

To learn more, visit:

https://digitalcloud.training/aws-certified-developer-associate-exam-training/

Apply Coupon Code
AMZ20
for a 20% discount

Get access to the **online Exam Simulator** from Digital Cloud Training with 390 Questions in 6 sets of practice exam. All questions are unique and conform to the latest AWS DVA-C01 exam blueprint.

Our AWS Practice Tests are delivered in 3 different modes:

Simulation mode: the number of questions, time limit, and pass mark are the same as the real AWS exam. You must complete the exam before you are able to check your score and review answers and explanations.

Training mode: You are shown the answer and explanation for every question after clicking "check". Upon completion of the exam the score report shows your overall score and performance in each knowledge area.

Knowledge reviews: Collections of practice questions for a specific knowledge area. When you complete a practice exam you can use the score report to identify your strengths and weaknesses and then use the knowledge reviews to focus your efforts where they're needed most.

To learn more on how to fast-track your AWS Certified Developer Associate Exam Success, visit:

https://digitalcloud.training/aws-certified-developer-associate-practice-exams/

Apply Coupon Code
AMZ20
for a 20% discount

AWS Certified Solutions Architect Associate Video Course

AVAILABLE ON DIGITALCLOUD.TRAINING

This popular AWS Certified Solutions Architect Associate (SAA-C02) video course is delivered through practical AWS Hands-On Labs.

You will be looking over my shoulder and building applications on Amazon Web Services. By the end of the course , you will have a strong experience-based skillset thanks to the guided AWS Practice Labs.

We will use a process of repetition and incremental learning to ensure that you retain the knowledge as repeated practice is the best way to learn and build your cloud skills. We take you from opening your first AWS Free Tier account through to creating complex multi-tier architectures, always sticking to the **SAA-C02 exam blueprint** to ensure you're learning practical skills and also preparing for your exam.

We back the 28 hours of AWS Hands-On Labs with high-quality logical diagrams so you can visualize what you're building and check your progress.

Our AWS Hands-On Labs teach you how to design and build multi-tier web architectures with services such as EC2 Auto Scaling, Elastic Load Balancing, Route 53, ECS, Lambda, API Gateway and Elastic File System.

To learn more, visit:

https://digitalcloud.training/aws-certified-solutions-architect-associate-hands-on-course/

Apply Coupon Code
AMZ20
for a 20% discount

AVAILABLE ON DIGITALCLOUD.TRAINING

Get access to the **online Exam Simulator** from Digital Cloud Training with over 500 Questions plus 6 sets of practice exams with 65 Questions each. All questions are unique, 100% scenario-based and conform to the latest AWS SAA-C02 exam blueprint.

Our AWS Practice Tests are delivered in 3 different modes:

Simulation mode: the number of questions, time limit, and pass mark are the same as the real AWS exam. You must complete the exam before you are able to check your score and review answers and explanations.

Training mode: You are shown the answer and explanation for every question after clicking "check". Upon completion of the exam the score report shows your overall score and performance in each knowledge area.

Knowledge reviews: Collections of practice questions for a specific knowledge area. When you complete a practice exam you can use the score report to identify your strengths and weaknesses and then use the knowledge reviews to focus your efforts where they're needed most.

Each exam includes questions from the four domains of the AWS exam blueprint. All questions are also available in the knowledge reviews where they are split into more than 15 categories for focused training.

To learn more on how to fast-track your AWS Certified Solutions Architect Associate Exam Success, visit:

https://digitalcloud.training/aws-certified-solutions-architect-associate-practice-tests-saa-c02/

Apply Coupon Code
AMZ20
for a 20% discount

The AWS Solutions Architect Associate certification is extremely valuable in the Cloud Computing industry today and preparing to answer the difficult scenario-based questions requires a significant commitment in time and effort.

The latest **SAA-C02 exam** is composed entirely of scenario-based questions that test your knowledge and experience working with Amazon Web Services. Our practice tests are patterned to reflect the difficulty of the AWS exam and are the closest to the real AWS exam experience available anywhere.

There are **6 practice exams with 65 questions** each covering the five domains of the AWS exam blueprint. Each set of questions is repeated once without answers and explanations, and once with answers and explanations, so you get to choose from two methods of preparation:

- **To simulate the exam experience and assess your exam readiness**, use the "PRACTICE QUESTIONS ONLY" sets.

- **To use the practice questions as a learning tool**, use the "PRACTICE QUESTIONS, ANSWERS & EXPLANATIONS" sets to view the answers and read the in-depth explanations as you move through the questions.

These Practice Questions will prepare you for your AWS exam in the following ways:

- **Master the new 2020 exam pattern**: All 390 practice questions are based on the SAA-C02 exam blueprint and use the question format of the real AWS exam

- **6 sets of exam-difficulty practice questions**: Presented with and without answers so you can study or simulate an exam

- **Ideal exam prep tool that will shortcut your study time**: Assess your exam readiness to maximize your chance of passing the AWS exam first time

The exam covers a broad set of technologies and it's vital to ensure you are armed with the knowledge to answer whatever questions come up in your certification exam. We recommend reviewing these practice questions until you're confident in all areas and ready to ace your AWS exam.

To learn more, visit: https://digitalcloud.training/cartflows_step/checkout-csaa-pq/

Apply Coupon Code
AMZ20
for a 20% discount

AVAILABLE ON DIGITALCLOUD.TRAINING

We have fully aligned this instructor-led video training with the AWS Certified Cloud Practitioner exam blueprint and structured the course so that you can study at a pace that suits you best. We start with some basic background to get everyone up to speed on what cloud computing is, before progressing through each knowledge domain.

Here's why this ultimate exam prep is your best chance to ace your AWS certification exam:

HIGHLY FLEXIBLE COURSE STRUCTURE: We understand that not everyone has the time to go through lengthy lectures. That's why we give you options to maximize your time efficiency and accommodate different learning styles.

6 HOURS OF THEORY LECTURES: You can move quickly through the course, focusing on the theory lectures that are 100% conform with the CLF-C01 exam blueprint - everything you need to know to pass your exam first attempt.

4 HOURS OF GUIDED HANDS-ON EXERCISES: To gain more practical experience with AWS services, you have the option to explore the guided hands-on exercises.

1 HOUR OF EXAM-CRAM LECTURES: Get through the key exam facts in the shortest time possible with the exam-cram lectures that you'll find at the end of each section.

HIGH-QUALITY VISUALS: We've spared no effort to create a highly visual training course with lots of table and graphs to illustrate the concepts. All practical exercises are backed by logical diagrams so you can visualize what we're building.

To learn more, visit: https://digitalcloud.training/aws-certified-cloud-practitioner-training-course/

Apply Coupon Code
AMZ20
for a 20% discount

AVAILABLE ON DIGITALCLOUD.TRAINING

Get access to the online Exam Simulator from Digital Cloud Training with over 500 Practice questions plus 6 sets of practice exams with 65 Questions each. All questions are unique and conform to the latest AWS CLF-C01 exam blueprint.

Our AWS Practice Tests are delivered in 3 different modes:

Simulation mode: the number of questions, time limit and pass mark are the same as the real AWS exam. You need to complete the exam before you get to check your score and review answers and explanations.

Training mode: You are shown the answer and explanation for every question after clicking "check". Upon completion of the exam, the score report shows your overall score and performance in each knowledge area.

Knowledge reviews: Collections of practice questions for a specific knowledge area. When you complete a practice exam you can use the score report to identify your strengths and weaknesses and then use the knowledge reviews to focus your efforts where they are needed most.

To learn more on how to fast-track your AWS Certified Cloud Practitioner Exam Success, visit:

https://digitalcloud.training/aws-certified-cloud-practitioner-practice-tests/

**Apply Coupon Code
AMZ20
for a 20% discount**

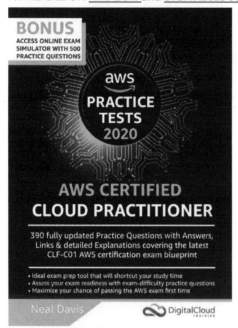

The **AWS Cloud Practitioner** exam is a foundational level exam that nonetheless includes tricky questions that test your knowledge and experience of the AWS Cloud. Our practice tests are patterned to reflect the difficulty of the AWS exam and are the closest to the real AWS exam experience available.

There are **6 practice exams with 65 questions each** covering the five domains of the AWS CLF-C01 exam blueprint. Each set of questions is repeated once without answers and explanations, and once with answers and explanations, so you get to choose from two methods of preparation:

1. To simulate the exam experience and assess your exam readiness, use the "**PRACTICE QUESTIONS ONLY**" sets.

2. To use the practice questions as a learning tool, use the "**PRACTICE QUESTIONS, ANSWERS & EXPLANATIONS**" sets to view the answers and read the in-depth explanations as you move through the questions.

These Practice Questions will prepare you for your AWS exam in the following ways:

Master the latest exam pattern: All 390 practice questions are based on the latest version of the CLF-C01 exam blueprint and use the question format of the real AWS exam

6 sets of exam-difficulty practice questions: Presented with and without answers so you can study or simulate an exam

Ideal exam prep tool that will shortcut your study time: Assess your exam readiness to maximize your chance of passing the AWS exam first time.

To learn more, visit:

https://digitalcloud.training/cartflows_step/checkout-ccp-pq/

Apply Coupon Code
AMZ20
for a 20% discount

Save valuable time by getting straight to the facts you need to know to be successful and ensure you pass your AWS Certified Cloud Practitioner exam first time!

This book is based on the CLF-C01 exam blueprint and provides a deep dive into the subject matter in a concise and easy-to-read format so you can fast-track your time to success.

The Cloud Practitioner certification is a great first step into the world of Cloud Computing and requires a foundational knowledge of the AWS Cloud, its architectural principles, value proposition, billing and pricing, key services and more.

AWS Solutions Architect and successful instructor, Neal Davis, has consolidated the information you need to be successful from numerous training sources and AWS FAQ pages to save you time.

In addition to the book, you are provided with access to a 65-question practice exam on an interactive exam simulator to evaluate your progress and ensure you're prepared for the style and difficulty of the real AWS exam.

This book can help you prepare for your AWS exam in the following ways:

• Deep dive into the CLF-C01 exam objectives with over 200 pages of detailed facts, tables, and diagrams – everything you need to know!

• Familiarize yourself with the exam question format with the practice questions included in each section.

• Use our online exam simulator to evaluate progress and ensure you're ready for the real thing.

To learn more, visit:

https://digitalcloud.training/product/aws-certified-cloud-practitioner-offline-training-notes/

Apply Coupon Code
AMZ20
for a 20% discount

ABOUT THE AUTHOR

Neal Davis is the founder of Digital Cloud Training, AWS Cloud Solutions Architect and successful IT instructor. With more than 20 years of experience in the tech industry, Neal is a true expert in virtualization and cloud computing. His passion is to help others achieve career success by offering in-depth AWS certification training resources.

Neal started **Digital Cloud Training** to provide a variety of training resources for Amazon Web Services (AWS) certifications that represent a higher standard of quality than is otherwise available in the market.

Digital Cloud Training provides **AWS Certification exam preparation resources** including instructor-led Video Courses, guided Hands-on Labs, in-depth Training Notes, Exam-Cram lessons for quick revision, Quizzes to test your knowledge and exam-difficulty Practice Exams to assess your exam readiness.

With Digital Cloud Training, you get access to highly experienced staff who support you on your AWS Certification journey and help you elevate your career through achieving highly valuable certifications. Join the AWS Community of over 70,000 happy students that are currently enrolled in Digital Cloud Training courses

Connect with Neal on social media:

 digitalcloud.training/neal-davis

 youtube.com/c/digitalcloudtraining

 facebook.com/digitalcloudtraining

 Twitter @nealkdavis

 linkedin.com/in/nealkdavis

 Instagram @digitalcloudtraining

Printed in Great Britain
by Amazon